CROTON

Book III

From Heaven To Hell and Back

By

Artur Tadevosyan

Library of Congress Cataloging-in-Publication Data

Croton: Book III by Artur Tadevosyan -1963-

A story anyone seeking answers to the big questions about life and death should read.

1. Reincarnation 2. Spirit Guides 3. Metaphysical 4. Spiritual
I. Tadevosyan, Artur, 1963 - II. Metaphysical III. Spirit Guides IV. Title

Library of Congress Catalog Card Number: 2025935627

ISBN: 978-1-950639-45-8

Cover Design and Layout: Victoria Cooper Art
Cover Art By: Grace Tadevosyan
Book set in: Times New Roman, Britannic Bold
Book Design: Summer Garr
Published by:

PO Box 754, Huntsville, AR 72740
800-935-0045 or 479-738-2348; fax 479-738-2448
WWW.OZARKMT.COM

Printed in the United States of America

Acknowledgments

I would like to express my deepest gratitude to my twin flame and beloved wife, Grace, for her unwavering encouragement and support throughout the completion of this final book.

A special thanks to Janet Erasmus, whose meticulous editing helped refine nearly every sentence. Your dedication and attention to detail are truly appreciated.

To my daughter, Eva Bruce, for elevating our online presence, ensuring this book reaches its intended readers.

Finally, I extend my deepest appreciation to my daughter, Diana Hatziandreou, for her persistent encouragement, always urging me to share the knowledge I have been called to give.

Table of Contents

DECISION

Henry and Rose remained sitting across the table for some time looking at each other. Each submersed in their own thoughts, trying to imagine any possible future without one another. Although Thales' last words seemed to leave them with the option to reject his proposal… the Planner's scenario began to take root deeper and deeper into their minds, leaving no space for any alternative to submit themselves to what now seemed inevitable.

Rose suddenly stood up and said, "I must go back to Earth. I have to see Croton and Gaya."

Henry agreed by saying, "I will be here waiting for you, my love."

While Rose rushed back to her duties, Henry chose to go for a walk, but it wasn't the beach that called him this time. He walked through Rose's quarters, into the back yard, where cascading pools were expecting him in anticipation to admire their natural beauty. But passing through Rose's extension, once created for him by Croton to ease his separation from Rose, brought back memories of loneliness.

"And I have to agree to this willingly?" he questioned, "Once reunited am I going to lose her again?"

Henry followed a long winding path through the majestic forest that presented itself in a full range of mid-autumn colors.

"How come I don't have a river to complete this perfection?" he asked himself.

A couple of steps further he heard the murmur of streaming water, and sped up until a few feet further he was standing in front of a crystal-clear brook playfully running down the hill. He found a perfectly shaped stone to sit on and dipped his hand into the water.

"You definitely look and feel real," he said to himself, "Real, what the hell is real? Are you the real one, or the ones on Earth?" Henry asked the cool water streaming through his fingers, "I don't know what is real anymore. Life here or life on Earth."

It was one of those moments when Henry would have gladly given up a lot to have his dear friend and mentor next to him, but unfortunately, he was on Earth, trapped in a physical body, and completely unaware of Henry's existence.

He looked tenderly at the water running down the hill saying, "Don't worry, you will find your peace when you reach the ocean…will I ever find mine, I wonder?"

Henry stood up and looked down the hill where he could almost see his entire reality. The lonely house standing on the border of a huge forest, the ocean timelessly striking the white sands, and the withering line between ocean and sky.

"My own peaceful universe," Henry said slowly with a great sadness in his voice. "Do I need all this without Rose? Three, possibly four Earth years, plus a couple of months of Gaya's pregnancy…should be a month or two in this reality."

Trying to convince himself Henry said, "Maybe Thales' plan is not so bad after all. The only sad one in this whole ordeal will be me. Croton and Gaya will have a beautiful girl for themselves. Rose will not remember anything, including myself."

His last thought hung in the air like a swaying sword above his neck. A state of panic embraced Henry's mind, leaving him disarmed to face approaching trouble. Henry tried to calm himself and pulled to the surface of his memory anything he knew about children crossing over to the world of spirit.

"As far as I remember, children still remain children when they cross into higher realms, and it takes quite some time for them to mature to their adult state of consciousness. Even so, will she remember me? And most of all, will she still love me? No, this is too risky, I need to raise these questions with Thales before making a final decision."

In the meantime, Rose appeared in Croton's living-room. The first soul to greet her was Lita.

"What took you so long?" she asked. "Since you left Croton's wedding with the old man, I haven't seen you. What happened?"

Ignoring Lita's questions Rose asked, "Is it true that Gaya is pregnant?"

"Yes!" exclaimed excited Lita. "Isn't it wonderful, and so quick. She fell pregnant in the first week of their marriage."

"Is it going to be a girl?" Rose asked, not sharing Lita's excitement.

"Yes," Lita confirmed. "I must say, you are quite well informed for a guide who's been absent for almost five months."

"I'm sure that you are quite aware of the time difference between here and up there," Rose answered, "It feels like I've been away only a day to me."

"It wasn't for me," replied Lita, a bit irritated with Rose's seeming lack of interest or appreciation.

Suddenly realizing the wrongfulness of her behavior, Rose said, "I'm so sorry, my dear Lita, for being absent for such a long time. Please allow me to express my gratitude for standing in for me and taking good care of my boy."

Rose stepped closer and hugged Lita.

Lita hugged her back saying, "It's quite all right. It was only a pleasure to be around him. I just wished you could have witnessed all the wonderful moments of their life together."

"I'm sure that there will still be many more," answered Rose.

After a moment of silence Rose casually asked, "Was Croton happy about Gaya's pregnancy?"

"He was ecstatic," said Lita.

"What about the news that he's going to have a daughter?" Rose continued.

"He wanted a son, but soon he got used to the idea. I heard him saying to Gaya, people say daughters are for fathers, and I'm sure that she will be as beautiful as her mother."

Rose smiled. Lita's last words somehow eased her tension, giving her comfort and a strange feeling of security. In some way, unknown to her, Thales' proposal had begun to work its way into Rose's mind, finding a tiny foothold and preparing to occupy her entire soul.

"Do you want to see them? I'm sure they are still awake," Lita suggested.

Passing through the living room wall into the couple's bedroom, they found Gaya lying on her back and Croton carefully placing his hand on her stomach.

"What are you doing, silly?" Gaya laughed.

"What? I'm trying to feel her," Croton explained.

"And?" Gaya giggled.

"When is she supposed to kick?" asked Croton.

"She already should be, and the fact that she is not is making me a bit nervous," Gaya answered.

Exposing her bloated stomach, Croton tenderly kissed it and said, "Please be kind to us." Then he placed his ear on her tummy in anticipation of any sign.

In that very moment Rose knew that she cannot let these kids down, and that she had to do what a moment ago seemed preposterous. She realized that this tiny, newly forming life was expecting her, and only she had the God-given power to become a gift of happiness. A gift which will present this young couple with an opportunity to experience unconditional love.

Rose lowered her eyes and whispered, "So much to lose, but even more to gain."

"Did you say something?" Lita asked.

"Let's leave them alone and I will explain," Rose suggested.

In the living room Rose shared with Lita her heartbreaking dilemma.

"I arrived here with huge doubts in my mind, but now none remain. I cannot explain, but it seems like it's the right thing to do."

"You should absolutely do it." Lita said convincingly, adding, "Don't worry, I will take care of you, too."

"No, there is no need. Henry is to be my spirit guide."

"That's the reason why I offered to take care of you," Lita replied.

"You don't like him much, do you?" Rose asked laughing.

"He's all right," Lita said indifferently.

"You shouldn't worry, he will take good care of me. Besides, my physical life span is going to be very short."

"What do you mean?" asked alarmed Lita.

"Yes, the Planner said maybe three of four years," Rose explained.

"No, this cannot be," Lita said in absolute disbelief.

"I know, it sounds horrible. To put our children through the trauma of losing their baby girl… but Thales explained that it will be very beneficial for their spiritual growth," Rose explained.

Lita didn't hear Rose's last words. Her only concern was to get to the bottom of this nasty surprise in the form of destiny prepared for her beloved Gaya by heartless Planners.

With great difficulty she waited for Rose to finish her sentence to say, "I'm sorry Rose, but I have to leave."

Left alone Rose went back to the couple's bedroom for a last glimpse at the peacefully sleeping Gaya. Due to the hot summer and the heat generated by the young mother's body, she had no blanket covering her. Rose carefully placed her hand on Gaya's tummy and for the first time felt movement of her future self. It was like an avatar feeling the touch of its soul and responding in anticipation.

"Hang on little one, in no time I will be yours, or you will become mine."

A second later Rose appeared in front of Henry. "You're back," he said with a sigh of great relief.

"Of course I am, silly" Rose smiled back.

Henry stepped forward and gently hugged her. Rose rested her hands on his shoulders and closed her eyes. No words were necessary. They both knew the recipe of their near future, but the taste of it was still unknown.

They stood intact like one creation.

Two bodies melted into one.

Dismay approaching separation and loneliness beyond this line.

"You know the decision has been made," said Rose in tragic desperation.

"I know my love, spare empty words. Don't make this harder than it is. You chose what is best for our son. Support of mine should be in order."

"Thanks for understanding me, my love. This separation will be swift. In the nick of time, I will be back to hold your soul again in mine."

"That's if you remember me at all—if memories created once will be intact when you are back."

"Forget, my love? Oh, what nonsense. Love is impossible to lose. If even so, I have no doubt you will find a way to win me back. To fall again in love with you, what can I ask from God above this? Besides, you know, each separation in its core holds anticipation of reunion."

"I know," said Henry with pain in his heart. "I'll set you free. Do what you must. I guess the balance has to be restored."

"What are you saying?" questioned Rose.

"The meaning of my words are simple. I left you once on Earth alone to suffer the pain of separation. The turn is mine to taste the dish once served by me for you to suffer the bitterness of a jilted widow."

Thales, who had been closely following their thoughts, had no doubt in the success of his plans. He knew that the bond between Gaya's fetus and Rose's soul was already sealed, and it was only a matter of time before they would melt together. Although the earth time was running out, he needed firm confirmation from Henry and Rose to close the deal and to stop looking for another soul to take up the task.

"Where exactly are we?" asked Rose noticing unfamiliar surroundings.

"We are in our reality," Henry answered.

"I don't remember there being a river?" Rose answered.

"I thought it would be a nice addition to our forest. Don't you like it?" asked Henry.

"Oh, it's perfect," Rose answered, leaning down to dip her hand into the cool water.

"Please forgive my intrusion," said Thales, appearing on the other side of the stream, right in front of Henry and Rose. "Did you give some thought to my proposal?"

Henry looked at the Planner and with undisguised irritation said, "Don't act like you know nothing. I have no doubt that our every word and thought has reached your sensitive ears. I know that you are here for Rose's soul."

"I will not deny my awareness, and that your decision is a remedy for my heart," Thales replied, and then fell quiet before saying, "I know that you are cross with me for now, but later you will see it all."

Rose stepped forward to end this aimless conversation and said, "I choose to go to Earth, and Henry has honored my decision. I am aware of the shortness of time, so please lead me to where the destiny of mine will be revealed."

Thales crossed the river by simply walking over it, and placed his hands on the couple's shoulders, swiftly saying, "Let's go."

The three of them were standing in the "Preparation Chamber", near the cafeteria that was so familiar to Henry and Rose.

"I just remembered our goodbyes to Croton," Rose said sadly.

"This place reminds me of a train station, with one difference," Henry said.

"And?" asked Rose.

"There is no arrival terminal," Henry explained.

"You are right, Henry," said Thales, and facing the loving couple apologetically whispered, "It is time to say your goodbyes."

"What are you talking about?" protested Henry, "I am familiar with the procedure. First, we have to see her life tree, and then…"

"There is no life tree," Thales interrupted, "If you want to see, be my guest." Thales stretched out his hand and in his open palm that was facing up was a three-dimensional holographic image.

"What is this?" asked surprised Henry, observing a short stick, vertically rotating in mid-air above Thales' palm.

"It is her life tree. Satisfied?" Thales said in irritation as time was running out.

"Actually, I am," Henry replied, "Especially with the length of it."

Rose stepped into the conversation, "I know you're in a hurry, and so am I, but don't you think that it's only fair for me to see the end of my physical life?"

"Unfortunately, I am not able to present it to you Rose," said Thales.

"Why?" Rose and Henry asked simultaneously.

"It is still unknown to me," explained Thales.

"This is ridiculous," reacted Henry. "How can you plan someone's life without a clear vision of it?"

"Calm down, my friend," said Thales, "There are multiple exits that we can arrange for Rose. The short period of time she has to spend on Earth is not going to be much of a lesson for her. This journey is all about Croton and Gaya, and the fact that Rose is going to be out of their life in the early years of their marriage. So, the way she exits physical life is irrelevant, the fact of its occurrence is what's important."

Without further ado, Thales walked toward a highlighted door. Rose and Henry followed him.

Thales stopped at the door, looked at Rose, and said, "I would like to express my gratitude for the sacrifice that you are about to make. The same goes to you, Henry." Then he bowed his head, putting his chin on his chest, and stepped aside to allow them some privacy.

"I guess this is goodbye," said Rose, and they hugged each other tightly.

"Everything is going so fast," said Henry. "I feel like I'm losing you. A minute ago, we were at the peak of happiness, and now we have committed ourselves to God knows what, and you're slipping through my fingers."

"I will be back in no time, my love," Rose answered, looking deeply into Henry's eyes.

Thales stepped forward saying, "They are waiting for you."

Rose turned around, placed her hand on the golden knob of the door, and without looking back boldly stepped through the opening. "Only three years," she kept repeating to herself as she passed through the seemingly endless corridor filled with white light. "I will be back momentarily. Back to where I belong. Back to Henry." A sudden warm feeling came upon her, wrapping her entirely like a cozy blanket in a chilling cold. Her chest filled to its brim with an ocean of love, which pushed aside all that was in her mind, replacing it with one strong desire…to be merged with the little newly forming life.

She suddenly appeared at the end of the faceless corridor,

standing in front of large double doors that looked strangely familiar to her. They had small glass windows in their center and no handles. Rose realized that this was the last frontier between now and after. She paused for a split second, then pushed the doors wide open and firmly stepped through them. For a moment she felt that she was back on Earth in a familiar hospital ward. A short distance away she noticed two nurses casually conversing at the reception counter. One of them stepped toward Rose. She stood straight, like a schoolgirl in a morning line-up, in anticipation of her fate. The warm smile on the face of the approaching nurse gave her comfort and assurance in her belonging to that place. The nurse stopped at the entrance of the nearest room and invited Rose to enter. Rose cautiously submitted to the invitation and walked into the quite ordinary hospital room, with a single bed placed in the center of it. Rose stopped at the bed and turned around to face the nurse.

"Yes?" the nurse asked.

"Am I on Earth?' Rose questioned.

"No, my dear Rose. Not yet, but you will be soon."

The entire setup was quite questionable, and Rose couldn't help but ask, "Is this going to be painful?"

"No, not at all," answered the nurse, still smiling.

"Then, why am I in a hospital?" Rose pushed.

"The descent of each soul into the physical world is a unique procedure and depends on a variety of circumstances," the nurse explained.

"Like?" Rose asked.

The nurse lovingly looked into Rose's eyes and said, "This setup is the most suitable in your case."

"My case?" questioned Rose.

"Yes, my dear," patiently answered the nurse, and explained, "Souls who commit themselves to such a short visit have an opportunity to preserve previously accumulated memories."

"Does this mean that when I am back, I will remember all that I know now?" asked Rose.

"Yes, you will," replied the nurse.

"Oh, that's a big relief," sighed Rose.

"Shall we?" said the nurse indicating to Rose that she should lie down on the hospital bed.

Rose lay down, stretched out her body, and froze in anticipation of the unknown. Next, two more nurses stepped into the room. They sat down at the edge of the bed on either side of her, while the first one stood at the head.

"Close your eyes my dear," instructed the first nurse.

For the last time Rose looked at the fluorescent light above her on the ceiling and closed her eyes.

"Don't worry," said the nurse, "In no time you will be back, and it will all seem like a bad dream."

The last two words pronounced by the nurse rippled through Rose's consciousness, but very soon they faded away as she submerged into a deep sleep. The three nurses held their hands in a circle around Rose's disappearing body and waited patiently for its complete transformation.

"Bon voyage," said the first nurse, and the three of them left the room.

Henry, who willingly let his token of happiness disappear behind the door, stood confused and completely lost.

"You mustn't worry. Everything will be all right," said Thales.

Henry looked at him and asked, "What now?"

"Now? Now she is all yours," replied Thales.

Henry smiled sarcastically and shifted his sight to the door separating him from Rose. Anger began to boil inside of him. Anger toward the unfairness of this entire situation.

He grabbed the golden knob on the door and without looking at Thales said, "You Planners so casually manipulate our lives on Earth, twisting and turning them to your will, but this is not enough for you, you have to juggle with our destiny even up here."

Then with great force he pushed the door, but it was firmly locked. Henry turned around to face Thales, but he was gone. Left alone, he realized the irreversible nature of this entire situation and instead of sitting and sulking, he chose to pull himself together and act rationally. Waves of thoughts began to crash their might against the rock of Henry's mind.

"I have to go and find Rose," he thought to himself, in an attempt to organize the line of rolling waves. "But how am I going to do that? The last time I saw Croton was at his wedding… so much time has passed. They have probably moved to a new place that I am completely unaware of."

Under the pile of crashing thoughts, Henry began to panic, feeling as though he was suffocating himself. "Stop it," Henry commanded himself. He shook his head, and with that all the debris of scattered scenes stuck in his mind and grabbed one that was the most inviting. "Croton," said Henry, "The last time I checked I was his spirit guide, which means that I can locate him anywhere in the physical world. Yes!" exclaimed Henry as he disappeared into thin air.

ARRIVAL

Rose opened her eyes into darkness, a type of darkness when you doubt that your eyes are open. She tried to move, but soon realized there were restrictions to her level of freedom. Strange and indescribably pleasant feeling overflowed her soul. It seemed like an unknown liquid substance she found herself in had a magical ability to cast complete tranquillity upon her. The word "trapped" did not enter her mind. If there were abundant other places to be she would, without any doubt, choose this one. For the last time she tried to stretch her legs, but realizing the uselessness of that act, fell into a deep sleep.

A strange feeling of discomfort woke Gaya early in the morning. She placed her hand over her belly and for the first time felt her daughter's presence. Relief, mixed with an enormous sense of happiness, seeped into every cell of her body. She kept holding her palm in the same spot in anticipation of more movement, but the baby seemed to have chosen to announce her presence with one kick. Gaya looked across at peacefully sleeping Croton and decided not to wake him and rather surprise him in the morning. She lay back, finding comfort in her goose-feather pillow and soon fell asleep.

Who Gaya couldn't see was a young man kneeling by her bed, who could have reminded her of a devoted follower of faith, praying in front of an icon. The icon was her womb, and the young man was Henry. Timelessly repeating Rose's name with a lantern of hope burning in his heart that she could hear him. From previous experience with Vivienne, his granddaughter, Henry knew that Rose should still be able to communicate with him, but the question, "Does Rose know about that?" was hammering his mind. Somehow, he had forgot to tell her about that, and now he couldn't forgive himself such an error. He had been so wrecked by the forthcoming separation from Rose that he completely forgot to share with her his accumulated knowledge about communication with unborn and newly born children.

An hour later Croton was up and ready to leave for work when Gaya shared her good news. Although he was already late, he nevertheless, fully dressed, lay down next to her and gently placed his palm on the place indicated by Gaya. The tiny, fragile body, seeming to feel her father's presence, rewarded him with a soft push.

"Did you feel it?" asked excited Gaya.

"Yes, yes I did," Croton happily confirmed.

Henry, standing as an invisible witness of this act, couldn't hide his emotions. Everything that mattered to him and defined his presence in the universe were in that tiny bedroom. For the first time, Henry looked into the eyes of this young man and saw there his mentor. Since Croton's descent into the physical world, Henry could not come to terms with the fact that Croton was still alive. Not only alive, but trapped in the body of this pleasant looking young man. His long-lost friend suddenly began its appearance in all of its might, and the only place that Henry could sense him was in this young man's eyes. Familiar emotions clouded his heart to an extent he'd never before experienced. The name of those emotions is love—a God given gift that unites his entire creation, and now the very same gift overpowered Henry's soul entirely, not leaving any piece untouched. He became love itself. Love toward his old friend who was about to become the father to his Rose, and love toward this young fragile girl who was about to become the mother to his Rose. Finally, love toward that tiny creation who had just earned herself the right to be called human, thanks to the sacrifice Rose chose to make.

From that morning on, Henry became an inseparable part of this newly formed family. He became a morning shadow to Gaya, following her to all doctor's appointments, making certain that nothing could harm her, and especially the growing baby inside her. Henry meticulously followed the baby's progress and was permanently trying to influence Gaya's consciousness to eat only healthy food. Days passed by, and the hope that one day he would see his Rose for one last time was still smouldering in his heart. Timeless prayers went unanswered, leaving him wondering if Rose would ever be able to hear him. Then, he convinced himself that probably after the birth, Rose will definitely learn how to leave the baby's body, even for a short moment, just to be with him. Sometimes he visited Croton at work, especially on the most difficult days. Although Henry didn't know much about Croton's work, still, he sensed all of his emotional ups and downs. Henry felt, at a very personal level, a mysterious bond that chained them and changing his entire perception of this young man and triggered the bloom of a most beautiful flower called love.

For the first time, Henry understood how Rose felt about Croton, or for that matter, what a protecting mother could feel toward her child. So often he had to stop himself, checking if he still saw himself as a male energy. Lita, sensing the change in the pattern of Henry's behavior used to tease him saying, "Two young boys in such a tight relationship?" The confusion expressed on Henry's face and his innate inability to respond to her gave Lita a tremendous amount of pleasure. Eventually Henry had to admit to himself that he was turning into a loving and caring mother. Just the thought of it placed Henry in a state of repulsion and the urge to change this pattern of transformation into a female energy was definitely in order. Suddenly a bright idea lit up his mind. "Why not?" he said to himself, and in his next meeting with Lita he appeared as a much older and mature man. Just the way he remembered himself the last time he lived in the physical world.

"Wow!" exclaimed Lita, "What happened to you? Are you hoping to get wiser by changing your appearance?" she teased him.

Ignoring Lita's sarcastic remarks Henry said, "That's how I stood in front of Croton when I crossed over into the world of spirit."

On seeing how sensitive this subject was to Henry, Lita regretted her cheekiness, and this time chose to just say, "Good choice."

Since Rose's decision to descend into a physical state, Henry completely forgot about exploring the universe and its multitude of realities. Realities that not so long ago were mysteriously calling him to be discovered. Everything fell into the past, to be replaced by this tiny family, in this tiny city, on this tiny planet. Timeless crossing of their paths as guides eventually warmed up his relationship with Lita. Soon she became Henry's best ally in protecting this family so precious to both of them. Knowing by now her protective character, Henry trusted her to take care of Rose and spent more time with Croton in order to get to know him better, hoping that deep under the mask of his physical appearance, Henry could find his old friend, the one who was so irritably intrusive, and also so dearly missed.

Since Rose's descent, Henry never returned to their common reality. Just the thought of being there without Rose, where each particle of it would remind him of her, was altogether unbearable, and not worthy of being entertained. Once, when he was left alone in the young couple's living room while everybody was asleep, Henry came to the realization of how cleverly he'd been manipulated by Thales to become a responsible spirit guide.

"You Planners definitely know your business," he said to himself.

"Yes, we do," he heard Thales' voice in his head, followed by his manifestation in the room.

"To what do I owe the pleasure of your visit?" Henry asked respectfully. The anger he had felt toward this man for quite some time had completely vanished through the routines of his activities as a guide.

"I came to warn you," said Thales.

"Warn me about what?" Henry jumped in.

"Nothing to worry about. Tomorrow you are going to see Rose, or to be exact, her physical manifestation."

Henry became overwhelmed by this news, but chose to hide his emotions and kept up the appearance of a vigorous guide attending to his duties.

"Thank you, I will be ready," Henry replied.

"If you have no more questions, I will leave," said Thales.

"I have just one," answered Henry.

"Yes?" asked Thales.

"Is she going to recognize me?" Henry cautiously questioned, hardly able to disguise his desperation.

"We will have to wait and see," answered Thales.

Henry nodded his head in respect and goodbye as Thales disappeared. Henry rushed to share the news with Lita, but to his great disappointment she already knew

It was just after midnight when Gaya gently pushed Croton's shoulder in an attempt to wake him.

With his eyes still closed in a shallow sleep Croton muttered, "Yes?"

Gaya, trying to keep calm said, "It's time to go."

"To go where, my love?" Croton said.

"To the hospital, dumb ass!" Gaya retorted with great difficulty to stop herself from screaming.

"How do you know?" Croton asked still half asleep.

"Look!" Gaya shouted running out of patience, tossing aside the blanket that was covering them both.

Croton switched on the lamp on his bedside table and was shocked by the sight in front of his eyes. Gaya was lying in a pool of water.

"What is that?" he asked in horror.

"What do you think, Brainiac?" Gaya replied.

Only then did Croton realize what had happened.

"Go, go quickly and get the car from the garage and I will be down soon," said Gaya meaning business.

Henry and Lita, standing nearby like muted ghosts, didn't know how to make Croton think and move faster. Realizing what had just happened, Henry completely lost it. He was expecting this to happen sometime during the day. Awareness of the fact that his Rose might be suffocated without amniotic fluid threw him into a state of shock.

"Don't worry, they're going to make it," Lita said as she tried to calm Henry down.

All the way to the hospital, Henry and Lita stayed next to the young couple. Henry placed himself on the passenger seat trying to keep Croton calm and not have an accident. Lita was in the back next to Gaya, holding one hand on Gaya's tummy, and the other on her heart to keep her balanced and her fetus safe. Luckily the road was empty of cars and twenty minutes later they made it to the hospital.

Gaya was rushed into the maternity ward, leaving Croton behind in the waiting room to worry all by himself. Lita and Henry were almost attached to Gaya's bed as it was rolled into the operating room. She was already fully in labor, but Rose was not in any hurry to show up. The appearance of a doctor to help the nurses planted a seed of panic into Henry's heart. Not knowing what exactly was happening, Henry concluded that things were not going the way they should. Lita, holding her hands over Gaya's body was not responding to Henry's questions, and the only thing left for him to do was to kneel and pray. It was practically the first time since he was a little body next to his father in church, calling to God. He pleaded with the supreme creator, the origin of whom, until now, remained the biggest unsolved puzzle in Henry's mind. All of his attempts to establish sensible ground to stand on and somehow to create even a slightly remote image of the Creator, were in vain. Nevertheless, Henry knew that he was up there somewhere. Somewhere in the highest vibrational dimension, hearing him, and undoubtedly would answer his prayer.

Thales, being invisible to all participants in this scene, was attentively listening to Henry's pleas. The sight of Henry kneeling plastered a smear of satisfaction on Thales' face. Self-satisfaction would have been a more accurate a description of what Thales was experiencing as he watched this free soul brought to his knees by the most powerful force of love diluted by fear. "Fear and love," said Thales to himself, "An undeniably powerful mixture. Love is the attachment to another soul, and the possibility of losing it gives rise to fear. This can definitely bring you to your knees."

Henry, in his prayer, was asking God to help his Rose. To bring her out of this entrapment which could lead to the death of the fetus. Henry knew that Rose's exit from the physical world earlier than planned would cause substantial problems and tremendous suffering. According to the large amounts of information he'd managed to gather by studying non-physical realities, Henry was certain that any mistimed exit would imminently create problems, not only for the exiting soul, but also for those who were responsible for them. In this case that would be him. Rose's consciousness was lowered to the level of a newly born child and would remain as such for God knows how long if it happened that she would crossover now.

Thales, who was patiently waiting and listening to what Henry had to say, kept stroking his beard. "Now you're praying," Thales observed. "Now you realize that the supreme Creator is up there, not only to be investigated, but to be acknowledged. To be believed in and trusted." After observing for a while longer, Thales chose to reveal himself, but before doing so he spoke into Henry's mind, *"When humans pray to God it is their spirit guides responsibility to answer their prayers. I wonder who you expect to answer to your prayers?"* With that last thought Thales boldly stepped into the scene.

"Get up son, your prayers have been answered."

He walked straight to Gaya, who was suffering in pain and great discomfort, looked at her and turning to the struggling doctor commanded, "Go for a C-Section."

Miraculously the doctor heard Thales' instruction and ordered the nurses to get ready for the operation.

Henry rose up from his knees with great difficulty, completely drained, but immensely relieved with the outcome of his request saying, "At least now I know who is the one that listens."

Since Rose's soul was enveloped within Gaya's fetus, her mind went into an unusual state of being, an on-and-off mode. When she was awake, everything was in perfect order, belonging to this place was unquestionable, and the pleasure that she was drawing from the entire experience was beyond anything she had encountered before. Anything that may have caused her slight discomfort was immediately fixed by a firm kick from herself. Besides, this constant sound that reminded her of a drum beat, and which resonated through her entire body, placed her a trance-like state. Later, during Gaya's pregnancy, Rose began to identify voices that managed somehow to reach her hearing over the rhythm of Gaya's heartbeat. Soon she learned to differentiate Croton's voice from Gaya's. This on-and-off mode wasn't accumulating any memory data in Rose's newly developing human brain. Each new day was being recorded over the previous one, soon to be erased by the next day's experience. So, the last five months of Rose's seclusion seemed to be only one day, and that day was the one when she would face all who were excitedly waiting for her arrival.

Rose woke up to Gaya's distressed voice and ultimate discomfort. The surrounding soothing liquid suddenly disappeared, and she felt the crushing weight of her own body. The chamber she was in was rapidly closing in on her, leaving her with no room to move. Rose pulled together all the strength that she had and with great difficulty changed her position. She moved her head up to find greater comfort and stability. A bit later, completely exhausted, as she was about to fall asleep, she felt an incredible force being applied to her. An unknown power grabbed her leg and pulled her from her heaven. Next, followed horrifying pain as she tried to open her eyes. A strong stream of light penetrated her eyeball, leaving the first image of a completely forgotten world in her blank brain. Her next attempt to have a glimpse was less painful, and a second later the unimaginable happened. The excruciating pain caused by a hard slap on her bum, followed by the rough handling of her body by some rude being dressed in blue, made her scream. That being began to toss and turn Rose's tiny and powerless body as though it was a plastic doll in the hands of a disobedient child. After some moments of juggling, she was passed to an incredibly beautiful being who was looking at her so tenderly. Rose's eyes, already adapted to the light, began to focus and differentiate not only colors, but images, also. The moment she saw the eyes of this magnificent being and heard her voice, Rose knew that she was back in heaven. A second later, a warm and incredibly tasty liquid filled her mouth and stomach, filling her with comfort and a sense of belonging to this being. Her eyes became heavy and soon she fell asleep.

"What should we name this precious angel?" asked Croton.

"What about Rose?" answered Gaya.

"Why Rose and not my mother's name?" protested Croton.

"I don't know, that was the name on my mind when I woke up this morning," explained Gaya.

Henry looked at Lita asking, "Was it you?"

"Guilty," replied Lita, "I just couldn't resist it."

"Okay," said Croton, "If that's the name that you want, I will talk to my parents."

Gaya placed her palm on his and looking straight into his eyes said, "Don't let them influence you. My decision is final."

"Okay, okay," agreed Croton.

"By the way, did you let your parents know that their granddaughter has arrived?" Gaya asked.

"Oh God, I'm going to call them now," said Croton leaving the room.

CELEBRATION

An early morning phone call awoke Raymond and Anne from their deep sleep. Raymond grabbed the handset expecting to hear the voice of his personal assistant about some problems at work, but it was Croton. Such occasions were so rare that regardless of the news, Raymond was so happy to hear his son's voice.

"Is everything all right son?" Raymond asked with genuine concern.

"Yes, Dad, everything is fine. I'm just calling to let you know that your granddaughter has arrived," Croton said happily.

"What. What did you say?" Raymond repeated doubting his hearing.

"You heard me right, Dad. Come to the hospital to meet her," Croton invited.

"What just happened?" jumped up Croton's mother, Anne.

"Happiness happened, our granddaughter is born!" exclaimed Raymond beaming.

"Oh my God!" exclaimed Anne, quickly jumping off the bed, only to sit back down due to a sharp pain in her stomach.

"Come on, hurry up!" Raymond pushed.

Anne forced herself to get dressed, and by the time she stepped into the car the pain released its clench, leaving her in peace until their next meeting. Neither Anne, nor Raymond, paid deserving attention to the first visit of this invisible guest which had begun its sideways crawl into the humdrum life of this family.

The door into the ward was opened wide and Raymond, followed closely by Anne, marched in bringing along enormous happiness and boundless love. They couldn't pull their eyes away from the newborn baby, admiring her beauty and perfection. Henry, who placed himself in the corner of the room to keep out of everyone's way, couldn't help but share in their joy, completely forgetting the pain that it had caused him, the pain of separation from his Rose who was still not responding to any of his attempts to leave this tiny human body at least once for an instant.

"How much happiness a soul's arrival into this world brings," Henry murmured to himself, "I guess, just for this moment it was all worth it."

Stepping into the life of this family, Rose gave them an opportunity to experience unconditional love and what it is to be a parent and grandparent. She filled their lives with love. She allowed Gaya the chance of becoming a creator. The creator of another human being.

Then Henry stumbled in his thoughts and an enlightenment came upon him…could all of this be designed by the Creator for humans to experience, in a miniscule scale, what it is to create life, and how to love their creation unconditionally. This first attempt to understand the Creator's logic left Henry feeling quite satisfied and he chose to entertain this line of thinking further.

"If God created all that is, then to love should be no problem. So, if the core principle of creation is love, then all that is should be love. That means that love is the building block of this existence and the force that holds everything in place. The entire universe above us and whatever is below—exists because of love. All light and dark also belongs to love. The Creator will prevail through love. We are punished or encouraged because of the love he has for us…"

A sudden bang of the door interrupted Henry's excursion into his mind. He realized that he was standing alone in the room with Gaya and Rose. He moved closer to get a better look at his new Rose. Gaya was lying nearby and with utmost delight was observing the product of her creation. Rose was peacefully sleeping in a cot next to her.

Henry leaned over, and almost touching the baby's face whispered, "Rose, it's me, your Henry." A stream of light poured from his face into hers, enveloping the baby's entire being in a blanket of love, draped with the pain of their separation. Baby Rose rewarded him with a wide smile, still in a state of deep sleep. A spark of hope lit up Henry's soul, only to be extinguished by the lack of response to his multiple attempts to awaken his Rose. To get her back for just one second. To hold her, feel her warmth, to be embraced in the caring arms of one who wants to be embraced by you. All that was missing in Henry's life right now and he felt so lonely and abandoned, like a hopeless lover patiently waiting for his date.

A flick of a switch extinguished the light in the room and the young mother fell asleep, submitting the consciousness of day to slide into unconscious night, making Henry's presence feel unwanted, and perhaps unnecessary, too.

He hadn't been back to his reality since Rose left him. All of this time on Earth, Croton's home had become his home, and his time alongside Rose became his work and place of belonging. But tonight, he wanted to go back. His last hope of seeing and feeling Rose was fading away with the only island of her presence being their common reality, their home. "I want to be back," Henry said firmly, with some anxiety in his mind that he may not find it the way he left it last.

News about Rose's arrival rippled quickly around the city. An endless chain of relatives lined up to visit the newborn granddaughter of Raymond and Anne, and to pay their respects to them. Croton's father had become one of the most influential and wealthiest men in the city. Accumulating substantial power, Raymond had become "one of them", those who subdivided the entire city into areas of influence and were in pursuit of sustaining this fragile status quo. It was fragile because what they were doing was against communist law, and an imminent end of this stolen power was self-evident, although they couldn't see it. Being heavily intoxicated by power and money, "they" were excited in the world created "by them, for 'them", where everyone else was obliged to follow the rules enforced by "them". In other words, Croton was the son of one of the untouchables. All of this weighed heavily on Croton's heart. While children of the elite cashed in at every opportunity, Croton, by his behavior, showed his disapproval of his father's lifestyle and lack of morals and virtues. Raymond constantly tried to shape Croton into his image, because he was certain that his son's future could not be cloudless until he passed to Croton his skills of survival in the murky waters of politics. A world filled with sharks waiting to take a bite of you the moment they see a sign of weakness. To secure himself in the early stages of his career, Raymond learned to collect any kind of compromising information on his colleagues, superiors, and anybody who was somebody. He soon discovered that others were doing exactly the same. This huge network of corrupt officials was bound together by the strongest possible tie—a tie of fear. To summarize, Raymond was basking on the laurels of his success.

Forty days after Rose's physical birth, according to their customs, Croton's parents hosted a huge party in celebration. Despite Croton and Gaya's protests, begging to keep it small and limited to close relatives, Raymond invited most of his colleagues, friends, and especially enemies to be kept closer. Adding to this, with Gaya's relatives, serving staff, and musicians…you could say close to half of the city attended. Seven sheep, two cows, and God knows how many chickens, were slaughtered for this occasion. All delicacies known to the guests were displayed just to amaze and indulge their glamorous tastes, leaving no room for any complaints. The party lasted until two in the morning. Exhausted from dancing, eating, and drinking, guests left this celebration of wealth to return to their humble dwellings, taking with them memories of foods that they'd never tasted before, and a perspective of the life of the city's elite that had been hidden from them.

A VISIT

To Henry's great satisfaction everything back home was exactly the way he'd left it. He sat down on his favorite sofa, leaned back, and closed his eyes. "I'm so tired," he murmured to himself. "All I want is to close my eyes and only open them again when Rose is about to return home. He sighed deeply and drifted into a deep sleep.

"I hope I'm not disturbing."

Henry heard a voice drifting in from a distance. Regaining consciousness, Henry woke up to find Thales sitting right in from of him.

"How was your nap?" he asked sarcastically.

"Did I miss something?" Henry asked, ignoring Thales' remark.

"A lot, and not much," Thales replied.

Noticing Henry's confusion touched with guilt, he continued, "Relax, I have Lita covering for you. Being a spirit guide can sometimes wear you out, especially in the beginning."

"Thank you, Thales," Henry answered appreciatively.

"So, tell me, how are you finding it to be a spirit guide?" Thales asked with genuine interest.

Henry sighed and answered, "In short, it's a handful."

"I'd like to hear the long version," insisted Thales, making himself comfortable in an armchair close by.

He placed his elbow on the armrest and his chin into his open palm in the pose of focused attentiveness.

"All of the responsibilities, endless worries, boundless love, a strange kind of attachment…" Henry said, falling quiet. "Oh, you know better than I do."

"No, no, I would like to hear more about the strange attachments," Thales insisted.

"Okay," agreed Henry, taking a short pause.

The phase he was going through was not completely clear to

himself, let alone to be explained to Thales. Still, he tried, "You see, it's as though you lose your identity and don't know exactly who you are."

"Are you talking about your gender identity?" Thales jumped in.

"Yes, this strange motherly instinct took over, and I don't know how to fight it."

Thales smiled, gently saying, "You shouldn't fight it, but rather embrace those feelings. After all, you are a genderless being."

"I understand that, but I still see myself as a man," Henry explained. "And all this is quite embarrassing."

Thales burst out laughing and then said, "So that's where this older look comes from."

"Yes," blushed Henry.

"Anything else you'd like to share?" Thales invited.

"Yes, one more thing," replied Henry. "I think I learned to love humans."

"Oh, this is interesting. Please tell me more," said Thales excitedly.

"Yes, regardless of their shortcomings, short sighted actions, and all of their imperfections, just the way they are, with a complete absence of judgement," explained Henry.

"Why is that do you think?" Thales asked.

Henry tried to explain, "Probably because I have the advantage of a broader angle of observation. Being outside of their reality, I can see and understand what they cannot, and this ability makes me pity them, urging me to help, but…"

Thales stepped in saying "Then you realize how limited you are in the physical world."

"Yes," agreed Henry, who unexpectedly asked another question that surprised even him, "But why is that?"

"What do you mean?" Thales asked puzzled.

"Why are things the way they are?"

"You're confusing me."

"I just want to know who came up with these rules, and why humans have to suffer?"

"Oh, I see," sighed Thales. "The answer to this question you have to discover for yourself, and you will when the time is right. But for now, there was another pressing question on your mind that needs to be addressed," Thales said, trying to change the subject of discussion that he was not willing to continue.

"Another question?" Henry asked.

"Yes, the question that is stuck at the back of your mind," Thales continued.

"Oh yes," remembered Henry, "Why I cannot see Rose. I know that she can step out of the baby's body, at least for a short while, to see me. I want to see my Rose in that tiny human, but I don't. Don't get me wrong, I love that child dearly…" Henry stopped as he ran out of words, "…Is something wrong?" he continued in desperation.

"There is nothing wrong, my friend, it's just that the bond between body and soul is too strong. There are no set rules for these things. Besides, I planned it to be that way." Thales tried to explain, "You should know that a soul's true character comes through much later in their physical age. For now, everything in that tiny body is focused on a single task. Survival. So, you should not waste your energy trying to see Rose in that child. At the moment, she resembles her parents more than your Rose. Remember, she is a human now."

Henry looked down as he realized the truth in Thales' words.

"I guess we're done for now," Thales said as he stood up ready to leave.

"Before you leave…" Henry stopped him.

"Yes?" Thales replied.

"Can I have a glimpse of how Rose will die?" Henry continued.

"Hmmm," Thales hummed. "If she was older and her exit was dependent on one life changing decision, I would have said yes, go ahead and study the possibilities to help her to make the right decision. But in this case, because her exist will not be due to a decision of hers, allow me to decline your request. Rather, let it be a surprise for you. Your reaction to Rose's early exit is as important to me as Croton's."

"My poor boy. He must outlive his own daughter," Henry stated sadly.

"That's not a fact yet, and we have to wait and see," Thales said.

"Are you suggesting that everything could still change?" Henry asked.

"Not in Rose's case," answered Thales, and nodding his head, disappeared.

Left with more questions than when he started this conversation with Thales, Henry walked to the center of the living room. He stood right in the middle, took a good look around and said to himself in despair, "Do I need all this? What a waste of space.

I think it's time to get rid of this house, and probably this entire reality. Yes, why not?"

He cast his eyes upward to the ceiling as it began its slow disintegration. A moment later, Henry saw a beautiful blue sky above the freestanding walls of the room. "This is actually fun, why not?" Henry smiled to himself. "This way I will have no place to retreat to and hopefully will dedicate my entire self to my Guiding duties. Yes, this will be the only right thing to do," he said as he concentrated his attention on the walls.

He suddenly heard Croton's voice in his head, then Gaya's, it seemed as though they were arguing. The next came a baby's loud cry. Henry tried to concentrate to better hear the physical reality, but he kept losing them. "Something must be wrong down there," Henry said, and before he had a chance to set himself back to where he was needed, some undefined force pulled him out of his reality into an unknown trajectory.

REVELATION

A second later Henry found himself in a huge hall standing in front of a humongous white wall, and a row of countless chairs stretching out on either side. After a quick observation of his surroundings Henry wondered, "Am I in a movie theater?"

"Yes," answered a soul standing in front of him, dressed all in black.

"Tatiana," exclaimed Henry in surprise. "What are you doing here?"

"I think the question should be rephrased to, "What am I doing here?" the multi-layered Tempter answered.

Completely lost in the manner of his transformation and the reality that he appeared in, Henry stumbled, feeling disorientated.

"Please have a seat," offered Tatiana, placing herself right next to him.

A single clap of her hands made the lights of majestic the chandeliers fade away, leaving the gigantic screen still lit up in complete isolation.

"Are we actually going to watch a movie?" Henry asked.

"Do you want to know the purpose of your presence here, or not?" Tatiana asked irritably.

"I do," Henry quickly replied.

"Then, be quiet and watch," Tatiana instructed.

A moment later the entire screen plunged into darkness, depriving the hall of the last remaining source of light.

Suddenly Henry could hear a long forgotten, but so familiar buzzing sound coming from behind him. He turned around to see a square window in the back wall. There was a stream of light that hit the screen, bringing it to life within the swaddling blanket of darkness. To Henry's amusement the movie began with a black and white advertisement. He looked at Tatiana with perplexity.

"What? Is black and white too old fashioned for you?" she retorted.

"No, I'm okay with black and white," Henry quickly replied.

"The last time I was on Earth as a human, cinema had just come to our village, and it became our ultimate form of entertainment. Something way beyond my imagination. Until now, I miss that feeling. The feeling of disguised magic. All the physical, and especially the non-physical, realities are so overwhelmed with colors that sometimes you want…" Tatiana stopped for a second, and Henry completed her sentence,

"…you just want black and white."

"Exactly," she said.

Five minutes later, the political advertisement about the achievements of the communist party, the wisdom of their leaders, and the devotion of comrades was over, and across the screen in capital letters appeared the title of the movie…*CROTON*.

Henry made himself comfortable in the old wooden chair that had a red leather seat and almost no padding.

"I imagine it would have been quite uncomfortable to be in such a chair for an hour and a half," Henry tried to break the escalating tension.

"It's okay," Tatiana commented abruptly, "it only makes people stronger."

For the rest of the viewing Henry chose to keep quiet so as not to agitate this Tempter who could at any time have a change of mind and withdraw to her duties.

One after another on the screen appeared pictures of commercial and residential buildings, technical documentation, blueprints, etc… From the beginning, Henry found this all boring and began to lose concentration, and then a picture of a document attracted his attention. It was the parallel comparison of what should have been done and what was actually done. For example, what type of cement the builders were supposed to use, and that which was actually used. The quantity of steel in the concrete was a lot less than it was supposed to be. The type of paint used on the walls, the quality of timber used in the flooring, electrical wiring—instead of copper aluminium, is used. Basically, wherever possible, and even impossible, all of the materials recommended by the architect engineers and many organizations who filled the blueprint were compromised. Henry intensely observed these documents and was satisfied with the fact that Croton's name was not mentioned once.

"Wait and see," Tatiana said, reading Henry's thoughts.

Then on the screen appeared a Board of Inspectors, with Croton among them, to sign documents releasing those buildings for inhabitation. One after another Henry saw Croton's signature highlighted on those release forms. Then came a scene of someone handing to Croton, filled envelopes containing sizeable amounts of cash. Henry leaned forward covering his face in his hands. The buzzing of the projector behind him stopped, and the majestic chandelier regained its life.

"So?" Tatiana remarked toward ashamed Henry.

"I do not understand. I don't get it. How could this happen? He was the brightest young man known to me, and I know the soul that resides in that body. He stood for nothing but integrity. What happened? Where did all of that go?" Henry questioned.

Tatiana sarcastically smiled and said, "You should know. How culture, traditions, friends, colleagues, the overall surrounding reality can influence the consciousness of humans, and as a result to lower the level of their vibration."

"May I ask you something?" asked Henry.

"Yes, my friend," Tatiana replied.

"Can you please leave Croton alone?" Henry pleaded, "I promise to persuade him to step back from this self-destructive path."

"You know that what you are asking is impossible. Besides, I am not sure that you can help him. I think he crosses the Rubicon. I hope you understand my reference."

"Yes, I know the river in Italy crossed by Caesar to seize power over Rome. A point of no return," Henry explained.

"Yes, exactly," nodded Tatiana.

"Are you certain?" Henry asked with a dying spark of hope in his voice.

"Let's go and witness for yourself," Tatiana said as she grabbed his hand and pulled him out into another reality.

"Are we back on Earth?" Henry asked.

"Yes, and this is happening right now," Tatianna replied.

They appeared in one of the apartments of a newly completed building and members of the Board were standing around a wooden door placed on trestles to serve as a table. After a short conversation it seemed as though all of the parties came to an agreement and the committee members began to place their signatures on a sheet of paper, as a token of a satisfyingly completed task.

"Listen now," whispered Tatiana.

"Well. We found lots of defects, some violations of the required standards, and incomplete work. Nevertheless, we agree to accept this building for inhabitation to help you and those citizens who are anxiously waiting to move in," a man said.

Everyone agreed and began to shake hands and congratulate each other. Before leaving, Croton approached the manager of the construction company and urged him to fix all of the problems before anyone moved in.

"Have no doubts, sir, everything will be in order," he promised.

Then everyone left the room, leaving behind Henry and Tatiana who had been invisible to them. The shock of what he had just witnessed seized his will to follow Croton.

After taking some time to regain his ability to think rationally, Henry asked, "What now?"

"You know the procedure," Tatiana answered.

"Procedure?" asked Henry.

"Yes," She replied.

Henry immediately recalled the time he spent in the hut with the Punishers. He remembered the reality embraced by snow, and the souls residing in it. A sudden cold invaded Henry's soul, squeezing his heart in its icy grip to extinguish the barely breathing light of hope.

"When?" Henry asked.

"I'm not sure, but it is inevitable," answered Tatiana.

Henry wanted to disappear from this physical reality to bury his shame in the sand of a most remote place of the universe. A place where no one could find him. He suddenly realized that all of this was the result of his actions. Feelings of guilt, accompanied with blame, came upon him, causing him to regret the moment he chose to go back home to his reality, leaving Croton on his own to face this sick world clouded with greed and ignorance.

Tatiana silently watched Henry's self-torture, drawing from it the satisfaction of a job well done. "If your revelation is now complete, I will leave," she said.

"Before you do," Henry stopped her.

"Yes?"

"I would like to say thank you for opening my eyes. I know that this is not what you usually do. But still, something doesn't add up in my mind. I've been studying this country with its political and economic systems, and I know for sure that everything here belongs to the government."

"So?" asked Tatiana, unclear as to where exactly Henry was going with this line of thinking.

"I am not getting it. What is the reason behind all of this bribery? What is the interest of the building company?"

ANNE

On the same evening, when Raymond and Anne returned from the celebration party for Rose's arrival, Anne experienced a sharp pain in her stomach again. As she got to her bedroom an excruciating pain gripped her internal organs, forcing her down to her knees. A cold sweat broke out on her face, and the undeniable awareness of rapidly approaching trouble stormed in, and settled permanently into her mind. It felt as though the cold, lifeless hand of death had plunged one arm deep into her stomach, and with the other, tightly squeezed her throat, preventing her from calling out for help. Only a deep and hardly recognizable moan managed to escape through her tightly squeezed teeth as she lay crumpled on the floor.

Raymond, a bit drunk, was lounging on a sofa about to turn on the TV when the unfamiliar sound reached his ears. Momentarily he froze, trying to establish its source, and with the second moan, this time a bit loader than the first, he was convinced that something was wrong with Anne. He found his poor wife lying on their bedroom floor, almost unconscious. Raymond couldn't see her spirit guide, Solomea, who was holding one hand over Anne's head and the other over her stomach. Solomea managed to ease Anne's suffering by knocking her almost unconscious. Such a procedure, as well as the outcome of it, were very familiar to Solomea. She had to use a tremendous outburst of energy to ease Anne's pain, and it was going to cost her a couple of hours of almost motionless existence. Knowing this, she managed to hold on for help to arrive. What Solomea performed that evening was known in the spiritual realms as an extreme act of self-sacrifice. The fact that a human body was able to knock itself unconscious at a time of extreme pain was well known to Solomea, and she was waiting for this phenomenon to kick in, but it was not happening. That was the reason why she rushed in to save her dear Anne some moments of painful existence. Her right hand placed over Anne's head was radiating a direct stream of light right into Anne's pineal gland. This tiny gland, the size of a pine seed, located between the two hemispheres of a human brain, is the doorway into the world of spirit. Solomea, being experienced and quite knowledgeable in the field of human anatomy, was well aware of the role of this essential organ. She understood that it is an important part of the body, often referred to as the third eye, and is an irreplaceable portal of connection between the human mind and the astral realms, where trapped souls could escape their physical limitations in the search of pleasant dreams.

"Anne, what happened?" screamed Raymond, falling onto his knees next to her, helpless and confused. Raymond had never seen Anne weak or not in control of any situation. He was so accustomed to the scenarios where it was he who was sick and being taken care of by Anne. To be entirely honest, they were his most favorite times, when he could act like a helpless child, to be pampered and nurtured by loving "mommy".

Anne was always a pillar of strength for the family, and not only for her family, but the whole community who depended on her giving hands and kind heart. So to Raymond she appeared to be eternally strong, with one tiny weakness, her affection for a life of luxury. But this weakness was so insignificant in Raymond's eyes. Besides, he could afford it, and the fact that his wife was in the possession of very rare diamonds placed him above all other husbands who couldn't afford it. Seeing Anne lying motionless on the floor placed him into a state of panic and the first thing he did was call for help.

He placed his left hand under her head to serve as a cushion, and with his right he held her waist and began to scream like a wounded animal. "Help! Somebody help us!" No neighbor could ignore such a painful call. Twenty minutes later paramedics made it to the second floor to find Anne just returning back to her senses, accompanied by escalating pain.

Solomea was still bravely holding her ground until the minute she saw the hands of the doctor reaching her lovely Anne in an attempt to help ease her pain.

"Finally," Solomea said as she let go of Anne. Her motionless body began to hover just above the floor next to Anne. No guide likes to be merged with a human body and tries by all means to avoid being in the same space as them. The corners of rooms are their preferred places to dwell and monitor the affairs of their guided souls. If someone could only see how, in their desperate attempts to help Anne, all these humans were stamping on the defenceless body of Solomea. She was like a fallen angel with broken wings, crushed into the ground for the sacrifice she gave.

A couple of moments later she was left alone in Anne's bedroom. Her attempts to transfer herself into her own reality failed. Although the sensation of complete immobility was familiar to her, it was still frightening. Fear began to test her mind and patience. "It's only temporary," she kept saying to herself, trying to shift her mind to focus on happy thoughts.

On arrival at the hospital, Anne was taken to a VIP room where the best doctors of the town were immediately called in to check on her. After extensive examination, one of them came out to see Raymond.

"What is wrong with my wife?" he asked.

"We have to wait for the lab results," answered the doctor.

Raymond grabbed his arm firmly demanding, "Tell me the truth, you know me, I can handle it."

After some hesitation the doctor replied, "We still have to…"

Raymond squeezed the doctor's arm so hard that he could feel the tips of his fingernails cutting through the man's flesh. "What is it?" said Raymond raising his voice as he ran out of patience.

The doctor looked at Raymond with sincere compassion and a heavy heart weighed down by the bad news he was to deliver, and after a moment of hesitation, in a low voice, he delivered the sentence, "I'm afraid it is cancer."

Raymond stood motionless, refusing to accept the doctor's verdict. He felt himself slipping into a strange and unfamiliar state of existence. It seemed as though his mind was separating from his body, and he became a distant observer of this strange and frightening reality. He felt as though he was dreaming. One of those dreams that you want to wake up from, but are unable to escape. Even after you manage to escape, wishful thoughts that soon it will be dispersed into the depths of time hold you for ransom. His body froze for a moment. He released the tight grip on the doctor's arm and felt as though he was going to faint.

The doctor caught him and guided him to a nearby chair.

A moment later Raymond came back to his senses, and the first question he asked was, "How long?"

"I beg your pardon?" asked the doctor, convinced that Raymond was still not himself.

"How much time does she have?" Raymond asked.

"I'm not sure. We need to wait for the results of the tests…"

"How long?" Raymond repeated, adamant for an answer.

“A couple of months…” murmured the doctor and disappeared into the maze of faceless corridors.

“A couple of months…” Raymond repeated automatically. A sudden overflowing of emotions borne in his chest, rose up to his throat, growing into a stubborn lump that refused to move, demanding that the unbearable pain be set free.

Raymond leaned forward, buried his face into the sleeve of his jersey to hide this moment of weakness and prevent his tears from wetting his reputation as a strong-willed man and an undisputed leader. His tears did what they do best. They eased his pain, but they still left him with a multitude of questions with no answers, one of them being, “What now?”

Raymond suddenly thought about Anne, lying in a hospital bed completely unaware of her condition. He wiped the tears from his face, pulled himself together, and confidently stepped toward Anne’s ward. As he placed his hand on the door handle, he paused. It was a defining moment. The question of how he was to bring this news to Anne hung in the air, stealing from him the power to turn the handle. He stumbled for a second and then pushed the door open. A pair of eyes filled with hope and expectation of good news met Raymond’s, moistened by sorrow and despair.

Still looking at each other and with false optimism, Raymond walked cheerfully to Anne’s side and sat on the edge of the bed. He tenderly picked up her hand and pressed it against his lips. This simple act of compassion reawakened the pain in his heart and undesired tears again surfaced in his eyes. In an attempt to stop them, Raymond squeezed Anne’s hand so hard against his face, and in that moment, the last hope that had been barely breathing in Anne’s eyes gave up its spark in the sudden realization, and she turned her face away to the pitch-black window and silently, almost motionlessly, began to cry.

Raymond, realizing what he had done, allowed his emotions to take over completely. Anne had never seen her husband so uncomposed, especially never crying so loudly, and that made her even more certain of her conclusion.

When Raymond had exhausted his tears, without looking at him, Anne said, “So, this is the end.”

“No!” exclaimed Raymond. “We are going to fight. Promise me that you’re not going to give up. We’ve been through worse, and we’ve managed…”

Anne looked at him tenderly and with her hand freed from Raymond’s tight grip, gently wiped his face and whispered,

"Don't worry, my love, you will be all right."

"Don't," said Raymond through tightly clenched teeth, forcing himself to subside a new wave of approaching emotions. "Don't talk about me being all right without you."

Anne covered Raymond's mouth with her fingers to stop him talking.

"Hush, we knew that this day would come, when one of us would have to leave, rewarding the other with pain and fading memories." She paused and then added, smiling softly, "Although I always thought that you would be the first to leave, but this is how God wants it to be. He wants me ahead of you, and you will have to live with that."

Raymond kissed her fingers covering his mouth, and putting her hand down in his lap said, "You know that I do not believe in God, and all those ancient legends have no meaning to me. The one thing I want you to know for definite..."

"Yes, my love," said Anne attentively.

"I'm not going to let him take you away from me," Henry continued.

"Let who?" asked Anne smiling.

"Whoever you think is waiting for you on the other side," Raymond replied sharply.

"Of course you won't, my brave knight." Anne answered.

Solomea, who had managed to regain her strength, cautiously walked into the hospital ward, afraid of spoiling this moment of fusion between these long-separated hearts. Since the time that Anne forced Raymond to take the deal against his conscience and to become a corrupt official, she had laid the foundation for the wall between them. The wall that grew higher every year, pushing them apart until they could barely tolerate each other's presence in the same house. But now, in this very moment, seeing Raymond and Anne holding each other's hands, filled her heart with tender love and boundless compassion. This would have been a defining moment for any guide who took upon themselves such a difficult mission, to guide humans to experience pure love. Love that humans are sometimes so reckless with, despite their very existence being borne by the force of pure love.

Solomea quietly stood in the corner, and taking a short excursion in her mind into the past of these two reunited hearts, had to admit that the love that once burned so vigorously, had burned out in the race for meaningless possession of lifeless goods. Suddenly this race had reached the finish line, tearing down the wall that had been separating them, and letting their once lost hearts find each other again. She knew that love has its own energy, unmistakable and unique. Just to be in the field of that energy uplifts one's soul to such a height that the Creator seems to be within arm's reach. Basking in the dazzling field of love, Solomea was observing waves of emotions frequently washing the bodies of these two intertwined souls. The ability of humans to express emotions through their tears was worthy of envy by the non-physical world. Tears to Solomea were the only true revealers of the depth of those emotions. Regardless of their cause, be it happiness or sorrow, their ability to deliver immediate relief she saw as a priceless gift by the Creator to these weak and vulnerable beings.

It wasn't that Solomea wanted to relive long forgotten emotional pain, but the absence of a physical body left her with memories of once being on Earth in a female body. Being around this family from the moment that Anne fell in love with Raymond, she'd seen it all, good and bad. She knew a time when Raymond couldn't have enough of Anne, and also a time when he first betrayed her trust. Collectively, the bad was overwhelmingly more than the good, from Solomea's perspective. She knew how their love could have potentially turned out, but...as any other guide she had no right to judge those who she was responsible for, or for that matter, to take a side. The guides duties were very familiar to her, protection from unplanned harm, try to advise within the range of your capabilities, and most importantly, learn to accept their choices and live with them regardless of whether they are right or wrong. Now looking at Raymond and Anne holding each other's hands, Solomea wanted to freeze time and to dwell eternally in the aura of a most bewildering and perplexing energy so handsomely gifted by the Creator, and named by us, love.

The rest of the night Raymond spent in an armchair next to Anne's bed. He fell into a deep sleep holding her hand in the hope that the approaching day would deliver better news and this one would perish into the past as a nightmare.

The new day arrived at 6am with the irritating voice of a chubby old nurse declaring that it was time for breakfast, knocking loudly on the door. Raymond stretched his body that had molded itself into the armchair, glanced at the still peacefully sleeping Anne due to heavy sedatives, and thoughtfully said to himself, "Here we are, standing right on the edge between life and death, between a familiar old routine and loneliness, between the known and the unknown."

After an intensive rubbing of his sleepy eyes, he went to the bathroom to fix himself up before the doctor's arrival. He discovered that the doctor wasn't in a hurry to show up. There were only frequent visits by nurses to perform their duties, completely unaware of Anne's condition and the reasons for the doctor's delay.

Tension was floating in the air and escalating in a geometrical progression. Raymond's continual visits to see the doctor were denied by his secretary, with the excuse that he was in the operating room Raymond deliberately chose not to tell Croton about his mother's condition until there was complete certainty of her diagnosis.

Around 2pm a soft knock on the door made Raymond jump out of his chair with the utmost assurance of the doctor's arrival, and with that, deliverance of Anne's and his sentence to heaven or hell. The doctor's slim figure and elongated and pale face appeared through the half open door. Raymond's attempt to establish eye contact with him failed.

He walked to the foot of Anne's bed and looked at her. "How are you feeling?" he softly asked.

Anne's glance at his sad eyes caused her last hope to evaporate into thin air. After a long pause she said, "No need for small talk, you can say what you came here to say."

The doctor opened the file in his hands to avoid direct contact with Anne and Raymond and began to shuffle through the laboratory's result to give him time to find the right words and to structure them.

The tension that was rising in the room was discharged by Raymond, "Tell us the truth."

The doctor lifted his eyes, sighed deeply and with great difficulty announced, "It is cancer, and it is spreading rapidly."

Raymond, knocked off his feet, fell back into the chair that he had been sitting in. Anne turned her face to the window now filled with daylight. The doctor stood motionless, filled with the guilt of delivering this death sentence. Raymond held his face in his hands and then slapped himself on his cheeks to clear his head, stood up, and approached the poor doctor.

"Is there anything you can do?" he asked.

"I'm afraid it is too late. We will only cause her more pain and suffering. If you ask me I would suggest that you take her home so that she can be surrounded by the love and care of her loved ones."

And then he apologetically left the room, leaving behind the crushing weight of his words and the rapidly approaching dusk to the union of these two souls.

Anne turned to face Raymond saying, “I think this will be the right time to inform Croton and Gaya. Go home and have a rest… yes, one more thing I would like to ask you.”

“Anything,” said Raymond.

“Can you bring me a Bible?” Anne asked.

“Bible?” Raymond asked to make sure he’d heard correctly.

“You heard me correctly, a Bible please,” Anne confirmed.

Raymond shrugged his shoulders in confusion. He had heard about the existence of such a book, but where to find one was completely unknown to him. Regardless he said, “Of course my love, I will.”

“Go now” Anne insisted, “I want to be left alone.”

Raymond quietly walked out of the room, leaving Anne behind with heavy thoughts, and a victorious Solomea who couldn’t hide her delight observing the sudden turn of events in the lives of her loved ones.

MEETING

Raymond's late afternoon visit on Sunday to Croton and Gaya plunged anxiety into their hearts. Croton's father had never before shown up without Anne, nor prior notice. A look into the face of Raymond standing in the doorway was enough to assume that something terrible had happened. The first thought that burst into Croton's mind was that his father had been caught, and that the long arm of justice had finally caught up to him and brought him down to Earth, or to be more exact, a jail cell. Croton could not judge his father anymore because he had become the spitting image of Raymond. The fear that one day someone will knock on his door and command him to step outside, put him in handcuffs, and instruct him to follow them was already growing in his young and untested mind. All of these thoughts rushed through Croton's guilty conscience like a blast of icy wind.

"What happened?" he asked cautiously.

Breathing heavily after climbing the stairs, Raymond answered, "Last night I took your mother to the hospital."

"What happened to her?" Gaya stepped in, "And why didn't you let us know?"

"It was late, and I thought that it was nothing serious, but…" explained Raymond.

"Please have a seat," said Gaya, showing her father-in-law to a couch.

Raymond fell heavily into the soft cushions and while trying to normalize his breathing thought about how to break this horrible news to his son. Then, without looking up he said to Croton and Gaya standing in front of him, "Mom is not well."

"What do you mean by not well?" asked Croton.

Raymond sighed deeply and said, "She has cancer."

Croton and Gaya sat down right where they were standing. The extreme emotional stress experienced by Croton immediately attracted Henry's attention, who had already developed the habit of not leaving little Rose alone, even when she was sleeping. On observing the heavy silence and the horror on the faces of all of the inhabitants in the room, Henry knew that something irreversible had happened. People usually reacted in this way to life changing news, especially to those that bring fear and uncertainty.

In painfully brief sentences, Raymond told them what had happened the night before, after the party, and the doctor's diagnosis of Anne's health condition.

"We would like to visit her," Croton and Gaya requested.

"I will wait for you downstairs," said Raymond, hoping to inhale a couple of breaths of smoke while waiting.

Twenty minutes later, Croton, Gaya, Raymond, and Rose were on their way to the hospital. Although Henry knew that nothing bad could happen to tiny Rose, he followed closely behind. He was uneasy leaving the young and inexperienced youths to handle his lovely Rose. This tiny body in Gaya's hands was all that was left of his Rose. All that was keeping him attached to this physical reality, especially after what he had learned about Croton. The person he had become and was turning into. Deep inside Henry knew that it was wrong and that he, being the guide to both Croton and Rose, should not choose between them or set priorities. Still, Rose was so small and vulnerable, and Croton so independent and certain in his fallacy. Despite the fact that Gaya's guide, Lita, was always available to stand in for him and take care of Rose, Henry chose to rigorously perform his "motherly" duties himself.

A while later everyone barged into Anne's ward. Preoccupied with Croton's reaction to his mother's condition, Henry did not notice a female figure quietly standing in the corner of the room. When the emotions finally settled, Henry focused his attention on the impeccably shaped slim figure that he assumed was Anne's guide. Usually, a respectful nodding of heads would have been quite appropriate and sufficient as a greeting between guides, and that's what Henry did. But then some uncontrollable force made him approach her and become acquainted with this perfectly dressed guide in the manifestation of a human form.

"Hi, I am Henry," he said introducing himself cautiously.

"I know who you are," answered Solomea.

"I'm sorry for what you are having to go through," Henry said politely.

"Really, why?" Solomea replied.

A bit confused by her response, Henry quickly regrouped his thoughts and said, "I'm sorry because you have to go through the very unpleasant process of Anne's slow death."

"Oh, that's why. Don't worry, and especially don't be sorry. This is the best part of my work," Solomea replied.

Her answer left Henry puzzled and he chose, as always, to get to the bottom of it. He thought to himself, obviously this galactic being knew something he didn't. With this thought Henry politely suggested that they step out and go somewhere quiet where he could satisfy his curiosity. Solomea nodded her head in agreement and smiled gently.

They moved into the waiting room for relatives which luckily was free of any visitors. Henry gestured and Solomea graciously lowered herself into a worn, but comfortable, armchair. Henry noticed that her unusually designed attire would have been more appropriate for lounging on a throne in some exotic place, rather than here. Solomea crossed her legs, revealing her thigh through the long slit in her white silky dress. Noticing Henry's fixation on her leg, she smiled and softly turned so that he could have a better look. Embarrassed, Henry quickly turned his gaze away to look at her face, but her deep cleavage was hard to ignore.

"Are you comfortable?" Solomea asked, pretending to care.

"I am okay," Henry answered, suddenly losing his confidence in front of this mysterious woman. He couldn't quite figure out what was different about her compared to other guides, but she was definitely a much wiser being, and the confidence she carried within was raising all kinds of uncertainties in Henry's mind.

"I am listening?" Solomea asked. "You asked me to step out for a reason, or am I mistaken?"

Henry felt completely lost and confused and only managed to squeeze out, "I did."

"So? What is it you want to talk about?" she pushed.

Henry looked into her eyes and cautiously formed his first question, "Who are you?"

"That's a very philosophical question, because none of us really know who we are, but not to overload your mind I will simply say I am Solomea, Anne's guide."

"Why do I have the feeling that you are more than just a guide?" Henry asked, his courage growing.

Solomea smiled widely revealing perfectly white teeth, and gently placed her hand on Henry's knee. Henry momentarily lost his sense of presence and awareness. Everything around him disappeared into darkness and a second later he found himself in a completely unknown reality belonging to a different time and space.

CRYSTAL REALM OF CREATORS

"What is this place?" asked Henry.

"This is the place where all humans are striving to be, but very few of them actually know about it," replied Solomea.

Casting his eyes around Henry said, "That doesn't make any sense."

"I'll explain it to you later. For now, let's take a look around," Solomea suggested.

In front of Henry's eyes an unusually constructed city began to reveal itself. What struck him first was the building materials used to erect massive structures. They looked like colossal crystal blocks in various geometrical shapes. They reflected rays from an unusually large sun that was hanging over their heads, dispersing a soft glow of irresistibly beautiful colors across the spectrum. This reflection of light from the facets of the buildings filled up the entire city, creating a pampering comfort and the desire to be swallowed by it and dissolved into the rainbow colors. A strange force of attraction amplified by a mind dazzling wish to surrender your entire being to this irresistible energy made Henry step toward it.

Solomea, silently watching Henry's reactions, momentarily grabbed hold of his hand in an attempt to stop him from moving forward. Her touch shook Henry back from his hypnotic state that he'd found himself completely submerged in.

He looked at Solomea and asked again, "What is this place?"

Solomea was so tempted to say "paradise", but on second thought she said instead, "A high vibrational reality."

Henry looked around again saying, "I can feel it with my entire soul. Thank you for bringing me here."

"You are most welcome," smiled Solomea.

A sudden realization came upon Henry, and he apologetically said, "I'm afraid that this is not a good idea."

"Why?" asked Solomea in surprise.

"Every time I leave the physical world something terrible happens," Henry explained. "I'm sorry, but we have to go back. Besides, I cannot leave Rose without my presence or guidance."

"Don't worry," smiled Solomea, "Regardless of the time we spend here, I will return you to the same time and space that we just left."

Eased and comforted by Solomea's answer, Henry felt this gulp of fresh air filling up the sails of this restless explorer. A new and untested before reality was waiting for him and was drawing him to itself leaving no fear of being trapped nor lost in it. A strong feeling of belonging to this place grew within him, filling his soul with light and clarity.

"Why is this city free of inhabitants?" Henry asked.

"It isn't, you just can't see them," Solomea answered.

"Why?" Henry asked.

"I'm working on it," replied Solomea, focusing her eyes on Henry's hand that she was still holding.

Suddenly Henry felt as though he was a vessel being filled to the brim with a strange substance. Any more of it and he would have exploded. Solomea released his hand, and the calmness of the universe enveloped him. With this, the silhouettes of beings slowly began to appear, gliding on the smooth surfaces of the walkways, finding their paths in a thoughtfully designed streets of this metropolitan city.

Henry gave himself some time to adjust his vision so that he could observe the inhabitants clearly, but they still remained hazy and blurry.

"Do you want to meet one of them?" asked Solomea.

"Yes, please!" Henry answered excitedly.

Solomea nodded her head gently and one of the beings walked out of the crowd and approached them. The distance to them was about fifty yards and once the being had covered half of it, Henry felt uneasy. ten yards away and Henry's heart was overwhelmed with love toward the approaching being. Frightened and confused, Henry stepped back. Solomea extended her hand forward, indicating to the being to stop his approach.

Standing ten steps away from this being, Henry had a better chance to observe them in finer detail. He, or she for that matter, because it was literally impossible to identify their gender, was a lot taller than Henry, reaching a height of eight feet or somewhere close to that. A slim figure, absent of any defining muscles on its limbs made them look like a simple but proportionate addition to the body.

Its head was slightly elongated, with no hair and no facial features. It was as though its entire body was made with a semi-transparent substance with a strange inner glow. Despite the absence of any visible facial features, Henry could swear that he was feeling a strong penetrating stream of light emerging from where their eyes were supposed to be, right into his mind. The being's entire body was radiating shimmering light and with it, all of what humanity had been striving to attain for the last 1000 years of evolution. Evolution of their consciousness in understanding and integrating all of the universal virtues. In short, in Henry's judgment, it was perfection itself, despite the oddness of its appearance and the dynamics of its body's movement. Each motion of its body was graceful and dignified at the same time. Despite the enormous amount of energy that it contained, it somehow remained calm and clearly self-aware of its superiority over Henry.

Allowing enough time for Henry to conclude his observations, the being turned its head toward Solomea and asked, "How can I be of service?"

"It came to my awareness that a meeting with you could assist Henry in his ascension," answered Solomea.

"Is he ready?" asked the being.

"You be the judge of that," suggested Solomea. After a moment of silence, she added, "If not, then all of this should be erased."

Her last words struck a note of caution in Henry's mind, which was immediately registered by the being who said, "It is for your own protection."

"To erase my memory?" asked Henry.

"If your soul is not ready to be exposed to the large amount of knowledge that I can impart, it could be harmed," explained the being.

"In what way?" Henry probed, certain in his ability to accommodate any amount of information to be possibly given.

"As you already know, all that you are is just a mind with only so much capacity to absorb and digest. If it is overloaded, the vessel could be destroyed."

"Try me," quickly replied Henry.

"On this positive note, I shall leave you," said Solomea. "Don't worry, you are in good hands, and remember, do not try to get back to Earth by yourself. Whenever you are ready, I will assist you to get back to where we started."

"Thank you," Henry said after the already disappeared

Solomea.

Once Solomea had left, Henry focused his attention on the being in an attempt to understand who, and exactly what, he was facing.

"Ask," said the being, ready to satisfy Henry's curiosity.

"Who are you?" Henry said slowly.

"Do you want to know my name?" the being replied.

"For the sake of starting our conversation it would help," said Henry.

Immediately Henry heard in his mind an unpronounceable, or to be exact, an unimaginable collection of sounds impossible to reproduce.

The being smiled and reading Henry's confusion said, "It was my name in my last incarnation into the physical world."

"The way it sounds, it seems like it wasn't on Earth," Henry commented.

"That's a smart observation," said the being.

"Is this the name that you go by in this realm?" Henry continued.

"We have no names here," answered the being.

"Then how…" Henry replied confused.

"Each of us possesses our own pattern of energy that is unique in the entire universe".

"That makes sense," Henry said, realizing how many Henry's exist on the planet Earth.

"You have your own pattern too, make no mistake about that," said the being.

A sudden realization came into Henry's mind, prompting him ask his next question, "Are you an alien?"

The being slightly leaned his head forward to ask, "Can you be considered an alien to Earth?"

Considering his current situation, Henry realized that he is possibly an alien to those who are living their current physical life on Earth, but the mission he was carrying out as a guide gave him surety to assume that he is not an alien to Earth. "No," he answered firmly.

"Nor am I," said the being.

The strange reality that Henry was facing was becoming even stranger due to the fact that he could see, or to be exact, perceive, all the facial expressions of the being despite the absence of any features.

Henry chose to probe deeper, "How should I address you?"

"As you wish," answered the being, confusing Henry even

further.

It seemed as though the being wanted Henry to establish his identity himself. Giving it some thought Henry said, “May I call you Bernard?”

“Why Bernard?” the being asked.

“I had a lecturer at university with that name and I have the deepest respect for him.”

“On what basis?” enquired the inquisitive being.

“He was a science professor and had a big impact on me, not only as a professional, but also as the embodiment of a perfect human being. He was…”

“That will be enough,” interrupted the being, “I can clearly see that soul and I will be honored to be called Bernard.”

Henry’s excitement was short-lived due to the beings next question, “So, you see me as a male?”

“I guess so,” Henry answered.

“This is very sexist of you,” the being commented, “because you are assuming that a female would have nothing to teach you.”

“I guess you caught me out,” surrendered Henry.

“So, Bernard it is,” concluded the being, adding, “Solomea brought to my attention that you are anxious to learn more about creation. If this is true, I will be happy to assist you in your quest.”

“Thank you,” Henry replied politely, and dropped his first question, “What is this place, who are its residents, and why does nothing here remind me of Earth?”

Bernard moved closer to Henry stopping about six feet away from him, which made Henry very concerned. “Our energies are compatible now,” said Bernard, picking up on Henry’s anxiety, “Let’s take a walk,” he invited, and side by side they walked into the depth of the strange city.

Humongous crystal shapes that Henry assumed were buildings had no doors, nor windows. Each facet was like massive glass windows. Inside the structures Henry could see one or two beings in each room engaged in some kind of activity.

“What is happening in these structures?” asked Henry.

“Before I can answer that question, let me begin with one that you raised earlier. If I’m not mistaken it was…what is this place?”

“That’s right,” Henry happily confirmed.

“This is a higher vibrational reality compared to the one that you are a part of. The difference in the rate of vibration is similar to the difference between Earth and your transitional realms,” Bernard continued.

"Does this mean that if Solomea hadn't raised my level of perception I wouldn't be able to detect you?" Henry asked.

"Not just me, but the city, also. Your second question was, who resides in this reality?"

"Yes," confirmed Henry.

"In short, students," answered Bernard.

"Students?" Henry asked surprised.

"Didn't you realize by now that regardless of the level of our development, and I mean in any aspect of it, we are all students in the quest of understanding creation?" Bernard explained.

"Or the Creator?" Henry jumped in.

Bernard laughed loudly saying, "Being an integral part of creation, all that we can do is to understand the fundamental laws of creation, but not the Creator himself."

"I thought that comprehension of the Creator itself would be a task of paramount importance," questioned Henry.

Bernard smiled knowingly and said, "You are still human."

"Why?" asked Henry.

"Humanity, since the beginning of their time on Earth, have been possessed by the idea of understanding and explaining the Creator. This urge soon finds satisfaction through different scriptures given to humanity by various higher spiritual beings in different time frames. The knowledge passed to humans through these scriptures was supposed to unite, and not segregate them. The latter is what has happened, and this separation brings great sadness to our hearts."

Then Henry said, "It just occurred to me that Solomea was saying that this is a place where humans strive to be. Do you know why she said that?"

"As a matter of fact, I do," answered Bernard, "I'm just not sure if you really want the answer to that."

"Oh, I do," Henry said, "I'm craving to be enlightened."

"Okay, let's find a seat and I will try to explain it to you," suggested Bernard.

Some coffee would have been nice, mused Henry with the expectation of being invited inside a "high-dimensional" coffee shop.

Bernard gestured toward a nearby crystal building. Unable to locate the entrance, Henry allowed Bernard to lead the way. To his amusement Bernard walked right through the facets of the gigantic crystal and Henry followed him. Right in the middle of a perfectly shaped hollow structure, Henry noticed a table with two chairs opposite each other.

Sitting down in one of them and casting a look around, Henry asked, "Why crystal?"

"Crystals manifest the perfection of creation's geometry. They have the ability to hold enormous quantities of data and information. They are living libraries of the entire creation and each one serves a different purpose," explained Bernard.

"What is the purpose of this one?" Henry asked inquisitively.

Bernard answered, "This one helps us to understand physical matter, how it is created, and the methods of its manipulation."

Noticing Henry's confusion as he tried to understand what he'd just heard, Bernard said, "Before going into detail about this, I would like to answer the question you asked earlier about humanity's striving to be here."

"Oh yes, I almost forgot that one. There is so much to learn here that one can be easily distracted," Henry said.

"Now, I'm going to reveal to you the core reason for souls' timeless reincarnation into the physical world," Bernard began and then paused, choosing to start his explanation with a question. "Do you know what the purpose is of these countless visits from the spiritual realms into the physical world and vice versa?"

"I think I do," Henry asserted firmly.

"And?" Bernard pushed for clarification.

"In short, the purification of souls through raising their consciousness," Henry replied.

"It's hard to disagree with such a statement," Bernard replied, "But can you tell me why we have to do that?"

Henry stumbled for a moment. It had never occurred to him, "*Why indeed do we have to be engaged in such a process? Why do we need to evolve our consciousness? Why are we continuously striving for more knowledge? Always in pursuit of new heights never before conquered, and just as soon as we manage to accomplish, it immediately devaluing it for the sake of new goals.*"

Bernard patiently followed Henry's train of thinking, wondering where he was going to end up.

A sudden realization came to Henry, "*How could I have missed it before, the purpose of all that was to become a spirit guide.*"

Bernard burst into laughter, offending Henry.

"My apologies," Bernard said, restraining his involuntary show of emotion, "I did not mean to offend you, but tell me please what about those who don't want to become spirit guides, or simply have no talent for it?"

"I became one," answered Henry adding, "Actually I was forced to become one."

"Forced?" Bernard asked.

"Yes, as a return of favor for my own spirit guide," Henry explained. "He asked me to guide him in his next physical incarnation. Then, my wife was ripped out of my heart and sent back to Earth, and I had to become her guide, too…I don't know, probably this all sound quite twisted to you."

"It sounds like you are complaining," Bernard said more seriously.

"No, not at all. I love them both and I see the reason and purpose for it, but my heart is always in pursuit of more knowledge," Henry tried to explain.

He looked around, lifted his eyes to the enormous sun and said, "The entire universe waits to be discovered…I feel stuck in the physical world, although I do realize that the name of this adhesive is love. So, where do I go from here?" he asked hopelessly.

"One thing I know for definite," said Bernard, "is that the core of this creation, the one that we are all a part of, is love. Love of the supreme creator toward his creation, and as you called it the 'adhesive' that holds all that is physical and non-physical intact is called love," Bernard answered.

"I do understand that," said Henry.

"Only with the perspective of love can creation be understood," Bernard continued. "Reasoning is a powerful tool, but blunt when used on its own. Knowledge without compassion can lead to the destruction of all creation. By the way, that almost happened on your planet and can still happen if humans don't learn to love each and every part of all that has been given to them by the Creator, how they should take care of it. Can you see how everything is entangled and dependent upon each other? The entire universe is like one living and breathing organism, and each of us is a vital organ within that organism."

Henry was listening attentively to all that this strange being had to say and was pleasantly surprised at how passionate he was about saving Earth.

"The time will come," Bernard continued, "when one by one all of the inhabitants of planet Earth will realize that they all came from a single source. That they are closer to each other than they realize, despite all of their differences, which by the way are less than their similarities. But humans still chose to concentrate on their differences, and you know why?"

"Why?" Henry asked.

"Because each soul is in pursuit of personal perfection. Perfection in any activities that they choose, although they are not fully aware of their behavior. Anything they do, they try to do better than the soul next to them and this pushes them apart. The higher they climb up the ladder of consciousness, the lonelier they become," Bernard answered.

"The way you put it…it is not entirely human's fault that they are unable to see their oneness. The way I see it is that the only being who can be blamed is God himself. Obviously, it was his wish for us to strive for perfection and probably never to be able to reach it," Henry interjected.

Bernard nodded his head in agreement, then placed his right hand on the table with the palm facing upward. It was the first time that Henry noticed that the being had only four fingers, an opposable thumb and the rest equally sized, almost double the length of Henry's. Henry focused his attention on Bernard's open palm, which he slowly clenched into a fist. Not knowing what to expect, Henry tried to keep his cool regardless of what he was going to have to face next.

Becoming aware of Henry's tension Bernard smiled, making his entire figure light up. Only now Henry realized how he was judging the mood of his new acquaintance. The absence of facial expressions was well compensated by slight changes in the shade of his body's color, which by some miracle was easily identifiable by Henry as a form of emotional expression. A moment later, Bernard opened his fist and spread wide his elongated fingers. To Henry's astonishment this revealed a most exquisitely shaped, and tastefully colored butterfly. The insect was peacefully resting in the middle of Bernard's palm.

"What is this?" asked Henry, unable to share the apparent delight which captivated Bernard's entirety.

"Don't you see it?" Bernard asked, surprised by Henry's indifference.

"I can do the same, it's just a figment of your imagination," said Henry, "Although I've never tried to create any type of animal or insect, but I am sure that with practice I would be able to do it."

Bernard looked at Henry and said, "Try and touch it."

Henry stretched his hand toward the peacefully resting butterfly and gently, so as not to harm its fragile wings, tried to pick it up, but he was unable to. Compared to the butterfly he was completely flimsy. His fingers passed right through the body of the butterfly without any resistance or harm to it. Henry suddenly remembered that since he crossed over into the transitional realms, that Croton used to call the place where all souls were residing, he'd never come across any animal, nor insect for that matter.

"Is this butterfly real?" Henry asked.

"Don't you see it?" replied Bernard.

"I mean, is it alive like those on Earth?" Henry continued.

"Not yet," whispered Bernard, "But it is about to become a living being in the physical sense."

The butterfly stood firmly on its six legs, with its wings spread wide apart, displaying their symmetry and arrangement of the most unimaginable colored patterns. The brittle antennas that were slightly shivering were the only indication of the soft spark of life dwelling in this creature. Bernard stretched his elongated neck forward, and lowered his head over the butterfly, and it seemed to Henry as though he softly blew life into the insect.

As though being awakened from an eternal slumber the butterfly began to aimlessly flap its wings, still standing on Bernard's hand.

Watching the poor creature struggle Henry asked, "Is something wrong with it?"

"Why?" Bernard asked offended, "It's absolutely perfect."

"It doesn't seem perfect to me. Its unable to fly," retorted Henry.

"Oh, that's what you mean," said Bernard, "Of course it won't fly."

"Why?" asked Henry.

"In order to fly it needs air under its wings," explained Bernard.

"Oh, I see," Henry responded sheepishly. "Lately I've been spending so much time on Earth that the distinction between physical and non-physical realities sometimes get blurred."

"That is understandable," said Bernard.

"What I am interested in is how exactly you gifted this creature with life?" Henry asked.

"That was the easiest part of this project," Bernard replied. "The difficulties lie in its manifestation. But we will discuss that later if you are still interested."

"I really am," confirmed Henry.

"So, what did I do to bring this butterfly to life…I just funnelled a tiny part of my personal energy into its body," Bernard continued.

"Are you saying that a part of your energy will now reside eternally in this insect?" Henry asked with genuine surprise.

"Just a tiny part. Enough to give it life, but not enough to join with common butterfly consciousness. Besides, that tiny part of donated energy will be retrieved once this butterfly dies."

"I think you lost me at 'common butterfly consciousness'", said Henry.

"I see, dear Henry, as I told you before the animal world is different to humans. They possess a common consciousness. Different types of animals have different types of minds and as a result different pattern of behavior," Bernard continued.

"Can you define that more for me please?" Henry asked.

"Of course. Elephants, regardless of where on the planet they are born, behave in a similar way. Any mammal, insect, or fish that belong to the same group, have similar patterns of consciousness, and as a result a similar pattern of behavior."

"So, why a butterfly?" Henry suddenly blurted out.

"In my last few lives in physical form I developed a deep interest in entomology."

Noticing Henry's confusion Bernard explained, "I was a scientist who was studying insects, and in particular butterflies."

"Did you have them on the planet that you came from?" Henry enquired.

Bernard fell quiet and so Henry continued apologetically, "I guess that was a stupid question to ask."

"Anyway, they have become my current love affair," said Bernard.

"A love affair?" Henry asked.

"Yes. We cannot create without love. After all, they are a part of me, and always will be," Bernard explained.

"If you don't mind me asking," Henry probed, "what exactly are you doing here in this so called high vibrational realm? And not only you, but all the others, too?"

"You, my dear friend, are in the place where magic happens," Bernard replied mystically.

"Judging by how easily you created that butterfly and breathed life into it, I have no doubt in your abilities as a magician," Henry commented.

"There is no magic in the creation of physical objects or beings," Bernard answered. "The process is similar to what humans do on Earth."

"Excuse me?" asked Henry.

"Down there humanity manipulates matter, and up here we

manipulate God given energy to create that very same matter… let me cheer you up," Bernard said energetically, "It seems as though I have overloaded you."

"Yes, it is a lot for me to take in," replied Henry.

"Let's leave this building," suggested Bernard as he slowly closed his palm, and the butterfly was nowhere to be seen when he opened it back up.

On their way out, Henry noticed again the enormous sun suspended over the entire reality. Its orange, smooth surface was easy, and quite pleasant, to observe. "What is that?" asked Henry pointing at the orange sphere.

Bernard raised his head to face the orb, and after a moment of silence said, "We believe that it is our source of life and love."

Henry commented, "That's quite a strange combination of words."

"There's nothing strange about it," replied Bernard. "This you should remember for your entire existence." Looking up again it seemed as though he was taking a moment before delivering his next sentence, in order for it to have a deeper impact on Henry's still simple, but very inquisitive mind.

"What should I remember?" asked Henry, becoming impatient.

Bernard turned his head to face Henry and, in that moment, Henry could swear that he saw Bernard's eyes. They were humanly placed on his head, but at a different angle. The corner of the eyes, closest to the nose, were a lot lower than the ones close to the temples. They were a bit bigger in size and had a deep blue iris and dark black pupils. This flash of identity did not scare Henry, on the contrary, he felt a strong attraction toward this being and an irresistible urge to keep staring into his deep eyes that appeared like space itself.

"Remember this, light stands for knowledge, and love stands for creation. One is always the outcome of the other, and they cannot exist without each other."

"The fact that life is knowledge I can accept," replied Henry, "But the outcome of love being creation can be debated."

"Please proceed," Bernard invited, getting ready to engage in debate despite being confident in its outcome.

"So many rulers on Earth created colossal monuments to immortalize their names, and as always, poor people have to pay for this with their sweat, blood, and lives. Looking at those structures, they deserve admiration for their size, beauty, and craftsmanship, but I do not see any love, just overextended human ego," Henry started.

"Only because your observation is shallow," argued Bernard. "Yes, you're right, those ruthless rulers raised monuments to glorify themselves, to satisfy their pride on the bones of poor people. But they were only the customers who ordered the work. The masterminds behind those projects were always talented architects who outshone most due to their ability to dream big."

"Dream big?" asked Henry.

"Yes, you heard me right," replied Bernard. "All those magnificent structures are materialized dreams. You should know that one who cannot love, cannot dream. Love for the trade they chose gives the architects the ability to create something that would withstand the tests of time and remain as a statement to manifested love through creation."

"I see your point," said Henry.

"Will you be interested to visit our zoo?" Bernard asked enthusiastically.

"Zoo?" said Henry confused.

"Yes, every animal that has ever existed on planet Earth has been well preserved in our bank of species," advised Bernard.

Noticing Henry's expression, Bernard continued, "You should know that nothing, once created, ever goes to waste or is destined for oblivion. Every materialized dream of these scientists remains for eternity to be studied and observed."

Henry noticed that Bernard was drawing enormous pleasure in this process of unveiling an entire new world to him. He understood that Bernard had carefully planned this entire trip to unfold gradually in line with his ability to absorb new information and stay interested. At the same time, Henry knew that nothing in the universe has been left to chance, and that his presence in this realm of creators was not a random coincidence.

Given this realization, the thought that some other force of higher consciousness was puppeteering his entire existence began to creep into his mind. This led him to question the origin of that force, and the motives which were stimulating his actions.

Caught in his thoughts, Henry didn't notice how they appeared in the so-called zoo. Perfection in the form of the crystalized city had disappeared, surrendering its place to what could be described as pre-historic nature. The surrounding landscape was remotely similar to Earth.

They appeared in the middle of a forest with wild vegetation. Most of the trees were familiar to Henry, but some he was seeing for the first time.

"Are we on Earth?" asked Henry.

"Not exactly," replied Bernard. "This is how Earth looked in what humans called pre-historic times."

"So, this is a replica of it?" Henry commented.

"The trees and vegetation unfamiliar to you were for a long time extinct before you chose to begin your reincarnation cycle on Earth."

The word "chose" completely missed Henry's attention due to his preoccupation with this zoo, with no cages, nor fencing, to protect visitors from possible danger. Before Henry could project his thoughts about coming across pre-historic animals, a dinosaur appeared in front of them, firmly erect on four legs that looked like pillars. It's extremely long neck was crowned by a disproportionately small head. In Henry's judgment it was as tall as a five-story building.

"Brachiosaurus," said Bernard.

"Sounds complicated," said Henry.

"It was not us who named this animal. A human scientist came up with this complicated name," answered Bernard.

"What would you have named it?" Henry asked curiously.

"We do not need to name any of the animals," said Bernard. "We just keep their images in our minds and when we have to refer to them, we just project their images to each other."

"Oh yes, I keep forgetting," said Henry, feeling a bit stupid. "Can I get closer to it?" he asked.

Bernard gestured with his hand that Henry could proceed.

They were about 100 yards away from the animal. The closer Henry got to it, the harder his heart was pumping, although he was quite aware of its absence, he could swear that it was there and was rushing adrenaline to his brain. On closer observation, the dinosaur was a lot bigger and more scary than Henry had imagined. The animal didn't seem to be moving, with only the gentle replicated breathing, and the gracious movement from side to side of its long neck giving away the presence of life in this humongous tower of an animal. Henry cautiously stepped up to its leg. He felt like an ant approaching a human foot.

He turned to look at Bernard and asked, "May I touch it?"

"What are you afraid of? No physical harm can come to you," Bernard replied.

"I know…still, it is quite scary," answered Henry. "I guess human reflexes are still deeply embedded in my mind."

"That's right, and it will take years spent outside of physical realms to lose it," said Bernard. "Fear is the most dominant emotion in the physical realm, and you know why?"

"I guess to protect humans from harm," Henry surmised.

"Not only," replied Bernand. "Fears keep you trapped in the re-incarnational cycle."

Bernard emphasized his last word, but Henry didn't pay any attention to them because of the miracle he was facing was way more interesting than any debates about reincarnation. Henry stretched his hand forward and carefully touched the animal's leg. He could immediately feel the strength of its muscles, carrying such a weight to withstand the force of Earth's gravity. Each vein that was visible was thicker than Henry's leg.

He felt the peaceful pulsation of the animal's heart pumping an enormous amount of blood to sustain life in such a creation of bone and flesh. While he was standing fearlessly touching a living skyscraper, Henry's heart filled with happiness and joy. He could feel an energy exchange happening between them and an unexplainable unity in that very same moment.

Bernard, who was observing Henry's revelation, felt satisfied and fulfilled.

The first spark of understanding how united the entire creation is had found its place in Henry's mind. In that moment, Henry felt an absolute merger of his consciousness with that of this majestic animal. They became one mind, one soul, and one body. The feeling itself was so overwhelming that Henry unconsciously hugged the animal's leg, wishing to be merged with it.

A second later the Brachiosaurus turned its head toward Bernard and began to observe him. Then he raised his head up to observe the surrounding nature. After substantial observation it leaned its neck forward and took a step, disconnecting itself from Henry's grip. This caused it to stand still again, and to return to its previous state of unconsciousness.

Henry immediately snapped back from the trance that he'd been in, and once he'd recovered his state of mind, he asked, "What was that?"

Bernard gently smiled and asked in return, "What did you experience?"

"I wasn't myself. It seemed as though I merged with the dinosaur. It was a strange, or should I say, a weird feeling of becoming one. One in every sense of that word. For a moment I desperately wanted to go and explore this forest, but mostly I had my eye on that tall tree." Henry pointed and said, "The leaves at it's top are irresistibly attractive."

"Did you feel hungry?" asked Bernard.

"Oh yes. For the first time since I left my physical body, I remembered what it is to be trapped in flesh again," Henry replied. "My senses came back…"

"Would you like to become a human again?" Bernard interrupted him.

"No," Henry immediately dismissed the idea. "I have duties to perform. I have souls to take care of, and to ensure their safe return back into the spiritual realms."

Bowing his elongated head, Bernard said, "I guess we have reached the end of our journey," as he vanished into space, leaving Henry in the presence of the splendid reptilian. The fact that Solomea had promised him to be returned to the exact time of their departure gave Henry a certain peace of mind and the will to carry on exploring this mysterious zoo. So many animals from a long-forgotten past emerged for Henry's observation. Some were so familiar to him from pictures in books. Some were only being discovered now, and completely overwhelmed with so many impressions and discoveries, Henry decided it was time to go back.

He concentrated his thoughts on Solomea, and she immediately appeared right in front of him.

"How was your journey?" she casually enquired.

"I'm still in shock and partially confused after being exposed to such revelations," Henry answered.

"What confused you the most?" asked Solomea.

"How far away I still am from understanding, or even having the ability to accommodate the size of love which it will require one day to stand amongst these semi-Gods. How will I learn to love humanity with all of their imperfections in order to deserve a chance to experiment with even the simplest forms of life," Henry explained.

"What can I say. This is a place of powerful Creators," said Solomea. "You saw yourself, they are shaping a physical existence that gives us the opportunity to descend to Earth into a human body, which by the way we all become so addicted to. All souls in their ascension are destined to be here, or in a realm similar to this. We have all been created by a Creator, and we will all one day become Creators ourselves."

"It's hard to understand, and even harder to imagine, the length of time we have to cover in order to become the one we are destined to be," said Henry.

"Eternity has been given to us by the supreme Creator to accomplish such a tremendous task," Solomea replied.

Giving Henry a moment to reflect she simply asked, "Should we get back?"

"I think we should," agreed Henry. "I've had enough and probably a lot more than I could have asked for, and for this I'd like to thank you. This was such a pleasant surprise and an opportunity for me to detach from the heavy weight of planet Earth. This break was definitely needed."

"I know, my dear friend," said Solomea, gently touching his hand.

BACK TO THE WARD

Momentarily they were back in Anne's ward. Solomea took her place at Anne's head and Henry stepped aside from everyone's paths, into a remote corner of the room. An hour later, when all emotions were settled and everyone came to terms with the unequivocal fact of cancer's presence in Anne's body, she chose to chase her visitors away.

"I want to be alone. Please go home," she said.

"I will walk you out," Raymond said to the visitors, standing up from Anne's bed.

"Will you stay for one more minute my son?" Anne asked Croton.

Letting everyone else out of the room, Croton sat on his mother's bed and gently took her hand into his. In that very moment Croton noticed how much his mother's hand had aged. Fine wrinkles looking like thirsty ground craving for a drop of water were crossing the back of her hand. The fact that his mother had aged suddenly hit him with a force of passing years. When she, the most important person in his life was gradually relegated to one who fed him, cleaned his room, washed his clothes, all without any expectation of appreciation. Now she was lying hopelessly in front of him, crushed by the irrevocable verdict and the sentence to that verdict was death. He tenderly looked into her eyes, something that he hadn't done for such a long time, since he was a child, and he felt his heart drop to his stomach. Anne's love of Croton was seeping from her eyes as glistening tears. A love that only a loving mother has for a child. A love that has no conditions, nor any judgements attached. The biggest mystery of nature is this form of love. The one that brought us one by one to life, raised and protected us from harm, and never dies with time, if anything becoming stronger.

"Yes Mom," Croton said.

"There is something that I would like to ask of you. I asked your father, but I have my doubts in his ability to comply with my request. You know that he is very busy…," Anne asked in earnest.

"What is it Mom," Croton said.

"It's very important to me. Just promise that you will not decline my wish," Anne answered.

"I promise Mom. No matter what it is, I will do it gladly," Croton said.

No mother is ever capable of wishing harm, especially when it comes to her only son.

"My request is simple, but not effortless," Anne said.

"What is it, Mom?" Croton pushed.

"My heart requires a Bible," Anne said.

After a moment to reflect on Anne's request, Croton answered, "Maybe a priest can be of help, but don't get ahead of yourself. Why don't you have a rest, lie back and have a nap. I'll ask my father to delay his return and when you are rested perhaps you will see things in a different light."

Anne smiled sadly and insisted, "See my request as a wish. I hope not my last one, my dear son. That book I have to read myself. I don't know why I am so certain about this, but it is so stubbornly persistent in my heart and mind."

"I'll do it Mom," Croton assured his mother, without a single clue where he could find this book in a communist country.

Solomea stayed behind with Anne in celebration of the victory of spirituality over a cold and calculating mind.

While Henry followed Croton who left not knowing where to start. He stood in front of the hospital completely lost. Although he knew of the book's existence, he wondered who could be of assistance to him. Book stores would never stock this book. As far as he knew it was illegal.

Henry stepped in front of Croton, looked straight into his eyes and kept repeating one phase, "Look at the church. Look at the church. Look at the church."

This idea found it's place in Croton's mind. He looked around, and then noticed a building right in front of him. Amidst the concrete jungle of faceless flats, he saw in the distance, like melting hope on the horizon, the soft shimmer of a cross. It was resting on the temple of the church that had survived demolition by some miracle. Brave citizens, some sixty years ago, protected the last one with their bodies so bravely placed between bulldozers and their ancient church. Without looking any further, Croton walked directly to the church. He knew that in choosing such an act he could jeopardize his high position. The party leaders may not forgive him such a weakness, not trusting science, and looking for help through religion. For future troubles Croton couldn't care less. His mother's dying wish was placed on the scale. His future was irrelevant in the quest to find this book and help his mother to find what she was hoping to discover.

An hour later Croton stood in front of heavy wooden doors so delicately carved by master carvers. Through intricate entangled ornaments created by the weaving lines, a cross emerged from ancient times, worn down by the elements and the touch of countless devotees hoping to find salvation through those doors. He pushed them open, finding them a lot heavier than he anticipated. Accompanied by a loud squeak from their rusted hinges, the doors finally gave in to the force of the Bible seeker.

Disturbed by the loud noise, the entirety of the church awoke from slumber. So seldom visited by congregation, those walls seemed as though they'd lost their purpose and connection. Connection with the multitude of people in search of God who used to visit such a humble institution. Croton cast his eyes from left to right in search of a priest, or someone who he could approach. Dark walls, handsomely splashed with bible scenes and hardly lit by candlelight, were so unfamiliar to Crotons mind.

Each step toward the altar echoed off the walls, and on reaching the cupola of the dome were one by one reflected back to the disturber of the peace. There was something magical about his approach under the surveillance of the watchful eyes of the saints depicted on the walls. A few more steps and Croton stood in front of a mighty wooden cross. He lifted his gaze upon the relaxed and lifeless body of Christ, and a revelation crept into his mind in the form of a question. "*Am I living right? Is something missing in my life?"* A chain of doubts visited his heart, touching his soul, and reflecting to his mind. *"For centuries our ancestors used to find salvation within the walls of churches. Were they wrong? To come with pain in search of a cure. Trusting their secrets to a man who was probably closer to God."*

His trail of thoughts was interrupted by a voice suddenly approaching him from behind, "How can I be of service, son?"

As if struck by lightning Croton jumped and spun around. Dressed all in black, a priest in his late 50s was standing in front of him, expecting Croton to explain what brought him to the house of God. Croton stumbled for a moment unsure of how to approach the priest.

"How should I call you…uncle?"

"You can call me Father," said the priest, modestly bowing

his head in respect.

"Father, I have an unusual request," Croton said, falling quiet for a moment before continuing, "I don't know where to start."

"Start from the beginning son," suggested the priest in a humble voice.

"My mother is in the hospital as we speak in an epic battle between life and death. I don't know how long she has to live, and with this she placed upon my shoulders quite a strange request."

"Yes?" said the father.

"She asked me to go and look for a book. I don't know why it is so important to her, or what she is hoping to find in it. But she is so adamant and so persistent, it seems as though she feels that her life depends on it."

"Let me guess, she's asked for a Bible," replied the priest.

"Yes, and the only place that I could think of was this church. Please don't decline her wish," Croton said.

The priest looked at Croton with eyes touched with compassion toward a son who couldn't understand his mom due to his age filled with ambitions, finding his place in a society of non-believers.

"You know I have this book in the church, but unfortunately each copy is under strict observance by servants of the government. To give that book to you would be considered a crime against our communist republic," explained the priest.

"I know about that. To be standing in front of you in these walls I am risking a lot," Croton answered. "I beg you. Don't leave my prayer hanging in the air."

"Prayer?" said the priest in surprise. "Are you familiar with any?"

"I am not, but I'm sure they will find my mind unless you choose to deny my supplication," urged Croton. "Please be kind."

Observing Crotons dedication, the priest took a step toward the young man and softly whispered into his ear, "I might be able to find a solution to your problem. One copy has recently been smuggled into the country. We call that book the breath of God. A book divided in two parts. The first is called the old testament and the second the new testament. I suggest that you take the second part, where the life of Christ is depicted. I'm sure that it will help your mom by shedding light on the Creator and will provide her with much needed comfort for the remaining time that she has."

He placed his hand on Croton's shoulder and with the wisdom accumulated in the last 2000 years by the church he said, "You shouldn't worry son, death is not the end. Her soul will remain, and it will find its path to our Father, Almighty God. But she must know that the passage leading up can only be found through our savior and guide, Jesus Christ."

"I see now. I'll make sure that my mother gets your advice. For now, I beg you, let me have it," asked Croton.

The priest disappeared behind the alter, coming back soon with the book wrapped in newspaper, saying, "Don't blow my secret, be discrete. I might lose my freedom over this."

"Trust me on this," insisted Croton, grabbing the book, which was much lighter than he anticipated.

He was about to turn and leave, and then suddenly remembered, sliding his hand into his pocket to retrieve his wallet, but the priest grabbed his hand and said, "There is no need. To spread the word of Christ is already my reward."

Thanking the priest Croton left the church with doubts seeded in his chest. Those doubts find their way into our hearts and minds once we step into the house of God, but then they swiftly vanish once we get out in the world again. A world based on the trade of any possible possessions including honor and dignity.

An hour later Croton was back at his mother's bedside, presenting the book to her, "Please be secretive about this," he said. "I gave my word to the priest."

Anne grabbed the book, pressed it against her chest, and landed a kiss upon Croton's forehead.

Henry was filled with hope that Croton might still find his way to the light, and looked at Solomea saying, "I think that this is a victory deserving a celebration, certainly to be admired. A tiny step toward the light on Croton's side, and a break through the darkness for Anne."

"Should we go to my reality?" Solomea asked casually.

Henry stumbled for a second juggling with the decision to either submit or respectfully decline such a generous suggestion. Solomea was so attractive in her feminine appearance that Henry, being so firmly masculine in his mind, was afraid of being attracted to her beauty. Solomea, reading Henry's unprotected mind chose to ignore and overlook his precautions and insisted.

"*Oh, what the hell, a short visit to a new dimension can't cause me any harm. Besides, my love for Rose is so intense no beauty in the world can weaken my devoted heart,*" Henry thought. Solomea, giving Henry time to reach consensus in his mind, gently touched his arm and immediately everything began to swirl with a pulling force into the unknown.

Solomea's Reality

Henry opened his eyes standing on an ancient terrace. Solomea was next to him expecting admiration for her creative drive. The scenery was breathtaking. They were standing on the top of a hill, and as far as Henry could see there was vegetation splashed all over the realm. Irregular in shape, terraces ran down the hill, creating a gradual descent into scattered clouds floating down below. Each level of this slatted serpent was planted with various types of flora. The most attractive of all were handsomely filled with colors reminding Henry of a messy artists palette, splashed with unimaginable colors, that by some magic, were turned into flowers.

Henry took a deep breath to fill his lungs with the aroma of wildflowers, but was quickly disappointed, and without facing Solomea he said, "It would have been nice for a change to inhale the freshness of the air and the scent of these wildflowers."

"All you have to do is to remember," Henry heard Solomea's voice from behind him.

"The problem is, I have never been to a place like this in my past life, and so it will be hard to recreate an experience that I have never been exposed to," replied Henry.

"I am sorry to hear that," replied Solomea.

The plateau that they landed on was paved with a flat rectangular tablet decorated with writings unknown to Henry, that were encrypted, or should I say, carved into it. On closer inspection they reminded Henry of hieroglyphics. The plateau was sizeable, about fifty yards in diameter. Six obelisks were firmly erected in each corner of a hexagon deck. Henry stepped closer to one of them to have a better look. They were made of solid granite, with Egyptian writings deeply carved along the four sides of the column reaching all the way to the top. Henry looked up to establish the height of the obelisk, concluding that they were about sixty-five feet tall with a defined sharp point at the top. Standing on the plateau, which was at the highest point of the entire reality, Henry felt as though he was at the top of the world.

Having satisfied his curiosity with the exterior, Henry turned around to face Solomea and to his astonishment she was wearing a very different outfit. More elegant and even more revealing of her body's beauty then the previous one. Henry could not hide his satisfaction. An emotion that was immediately sensed by Solomea. Her garment was light, not only in its texture, but also, it's color of blue. The fabric hardly covered her naked body, leaving very little to Henry's imagination. A golden lining was visible on the edges of the fabric, adding even more mystery to her appearance. The long dress, reaching to the floor, covered only the front and back of her body, leaving the sides exposed. The cleavage reaching to her belly was restricted with a thin golden belt gently hugging her waist.

She was standing between two completely white marble chaise-lounges covered with red velvet cushions. They were about six feet apart from each other, poised in readiness to comfort the visitors to this unusual reality. Solomea invited Henry to lounge on one of them and offered him a heavily encrusted golden cup filled with red wine. Henry accepted her offering, and as he did so he noticed a strange bracelet in the shape of a snake wrapped around her wrist reaching to her elbow. What was strange about it, was that for a second Henry felt that the snake was moving, but when he paid attention to it, it became still.

"Nice touch," said Henry referring to the bracelet.

Solomea smiled, and gracefully laid down on the chaise.

She made herself comfortable, putting her left arm up to support her head, motioning to Henry to follow suit. Henry copied her action, but a moment later he sat up.

Noticing the question on her face, he said, "I feel more comfortable this way." Then, taking a sip from the cup that was still in his hand, he looked for somewhere to put it down. Solomea instantly created a white coffee table made from marble that formed a barrier between them.

With great difficult Henry tried not to fixate his gaze on Solomea's completely exposed right thigh that was elegantly resting on top of her left leg. The blue fabric on the upper part of her body was by some miracle still covering her breasts, only disclosing a slight glimpse. Henry noticed that this game of exposure and his reaction to it was giving Solomea pleasure and she was pushing it to the edge of acceptable decency.

Trying to redirect his attention Henry looked up saying, "So, no roof?"

"Who needs a roof," Solomea said seductively adding, "where even the sky is no limit."

"Yup," said Henry as his right leg began to tremble nervously.

He remembered the purpose of his visit to Solomea's reality, and like a drowning man clutching at a straw he asked, "Is Anne going to die?"

Solomea answered, "Of course she will."

"Soon?" Henry asked.

"It will depend on her," Solomea answered without taking her eyes off Henry's face.

"What do you mean?" Henry questioned.

"It will depend on how soon she will accept with her heart Christ Consciousness," answered Solomea.

With great disbelief upon his face Henry responded, "Are you kidding me?"

"Not at all. Why should I?" replied Solomea.

"What is it anyway, Christ Consciousness?" asked Henry.

Solomea smiled and answered, "I see that you have complete disregard for the Christian religion."

"Not only for Christianity, but for any other religion, also," Henry answered.

"Here you are completely wrong, my friend," Solomea replied. "Religion plays an enormous role in the shaping of human souls. It is a necessary period in our development. Each soul must go through this, to let those teachings in, and to plant fear in their hearts of the Creator's judgement and imminent punishment. You can not underestimate the importance of religion."

Henry listened silently to Solomea's explanation, and then burst out with a question, "Why don't we tell humanity the truth?'

"What truth?" asked Solomea.

"The truth about the spiritual realms. The truth about the infinity of life and the eternity of our souls.

Why don't we tell them what to expect, or what is the meaning of their lives, and what the Creator expects them to become? Why don't we tell them that one day they are all going to become powerful creators of physical realities, and probably become Gods in their own right?"

Solomea listened quietly to Henry's emotional outburst, and then answered, "There are rules to the game of reincarnation. They were not set by us, and they are not for us to break. Even if we wanted to, we will not be able to."

"Why?" Henry reacted angrily.

"Those higher dimensional beings, or should I say Creators, who came up with the paradigm for a soul's evolutionary development on the planet Earth, also designed protective mechanisms to prevent the matrix from self-destruction."

Before Henry had a chance to throw his next question, Solomea slowly lifted herself up from the chaise. She did so gracefully and irresistibly sexily that for a moment Henry forgot about all of his complaints regarding soul's development. Solomea gracefully turned her back to Henry and with one stroke of her hand released the fabric covering her body. It slid off her silky skin and softly landed at her feet. Henry swallowed hard in complete confusion. Solomea deliberately held this pose for some time to allow Henry time to observe and appreciate her beauty. The radiating inner glow of her olive skin was irresistibly inviting to not only be observed, but also to be touched and possibly to be possessed.

Henry squeezed the cushion that he was sitting on with such force that his knuckles turned white. Although he wanted to take his eyes off her, his hypnotic state of mind prevented him from doing so.

Solomea gently turned her head to expose her perfect profile and glanced at Henry. Satisfied with the effect she had achieved, she stepped forward over the blue gown and away from Henry. After a few steps Solomea began to shrink in height. Henry thought that she was sinking into the ground. He stood up to see what was happening and saw that she was slowly immersing herself into a bright turquoise swimming pool. A few steps later she was immersed up to her waist in water. Her long shiny hair touched the surface of the liquid forming the shape of a floating fan behind her. After a few more steps Solomea reached the center of the pool and stopped. Henry, like a powerless prey under the spell of a serpent could not take his eyes off her. Solomea slowly turned around, completely revealing her upper body for Henry to observe and admire.

To anyone watching from afar, Henry would have appeared like a firmly erect statue of a man, a bit lost in uncertainties as to how to react to such an obvious seduction.

"Do you care for a swim?" Solomea casually asked.

Stepping back from his hypnotic state of mind Henry answered, "You know I have a reality situated right on a beach, but to go into the water, or even to try and swim, never crosses my mind."

Solomea gently smiled and said, "Do not tell me that back on Earth you never swam in a pool."

"I did…" replied Henry.

"Then it should not be a problem," Solomea interrupted. Her posture and the look on her face expressed an invitation to join her.

"Where are you when I need you most?" Henry thought about Croton, the one with an ability to appear at the right time and the right place. Croton's absence in Henry's life as a mentor created an unimaginably large void. A void that was expected to be filled by Henry's ability to commit himself to a decision making process alone. With no one around to agree, or even argue about the choices he had to make. He was alone. A part of him wanted to jump into the shallow pool headfirst and to explore whatever this beautiful being in front of him arranged for him. But there was the other part that was worrying about the trouble that would follow such an act.

A short juggle for and against ended up with the choice to test the waters, and not only literally. Henry closed his eyes and, in an instant, appeared at the edge of the pool wearing his favorite swimming trunks.

Solomea looked at him and asked, "What the hell are you wearing? Is that in fashion on Earth these days? I don't know about Earth, but in my realm, you do as I do" Solomea almost commanded.

Henry stood indecisively for a moment and then against his nature removed the remaining article of clothing.

"Good," said Solomea, "Now test the water."

Henry stepped forward holding both hands in front of his private parts, and carefully lowered one foot into the pool. He quickly pulled it back saying, "It's cold."

"Haven't you ever been into a heated pool?" Solomea asked irritated.

After a short excursion back in time, Henry answered, "Actually no."

"Just imagine it is warm and you will be all right," Solomea advised.

Before his sexuality could take its natural course, Henry rushed into the pool leaving only his head above the surface.

Solomea waited a while for Henry to get comfortable and then took a first step toward him. Ripples caused by her movement reached Henry's body, resonating with the uncertainties in his mind, making them stronger than before. Solomea stopped about three feet away from Henry and whispered, "What are you afraid of?"

Henry stood up exposing his upper body and realized that he was actually a lot taller than her. He gazed at her face which seemed even more captivating.

She carefully took his right hand in her left and asked again, "What are you afraid of?"

"I am not sure if I am doing the right thing," Henry said.

Solomea smiled and answered, "There is no right and wrong, my dear Henry, as there is no universal scale to measure or to judge our acts. Every act is just an event which goes down into history to be reflected on later. Why don't we follow the call of nature and enjoy this moment that the universe has so graciously provided us?" She smiled and added, "You might learn something new."

Before Henry had a chance to answer she pressed her entire body against his and landed a hot kiss on his lips.

Henry, confused by the course of events, stood uncertain of his next action. She softly reached for his hands and pulled them up to the level of his shoulders. Henry stood as a crucifix, without any cross supporting his posture. Then she began to slowly move her hands down his arms and along his sides, touching him only with the tips of her long, elegant fingernails.

This almost non-existent contact filled Henry's lower body with an unfamiliar energy. The closest thing that he could compare it to would have been a tiny sun, or unknown source of very pleasant warm energy placed between his thighs.

Solomea began to move her hands up along his body. With each conquered inch the sun moved higher, growing in size. When she reached his underarms, Henry felt as though he would lose consciousness. The sun was positioned where his heart used to be and the energy illuminating outward could only be compared to a nuclear reactor placed in his chest. His entire body glowed like a light bulb ready to explode with ultimate pleasure. All this time, Henry was fighting to hold onto his last bit of consciousness and finally succumbed to whatever was about to happen. Surrendering his will to the overpowering force of euphoria placed upon him by this irresistibly attractive being. Unable to withstand the ultimate seduction, Henry grabbed her waist and forced Solomea into full contact with his body, an act that he would regret later, but for now that was no matter.

BACK TO THE HOSPITAL

The moment that the door closed as Croton left the ward, Anne, with the utmost desire, opened the Bible and began her climb, much like the mountain named Golgotha. She was well aware of the risk that she was taking to be caught while reading. An unexplainable thirst for knowledge forced her to fly through pages of this forbidden fruit, and to indulge in its sweetness. With each new chapter, she was discovering a world that made perfect sense in its unbelievable stream of pure light rapidly finding its way into Anne's mind and heart, lighting up her future and plunging into darkness her past.

The sudden realization in the form of a revelation about her deeds in the past made her heart sink deeper and deeper into a world of regrets and remorse. The shortsightedness of choices over her entire life, and misplaced values of physical wealth over spiritual, gave her hope that this tiny span of time that she had left would be enough to share the light that she had suddenly come across. To warn her loved ones to change their perspectives on life and to finally help them to find the path to God. To the one who was so recklessly eradicated from the lives of so many generations, and forcefully replaced by comrade party leader.

Anne always suspected that there must be a higher power. A power above all Earthly powers. Someone who can see everything. That no one can escape his judging eyes and justly punishing hand. Strangely enough, this newly discovered knowledge did not place fear in her heart. Utmost certainty that she had done more good in her life than harm was tilting the scale of justice in her eyes, into her favor. Something that she would never have said about Raymond. His seemingly successful career which had always made Anne a proud wife, suddenly lost its glamour by revealing the bad side of the coin. A side that had never been revealed to her before. She remembered the day when Raymond came home with a thick pile of money and threw it into the air.

She remembered the boundless happiness she felt watching the spectacular shower of bills falling in a crazy dance of victory. Her victory over Raymond's unwillingness to be and act like others.

Although her eyes were still following the words of the book, her mind drifted away with the realization of all the grief that her husband had caused others by breaking laws set by humans, but above all those set by God. She suddenly released the Bible and began to rigorously rub her hands against the white folds of the blanket, as though she was trying to wipe them clean from invisible filth. By now she knew for certain that the name of that filth was money. Money made her force Raymond to take bribes. It was this urge for more money that made her ignore Raymond's drift away from her in fear of interrupting the flow of that same damned money. She realized that money stood between her and Raymond, like an indestructible wall covered with the sorrow of all unjustly treated poor people.

Anne lifted the book off her chest trying to find the place where she had lost track. Finally finding it she began to read again. A couple of lines later she surrendered her trail of thoughts to new waves of worry. *"Croton, my son, what if he follows his father's path? No, this cannot happen. He is way too clever to repeat his father's mistakes. I have to warn him before it is too late. He will not..."* Convincing herself, Anne surrendered her consciousness to heavy slumber caused be the sedatives that she had to consume to relieve the unbearable stomach pain.

An hour later, Raymond quietly entered Anne's ward. Afraid to wake her up he gently lowered himself on the edge of her bed and observed her face. For almost forty years he had been living with her, seeing her every day, but somehow, he never took the time to observe her. He used to look at her but never actually saw her. Wrinkles that Anne had always so skilfully disguised with make-up suddenly appeared on her unattended face, wounding Raymond's heart with the sharpness of their reality. The sudden realization of the lengths that Anne had to go to in order stay attractive to him, living in constant fear of being unable to compete with the young mistresses he had from time to time, that Anne was undoubtedly aware of, made him feel heartbroken. Only now when he noticed the touches of silver on her temples, mercilessly revealing her age, Raymond realized the necessity of those frequent visits to the hair salon and their justification. Now he, an insensitive asshole, as he called himself, was looking at the only soul who had devotedly served him his entire life, loved him unconditionally regardless of how much he had hurt her. Emotions blocked his throat, seeking the pathway to his eyes to manifest themselves as tears, delivering relief from the heavy weight of guilt piling up. A weight that plunged him deeper into the past.

"How did we come to this?" Raymond asked himself. He stopped noticing the one and only being entirely devoted to him. Now seeing her pinned down to a hospital bed by an invisible disease that was destroying her body from the inside out, he realized that the only soul who had chosen to share with him all good and bad, and stick with him no matter what, was about to abandon him, leaving him completely alone. Alone in the entire universe. Relinquishing him of her care. Something he had always had in abundance, taking it for granted because of the man he thought he was.

Always proud of his achievements, Raymond suddenly felt small and insignificant. Like a boy who was about to lose the only lifeline to his mother, and the name of that line was love. This last thought helped the trapped emotions to find their way back to become tears. He lowered his head, allowing the pool of salty substance on the surface of his eyes to release themselves into a freefall to crash onto the floor and vaporize into nonexistence. Each tear was bringing relief from the stubbornly surfacing realization of him being the cause of Anne's sickness.

A sudden loud knock on the door made him swiftly wipe the moisture away, and to face Croton as he entered.

"How's Mom?" the concerned son addressed his father.

"I'm okay," answered Anne, awakened by the sound of his voice.

Croton moved to Anne's bed and lowered himself to face her, carefully taking her hand in his. Her other hand was still resting on the book.

"So, how's it going?" asked Croton pointing at the Bible.

"It's interesting. Was easy in the beginning, and then it's becoming complicated. But I am adamant," replied Anne.

Croton looked lovingly into his mother's eyes and asked, "What is it that you are looking for?"

"Truth," answered Anne.

"Truth? Truth about what?" asked Croton.

Anne fell quiet, drawn into herself in search of an answer.

Raymond, who was sitting at the end of her bed, placed his hand on Croton's shoulder and slightly squeezed it.

Realizing the pressure that was mounting on his mother, Croton immediately backed down by saying, "I'm sure that whatever it is you are looking for, you will find it."

Anne gratefully looked at him and releasing her hand from Croton's palms, placed it on his cheek with the words, "Sometimes I wonder what did I do right to deserve such a good boy."

Croton placed his hand over hers, squeezing it to his cheek. Anne turned her head toward the window. away from her husband and son. and let out a deep sigh.

"What is it?" asked Raymond.

"There is something that I would like to share with you," Anne said, still facing the window. "While I was reading this book many things have been revealed to me."

"Like what?" asked Raymond and Croton simultaneously.

After a moment of silence she said, "We are not living our lives righteously."

"Righteously?" asked Raymond.

"Yes, righteously. You heard me right," Anne replied. "We are all sinners in God's eyes."

"What are you talking about Anne? Do you really believe that God exists?" asked Raymond.

"Yes, I do. I suspected before, but now I am certain, and I will tell you more. I strongly believe that this sickness of mine is a direct result of the life I have lived."

"Stop it, Anne, you are scaring me!" exclaimed Raymond.

"No, please hear me out," Anne replied. "I might have no other chance to tell you this. You cannot keep living your lives the way we have been up until now. Many things have to change."

Raymond sighed, "Trust me, things will change."

"I am not talking about a time when I will be no more," said Anne. "I am talking about our opulent lifestyle. The false standards that we try to live up to. The messed up priorities. Corrupt virtues. The way we make money, and so much more."

After saying all of this Anne fell quiet, plunging the room into a deadly silence.

Confused by such direct accusations, Raymond stood motionless, looking at Anne, giving her space and time to come back to her senses.

Instead she looked him straight in his eyes and said, "I wish I knew all of this earlier. I would have lived my life so differently."

Raymond wanted to argue with her by saying that life itself had forced us to be who we became. Circumstances necessitated him to become a person he didn't want to be. The rotten society that they were unfortunately a part of molded him into who he is now. The expectations of others, and yours in the first place, my dear Anne, pushing me for the chance to create the lifestyle that you wanted to have. All of the sacrifices I have made for you, to provide my family with the best, or at least better than most, and now you are saying that all of this has been in vain! But he didn't say any of this to Anne. How could he break her heart, blaming her for the creation of the lifestyle that she is now suddenly choosing to deny.

"I think this is God's way of punishing me for being so self-absorbed and fixated on material things. It seems that I was blinded by the irresistible shine of gold," Anne said. Then she grabbed Raymond's hand and passionately said, "I know now that it is all empty, all meaningless."

"Then what is?" Raymond said angrily.

Croton sensed the rise in his parents' emotions and stood up to leave the room, but Anne stopped him saying, "I want you to hear me out, too. Please stay."

Facing Raymond she answered the question, "The love that we once had was, and is still, all that matters."

Raymond replied cautiously, "But we still have it. Or am I wrong?"

"No, we don't. We lost it in the race," Anne replied.

"What race?" Raymond spluttered.

"The race for success," Anne answered.

"I think you should stop reading this book," said Raymond. "Next you are going to say that our life was all a lie."

"Yes, my love, it was a lie," Anne replied. "Trust me, I am not trying to blame you for all of this. I was aware of all of your affairs, too. I chose to keep quiet, not only to save my family, but also to… "

Raymond jumped off Anne's bed and abruptly pronounced as he turned around to leave, "Take your medication and stop reading that damned book. It is clearly messing with your mind. I will see you tomorrow hoping to find you in a better mood." He slammed the door on his way out leaving Anne broken hearted, and Croton puzzled about his mother's sudden revelation.

RESTING MONK

When Henry regained consciousness, he was flying next to Solomea through a milky substance which could be compared to a dense cloud formation. From time to time, it seemed as though the substance was thinning out and would give up what lay beyond, but then again, the veil of the unknown dropped to prolong the mystery. The suspense and anticipation of discovering something unknown filled Henry's heart with happiness. The uncontrollable spirit of the explorer took over his entirety, occupying every cell of his soul, calling him toward whatever was waiting to be revealed.

Flying hand in hand with the most beautiful woman in the entire universe, he forgot every Earthly attachment. Neither Rose, nor Croton were on his mind. He was racing toward the unknown, toward whatever Solomea had planned for him to explore and to indulge his senses. They were two completely naked figures streaming through the mists of the universe symbolizing absolute freedom, something Henry was experiencing for the first time. Complete detachment from the past and all obligatory knots tying them to anything or anyone, and Henry's heart was filled with boundless joy and happiness. All that used to bother him was gone, and he found himself in a state of absolute bliss.

Afraid of missing the moment of revelation ahead of him, Henry cast a quick look at Solomea to express his gratitude and deep appreciation.

Solomea lifted her left eyebrow as a sign of acknowledgment of his sentiment and gestured forward to indicate that he should keep his eyes on the course ahead.

The haziness began to give up its intensity and through hesitantly parting clouds, Henry began to distinguish the outline of two enormous statues of horses facing one another. Solomea was aiming for the gap between them. On closer observation Henry could see that the statues were not horses at all, but rather powerful creatures that were half man and half bull. Built with a humongous bull body and a muscular human torso, topped with regal heads with magnificent beards. Torrential waterfalls flowed from their mouths, vaporizing before reaching the river far below, creating an indescribably beautiful rainbow made up of many more colors than what is seen on Earth.

Successfully passing through what could only be described as city gates, Henry could see silhouettes of urban structures in the distance. Soon they were flying above an unusual city with architecture and a layout that was definitely not of Earthly origin. The tall buildings were nothing like the faceless skyscrapers that Henry was familiar with. To be exact, they were not buildings at all, but rather still statues. They were a lot smaller than the statues passed through at the entrance, but they were still impressive. Some stood as high as twenty story buildings on Earth, with most being shorter. Their size was determined by the figure that they were representing. Some were familiar to Henry, reminding him of eastern gods and goddesses, or to be more exact, Hindu statues. Most were unfamiliar to him, and quite spectacular in their appearance, handsomely dressed in the brightest colors that could be fantasized by the most adventurous artists.

They dropped their altitude, aiming for the lap of a monk made from a dark gray substance, sitting peacefully in a lotus position. Henry glanced at Solomea, checking her intentions for the landing. She just blinked her eyes in agreement and a moment later they gently landed on blades of the softest grass that stretched for 100 yards on either side. The feet of the meditating monk were placed on the banks of a wide river, carrying its waters from the tips of remote mountains, and flowing into the heart of this strange city. A city of still idols harmoniously bedded amongst flourishing nature.

With the sudden realization and discomfort of his nakedness, Henry asked Solomea if it would be okay for them to wear some clothing.

“Allow me to help you with that,” offered Solomea. “We still need to blend in with the crowd.”

“What crowd?” Henry asked cautiously.

“Be patient, my friend,” Solomea replied, covering his eyes with the palms of her hand.

When she withdrew her hands, a “Goddess of Love” was standing barely dressed in front of him. This was the only way that Henry could describe her appearance.

“Look at yourself,” Solomea said, proudly observing her

creation.

From the entire variety of possible outfits she could have chosen, Henry saw that he was wearing a mini skirt. Admittedly, the design was undoubtedly intricate, made of overlapping golden strips of fabric attached to the belt, and handsomely showered with a variety of colored gemstones.

"A skirt?" Henry questioned Solomea's choice of outfit.

She slowly circled her creation and concluded, "Perfect!"

Henry shrugged his shoulders in submission to her will.

"How do you feel?" asked Solomea.

Checking under the skirt Henry replied, "Still naked."

"You will be all right, trust me," comforted Solomea.

She grabbed his hand and pulled him toward the opening in the belly of the resting monk. The darkness of the rectangular doorway called him to discover whatever was dwelling beyond. With every step the passage grew, gradually revealing the mystery of the resting idol's inner world. Blinks of red lights found their way into the interior, and Henry became aware of unusual music that was quite pleasing to his ears. This combination of music and lighting made Henry feel at ease with a real sense of belonging to whatever was about to be revealed.

Ten steps further they arrived at the opening of the interior of this unusual structure. What struck Henry most was the immense hollowness of the space, stretching upward the full length of the statue to the top of his head with a tiny hole visible right at its tip. Softly streaming light dispersed midway, with the rest of the inner world of the monk being filled with an overpowering red light with occasional glimpses of orange.

After observation of the upper levels, Henry concentrated his vision on the lower level, the one that they were about to step into. The diameter of the floor seemed to Henry to be fifty yards across. What astonished him most was the strange nature of the floor. It appeared to be alive with barely noticeable movements of the tentacles of a carpet, orchestrated in rhythm with the divine music, the source of which was hard to establish. It completely emersed Henry, filling his soul with warmth and a sense of oneness with the space. The vibrant carpet covered everything but the center of the floor, reminding Henry of a dance floor.

Without taking his eyes off the spectacular show of light conducted by the meditative, soothing music, Henry asked, "What is this place?"

After a moment of silence, Solomea answered, "Heaven."

"Heaven?" Henry asked surprised.

"Shhh, do not speak," commanded Solomea pressing her fingers across his lips. "Do not try to make sense of this. Just allow it to seep into you and enjoy every bit of it. Above all, do not judge, no matter what you see." She softly touched his hand, and invited, "Shall we?"

Surrendering to her strong will and his own irrepressible curiosity, Henry stepped forward into the perimeter of this huge hall. As his bare foot encountered the strange floor, Henry experienced something he had never felt before. After a while he sensed the softness of the carpet and sacredness of this forgotten sensation of feeling through touch. He immediately lowered himself, allowing his fingers to explore the tentacles of the moving carpet. In return, each fiber that could reach him, gently stroked his hand, leaving him completely mesmerized and puzzled at the same time. Tactile sensations found their way into his body and his soul. Something that he had not been able to experience since leaving the physical world.

He looked at Solomea with eyes filled with emotion, "My senses are back. I can feel it all."

Solomea, satisfied with the results of her master plan said, "Wait, there is still so much more to see and to sense."

Henry stood up moving his toes to indulge further in this wonderful sensation created by the magical carpet beneath his feet. Solomea led him toward the center of the space, and after few steps Henry noticed human figures engaged in dance. The half-naked dancers swirled around a silver ball placed in the middle of the arena. The ball was about a foot in diameter. Nothing seemed unusual about the sphere, other than the fact that it was suspended in midair, about six inches above the floor. The dancing figures struck it gently with their hands during their performance. Moving closer, Henry could see the dancers more clearly and distinguish their genders. There were five of them, two males and three females. Their bodies were covered with a semi-transparent silk-like fabric. The style of dance that they were performing revealed the extreme flexibility of their bodies. It was like no other choreography that he knew, but one thing was for certain—it was filled with passion and sensuality.

With his curiosity about the dancers completely satisfied, Henry shifted his attention to shadows moving around the arena. How shocking it was for him to discover that the shadows were actually naked human bodies engaged in a strange act. Henry wanted to move closer to have a better look, but Solomea stopped him with a soft touch on his shoulder. He momentarily stepped back from the hypnotic state that he was slowly being plunged into. He could still see a couple in their mid-thirties lying together and gently stoking one another's bodies. Moving up and down along their entire bodies like blind people exploring their shapes. Henry thought that it was a strange way of showing affection.

"Henry," whispered Solomea to shift his attention.

Henry looked at her in a completely detached manner. "Yes," he answered, barely moving his lips.

"I would like to introduce you to my friends if you don't mind."

Henry, hardly able to stand, nodded his head in agreement. Slowly through the moving ocean of naked bodies, two figures began their approach. As they moved closer, Henry could establish their identity. One was an African lady, slightly curvier than the lady next to her. The light chocolate color of her body was the first feature that caught Henrys attention. Her silky-smooth skin captured the restless blinks of orange light, engaging them in a crazy dance across the entire surface of her body. As she came closer, Henry noticed a soft touch of glitter covering her skin, making her even more mesmerizing.

Her companion's racial identity was more difficult to determine from the distance, but as she appeared in front of him in her entire beauty, Henry saw that she was Asian. Handsomely applied mascara around her eyes made them mysteriously soft and inviting. Her entire face radiated pampering comfort that she was ready to offer to anyone who would choose her, who would dare to indulge in the fountain of her love and be willing to be showered from head to toe with waves of absolute pleasure and ultimate satisfaction.

In comparison to her, the African lady was not wearing any make-up. Her black curly hair was firmly pulled to the back of her head and covered in a glossy substance. Her big sensitive lips were hard to miss, and especially to resist. The only thing that was quite unusual, and which caught Henry's attention, were her extremely long eye lashes graciously framing her big eyes. Her eyeballs were almost pitch black, surrounded by a pink sclera, radiating a wild and untamed energy that seemed ready to explode into a passionate outburst. Her entire body expressed barely controlled emotions that could be described by a single word… eros. A sizeable brass ring rested on her broad shoulders, circled by a multitude of colorful beaded threads cascading down to cover her voluptuous breasts. A leather belt embraced her slim waist, holding two narrow strips of fabric that fell to her feet at her front and back, leaving her powerful thighs completely exposed to curious observer.

The outfit of the Asian lady was less flamboyant and attractive, although in its design did not reveal less flesh. A semi-transparent silky fabric was draped around her neck and crisscrossed to a silver belt at her waist, barely covering her less sizeable breasts, and tumbling to her knees at the front. A second, longer piece of fabric was attached to the back of the belt falling to her feet, leaving her back completely uncovered. They were both irresistibly attractive in their own way.

Solomea stepped back, allowing her acquaintances to take care of Henry who was barely able to stand. Since he had crossed over into the world of spirit, Henry had not experienced such a crushing weight across his shoulders. It seemed as though gravity had found its way into Henry's non-physical body. The two ladies positioned themselves on either side of him and escorted him to a nearby available spot on the floor where they invited him to sit down on the vibrant carpet. Henry could not wait and dropped like a sack of potatoes, relieving the unbearable crashing pressure.

Both ladies lay next to him, finally at rest. "What is your name, handsome boy?" asked the African lady.

Henry answered and being polite asked them their names in return.

The African lady replied, "Ayanda", and the Asian said, "Taka".

"Excuse me for asking, but are your names of Earthly origin?" asked Henry.

"Yes," they both replied simultaneously.

"The reason I am asking is because your outfits are not at all Earthly in their design."

Ayanda laughed loudly saying, "It may not seem like much of an outfit, but a lot of thought went into its design."

"One thing is for sure, they are very sexy," Henry commented.

"That was our intent," answered Ayanda.

Henry cast one last look at the dance floor before shifting his attention to the ceiling of the dome which seemed to be the source of the background music that was soft and unpretentious. Henry suspected that this music was the cause of the drowsiness that overcame him. It was draining him, but not in a bad way, rather making him relax, letting everything go, surrendering to the rhythm all of his worries, and especially his responsibilities.

With the last drop of strength left in him, Henry asked, "What is this place anyway?"

"What does it look like to you?" Taka replied.

Looking around at the countless half naked bodies lying next to one another, Henry said, "No offence, but it looks like one big orgy to me."

They both laughed, and then Taka said, "No, you are wrong. This place has nothing to do with sex. The absence of physical bodies prevents us from experiencing our sexuality. Instead, we are exploring the emotions of sensuality."

"Seems the same to me?" Henry questioned.

"Sensuality, as any other emotion, has to do with our soul, while sexuality, like any other feeling has to do with the physical body," explained Taka.

Ayanda stepped in to help Taka, "To summarize, this is a place of ultimate bliss and happiness. And yes, we are helping each other to awaken the hurricane of emotions so deeply concealed deeply within each of us."

Taka suggested, "Don't you want to lie down?"

Henry, knowing where this was all leading to, surrendered his will to the force of gravity. The moment his head touched the soft carpet, he felt weightless again. The women moved themselves closer along the length of his body. While he was facing upward toward the temple of the hollow Buddhist monk, the women faced him with their heads resting in their hands.

"And now?" Henry asked.

"Now, you relax and enjoy the ride," Ayanda whispered gently into his ear.

Before she finished her sentence, Henry heard a strong drumbeat that was very distinctive, and in a completely new rhythm. Henry sought the source of this loud disturbance, sitting up to witness five large vertical drums standing around the silver ball, with five naked, very masculine men wearing long skirts striking them in unison. Suddenly the air around Henry became more vibrant, infiltrating his senses. Each beat awakened the fibers of his soul in a very unusual manner, placing fear in his heart as long forgotten primeval instincts were aroused, followed by an enormous sense of pleasure casting over his consciousness.

Taka softly touched his shoulder inviting him to lie back on the carpet. Powerless and drugged, Henry submitted, ready to face all that was prepared for him to experience.

"Now, close your eyes and ease your mind," said Taka.

Henry allowed his eyes to rest in anticipation of the unknown.

Once he did, the ladies softly stroked his upper body with the tips of their fingers.

Long forgotten feelings and sensations that once possessed his physical body filled up every particle of his metaphysical essence. A calming and comforting energy entering from Taka's side merged with the waves of fire pouring in from Ayanda along Henry's spine. Waves of extremely pleasant sensations traveled from the base of his spine to the top of his head, lifting his mind into a state of ecstasy. A state of complete detachment from past, present, and any possible future, regardless of their contents. Every stoke of the girls' hands, depending on which part of his body they were touching, awakened unique excitements previously hidden from him.

Without opening his eyes, Henry murmured, "What is this?"

"It is the merging of the energy of our souls with yours. It is always unique and unpredictable," Taka answered.

"Do you feel the same?" Henry asked.

"If you touch us in return, we will," answered Ayanda.

Henry lifted his hands, lowering them on their thighs, the affect immediately showing on their faces. This sudden strong bond with these souls previously unknown to him, raised questions in Henry's inquisitive mind. *"Maybe this is what the Creator expects of us,"* Henry wondered. *"To experience other souls through the exchange of energies and emotions. Why not? Does it always have to be through pain and suffering? Or should it be done in this way, a most pleasant and...loving way."*

The moment that the word love entered his mind, Henry remembered the soul that had been left all alone by him. The soul he could not imagine his life without. The soul who was helplessly trapped in the body of a child, whom he had promised to take care of, and wait for no matter what.

"Rose," whispered Henry, opening his eyes and trying to sit up as he regained consciousness.

But Ayanda's heavy hand placed on his forehead forced him back to the carpet. "Relax," she whispered, "You are doing nothing wrong." She softly kissed his eyelids closed. The drums became louder, with each strike the drummers applying more and more power with an accelerating rhythm, causing each and every soul to align their own vibrations to the flow of the beat, sending all participants in the act to a deeper state of trance and involuntary movement of their bodies to follow each strike of the heavy drumsticks.

The entire hall became an ocean of souls caressing each other in the most gentle and seductive manner. With the last drop of consciousness left in him, Henry opened his eyes to see the hands of other souls reaching out to him, while Taka and Ayanda had their hands on him as well as other neighboring souls at the same time. The entire multitude of souls became a single orchestrated sea of pure energy, energy that connected them to each other, moving around the circle, rising in its frequency.

Henry forced himself to sit up and observe this strange act and then the unimageable happened. Accumulating to its peak, energy in the form of emotions shot from each participant as a beam of light into the silver ball at the center of the hall, and then reflecting from it as a single stream of light through the hole at the top of the dome into the universe beyond. It was the last thing that Henry could remember before someone's strong hand pulled him back into the ocean of souls melting into each other.

The amount of time that Henry spent in the flow of bodies indulging themselves in a dance of ultimate of joy he couldn't establish, but when he opened his eyes and returned to his senses everyone was gone. Henry found himself in the humongous cavity of the statue completely alone, feeling abandoned and robbed by those who had accompanied him in this dream land.

He cautiously stood up checking to see if the gravitational pull was still there, satisfied with the weightlessness, Henry moved toward the center of the hall to have a closer look at the epicenter of this "pleasure land". The silver ball surrounded by the five drums was still there. He walked straight to one of the drums and carefully touched its surface. It was hard to imagine that only a moment ago they had been so active.

Henry stood back and cast his eyes to the floor. What he discovered cast an enormous fear in his heart. *"No, this cannot be,"* Henry said to himself. He took a few more steps back and saw the entire setup of the silver balls and surrounding drums. They were placed on a huge pentagram, with the ball in the center and the five drums placed upon each acute point of the star.

From what Henry could remember, pentagrams were never associated with light or love, but rather quite the opposite. His first reaction was to run from this place as far as possible. He immediately searched for the exit and moved toward it. Stepping out into the green field, Henry felt liberated in every sense of that word. He looked up into the clear blue sky and tried to let in as much light as was possible. He wanted to dilute with the light all of the darkness he had just been exposed to.

Solomea was nowhere to be seen to accompany him back, although he had no need of her, the damage was done, and the only thing left to do was to get back to all that he loved and had left behind, and to leave with remorse for visiting this forsaken place.

BACK TO CROTON AND ROSE

Croton was driving home, deeply concerned with his mother's deteriorating state of health and mind. He couldn't wait to see his wife and lovely daughter. Little Rose had begun to learn, with her first steps, to balance herself in a world of harsh physics with its unforgiveable laws of gravity. A law ready to throw you off balance at any given moment in your human life.

Soon his mind drifted to another level of consciousness, leaving his body solely in control of the car. His mind slipped into the land of love where he had been a resident for quite some time. To be exact, from the moment that he first saw Gaya. The love that he experienced for her had not faded away with the arrival of Rose. To the contrary, it gained new dimensions. In each of those dimensions Gaya had a leading role firmly occupying his entire world, leaving little space for him to exist. Even at work, which he was not much fond of, he could not stop thinking of her, counting the hours until he could back home and embrace her....

The love that had finally found its way to the Roman senator's heart touched his soul to its very core, occupying not only each cell of his current physical body, but his mind as well. The mind which was stretching its existence for millenniums. By embracing love, Croton had come to the realization that there is no opposite emotion to love. Some say it is hate or fear, but they were wrong. Love became to him the ultimate emotion. The pinnacle of all emotions that humans could possibly hold and experience. A blend of them all, both good and bad.

Deep inside he knew that love does not come to doors that are not open to it. Observing others around him, Croton felt privileged and undeservedly lucky to have Gaya in his life. One who taught him how to stay in love, and how to grow into each other, not only by interweaving their roots, but in their crowns as well, like two trees growing tall, side by side.

He kept convincing himself that this love will remain forever, until the end of their days. He could see them growing old and one day being surrounded by grandchildren, but above all, being hand in hand with one that he had completely immersed himself into, leaving no space for anyone to come between them. From time to time, Croton caught himself thinking that the life they were living was too good to be true, or to remain as it was. But then, he pushed those thoughts aside, convincing himself that he had been born under a lucky star.

Just one thing spoiling the perfectly arranged colors of his life, the frequent fights that he was picking with Gaya, although they were minor and probably caused by the stress he was dealing with due to his mother's sickness. Despite this, he felt truly blessed. Observing his parents and the situations that they found themselves in, Croton realized how short human life is. The rolling years of our lives felt like waves in an ocean, continuously pounding the beach sand, and swirling inward our irretractable moments of happiness, vanishing into the oblivion on the ocean's depth. He recognized how quickly tomorrow would disappear into the past, taking with it all that we had come to value, to live for, and to love.

He arrived, unnoticeably, in front of his garage door situated on the ground floor of the apartment in which he lived. After locking the car in, he flew up the stairs to ring the bell of the world where Gaya and Rose were waiting for him. The world he would give up his life for in a blink of an eye without thinking twice.

The loud door buzzer disturbed the serenity of its inhabitants and Croton heard Gaya's steps approaching the door followed by, "Daddy's home." Standing in the doorway, Gaya appeared different to him in a strange way. Apart from the fact that she was as always dressed for her husband's homecoming, she had a strange inner glow reflected in her gentle smile, and an aura of soft light framed her entire body.

Croton stepped inside and firmly embraced her. This hug was a customary part of his arrival home from work, but this time it was different. It was longer and stronger, making Gaya uneasy and a bit alarmed.

"How is your mom?" asked Gaya.

"She's okay."

Ready to release her arms from her husband's neck, Gaya felt that he was not ready to leave the embrace. In that moment Croton felt that he was hugging her for the last time, and his heart was pounding, pushing up into his throat overwhelming emotions. He pulled her closer, applying just enough force so as not to hurt her. He wanted to melt into her and seize this moment of ultimate union of their bodies for eternity.

The rapidly growing fear of how temporary everything was clouded his mind leaving no space for light to break in.

"Are you okay?" Gaya asked, concerned by her husband's unusual behavior.

"I am, my love," answered Croton, releasing his grip, but still holding her waist. He looked into her big brown eyes saying, "Promise that you will never leave me."

Gaya plastered a wide smile on her face and tenderly looked at Croton. "How can I leave your dumb ass, you will get lost in this world without me. Besides, this cage that you put me in with our daughter leaves me not much chance to do so." Then she planted a long kiss upon his trembling lips.

Henry suddenly appeared catching the young couple in a moment of utmost intimacy. Satisfied with what he witnessed, Henry stepped into Rose's room, afraid to find her all grown up in the time that he had been absent. He found her sitting amongst pillows playing with a doll. "Thank God, it seems as though everything had been a bad dream and I have not even left her."

"Oh really," Henry heard a voice from behind him.

The tone of this voice can only belong to one soul, "Thales," said Henry without facing him.

"You can look at me, unless you have no heart to do so," said Thales.

Henry slowly turned around and in front him stood the great philosopher in all his might. His deeply wrinkled eyes pierced him with such intensity that Henry had to lower his head and ask, "Did I do something wrong?"

"What do you think?"

After a short hesitation, Henry said, "At first it seemed like a good idea and opportunity to learn something new, but then it turned into something I had no intention of doing."

Thales then spoke, "I am not asking about your little adventure into the land of pleasure. I am referring to the fact that you deserted Croton and Rose, leaving them alone and unprotected, completely exposed to external harm."

"From what I can ascertain on my arrival, nothing much has happened, and everyone seems okay."

"Oh," replied Thales, "Allow me to enlighten you. How long do you think that you have been absent?"

"A day, maybe two," answered Henry.

"Six months," Thales threw into Henrys face.

"Six months?" Henry exclaimed in complete disbelief.

"Yes, my friend, six agonizing months these poor souls were left on their own while you satisfied your uncontrollable hunger for adventure. What is it that you are searching for, anyway? The universe and its physical and non-physical manifestations is so vast that to comprehend even a tiny part of it is beyond your abilities." Thales became quiet with an expression of big disappointment still on his face.

Henry stood lost and confused, not knowing what to say, but then he remembered something that could excuse him saying, "I was assured that I would be back in the nick of time. I trusted another guide, believing that she would never cause trouble for the souls that we were responsible for."

Thales lowered his head and took a deep sigh. "You still have so much to learn. Instead of discovering new realities and new etheric emotions, rather study the inhabitants of those realms, study those who created those realities that you are so adamant to discover. Each realm is created by the desires of various groups of souls to materialize their dreams, and by stepping into one of them you lose your identity as you become a part of their dream, wasting your emotions and vital energy on someone else's imaginings. These opulently constructed and skilfully designed realms that imitate physical realms are countless, spread all over the universe. Are you going to explore them all?"

Thales' rising voice echoed around the room attracting little Rose's attention to the disturbance in the air.

Thales lowered his voice and with less emotion said, "Now, about the benevolent spirit guides, let me enlighten you about their role in this ordeal. Yes, spirit guides are here to protect incarnated souls and to influence them, but you must remember that they were not long-ago humans themselves, flesh and blood just as you used to be, with all of the weaknesses belonging to humans that are not dropped when they become spirit guides. Sometimes, instead of influencing the souls that they are guiding up to the light, they drag them into darkness."

"What are you saying?" Henry asked Thales.

"I am saying that this tremendous shift in Anne's consciousness due to her sickness, pushed Solomea away. In short, she lost interest."

"Are you saying that she is not coming back to Anne?"

"No," Thales replied.

"Then…?" asked Henry.

"I have appointed a new guide to her. One who can help her in her journey toward light, love, and forgiveness. By the way, you will have the chance to meet her, a very interesting character."

Leaving the last sentence unattended, Henry asked, "So you are saying that Solomea took a hike, and me along with her?"

"Yes," came the answer from Thales.

"Doesn't she deserve some kind of punishment?" Henry enquired.

"There is no punishment in the spiritual realms, and you know this. No one can punish you except yourself," Thales answered, continuing, "For that to happen, one has to accept one's own faults."

"Yes, I remember that now," said Henry, recalling his time in the court with the judges.

Thales spoke again, "Solomea did nothing wrong. To the contrary. she helped you to find what you were looking for. Isn't that so?"

"Now, when I think about it, perhaps in the back of my mind I asked for it," considered Henry.

Thales smiled and nodded his head.

Henry looked at the peaceful Rose sitting on the carpet, meticulously undressing her dolls.

"Please, fill me in. What did I miss in her life?" Henry asked. "And what trouble did Croton manage to get himself into?"

Thales became serious saying, "Since you left, she lost her peaceful sleep."

"What do you mean?" asked Henry.

"I mean exactly what I said," replied Thales.

"I didn't know anything about providing her with good sleep. No one told me about that," said Henry.

"Your job is not to provide, but rather to protect her from dark entities," Thales explained.

"Dark entities?" asked Henry. "I have never heard of them?"

"Now you have, and one, if not the most important duty of yours, is to protect this child from them," replied Thales.

"What do they look like? Where do they come from? Why have I never heard of them before now?" Henry continued.

"You haven't seen them because your very presence makes their appearance in the room impossible. But let me enlighten you on this matter. I will take you back in time to just two nights ago," Thales answered, raised his right hand swiping it from left to right as though he was turning the pages of a humongous book.

The lights in the room dimmed and little Rose appeared in

her bed. Henry moved closer, leaning over her and confirmed that she was in a deep sleep.

"Wait," urged Thales, pointing his finger to the corner between the walls and the ceiling. "Look," he continued.

Henry noticed a rapidly growing darkness. "What is this?" Henry asked alarmed.

"A dark entity," Thales answered. Henry stared at the dark spot as it grew, gradually taking the form of an irregularly shaped object. It was hard to identify it as anything that Henry had seen before. The slimy, pitch black, and slow-moving substance with multiple short tentacles waving in the air, suddenly pushed itself off the wall right onto Rose's bed.

Henry wanted to throw his entire body between them to protect his one and only, but Thales stopped him with the words, "You cannot protect her now. This was two days ago. I just want you to observe patiently and learn the lesson."

Henry placed himself on the opposite side of the bed to face the dark matter. He kept staring at it with the utmost anger and hatred. The entity leaned over Rose's head and the baby sat up crying. Rose looked at the black mass with horror filling her eyes. Henry could hardly suppress his natural instincts as the entity continued to grow in size, occupying twice the space it had before. A minute later Henry saw Gaya, in her pajamas, walking into the baby's room to calm baby Rose. When Henry looked back, the slimy substance was gone. Gaya picked Rose up and walked back with her to her bedroom.

Henry stood completely shocked and traumatized by what he had just witnessed.

"What the hell was that?" Henry addressed Thales.

"What do you think?" Thales asked in return.

"It seemed like a nightmare from hell," Henry replied.

"What a meaningless composition of words!" Thales rolled his eyes.

"Do you have a better explanation?" Henry replied.

"As a matter of fact, I do," retorted Thales.

"And?" Henry pushed.

"Some call it a dark entity; I call it a Fear Hunter," explained Thales.

"Fear Hunter?" asked Henry.

"Yes, my friend. It is pure fear materialized as dark energy."

"Can you be more specific?" Henry pushed. "I just need to know more please, in case it appears again tonight. Then I will know how to deal with it."

"Do not worry, it will not visit the child while you are next to her," Thales assured.

"That's a relief, but still, why Fear Hunters?" Henry continued.

"I will explain to you how I see them based on my own encounters with them."

Henry sat on the edge of Rose's bed ready to absorb all that this old and wise Greek had to convey.

"I call them Fear Hunters because they are scattered around the world in search of negative emotions which unfortunately, are most common amongst human beings," Thales began.

"Fears?" Henry added.

"Did you notice how it expanded when Rose was crying?" Thales continued.

"In order to sustain themselves, they have to find a source of negative energy, and you should know that when humans are frightened, their bodies and souls expel huge amounts of negative energy into space."

"And…?" Henry prompted impatiently.

"Nothing goes to waste," replied Thales. "Due to the law of energy conservation, it travels from one entity to another. An outburst of negative energy is immediately captured by Fear Hunters. Fear by its very definition is an extremely destructive energy, and so it is no wonder that it creates such an unattractive form."

"So, the energy contents determine the look. But why did it stick to my Rose?" asked Henry.

"Rose, as with any child, left alone for an entire night in a dark room, is easy prey for them due to their ability to sense what adults are incapable of anymore," Thales explains.

"Wait a minute, are you saying that those characters belong to the world of spirit?" Henry asked.

"Yes, they do," confirmed Thales.

"Something is not adding up for me," said Henry. "If these creatures belong to the spiritual world, then why do you, as a Planner, or for that matter God himself, not destroy them?"

Thales smiled because he anticipated this question from Henry as he, more than anyone else, understood that if you don't ask you will never learn. After a short pause he delivered, "As you probably know, everything in the universe exists by the will of its creator. All spiritual and all physical realities, including this planet itself, are in existence by the Creator's intention."

Upon saying this Thales looked into Henry's eyes, checking to see if he understood.

"Okay," Henry agreed cautiously.

"So, all that is, regardless of whether or not we have the ability to perceive, will remain as originally created for as long as the Creator is willing to supply sufficient energy to sustain it."

Henry, trying to follow Thales' line of thoughts said, "Okay. So, fear as an emotion was not created by God and sent to Earth to frighten people.

It is created 100 percent by humans. If you observe closely, you will notice that fear is a primordial negative emotion constantly experienced by humans. They are always afraid of something."

"That is very true," agreed Henry. "I remember how, back in my physical body, I was often fearful. Afraid of being unable to pay my bills, or of something bad happening to my loved ones, the risk of losing my job, or having an accident…the list goes on and on. But above all there was the fear of death."

"Look," Thales smiled, "most of what you mentioned humans consider as worries, but still they are all fear based. The biggest contributor to the creation of those dark entities is wars. Meaningless, self-destructive acts nurtured and raised by human egos. Throughout the entire history of life on this beautiful planet that has been so thoughtfully created for them to stay and enjoy every bit of it, but instead what do they do…they wage war. The bigger the battle, the greater the contribution to the dark energies."

Thales fell quiet for a moment as he paged through the pages of the history of humanity.

"Although the one thing that I have to admire about them…"

"What is that?" enquired Henry.

"They are powerful Creators," Thales remarked. "Although most of them are completely unaware of that fact. Along with all of the negative emotions such as hate, envy, anger, jealousy, regret, guilt, shame, fear, frustration, and so many more, they are capable of creating many positive emotions also like empathy, joy, happiness, forgiveness, excitement, appreciation, gratitude, consideration, care, compassion, and above all, they are able to experience love, the ultimate crown of all emotions. In comparison to dark entities, positive emotions create and feed light, counterbalancing the darkness."

"Will there ever be a time on Earth when dark energy ceases to exist?" Henry asked.

"That's all in the hands of humans, collectively and individually," Thales explained. "Any darkness created by them can only be destroyed by them and no one else."

"I don't see how it can happen," Henry sighed.

"Neither do I," agreed Thales. "Look at me, the last time I was on Earth in a physical body was almost 3000 years ago, and here I am still running around worrying for each soul sent by me down to Earth, checking on unfit guides, such as yourself," Thales continued breaking into laughter.

"I guess one can call it responsibility," Henry responded.

"Yes, and this is how God created us. No matter where we are here on Earth, or up there in the spiritual world, we still worry," agreed Thales. "Although there is one distinctive difference. When we are in the world of spirit we worry about those having their physical incarnations, and you know why?" Thalles continued.

"Why?" asked Henry.

"Because we care. Because we care," Thales repeated slowly.

Looking back Henry realized that since he had crossed into the world of spirit, he had not experienced fear for himself. His fears were always for those for whom he cared the most. For those he loved the most. Those who gave meaning to his entire existence.

Reading Henry's thoughts Thales added, "For now, please, do not leave Rose's side, especially at night until that creature becomes completely detached from her."

"I will not," Henry promised sincerely, "If only I knew all of this before..."

"Now you do," Thales replied. "Do you remember how afraid you were to look under your own bed when you were small?"

"You are so right. I was terrified. Are you saying that a similar creature was under my bed?" Henry asked.

"Yup," Thales confirmed.

"Thank God, I do not remember it," Henry replied relieved.

Sensing that this conversation had come to its logical end, Thales said, "Should we go back to our present time to check up on the family?"

"Yes please," said Henry.

Thales raised his right hand and waved it from right to left, transporting them into the dinning room where Croton, Gaya, and little Rose were peacefully enjoying their dinner together.

Henry went around the table, observing them one by one, while Thales stood leaning against a wall with his arms across his chest.

"Aren't they lovely," asked Henry.

"They are now," Thales remarked.

"What do you mean?" Henry questioned suspiciously.

"Let me take you back in time again, just to yesterday

evening," Thales invited.

Thales waved his right hand again and instantly there appeared in the same room a different scene. Gaya and Croton were standing at opposite ends of the very same dinner table, screaming at each other. Rose was hiding in her room. In complete silence Henry and Thales observed the scene of the couple's fight, taking turns at yelling at one another, adamant to prove their point.

"Where is the sound?" Henry asked in surprise.

"It's not important," Thales answered.

"What are they fighting about?" Henry pushed.

"It is not important," Thales repeated.

"If they are fighting with such intensity about something unimportant…" Henry replied.

"That is my point exactly," Thales replied. "Their relationship is taking a big strain, and is about to be destroyed, and with that you know that Croton's mission to find his one and only will be jeopardized."

Henry lowered his head realizing that he has a part to be blamed for. Croton furiously slammed the table with his fist, and without saying anything more stormed out of the apartment. Gaya went into Rose's room, picked up the crying baby, pressing her against her chest. Her eyes filled with tears and her heart overflowing with anger could only leave a heartless soul indifferent to the pain that she was immersed in. Henry was standing right in front of them looking straight into Gaya's eyes, and he could feel the mother's pain and the daughter's fear.

Absorbing these emotions tore his soul apart, filling up cavities with regret and self-blame. He felt cheated and tricked by another soul. A soul that he had respected and trusted had deceived and misled him to take a journey that he had had no intention to be a part of.

Thales gently touched Henry's shoulder saying, "You know, Solomea is not the only one to be blamed."

Henry lowered his head saying, "Yes I know, and that is what is tearing me apart."

Then, pointing at the distressed mother and daughter with a deeply sincere voice, Thales said, "If you do not fix this, I will take drastic measures, and I warn you that you will not like it."

Thales' last words hung in the air like an axe hanging on a thin thread above Henry's neck as he evaporated into thin air.

ANNE'S JOURNEY BEGINS

Anne's health was deteriorating rapidly. Being constantly under the influence of drugs she was unconscious most of the time. In the short moments when she came back, she read the Word of God which irritated her frequent visitors. Raymond could hardly tolerate her condemning remarks about their life choices. With every visit Anne loaded his mind with guilt and regrets, drawing parallels between stories in the Bible and their life.

Gradually, but steadily, Raymond was losing his Anne, the one who was always there for him no matter how badly he had screwed up. But now that was no longer the case. She was drifting away from him, not only physically, but mentally and emotionally as well. Every day he had to force himself to steer his car to the hospital, taking his time to climb the stairs, hoping that today he would find his old Anne, the one he had known his entire life.

After the meeting with Thales, Henry was glued to Rose, following her on each new step and timelessly watching her in peaceful sleep. And when, a few days later, Gaya said to Croton, "Did you notice that Rose has stopped waking up during the night?", Henry felt proud of himself, realizing just how much his presence could do for his Rose.

A while later, when things settled down and the trail of dark energy was completely gone, Henry chose to pay a visit to Anne in the hospital. News from Thales about the newly appointed spirit guide made him inquisitive, and he could no longer wait.

One day, he followed Raymond to the hospital. Stepping into Anne's ward Henry noticed an odd-looking nun sitting on a small wooden stool at Anne's head. Just by her appearance Henry guessed that she did not belong to the world of the living. She was dressed all in black, except for the white scarf that completely covered her head and rested on her shoulders. A sizeable silver cross rested on her chest, leaving no doubt in Henry's mind that she belonged to the Christian faith.

She was reading the Book, only to be distracted by their sudden intrusion. She raised her head to look at Raymond as he entered, then concentrated her attention on Henry. The hardly noticeable nod of her head indicated to Henry that she had noticed him. He nodded in return as a sign of respectful greeting.

Somehow this nun's presence at Anne's side gave him a sense of relief and assurance that whatever Anne's soul had to face, that she would be all right. Her pale face and big brown eyes conveyed confidence, leaving no doubt in Henry's mind about her belonging with Anne. Although it looked as though she was reading a book placed in her lap, Henry noticed that she was intensely listening to the ongoing conversation between Raymond and Anne.

"I spoke to the doctor about further treatment…" started Raymond.

"And what did he say?" asked Anne.

Raymond paused in search of the right words to break the news.

"Do not worry, my love, whatever life has planned for me I will take it," Anne continued, placing her hand over Raymond, "You can tell me now".

After a deep sigh Raymond spoke, "The doctor suggested that I take you home."

"This is good news," Anne replied optimistically, "Why are you so upset."

A big lump stuck in Raymond's throat prevented him from saying a word.

Anne squeezed his hand and asked, "Are you giving up on me?"

"No, never," Raymond spluttered, suppressing tears.

"Come on, love, we knew that this day would come," Anne said gently.

"Yes, but I was hoping…" Raymond said as Anne placed her hand over Raymond's lips saying, "What could be more pleasant than dying surrounded by loved ones in your own bedroom, in your own time."

Raymond kissed her hand and managed to dissolve the lump in his throat by letting his tears loose.

The next day they went back home along with Anne's new spirit guide. Once everyone was settled and Anne had fallen into a deep sleep, Henry chose to approach her guide. She was still sitting on the same stool at Anne's head. It seemed to Henry that she was glued to it, or that it was an integral part of her soul.

Henry carefully approached her, and as she moved her

attention from the Book to him, Henry introduced himself.

"Gertrude," said the nun.

Trying to start the conversation Henry said, "I assume that you are Anne's new guide. Excuse me for saying this, but I have not seen you before."

"Yes, you are right. I have been approached by the Planners to accompany Anne in her journey to our world," the nun answered as she smiled softly.

Her humble manner placed confidence in Henry's heart and a desire to know more about her and her mission.

"Forgive me for asking, but what world are you speaking of?" he questioned.

"The world of spirit, of course," answered Gertrude.

"Oh yes, right," said Henry, juggling with the idea whether to dig deeper or to retreat.

Gertrude looked straight into Henry's eyes and invitingly said, "We can talk while Anne sleeps."

Her last words left no doubt in Henry's mind that he should explore further into the mind of this, the humblest being that he had ever encountered in either the physical or spiritual worlds.

"So, why you?" Henry began.

Gertrude looked quizzically at Henry, completely missing the point of his question.

"I mean, why did the Planners appoint you and what was wrong with her previous spirit guide, Solomea?" Henry clarified.

"I didn't have the pleasure of meeting her," Gertrude smiled, "But this is common practice as most humans, toward the end of their physical life, initiate a process of re-evaluation of their life's journey, and most of the time they invite faith into their heart. Not that it wasn't initially there, but that it was just dormant waiting to be awakened in a time of great difficulty."

Despite being humble, Gertrude happened to be quite talkative to Henry's great satisfaction.

"Judging by your outfit I presume that you belong to one of the Christian denominations," Henry suggested, "and when you speak of faith, I assume that you are talking of the Christian religion."

"Faith has nothing to do with religion," Gertrude answered confidently. "Religion is a man-made institution, while faith is a direct line to God."

"Direct line?" Henry said surprised.

"Yes, didn't you know that?" Gertrude replied.

"It seems like I have missed some lessons," Henry answered

ironically.

Ignoring his irony Gertrude kept going, "Faith has to do with what you believe in and who you pray to. I'm quite sure that each human has their own image of God. Some see God as Christ, some see him as an old man dwelling somewhere above. If you ask me, I would say that the best validation of their image of God comes through their answered prayers."

"I guess you are right. Once someone joins their hands together in prayer and a miracle occurs as a result…then who am I to say that they are praying to the wrong God," Henry said.

Gertrude smiled with great satisfaction as she connected with Henry's mind.

Henry shifted his attention asking, "How long?"

Gertrude placed her hand over Anne's forehead saying, "Soon."

"Are you ready?" asked Henry.

"Yes, I am," Gertrude answered confidently.

Henry excused himself politely and went back to his duties as caretaker of his wife with whom he could not establish a connection with, and to be a guide to Croton who had become completely out of hand. All that he could do was to be a witness to his soul's self-destruction, falling deeper and deeper into the hole of corruption and misplaced values.

Suddenly Henry heard the deeply troubled voice of Raymond reaching him through the staircase calling Croton and Gaya to come up to check in on Anne. "Please hurry, she is not doing well, and please call an ambulance."

While Croton was making the phone call, Gaya quickly checked on the sleeping Rose and then rushed upstairs, leaving the baby girl all alone in their apartment. With each fiber of his non-physical body Henry wanted to be upstairs to see what was happening in Anne's bedroom, but he would never dare to leave Rose alone after what he had been shown by Thales.

Soon his inquisitiveness overpowered his sense of responsibility. To be a witness of Anne's last hours in her physical body and the very moment of her departure, Henry couldn't miss for the world. Suddenly he realized that he was airborne, and his head was about to hit the ceiling of Rose's bedroom. A second later he passed through the ceiling and appeared in Anne's bedroom. Raymond was sitting on the edge of her bed holding her hand. Croton was waiting impatiently by the window so as not to miss the ambulance's arrival. Gaya was at the foot of Anne's bed wiping away rolling tears.

The last for Henry to notice was Gertrude, on her stool, seemingly detached from all of the buzz and deep in her reading. Part of Henry wanted to stay and witness the upcoming drama, but the other part knew that Rose needed him. Torn between the two places he wanted to be, Henry suddenly discovered that he had the miraculous ability to be in two places at once. He could see the peacefully sleeping Rose and the scene in Anne's bedroom at the same time. Henry experienced for the first time this extraordinary power of split consciousness. The realization of this newly gained ability was so great that Henry wanted to rise above the world and scream into the universe, *"I've found it! I did it!"*

With great difficulty Henry calmed this flow of emotions saying to himself, *"Okay, I can be simultaneously in two different places on Earth, now let's check if I can be both in and out of the physical reality at the same time."* He momentarily thought about his and Rose's forgotten reality, their private home on the beach with the magnificent forest in the back yard. As the thought crossed his mind, Henry found himself standing on the balcony watching the cascading crystal clear pools disappearing into the deep green forest, with slow waves rolling through the treetops created by the soft ocean breeze. Henry wanted to take in a deep breath of the fresh air filled with the fragrance of the myriad of plants, but with the absence of his physical body and all of its senses, Henry stood disappointed and saddened. *"Why can't we be satisfied with what we have?"* Henry chastised himself.

Then he noticed the walkway disappearing into the forest, leading to the waterfall that he had created for Rose, and before memories of his past had their way with him, Henry turned away and walked into the room, the room which had once been all white and had been redecorated by Rose into a spectrum of the brightest colors. Everything reminded him of her, the magical short-lived happiness that they had together evaporated almost instantly, leaving scattered patches of memories which were too painful to be dwelled on. Henry felt sick to his stomach.

Since Rose had left, he hadn't wanted to visit this house, but now that he was back again and the crashing weight of loneliness made its home on his chest. Henry began to run out of breath despite being consciously aware of the absence of lungs. Feelings so deeply rooted into the minds of each human started to surface into his soul, plunging him into a field of regrets and deep remorse for letting Rose out of his sight, the decision by which he condemned himself to a confinement of loneliness and separation from all whom he loved and cared for. Henry took a deep breath and with the last air left in his lungs screamed, "Rose!"

By some miracle, he was instantly transferred to little Rose's bedroom whilst still remaining in his own reality. He experienced both realities simultaneously. The effect of this discovery was so shocking that Henry took a step back to observe and hopefully understand what was happening. Regardless of his retreat he remained in the double realities. He took a few steps forward to stand in front of little Rose's bed. He looked around and realized that whichever reality he focused his attention on was the one that came to the fore. Filled with these newly adapted powers, Henry sat back into the sofa in his realty thinking to himself, *"How come I never knew this before now? This is the coolest thing that I have learned since my arrival in the world of spirit."*

His next thought puzzled him, causing him some despair, *"How is it that neither Croton, nor Thales who obviously know about this, never taught me to exercise it?"*

"Because some things you have to learn for yourself," Henry heard Thales' strong voice as he appeared in front of him. Henry jumped up from the sofa to greet the old Greek.

"Thank you for showing up, dear Thales," Henry said, "My excitement has no boundaries."

"I can see that," replied Thales, "To be honest, forgive me for stating this, but I am not ecstatic by your discovery."

"Why?" exclaimed Henry.

"Because this will motivate you even more to sneak into realms that you are not yet ready to encounter." Thales explained.

"How about I ask for your permission before going anywhere?" suggested Henry.

"Deal," Thales agreed abruptly.

While observing Henry's findings, Thales said, "I am going to regret this, but let me extend your vision to the next level."

"What do you mean by the next level?" Henry asked.

"Think about Anne's bedroom. I am sure that you are dying to know what is happening to Anne right now," Thales suggested.

Henry sat back into his sofa and concentrated his thoughts onto the apartment above Croton's. Slowly the third reality began to reveal itself, taking the place of the others while leaving Henry very aware about where he was. Henry saw two doctors leaning over Anne's body. Gaya was holding Croton's hand with her eyes filled with tears, and a crushed Raymond sitting on the edge of his chair like a convict just before his execution.

Alarmed by what he saw Henry asked, "Is she dying?"

"Not yet, but I recommend that you be a witness to the journey that lies ahead of her," answered Thales.

"Do you want me to follow her to the world of spirit?" Henry asked in surprise.

"Yes. Since you have learned how to be in multiple places at the same time, you should be able to go with her. By the way, I call this the multi-dimensional existence of souls. A very powerful tool for spirit guides to gain back the freedom lost by being assigned to a human soul in the physical world," Thales continued.

"So, you are advising me to follow Anne?" Henry asked again.

"Yes, but first you need to get permission from her new guide," Thales agreed.

"Gertrude?" Henry asked.

"Yes," Thales confirmed.

"Consider it already in my pocket," Henry stated confidently.

"Don't be too certain about it," Thales warned, "An invitation into the world of…," Thales stumbled with his words for a second.

"World of?" Henry asked anxiously to hear the rest of the sentence.

"The world of strong faith and ultimate belief," Thales finished.

"Don't worry, I will do my best to get in," Henry said.

"I know you will," Thales said supportively, "I remember you visiting your father right after his passing in a similar reality, although this one is different."

"How different?" asked Henry intrigued.

"Let it be a surprise for you," Thales said. "If you manage to get in you will meet with a quite extraordinary soul who has been glorified, not only for his wisdom, but mostly for his approach to his own fame."

"I am already intrigued," Henry said, rubbing his hands.

PASSAGE GRANTED

"How's she doing?" asked Henry while carefully approaching Gertrude, afraid to disturb Anne's sleep.

"Not so well," answered Gertrude, with a pleasantly inviting smile. This warm welcome left no doubt in Henry's mind about getting safe passage into Gertrude's reality.

"When?" asked Henry.

"Tonight," replied Gertrude while looking at Anne with eyes filled with compassion and empathy.

"Did you arrange her welcome party?"

"What do you mean?"

"I mean her loved ones who are already in the world of spirit, and anxious to welcome her."

Gertrude gently placed her hand on Anne's chest where she was still holding the Bible while in a deep sleep.

"No, there will be no bunch of deceased relatives."

"Oh, I guess you want to welcome her personally," said Henry, remembering Croton's approach to his own crossing-over.

"Not exactly," answered Gertrude, lifting her left eyebrow hinting at some secret that she was reluctant to share.

"Aren't you going to tell me?" prompted Henry, playing the game set by Gertrude.

"No," she slammed the door right in Henry's face, leaving him unpleasantly surprised.

A while later, he tried a different approach.

"Would you please at least allow me to follow you and Anne to wherever you are going to accompany her?"

"Absolutely no," struck Gertrude with a serious tone.

"Why not?" pleaded Henry.

Gertrude leaned forward and looked straight into Henry's eyes. A look that would have frozen all of his insides if he'd had some. Then in the same cold voice, she said, "Why should I take a non-believer into something that I believe so dearly?"

"Whoa, whoa," exclaimed Henry, "Who said I am not a believer?"

"Did you ever read the Bible?" Gertrude asked, already knowing the answer to her question.

"Not entirely, but I am familiar with the concepts."

"Do you believe in Jesus Christ as our savior, and only son of God?" As she asked this she froze in anticipation of Henry's answer.

The dilemma thrown right into Henry's face by this small and fragile nun with the demand for a definite answer left Henry stumped. *"To tell the truth and be left out of the promising adventure, or to lie and gain passage?"* Henry chose the second option.

"Yes, I do," Henry answered firmly.

Gertrude squinted her eyes and said, "I do not believe you."

Henry suddenly remembered himself as a small boy, every Sunday dragged by his father to church. Sitting and listening to all of the reverent words containing no meaning to his young mind. *"This might help to convince her,"* Henry thought to himself, and he began to convey to Gertrude's mind, scenes of him in church.

Patiently absorbing all that Henry had to show, Gertrude said, "I have to get permission."

"Okay," said Henry filled with hope as he retreated to his reality full of hope and anticipation.

This latest discovery of his ability to be in different realities at the same time left the door into Rose's reality wide open. From here he could keep his eyes on growing up Rose, monitor Croton's dodgy affairs, and to have his hand on Anne's pulse almost literally.

Later in the same evening, unusual activity in Anne's bedroom attracted his attention. Realizing that this could be the moment, Henry transferred his light body into her bedroom.

"Should I call an ambulance?" asked Croton, directing his question to Raymond who was sitting at the edge of Anne's bed.

"No. Let her leave in peace. I do not want anyone here except us."

Besides Raymond and Croton, there was Gaya with Rose in her arms in physical form, and Gertrude with Henry in spiritual form. Anne's breathing was irregular and quite heavy. Suddenly she opened her eyes, and looking around, seemingly not knowing where she was, said, "Save yourselves…everything is falling apart…" The she closed her eyes, a moment later coming back to her senses, and with great difficulty pronounced, "My home, my children, save them." With the last strength left in her, she squeezed Raymond's arm, closed her eyes and left out the remaining air in her lungs.

Henry, quietly observing this scene while standing against the wall, as though someone had closed the book of Anne's physical life just to open another one. A book filled with upcoming adventure and endless revelations. Not only for herself, but also for those who were about to welcome her into the world of survived souls.

Completely ignoring the reaction of all of the relatives to the fact of Anne's death, Henry concentrated his attention rather on Anne's soul's departure from her body. He did not want to miss a bit of it, being afraid to lose her from the field of his observation, and with that, being unable to follow her and Gertrude to wherever they were about to go.

Henry still didn't have Gertrude's approval as yet, but deep inside he knew that the green light was given…by who exactly he didn't care, but the fact that Thales himself recommended this trip gave him a pair of invisible wings to overcome any obstacles. Just to find out about the "great" soul that Thales spoke of.

EXIT

As Anne closed her eyes for the next pass out, she found herself in a strange city, walking along unfamiliar streets surrounded by unknown buildings. Suddenly she felt the ground beneath her feet move to the side, plunging her down to her knees. She quickly stood up trying to find her balance, but then again, a much stronger force beneath her feet launched her high up into the air. As she fell back to Earth, Anne saw all the surrounding building crumbling like a house of cards. The ground was still shaking, and she battled stand up straight, dodging falling debris. When everything came to a standstill she opened her eyes, and with great difficulty forcing her way out of the strange dream, Anne said to Raymond, "Save yourself. Everything is falling apart." She closed her eyes to be drawn into the devastated city again. This time everything was painfully familiar. It was her neighborhood, her street, and the remains of her apartment building.

"No," screamed Anne, and grabbing her head she fell into the dust and rubble. On her knees she observed the scene, refusing to believe her eyes. Then she leaned forward, plunging her hands into the gray powder that had once been concrete walls, screaming in pain. Tears rolling down from her eyes couldn't get off her cheeks being trapped in the powder completely covering her face. Mixed with the dust they turned into concrete and falling to her knees she clenched her fist filled with dust, releasing it over her head. This repeatedly performed act turned her into a cement sculpture with horror etched into her face.

Suddenly she was out of the horrifying dream again. Anne opened her eyes to see Croton, Gaya and little Rose standing at her bedside. She looked at Raymond, grabbed his arm with the last of her strength, and on the verge of losing consciousness said, "My home, my children, save them." Then everything was plunged into darkness.

When she regained consciousness again, Anne was still in

her bedroom surrounded by her loved ones. Every one of them was crying, and she couldn't understand why she suddenly felt so much better. The pain that she had experienced earlier was gone, and the most amazing feeling of absolute weightlessness came upon her.

Soon she realized that her perspectives had changed, and she was actually floating just above the bed. A moment later she was elevated to the ceiling. Her heart was singing. She shouted out, "Look at me, I am levitating!" But no one heard her or even looked at her. With no effort she brought herself upright and looked down to see their mesmerized faces. Instead, Anne saw herself lying motionless in the bed. She saw her own pale, frozen face. She saw Raymond's torso laying over her with his face down in her blankets, surrendering himself to the overflow of emotional pain. Her son was on his knees and holding her hand. Crying Gaya, with confused little Rose looking at her granny's lifeless body. Seeing all of this Anne came to the realization to what had actually happened to her. "Did I die?"

The question which every soul placed on this planet will release into the universe at least once. Into the space filled with consciousness on every level of its existence. The question as such cannot be left unanswered.

"Yes, my dear," Anne heard a voice which at first frightened her, but then she reasoned that if I can hear…perhaps I am not dead after all…

"Yes, you are, my dear," Anne heard the voice again from an unknown source.

Although the tone of the voice was so soothing and pleasant it did not place fear in her heart, rather the uncontrollable urge to see and meet its owner.

"Who are you and why can I not see you?" Anne asked boldly.

Henry, who was standing by the wall a distance from everyone else, stepped forward so as not to miss a fraction of the act which was meticulously orchestrated by Gertrude. He knew that she would not leave any loose ends and will execute her mission to the T. "Will he be a part of this plan?" remained a question to him. So far he was a distant observer to a quite unusual scene.

Anne, hovering just below the ceiling with Gertrude right in front of her, although for some reason Anne could not see her.

"Who are you," asked Anne again, "Please show yourself."

Realizing the importance of this moment, Henry looked straight into Gertrude's eyes and asked, "May I?"

Ignoring Henry's request, Gertrude answered Anne, "You will see me if you truly wish for it."

Anne squinted her eyes trying really hard to visualize the owner of this pleasant voice. Gradually, in front of her appeared the silhouette of a woman dressed in black. At first, she was all hazy and blurry, but soon Gertrude stood in front of Anne in her fullness. Anne looked at Gertrude, trying to make sense of what was happening, her motionless body down below surrounded by undertakers who had just arrived to announce the fact of her death and to collect her body, this strange nun suspended in the air... everything was happening so fast and out of her control. She did not know what to concentrate on. Torn between the physical and upcoming spiritual life, she chose to focus on her future.

Anne boldly stepped forward to look closely at Gertrude, whose face was lit up with love.

"Who are you?" Anne asked.

"I came to welcome you to the next place," answered Gertrude.

"What place?" Anne asked suspiciously.

"I came from the kingdom of our Father to guide you home."

Anne stepped back, rewarding the nun with a cold look, and then said, "My home is here."

"I know that, but you should understand that you do not belong to this world anymore. The time has come for you to follow me."

Watching men in black suits place her lifeless body into a black bag on a stretcher to take her to the mortuary, Anne panicked.

"Where are they taking me?"

"This should not worry you," Gertrude's comforting voice tried to calm her. "You do not belong in the body anymore."

Suddenly, they were plunged into darkness and the only figures visible in the light were Gertrude, Anne, and frozen Henry. In that very moment Henry realized that something did not go as Gertrude had planned and that the situation may get out of her control.

"I do not know you," Anne cried out fearfully, "And I do not know where you are trying to take me."

"Please clam down," Gertrude pleaded, continuously conveying love and compassion. "I am here to accompany you to paradise. The one that you learned about in the Bible."

"Paradise," Anne whispered to herself. A smile appeared on her face which assured Gertrude that she had finally found a way to Anne's mind and heart…but then again, Anne cast herself into darkness and with a voice filled with remorse said, "I do not belong to paradise, I was not good."

Anne fell silent, and looking at her, Gertrude realized that Anne was about to drift away. Before the curtain of the final act was about to drop between them, Gertrude launched herself forward to hug and comfort Anne…to prevent her from drowning in a pool of self-condemnation that would raise nothing but regrets.

Anne stepped back and pushed her arms forward to prevent Gertrude from getting close, saying, "I don't trust you."

"Why?" asked Gertrude.

"I have seen that I do not belong to paradise. You must be here to take me to hell." As Anne stated this she disappeared into the darkness, leaving Gertrude in absolute despair.

Realizing that now would be a good time to step in Henry stated, "I guess that did not go the way that you planned."

"No," Gertrude answered, feeling both irritated and disappointed.

"What now?" asked Henry.

"I will find her," Gertrude replied confidently. "She cannot be far."

"And where exactly are you expecting to find her?"

"There are only two possible places that she can be."

"Two?" Henry questioned.

"Yes, it will either be the mortuary or with her relatives. I will find her in no time. I have no doubt. This is standard procedure," Gertrude reassured herself.

"Okay, good luck," said Henry, stepping back into little Rose's bedroom.

THE SEARCH

Days went by with Henry, unable to reach Gertrude to get news on Anne floundering between realities, he was keeping an eye on Rose's progression in terms of her growth, and Croton's affairs in term of their decline. Day by day his hopes of an exciting journey promised by Thales were now melting into oblivion. Numerous attempts to reach Thales went unanswered, most likely ignored, which could mean only one thing … that he had to sit back and wait.

One night when Henry almost forgot about Gertrude's unfortunate fiasco, he noticed a dark figure in the doorway of Rose's bedroom. He immediately jumped up to shield sleeping Rose with his body, but to his relief it was Gertrude. Her face was pale, and the presence of once eminent confidence was nowhere to be traced. Instead, Henry found her eyes expressing nothing but deep disappointment in her own powerlessness. Forgetting all formalities, Henry said, "Let me guess, you couldn't track her."

"No," Gertrude answered abruptly.

"Then, why are you here?"

Looking straight into Henry's eyes, Gertrude said, "You are my last hope."

"Me?" Henry asked in surprise.

"Yes, you. You have been the longest around Anne and I have developed the feeling that you are the only soul who can help me to find her."

"I am flattered, but how?" said Henry feeling confused.

Then after rewinding the past chain of events, Henry said, "Yes, I have been around her while taking care of Croton, but to be honest I wasn't the best at it. Most of the time I was absent, and it was my wife who was taking care of Croton. Unfortunately, we cannot ask for her help."

"Why?"

"Because she is sleeping in this very bed," Henry answered,

pointing at little Rose.

"I see," Gertrude said with disappointment.

"Other than that…" Henry kept thinking, trying to grab any loose end that may lead to someone who could assist them to find lost Anne.

"Wait a minute!" Henry exclaimed suddenly. "I am familiar with Anne's previous guide, the one before you."

"Really?" sparks of hope lit up Gertrude's eyes.

"Yes, her name is Solomea, and I am sure that she can assist us," Henry said optimistically.

"Will you please get in touch with her?"

"Remembering how his last encounter with Solomea turned out, Henry hesitated for a moment unsure if he wanted to see her again or not.

"Please," Gertrude pleaded.

Henry closed his eyes, and a moment later he stepped toward Gertrude, grabbed her hands, saying, "Let's go."

A second later they were both standing on top of a hill surrounded by six obelisks. It was Solomea's reality. Once so impressed by it, Henry approached it cautiously this time. Everything was exactly the way he saw it the last time. Chaises were in the same place with the coffee table between them, and of course the turquoise, sparkling pool. Everything began to trigger unwanted memories of his downfall which was soon interrupted as Solomea stepped into the scene to face her guests. Henry stepped forward to greet her. Observing this magnificent women Henry was assured again that the art of ultimate seduction was Solomea's strongest suit, as well as being an integral part of her true nature, although not so prominent while she was guiding Anne.

Being only a few feet away, Henry had a glimpse of her outfit, although to call it an outfit would not be entirely correct. She was wearing a semi-transparent nightgown draped loosely over her shoulders, leaving nothing to the imagination. To Henry's judgement she was still the most beautiful woman he had every seen in both worlds.

Spreading her arms apart and with a wide smile Solomea stepped forward saying, "Welcome back, pretty boy," and pressed her entire body against Henry.

A strong current of rapture traveled through Henry's body, and before reaching his mind with irreversible effect Henry managed to gently pull back, and while gesturing to Gertrude said, "I am not alone. Please let me introduce Gertrude."

All delight on Solomea's face was wiped off like rain drops on a windshield by a wiper blade. All this time Gertrude was standing right next to Henry and to miss her presence would have been impossible. Still, Solomea acted deeply surprised to see her there.

"Oh, hello there. I did not notice you," Solomea tossed casually as she turned around and walked away to one of the chaises. Slowly and in the most seductive manner she lounged on her chaise bending her right knee, completely exposing her elegant leg for her guests' admiration.

"How can I help you?" she asked, observing her manicured fingernails, groomed to perfection.

Unable to hold back and tolerate such disrespectful behavior, Gertrude stepped forward, hardly suppressing the anger she felt, she said, "We have lost contact with Anne and are hoping that you can help us to find her."

"And who are you, if I may ask?" said Solomea.

"I am Gertrude."

"I heard that the first time. What I want to know is what are you doing here?"

"I am Anne's new guide, and Henry is helping me to find her."

Solomea theatrically burst into laughter.

"Let me refresh my memory. So, you are the guide who managed to lose the soul you were guiding?"

"Yes," Gertrude replied impatiently, but still managing to keep her cool.

"What kind of a guide are you if such a simple task as the safe passage to the world of spirit you couldn't provide to poor Anne!"

"I was newly appointed…and I guess I did not know her that well."

"How could you know her?" Solomea burst out angrily. "It wasn't you watching her peaceful sleep through countless nights. It wasn't you wiping her tears every time she was hurt. It wasn't you following each step into adulthood, protecting her from any harm that she may find…and now you stand here with the audacity to call yourself Anne's guide."

"I was appointed."

"She was appointed," paraphrased Solomea.

Then, by scanning her from head to toe, Solomea said, "Judging by your appearance, I presume that the book you are holding is a Bible."

"Yes," Gertrude stated proudly, "What is wrong with that?"

"I will tell you if you insist. You, and others like you, think that the answers to all questions can be found in that book. A book written by humans, for humans. One book to have it all. One book to have it all," Solomea stated, bursting into sarcastic laughter. "Ha ha ha. Don't you see how pathetic you are. Hiding your entire life behind the cross. The very tool of your leader's execution."

As she said that, Solomea pointed to the silver cross on Gertrude's chest. Gertrude immediately covered it with her hand.

"Loaded with fear yourself, you spread fear into the hearts of poor humans, feeding their minds with the nonsense you call virtues. Teaching them to separate good from bad like you know it. Let me enlighten you, my dear. Your knowledge is old, and it stinks. No, it actually sucks how you have managed for 2000 years to fill up humanity's minds with guilt for the most innocent deeds."

Solomea got louder and louder and Henry chose to step aside so as not to be caught in the line of fire between Solomea and Gertrude. What was puzzling him most was how long Gertrude would tolerate this direct mockery and insult of her faith and all that she stood for. She reminded him of a brave and unfairly accused convict facing a firing squad.

Solomea kept on blasting, "Your so-called virtues are nothing but a breeding ground of regrets and the need for repentance, and you are the almighty ones who reserve for themselves the rights to grant forgiveness. Forgiveness for all the sins that poor humans believe they have committed. Sins…," Solomea exclaimed pointing up at the heavily clouded sky. Her voice echoed across the surrounding valleys and once it settled she continued …"What the hell is sin anyway? You came up with a set of rules, called them divine laws, and whoever dared to not follow them you called them 'sinner'. You are the main reason why humans stopped perceiving the Creator as the most loving and forgiving being. You are responsible for manifesting into reality the most ridiculous realm called hell. Planting it into their simple minds, frightening them with eternal damnation. Of course, they will end up in hell because they start to believe that they really belong to that damned place."

It seems as though Solomea was not going to stop until her cup filled with anger had been completely emptied over the head of poor Gertrude.

"You, and those like you, religious maniacs, who are posing as protectors of virtue are nothing but hijackers of human minds for your own sick agendas. You are the ones who are crushing those free spirits, chaining them to your vision of right and wrong, and reserving for yourselves the right to judge where they belong, to hell or to heaven."

Having said that, Solomea fell quiet. It seemed as though she had said it all. All that she had been carrying for God knows how long. Dumping it all right there with no remorse for poor Gertrude, who was still standing quietly without saying a word, waiting patiently for Solomea to run out of steam, and hopefully to later assist to find her lost soul.

In a more settled tone, Solomea said, "How can you not see it. That this scripture in your hands, and any others for that matter, are designed to kill any spirit of fun, fun which souls can actually find while being in a human body. The very same act of procreation you call sin. How could you."

With this Solomea let out a deep sigh, lowered her head, saying to herself, "Poor Anne, I can only imagine what she is going through."

Thinking that this would be the right time to step in Henry said, "Let's put aside all of our differences and focus on helping Anne. After all, it was her wish to study the Bible, and we should all respect her choice."

Solomea stood up sharply in a more modest dress. She was all in white with a slight shimmer of silver glitter to it. With the exception of her head, her entire body was covered. Her usually soft and sensual face now became an adamantly chiselled mask of determination. Without looking at her visitors she almost commanded, "Let's go."

CONFINEMENT

A strangely dressed nun, all in black and suspended in mid-air, raised an enormous feeling of fear in Anne's heart. Seeing her own body down below, and the appearance of this priestess out of nowhere asking her to follow her God knows where, was too much for Anne to take in. Her first thought was, *"Run. Run away from this weird and scary situation. Run somewhere safe. Somewhere where she could gather her thoughts and plan her next steps."*

Suddenly with the utmost clarity she pictured a special hiding place that she used to have on her Granny's farm, a place known only to her, a place where she could hide from the world and not be found. For many years in a row, Anne's parents used to take her for the summer school holidays to stay with her grandparents. She fondly reminisced of the times of carefree existence in the bliss of Gran's unconditional love and absolute tolerance. On the farm filled with livestock she was most attracted to nature. She was familiar with the oldest trees. Every morning she used to greet them by touching their bark. Something magical was in that touch. It seemed that the trees were greeting her back. They seemed to be conversing with her in a very special, undetectable way, and with that filling her heart with joy and delirious happiness. According to their appearance Anne would reward them with character and personality which helped her to speak with them and read their minds. Her favorite was the old oak tree that she loved to hug, placing her ear to her trunk to listen to stories that Anne made up on the tree's behalf. Overpowering all the other trees with her size, she placed in Anne's heart a sense of absolute safety. Not that she had anything to be afraid of, but in the absence of her parents she felt safer just being in contact with this old tree. She had a very special place between the powerful roots standing above the ground that created the perfect resting place for Anne to lounge…like a most comfortable armchair.

In this very spot, by some miracle, Anne found herself. How she managed to escape that horrifying reality she could not explain. With just a thought that she did not have to face that strange priestess and her own dead body already gave her great relief. She firmly grasped the mighty roots and sat back to organize her scattered thoughts into one sensible notion which could reflect, or at least explain, all that had just happened. A while later she said to herself, *"If this is the afterlife I could stay here forever. Yes, that is exactly what I am going to do. There is no better place to hide from the possible punishment for all that I have done."*

She tried to push away any unwanted thoughts about a feasible future and forced herself to the most from this unexpected gift. The gift of being in this most missed and magical place. Her entire surroundings were exactly the way that she remembered. It seemed as though this little forest managed to escape the touch of ever-aging time.

Soon, she chose to release her clenching grip of the roots and effortlessly lifted herself off the ground. The absence of pain and her weightlessness reminded her of the times of her childhood when the last thing she did was think about her body or its limitations. Running and jumping felt like the most natural thing to do, only later with age did she realize how reckless youth could be with the God-given tool of our bodies. Anne felt young again.

The path to her grandparent's house she could find with her eyes closed, and a moment later she was standing in front of it. A quick glimpse let her with no doubt that this was the house. She ran up the wooden steps to stand in front of the large wooden door. After a short hesitation she knocked, hoping that the chain of miracles could be extended, and that Granny would open the door to her. But there was no answer. Anne pushed the door which gave a familiar squeak inviting the unexpected guest into itself. Appearing at the center of the foyer Anne looked around hoping to find someone there, but then, the sudden realization that her grandparents were long gone snuck in. Even though it was the very same house that she was standing in that had been sold when they passed away, and as far as she could remember it had been demolished to make way for a holiday resort. Clouds found their way into her mind. She went to check each room one by one. Everything was exactly the way she remembered, but something was wrong with this entire picture. *"Am I back in time?"* Anne asked herself. *"Is this possible? Considering the circumstances*

I am in, anything is possible," she answered herself. Then she remembered about the full-length mirror in her granny's bedroom, and she rushed upstairs to face it. She stepped into the room, and then stumbled for a moment to prepare herself for whatever she may face. Then she began a slow approach toward the mirror. Her heart was pounding intensely, defining the importance of the moment. Anne closed her eyes before she could face the mirror, and only by standing tall and proud in front of it she dared to look. The astonishment that she experienced had no limitations. Standing in front of the mirror she was looking at the mirror itself. There was no reflection of her.

The confused state of mind that she was already in became even more demented. She stepped back and stormed out of the bedroom, literally flew down the stairs and stopped at the porch of the house, to sit down at the top of the wooden stairs to gather her thoughts and think about what is next.

The realization of her loneliness and complete abandonment by the world she knew squeezed her chest. To be stuck in the past all alone and seeing it as a safe haven from what she might face was not ideal at all. The occurrence of the fact that sooner or later she will have to face the music and whatever had to accompany the tune was becoming clear as day, revealing a vision of unpreventable events named "Judgement Day", waiting for her to unleash its retribution with full force. She held her head between her hands and closed her eyes with indecisiveness of her next move.

A party of three appeared in the middle of the forest right in front of the hole in the tree.

"Strange," said Solomea, "I was so sure that she would be here."

"Why here?" asked Henry.

"This was her favorite spot in her childhood, and I cannot think of any other place that she would have tried to escape to."

"Are we in the middle of a forest?" asked Gertrude.

Ignoring her, a sudden realization visited Solomea, and she exclaimed, "House!" Henry and Gertrude followed swiftly moving Solomea, and the next moment they were standing at the edge of the little forest.

"I see her," whispered Solomea. "This is as far as you can go. Let me handle this my way!" she demanded.

Henry and Gertrude stepped back so as not to be seen by poor Anne. Solomea stood motionless looking at despairing Anne as she surgically planned her next move. Then she faced Gertrude and asked, "Do you know where you are taking her?

Gertrude confidently answered, "Yes," adding a bit later, "Only if she will follow."

"To begin with, please change your gloomy outfit." "What is wrong with my outfit?" protected Gertrude. "I was a Missionary…"

"Just turn into white," Solomea interrupted commandingly.

Gertrude placed her right hand over the cross on her chest and closed her eyes. A second later she was robed all in white.

"Good," said Solomea. "Now you wait for my sign. Do not show yourself before. Is this clear?"

"Yes," answered Gertrude.

Solomea turned to Henry and said, "You can leave now. I located her. The rest is technical."

"I would like to stay and observe if you don't mind," pleaded Henry.

"Deal," agreed Solomea. "Do not show yourself at all."

"How long can I remain in this isolation?" Anne wondered to herself. *"I wish someone would tell me what to do."* In the very moment that this thought crossed her mind she noticed a white figure emerge from the forest and approach her. She immediately stood up straining all of her senses to concentrate on the lady in white gliding toward her. As Solomea got closer, Anne could see her immaculate beauty. *"Only wings are missing,"* thought Anne to herself. Waiting until Solomea stood in front of her in all of her glamour, Anne asked, "Are you an Angel?"

"I could be, my child," said Solomea, smiling gently.

The word child alarmed Anne. "Why are you calling me child?"

"You will always be a child to me, my dear Anne. I knew you before you knew yourself. I have been a witness to your birth, to your first steps and words, to your first love and first kiss. I stood next to you at your wedding and the birth of your son, Croton. I have been witness to Raymond's love and his betrayal. Your success was my success, and your failures mine, too."

The word failure downed her.

"So, you are aware of my failures?"

"You must stop judging yourself, my dear Anne," said Solomea as she gently touched Anne's arm.

A warm feeling rushed through Anne's body filling it with ease and contentment. A bit more relaxed she sat back on the wooden stairs and Solomea sat next to her.

"I have done so much wrong in my life and I am certain that I belong in hell."

"You have done nothing wrong, my child. Besides, there is no such thing as hell in existence. At least not in the way that you perceive it."

"There is no hell?" asked Anne in surprise.

"No, my dear, unless you chose to be there."

"Why would anyone choose such a thing?"

"You almost did," said Solomea, turning her head to face Anne, she continued, "To reject the one who came to greet you and welcome you to the next place was not a smart thing to do. Do you agree?"

Anne lowered her head and said, "I was terrified."

"I know, my child, but it is all over now. The important thing is that you are safe and please trust me, I know what is best for you."

Anne looked straight into Solomea's eyes and asked, "Why do I have the feeling that I know you? Solomea smiled gently.

"Above all, I would like to know who are you? Are you an angel from above?"

"I am not. I am just your spirit guide. The one responsible for your safe journey on this planet. The one who was always next to you, and sometimes the one whispering into your ear the right things to do."

"Why didn't you whisper a bit louder so that I didn't mess up my life, and probably my husband's, too. I am the one who forced him to accept bribes. Why didn't you stop me?"

"Humans are in possession of the God-given gift of free-will. We spirit guides, are obliged not only to respect it, but to assist in its execution as well. Regardless of being right or wrong, we cannot judge. All we can do is accept your will without interference."

"I see," sadly acknowledged Anne.

"Don't be sad. I would like to reveal to you one very important secret," Solomea whispered into Anne's ear.

"What secret?"

"Not many know that there is no ultimate right or wrong."

"What do you mean?"

"I'm saying that right and wrong are quite flexible."

Anne squinted her eyes showing distrust in Solomea's words.

"Yes, my dear Anne. What is right for you could be completely wrong for another person, and vice versa. What I am trying to tell you is that whatever you consider to be the most sinful thing to do, we see it as an experience, or a lesson for you to reflect upon later, and probably to be laughed at."

Solomea smiled and nudged Anne's shoulder saying, "Come on Anne, your physical life dealt with pain and suffering. It is over now, and new adventures are waiting for you. The entire universe is out there in suspense to be discovered and explored by you. All you have to do is allow yourself a last chapter of your 'Being a Human' book to be closed, and then start a new chapter, or even a new book if you will, by the name 'Birth Into the World of Spirit', where each and every soul is waiting to welcome you and shower you with love and happiness.'"

Anne looked at Solomea saying sincerely, "Are you saying that I will be allowed to enter into the kingdom of our Lord Jesus Christ?"

Solomea lowered her head to suppress her first reaction to Anne's question, but then seeing her eyes filled with hope and anticipation she said, "For that exact reason I brought to you a guide to that place of your desire."

As she said that, Gertrude appeared from behind the trees and approached Anne.

"What about you? Aren't you coming with us?"

"I have another task to perform, and Gertrude will be the perfect guide for this journey. You must trust her," insisted Solomea.

"When can I see you again?"

"Soon, I will visit once you are settled in the new place."

Before Gertrude reached them, Anne grabbed Solomea's arm to stop her from leaving, and asked one last question, "Should I be afraid?"

"The place you are about to go has no fear by definition and you will find nothing but happiness and abundance," were Solomea's last words to Anne as she stood up. As she walked past Gertrude, she said, "She's all yours," vanishing before reaching the edge of the forest.

Gertrude stood in front of Anne still sitting on the stairs, stretching her hand out, "Should we begin our journey?"

Anne placed her hand into Gertrude's, stood up, smiled sadly and said, "I am ready."

"Please close your eyes," lovingly asked Gertrude and they were both dispersed into the essence of the fresh air.

Henry, watching and listening to everything that occurred on the porch of the house was suddenly left alone. Forgotten and rejected by everyone. He came out of hiding and said, "Hello. What about me? Gertrude?"

Unable to reach Gertrude, Henry said to himself, *"Go and help them...after all this not even thank you."*

In absolute despair and disappointment Henry felt like the doors had slammed shut right in front of his face and along with that his hopes of the adventure recommended by Thales.

"Home," thought Henry and was immediately transported to his own reality.

HEAVEN

When Anne opened her eyes, she was standing next to Gertrude at the center of a humongous square surrounded by single story houses, all similar in appearance, stretching along streets running from the center of the square into the depths of the city.

While Anne was looking around to establish where she was, Gertrude changed her outfit to the original black. From the beginning of their arrival, the square which had hardly any inhabitants slowly began to fill up. Citizens were appearing from out of nowhere, like forest mushrooms after heavy rains. They were popping up in pairs, exactly as Anne and Gertrude stepped into this reality. Each pair, regardless of their gender, one wearing white and the other black.

Absolutely amazed by what was happening around her, Anne looked at Gertrude and asked, "Where are we and what is going on?"

"Newbies with their guides are arriving, just like us," answered Gertrude.

After giving Anne some time to absorb all that was happening around her, she continued, "Shall we locate your new home?"

"Do I have a house here?" asked Anne in surprise.

"All souls do."

"This must be a huge city to accommodate so many people," said Anne observing the ongoing, unstoppable process of arrivals of new souls, liberated from their bodies, just as she was, confused and surprised next to their guides who were projecting calm and confidence.

"Do you like your new outfit?" asked Gertrude.

Anne checked and realized that she was wearing a white robe.

"I love it," said a more relaxed Anne spinning around.

Seeing the smile on Anne's face, Gertrude could not hide her delight. "You are going to love being here."

"I already am," replied Anne as she slid her hand under Gertrude's arm. "Okay my guide, guide me to my house. I am dying to see it."

Side by side they walked into one of the streets leading toward the outskirts of the seemingly endless city.

"I guess my house will be one of the last ones," commented Anne cheerfully.

"Why so?" asked Gertrude.

"They are popping up non-stop," said Anne looking back at the fading square.

"What do you expect. Almost 30 percent of the human population are practicing Christians. That means that there are roughly 100 thousand souls arriving daily into this and many other similar cities."

"Do they all have to be accommodated?"

"Yes, with no exception."

"You must have a good team of builders to build 100 thousand houses a day."

Gertrude laughed loudly, unable to express her excitement at Anne's engagement.

"Why are you laughing? Did I ask a stupid question?"

"Not at all Anne, anyway, let me explain. The number of souls arriving are almost equal to those who depart from this city."

"To where?"

"Back to Earth to be born as humans again. So, you see, there is no need for big construction teams. Nor the continual development of new houses."

"So, the idea of rebirth is true."

"Doesn't that excite you?"

"That's not what the Bible teaches us."

"Don't be upset. Lots of revelations are still to come. Especially with regards to what the Bible teaches and what Christ himself teaches."

Before Anne had a chance to reflect on Gertrude's last statement, they stopped in front of an adorable little house.

"Is this mine?" Anne asked excitedly.

"All yours, as promised."

"I can't wait to see inside."

As they passed through the waist high gate Anne couldn't help but notice the well-groomed tiny garden, rich in colors with green grass surrounded by the most beautiful blooming rose bushes. Anne rushed toward the entrance door and opened it. The interior of the house did not have much décor. A small white table surrounded by four chairs found its solitude in the middle of the small room. The room was approximately twenty by fifteen feet. There was no trace of any other furniture. The back wall of the house facing Anne was missing, allowing the interior of the room to flow into the back yard, which was about the same size as the room. The entire ground of the back yard was covered by grass and surrounded by white walls.

A bit distressed, Anne observed the entirety of the house allocated to her, saying, "So, no bedroom, or bed for that matter?"

"No," confirmed Gertrude, "Disappointed?"

"Not really, I can sleep on the floor. Just a blanket would have been nice."

"No."

"Not even a blanket? Okay, this must be part of my punishment."

Gertrude burst into laughter and asked Anne, "Please sit down and I will explain to you how everything works in this place."

They sat down at opposite ends of the table, and Gertrude let out a long sigh as she prepared to unwrap the big box of knowledge that Anne had to be presented with. Even at its basics, there was so much to be absorbed by poor Anne, just to be able to sustain her existence in this land.

"How do you find your house?" began Gertrude.

"It reminds me of a white canvas."

"That is exactly what it is."

"What do you mean?"

"It's as you said, a white canvas for you to become the creator of your own reality."

"I'm not following?"

"You can make any changes to this room using the power of your imagination."

"Really?"

"Try."

"Okay," said Anne, and looking at the walls she continued, "I do understand that the white is the color of purity and innocence, but it is a bit too much for my liking."

"Just close your eyes and imagine the color that you want to see on your walls."

Anne closed her eyelids and in front of Gertrude the walls turned to light beige.

"Wow!" exclaimed Anne observing the change. "Back home, I could have spent a lifetime forcing Raymond to repaint the walls. This is amazing!"

Anne stood up from her chair and touched the newly painted walls. "Can I change the color of the floor, too?" asked Anne.

"Not only the color, but the texture, too. But before you jump into your interior decorator mood, let me explain your limitations."

"Yup, just as I get excited limitations have to step in."

"Nevertheless, you have to know about them so as not to waste your vital energy into something that you cannot manifest."

"Okay," grounded Anne answered.

"With this space given to your disposal, you can do whatever you like. I would advise you to keep it simple and modest. Do not forget the reason for you being here is your acceptance of Christ's teachings."

"I do understand that," Anne replied more seriously.

"You cannot change the size of this house." As Gertrude said this she looked straight into Anne's eyes to assure that Anne understood.

"I do understand that," said Anne.

"Since we are clear on this, I will share with you the daily routine." "Daily routine?" asked surprised Anne.

"Well, despite the fact that there is no such thing here, but we still call it daily."

"I don't get it?" asked Anne.

"There is no night here, Anne, and so there is no distinction between day and night as there is on Earth. All that we have here is one long day."

"That explains the absence of a bedroom and a bed."

"You will hardly ever be in this house. Only when you feel tired or overwhelmed by other souls."

"Okay, I am still interested to hear about our daily routine."

"Yes. There are lots of activities happening in this place. Most of them serve an educational purpose. Some are just for entertainment."

"Okay," said Anne.

"One more thing. If you choose to change your outfit, you will be able to do this, but only in your private space. Once you are outside, the robe you are wearing now will automatically find you."

"I like this robe," said Anne while cuddling herself deeper into it.

As Gertrude stood up to leave, Anne asked, "Are you leaving me?"

"Yes, you have a lot to do in your private space. Be creative, but modest. I will see you later."

"When?" pleaded Anne.

"The moment you call me I will be around."

"How do I call you? I see no phones around."

"Just a thought will be enough," said Gertrude as she withdrew.

With that Gertrude disappeared leaving Anne feeling a bit anxious. She looked around her new, humble accommodation and came to the sudden realization, except for the bedroom, the kitchen was also missing.

"Did she leave it for me to create?" Anne asked herself, *"Or is it considered an unnecessary luxury?"*

Choosing not to bother Gertrude, given how much trouble she had caused Gertrude to trace her, Anne decided to explore her new God-given gift of being a creator in the big, broader aspect.

"Why not?" thought Anne and closed her eyes.

When she reopened then, one entire wall of her one room house was plastered with an exact replica of her kitchen back home, her most favorite things, even with the loveliest stove, fridge, toaster, mixer, even the kettle that she used to boil was there. Unable to hold back her emotional excitement Anne screamed and stepped forward to check it was all real. To begin with she carefully touched it, checking each drawer and cupboard for contents. Everything was exactly the way that she'd left it. Her favorite and most precious set of plates with a golden trim was complete. Her crystal glasses, expensive cutlery, never mind the cheap ones, all her appliances were in a brand-new condition. The fridge was filled to the brim like always. If there was one thing Raymond was good at it was the constant supply of fresh produce, never mind the delicacies that only a few could afford. Her exuberance was boundless. Only one thing spoiled her excitement…the kitchen occupied half of the house. "It's okay," Anne convinced herself. "I can survive without the rest." She sat down in one of the chairs and couldn't take her eyes away from her own creation. "Wait a minute, what about more comfortable chairs, and maybe a table along with the chairs. I will just replace this ugly one with mine. It will occupy exactly the same space."

A second later she was sitting at her own mahogany table. The heavily carved dinning table had eight chairs to go with it. "Although my calculations were a bit off concerning the size of this suite, I still managed to fit it in," proudly admitted Anne, tapping herself on the shoulder. Then, the white floor grabbed her attention. "This is very impractical," said Anne and soon a brand-new wooden parquet floor came into existence. "Perfect," Anne said observing its texture and color variations. Considering what more she could fit in without taking up more of the space, and obstructed her already limited freedom of movement, she concentrated her attention on the ceiling. "A chandelier will not take up any space," said Anne closing her eyes again. A state-of-the-art crystal chandelier that she had back home did not look so big there as it appeared in her new home. To pass it she had to lower her head, but to ruin it by making it smaller she wouldn't dare. The emptiness of the tabletop caught her attention. "Maybe my two 15th century Ming dynasty Chinese vases that I spent a fortune on will complete the interior of this room."

Looking around Anne noticed that she had run out of space in the room, but the big yard remained untouched. She stepped out onto the evenly trimmed grass, looked around and said, "Maybe I can utilize this space too. Why not?" But then she remembered that wooden furniture could be ruined by being exposed to direct sun rays and possible rain. She looked up into the sky to check for any clouds and found the complete absence or even one. "What about the sun?" Being unable to see the sun she tried to locate it by shadows on the grass, but there were none. Even her own body did not cast any shadow. "This is strange," Anne admitted to herself. "I will have to check with Gertrude." The absence of sun and clouds encouraged her to keep going with her most joyous process of creation, or to be exact the process of re-creation of some of the furnishings she had grown attached to over her entire life. An hour later Anne's back yard was completely finished. Her favorite sofa with two occasional chairs and a coffee table in between found themselves on top of the most beautiful Persian carpet that completely masked the entire presence of outdoor grass. Exhausted from all the work she had done, Anne launched herself onto her sofa and observed the product of her creation. All the famous art pieces she used to have had found their new places on the walls previously untouched. Then Anne's attention fell to her hands. The absence of all jewelry on her was very unusual, but remembering Gertrude's advice? to keep it simple she thought "at least one…" and she crowned her hand with one of her precious rings. The only one that she always kept in her safe, never daring to wear it in public…the 25 carat flawless diamond was mounted on the golden band and circled by smaller diamonds. One more Cartier watch will complete this picture, Anne convinced herself, and sat back with the utmost satisfaction depicted upon her face.

"What now?" said Anne, and after a moment's hesitation, she chose to step out of the house and hopefully meet some of her neighbors.

With great difficulty she found her way to the door, squeezing herself between the dining room chairs and the kitchen on the sides and the chandelier on top. Reaching the door, she almost opened it, but then stopped looking at the empty space next to the door and said, "A mirror is missing." Having had an unpleasant experience with the mirror in her grandparent's house, Anne approached this task cautiously.

When she opened her eyes, she was looking at her own reflection. With a couple of short strokes, she fixed her hair, but her outfit left her completely unsatisfied. The white robe was no match for all that she had managed to manifest.

"Let me do something about this," said Anne, and a second later she appeared in her best designer dress. Pleased with the results of her rich imagination, Anne stepped closer to the mirror and by touching the wrinkles on her face said, "If I only could… What if…"

The transformation of her skin made Anne shriek with excitement. A few more touches and she was young again. "Hallelujah," said Anne, and she boldly stepped out of the house.

As she was warned by Gertrude, her newly created outfit vanished without a trace, to be replaced by the simple white robe. Anne checked her hands, and the diamond ring and watch were gone, too. Disappointed she looked her reflection in the window by the door with not much expectation, "Hooray!" celebrated Anne jumping up and down with ultimate excitement, "My youth is safe."

Stepping out of the house Anne felt liberated from all the clutter that she had managed to create in a matter of only a few hours. She went to check on her neighbors to hopefully meet them and say hello. But no one answered her knocking. She walked out onto the street. It was empty of inhabitants. Standing in the middle of the road she felt alone and abandoned.

"I think now would be the right time to disturb Gertrude."

As the thought crossed her mind Gertrude appeared and asked, "So how is your moving going?"

"I have to get used to your sudden appearances and disappearances," said frightened Anne.

"Didn't you call me?"

"I just thought about you."

"That's good enough. So, what can I do for you?" asked Gertrude excitedly.

"I guess I am a bit bored."

"I see that you have discovered your youth again."

"It brought me so much happiness," Anne said as she touched her face.

"I am glad to hear that. Did you finish with your home decorating?"

"Yes!" Anne answered excitedly. "Do you want to see it?"

"Of course I do."

They went back to the house and Anne proudly opened the door expectant of compliments.

"Wow!" exclaimed Gertrude.

"Delighted, I tried to keep it simple and modest as you advised. Do you like it?"

"Yes, I can see it," said Gertrude with a hint of disappointment in her voice.

"Do you think it is too much? But this is not even one percent of what I had back home!"

The word home pronounced by Anne cast sadness across her young face.

"Is something wrong" Gertrude asked in concern.

"Suddenly I remembered my family. How are they coping? I really miss them."

"Do you want to see them?" asked Gertrude.

"Is it possible?" A spark of hope lit up Anne's face.

"Only if you wish it."

"Of course I do. When can we do it?" Anne asked impatiently.

"Right now," answered Gertrude, unable to hide her delight.

"I'm ready," said Anne as she closed her eyes.

"But before we commit to such a journey, I must warn you that we cannot stay there for long. We basically will go in and out."

"Why?" asked Anne disappointed.

"To visit Earth, we must lower our level of vibration and if we stay too long, I may lose you again. You don't want that to happen, do you?"

"Definitely not," agreed Anne, "I will do as you say."

"One more thing, since I left the physical reality along with you, I have completely lost track of time and my connection with your family. Why I am saying this is so that you are ready for any scene that we may step into."

"Okay," said Anne not entirely grasping the meaning of Gertrude's words.

Gertrude gently took Anne's hand in hers and they both closed their eyes.

TRADITIONS

They appeared in the middle of a crowded corridor. Some people were sitting on chairs placed along the walls, and others were walking in and out of Anne's flat. Anne looked at Gertrude standing beside her with her eyes expressing deep appreciation for all that she had done.

"You go ahead, my dear,' Gertrude said lovingly, "I will be nearby."

Making her way between the multitude of people, Anne made her way to the dining room. What attracted her attention first was the coffin placed on top of the dining table with her own body in it. Her entire body, except for her face, was covered with a layer of red roses. Music, traditional for such occasions, added a shade of sadness to the palette of dark colors present in the room. Anne slowly floated toward the coffin not noticing anyone surrounding it. She stood by for some time completely disappointed by the way she looked.

"Is this all that is left of me? Even this will soon perish." She placed her hand on the edge of the coffin saying, "You caused me lots of pain lately, but I forgive you. Rest in peace."

She turned around and stood right in front of Raymond. He was sitting in a chair with a blank stare across his face. As though sensing her presence Raymond's heartbeat raised and substantially affected his breathing.

"Keep your distance please," Anne heard Gertrude's voice in her head.

"I wish he could see me. He would fall in love with me all over again."

Next she noticed Croton sitting beside Raymond. She stood in front of him and in the most loving voice said, "Look at my boy. I am so proud of him. I just hope that he won't follow his father's footsteps."

There were many other relatives, friends, and people who

she used to support financially, some who she didn't know at all. Every new arriving guest offered their condolences to Raymond and Croton, and by walking around Anne's remains, then left the room.

"It's time to leave," Anne heard Gertrude's voice.

"Wait a minute, I have not yet seen my little Rose, my granddaughter."

"We will be back soon, but for now we have to leave," insisted Gertrude as she approached Anne.

As a humble child she moved her hand toward Gertrude, but before Gertrude had a chance to touch her, Anne pulled back saying, "One more second please." As she said that Anne disappeared.

This last act placed Gertrude in shock. One moment she had everything under control, and the next, without any warning, everything fell apart. Fear crept into her soul revealing her weaknesses, if not her incompetence in managing Anne's spontaneous swings in behavior. Gertrude knew that the moment that Anne began losing clarity of vision she could be lost, or to be more exact, stuck between realities and become ghost in her own flat. Without losing any vital time she rushed from room to room searching for Anne, but with the flat being so full of people this was not an easy task. Finally, Gertrude located her. Anne was standing in the kitchen right in front of one of the cupboards helplessly trying to open it.

"What are you doing?" Gertrude almost screamed.

"I must warn them…I have to…" Anne whispered on the verge of losing consciousness.

Gertrude swiftly moved in, grabbed Anne's entire body, covering her eyes with her hand and then closed her eyes, too. The last words that Anne heard through the haziness was Gertrude strained voice, "Home!"

Anne gained consciousness back in her new house. Still embraced by a frightened Gertrude, she pulled back and asked, "What was that? I almost fainted."

As Gertrude helped her to sit up in a chair Gertrude said, "Didn't I warn you. I nearly lost you again. How could you!"

"Sorry," apologized Anne holding her spinning head in her hands.

"Will you tell me, please, why did you go into the kitchen? What was so important there to risk everything?" Gertrude kept going unable to contain her anger.

Anne slowly stood up and opened the very same cupboard

door that she failed back home. A sizable tin jar appeared on the kitchen counter.

"What is this?" Gertrude asked.

Anne removed the lid and Gertrude saw a white substance filling the container to its brim.

"What is this?" Gertrude asked again.

"Salt," answered Anne.

"Salt?" asked Gertrude confused.

Without saying anything Anne poured the contents out onto the counter. Unable to contain her curiosity Gertrude stood up to have a better look at this mysterious salt. With one swipe of her hand Anne revealed what was hidden inside the jar…various rings with precious stones, bracelets covered with diamonds and many more items of expensive jewelry.

"It was for all of these toys you risked being trapped in hell!"

"Not for me," Anne confessed. "Lately I was so centerd on my killing the cancer within my body that I forgot to tell my family where I had hidden all this. Now I don't know if they will ever find it, except by accident."

"I see," said Gertrude, "but don't ever do that again. Here I can locate you with no effort, but on Earth my powers are extremely limited and that is why most guides try by all means to avoid accompanying newly arrived souls back to Earth."

"Too risky, I understand," Anne apologized.

"By the way," Gertrude asked changing the subject, "what was the coffin with your body doing on top of the dining table in the middle of the living room?"

"Obviously you are not familiar with our traditions," answered Anne gradually coming back to life. "Isn't it the same in other countries?"

"No!" exclaimed Gertrude. "No one brings the corpse back home, and especially not displaying them on top of a table like that."

"I can see how barbaric that looks, but is the tradition in my culture." Anne smiled and added, "I can tell you more!"

"What could be stranger than this!"

"The coffin with my body in it will remain in that room for the entire night, and at least two adult males have to stay throughout the night in that room to watch me."

Gertrude exclaimed in stunned disbelief "Are you kidding me?"

"No, but the worst part is that trying to stay awake all night they get drunk and pass out instead in the next room."

"Who wouldn't. It's scary enough being in the same room with a dead body for the entire night."

"And that's not all of it."

"Is there still more?" Gertrude asked.

"Yes, tomorrow they will bury my remains and all participants of the burial will go back to my flat to feast at the very same table."

"That's weird," commented Gertrude. "What about the church? Aren't they going to take your body to church?"

"You're forgetting one important thing. I lived in a Communist state and atheism is the state's philosophy and belief. So, as a result, no church."

"Sorry to hear that," said Gertrude.

"It's okay, you are born into traditions and you follow them, seeing nothing wrong with them. Above all you do not questions them," Anne admitted sadly.

The sounds of ringing bells caught their attention,

"Sounds like a church bell," said Anne.

"Yes, it is."

"Any meaning to this?" Anne asked.

"This is how the inhabitants are informed of a gathering."

"What gathering?"

"We should get back to the square, the one where we started."

"Do we have to walk there?" asked Anne, still feeling drowsy.

"No, just visualize yourself there."

"Are you coming with me?"

"No, it's for only newbies."

"I guess I will see you later," said Anne as she left the house.

Gertrude passed a casual look at the jewelry splashed across the counter, the cluttered room, backyard once green and said, "She still has so much to learn."

GATHERING

The multitude of souls gathered at the square was growing bigger by the minute. All dressed in white, a bit confused and disorientated, not knowing what to do or where to go. Everyone was looking at each other. The braver ones were asking questions or making acquaintances. In short no one knew what to expect, but most of all, who to expect. Anne did not miss the chance to make friends with an older lady standing next to her. First, she established that her name was Maria and that she had died of old age.

"I am so sorry you died so young. You didn't live at all," Maria said compassionately with sadness in her voice.

"No, I didn't die young."

"Then how?"

"I discovered a remedy," Anne whispered into Maria's ear.

"A remedy of eternal youth?"

"Yes," answered Anne.

"Please share with me. I feel so ancient in this crowd."

Anne clued Maria in and a moment later, in front of her eyes, the old caterpillar transformed into a beautiful butterfly.

"Metamorphosis," said Anne very satisfied that she could help somebody to find happiness.

"Welcome, welcome, my brothers and sisters to our humble abode," Anne heard a prominent voice in her head.

"Did you hear that?" asked Anne and Maria asked each other simultaneously.

Noticing where everyone was looking, they saw a podium in the middle of the square with an old man standing on it. He wore a beige robe, heavily worn by time. The most prominent features of his face were the gray bushy beard, bald head, and small and perky eyes. His short and wide nose settled on top of a rich moustache that melted into the beard, disguising the presence of his mouth.

"Yes, that's me, the one who is talking to you," said the old man raising his hand.

Everyone focused their attention on the figure on the podium, afraid to miss a word that he had to say.

"Welcome to you all my brothers and sisters in faith. To begin with, I would like to introduce myself. I was named Simon at my birth on Earth, but I was known in the history of Christianity as Peter."

He then fell quiet to allow the audience to digest the information shared.

"Saint Peter," waves of whispers traveled through the crowd.

"Yes, you are absolutely right, but please just use my name with adding Saint to it. I was not Saint back then, and neither am I now."

As he said those words his wide smile revealed a perfectly white row of teeth. Laughter rippled through the multitude of souls lifting everyone's spirits and easing their built-up tension.

"Since you know who I am, I would like to say congratulations, you did it."

Silence grabbed the sea of souls.

"Come on, give yourselves a round of applause."

Random and isolated clapping turned into a loud ovation.

"We made it…we made it…!" reached Anne from all around.

Peter kept going, "As you see there are no golden gates, and I am not standing on clouds, and above all I am not passing judgement of all that you have done on Earth. You are all here through your own choice."

Everyone looked at each other confused.

"Yes indeed, by choosing to believe the teachings of Jesus Christ you set your destiny. It is your belief that led you to this place. The place where you will have the opportunity not only to learn, but also to teach. Not only to be healed, but also to heal. The place where you will leave in the past all Earthly problems and embrace joy and happiness that you all so rightfully deserve. Your stay with us will be filled with many activities of your choice, and lots of entertainment, also. In short, welcome to paradise," Peter pronounced loudly spreading his arms wide apart.

The entire crowd burst into applause. Once they had settled, Peter said, "For now, you will be led to your classrooms where you will have the chance to meet with classmates and teachers."

"Sounds like we're back at school," Anne whispered into Maria's ear.

"This way please," said Peter, gesturing the direction for

everyone to proceed.

A white passage leading from the square funneled the white robes into a river of curiosity and mystical expectations. It flowed to its final destination to be dispersed right at the end like a river into the sands before reaching the ocean. An ocean of knowledge and infinite wisdom that soon enough would lead the souls to discover their true selves and their belonging to hierarchy of spiritual realms. The flow of white robes narrowed as souls were pulled from it to their designated classrooms. Anne waited anxiously for her turn. Between the so-called classrooms, that were more like separate buildings, lay dense tropical vegetation covering them completely from view by curious spectators. The distance between the building probably measured fifty yards They stood on either side of the road, but did not face each other. At the entrances to each building Anne noticed nuns dressed in black robes who seemed to be randomly picking souls to join their classes. Soon she noticed Gertrude standing at the entrance to one of the structures made from shimmering pure white marble, standing three stories high, with rows of columns supporting a heavy triangular roof. There were no windows, just wide openings in the walls between the columns forming arches. Gertrude, armed with a wide welcoming smile, called Anne to step out of the white river. Approaching Gertrude, Anne hugged her, feeling liberated and relieved to be free of the dense current of marching souls.

"Come on, get in," said Gertrude guiding Anne toward the entrance.

"So, you are going to be my teacher?" Anne asked excitedly.

"No, I'm not." Noticing sadness on Anne's face Gertrude asked, "Disappointed?"

"No, not at all, it would have exceeded my expectations anyway."

"Thank you," said Gertrude. "One thing I can assure you of is that you will never be disappointed." Anne hugged Gertrude again and stepped into her classroom.

CLASSROOM

Anne appeared in a dim corridor plastered with the same smooth marble. The end of the passage was flooded with an inviting light, which somehow did not light up the corridor itself. Anne sped up her steps to reach her classroom and finally to check out her classmates. Long forgotten emotions of stepping into a new school raised anxiety in her heart. She came to the realization that this was the beginning of a new chapter in her life. Her future was still unknown, but one thing she was sure of was that her past would be abandoned at the shining entrance to the classroom. Anne slowed her steps to take one last glimpse at her past life, and with the speed of light scenes from her forgotten past rushed in front of her to disappear into oblivion, leaving space for what was waiting ahead. The light at the end of the corridor began to blind her vision, camouflaging the classroom and its inhabitants. Anne covered her eyes and stepped into the light. A second later she gained her sight back. What she expected to be a classroom, or at least a school hall, was in reality beyond her wildest expectations. She was standing at the doorway to another world, the magnitude of which was impossible to imagine from the outside. She was standing at the edge of a huge yard, probably 100 yards in diameter filled with scholars. The yard was covered by well-maintained grass, scattered with multiple walkways formed by wooden planks neatly laid for the student's comfort. Anne chose one of them leading to the center of the yard. The closer she got to the middle, the horizon transformed from a light blue into a breath-taking turquoise. A few more steps and she could see the entire scenery. The green field that she was standing on was placed right at the edge of the most beautiful white sandy beach. Palm trees leaned over the water, elevating the picture to the level of perfection which could have been expressed by the human mind only with one word, "Paradise," whispered Anne unable to move from the spot where she was standing to absorb more of this moment and this picture. One by one the newbies visited the beach with absolute disbelief and utmost satisfaction depicted on their faces. Satisfaction in the choice that they had made by allowing the words of Christ into their minds and hearts.

"So, this is the paradise that the Bible was promising. It really does exist," Anne said contentedly to herself.

But then a dark shadow fell over her joy.

"I'm not sure about Raymond, but I hope that my son Croton will deserve to end up here. Time, I just ran out of it. If I had a bit longer to live, I would have convinced my boy to read the Bible. It changes your life completely, turning your life upside down to the point of no return.

Thoughts impregnated with regret began to flow into Anne's consciousness leaving not much space for her to enjoy all that lay in front of her. The realization that none of this would be available to her son or her husband spoiled her happiness. Anne moved closer to observe the fading line between the beach and the ocean which was hardly visible due to the calmness and clarity of the water. The gradual disappearance of the whiteness of the sand into the depth of the turquoise waters mesmerized her until Gertrude's voice in her head snapped her back from her meditative state.

"Anne, will you please proceed to your class."

Anne turned around to see Gertrude standing at the end of the pathway, the one that ran along the beach to disappear into the horizon. As she stepped forward toward Gertrude, Anne noticed a string of buildings all facing the ocean, made from the same white marble, and proudly standing tall, reminding Anne of the Greek structures that stuck in her mind from the history books at school. Right in front of one of them Gertrude stopped her.

"Shall we," Gertrude invited her to step inside.

They appeared in a long school corridor filled with lights and anticipation. Anne had no fear, instead she was excited to meet new souls just like her, and begin the new chapter of her life, which against all odds she kept writing, experiencing the most surreal reality in the craziest of circumstances. Everything was evolving so fast since the time of her departure from the physical world? that she had no time to absorb the magnitude of the world that she had stepped into and become integrated with. The chain of events overlapped each other forcing her into a flowing stream where she had no control over her own destiny. The strange feeling that some invisible hand was conducting her every step was rising imminently, leaving no fear, but rather a sense of security and boundless trust into those who were leading her.

Doors to classrooms were placed on either side of the spacious of corridor. Gertrude stopped in front of one of them announcing, "This one is yours."

Anne looked at the door and unable to find any identifying number or name asked, "How am I going to find it on my own?

"Don't worry, it will be just like anything else…one thought away."

"I get it," replied Anne, and opening the door she cautiously stepped in.

The class was filled to capacity with students. Suddenly she heard one of them call her name. Maria's excited face stood out from the crowd. Without any hesitation Anne went to sit beside her.

"Can you believe it, we are back in school again. I feel like a teenager," Maria said enthusiastically.

Before Anne had a chance to respond, the door opened wide, and a teacher stepped into the classroom. Not knowing how to react to his entrance, some students stood up, but the teacher's "Please be seated," solved all uncertainties. The teacher was dressed like a Franciscan monk wearing a light brown loose robe with a hood attached at the back. A wide white rope was wrapped around his waist and dropped nearly to the floor, with a couple of knots at its end. As he approached the table at the front of the class, Anne noticed that he was wearing heavily worn leather sandals on his feet. His most prominent feature was the shiny bald patch on top of his head surrounded by bushy hair covering his ears and half of his neck. He had the features of a Mediterranean man. Once dark facial hair was now a gray, well-groomed short beard. A straight nose, big sharp eyes surrounded by a network of fine wrinkles making his face pleasant to observe.

He strode toward his designated table, and with a deep strong voice pronounced, "Hello everyone. My name is Bartholomew, and I will be your coach for the duration of your stay in this paradise created by our Lord for your utmost convenience. One of my duties will be to accompany you into your past, openly discuss different segments of your life on Earth for the purpose of examining it to see if you could have orchestrated it better than you did in reality."

Everyone looked at each other confused and frightened.

"It sounds like judgement day has arrived," Anne heard a voice from the back row.

Bartholomew smiled, "No Simon, no one is going to judge

you here except yourself, and only if you choose so. But before we get into the details of that procedure, I would like to answer some questions that you will ask sooner or later. There are twenty-four souls present in this room. For the next period of time, which by the way does not exist here, you will spend together, so get to know each other well. Most probably you will be accompanied on your next visit to Earth by one or more souls from this room."

The students looked around the room at each other.

"The reason why you have been assembled into this class is your acceptance of Christ's teachings by the end of your physical life. If you are interested, all of you died after your 60s due to a variety of sicknesses."

He then cast his eyes over the class with an enquiring look, "I see that you have all discovered your infinite youth and let me congratulate you on that. But sorry to disappoint you, this appearance does not resonate with you true age, nor your true essence. Why I say this is because you have all lived multiple lifetimes on Earth with different features and personalities. I see many surprised faces, and yes you are eternal beings in the process of ascension of your consciousness. No more and no less. If you ask me the reason for you being sent to Earth, it is simply for you to have a practical study of all the theory that you learn here. Yes, Earth is a harsh planet to live on, not the most difficult, but the most revealing of your true colors."

It seemed that Bartholomew was raising questions in his mind and vocalizing the answers for the students to hear. "The harshness of life on Earth as a school lies in its polarities, extreme diversities of all that has been created for you to have a physical experience. In case you want to ask who in their right state of mind would leave this paradise to return to Earth…I will answer, each and every one of you. No, we will not force you to go back, it is you who will ask us to do so.

With each sentence pronounced by the teacher, a rising level of confusion was overwhelming the students, and limiting their capacity to absorb further information. Each line turned their world and all that they knew and believed upside down leaving no room for any doubts to exist. "Let me reveal another big secret. Although you are not yet aware, all of you are deeply addicted to Earth. Addicted to the state of existence in a physical body as human. Addicted to the wide range of feelings and emotions that human bodies allow us to experience and indulge. Physical pain and pleasure will keep calling you back just to feel the sensations of being alive again. Despite all that we can offer you here, you will soon get bored, and new adventures filled with excitement will call you back to Earth. A beacon of light seated deep in your soul will awaken the search for the mother we all call Earth." Bartholomew paused for a moment and scanned the class with his perky eyes to determine the impact of his words. Then he grinned with a sarcastic smile saying, "Before I forget, you have no body. This pure excuse of a body that you are all wearing now is nothing but an illusion. You look like this to yourself and one another only because you see yourselves as such."

The students began to touch themselves to check if what he was saying was right. Each of Bartholomew's statements placed them into increasing states of shock.

"Yes," the lecturer kept going, "One more thing, you have no gender for the same reasons, too. You heard me right, you have no gender identification. You are energy in the form of consciousness. Consciousness that identifies itself with the last incarnation you had on Earth." After these last words Bartholomew fell quiet and so did the whole class. The information that he had shared was so vast in its volume that each student was led into its own maze of thoughts, lost and disorientated with no exit sign on the horizon. Bartholomew looked at each and every one of them satisfied with the results of his delivered punches. A moment later he said, "Okay, I will leave you now to have a break. I will see you soon." And he left the classroom the same way he entered.

For some time everyone sat motionless until one of the students stood up and then everyone followed them out to the beach.

Anne walked to the edge of the water, casting her eyes to the horizon saying to herself, *"Where the hell am I? Is this the promised land or purgatory? The old man turned my world upside down, not that it was steady to begin with, but now everything is so much more complicated."*

"Is everything all right?" Anne heard Gertrude's voice. She turned around and there she was standing next to her.

"You seem distressed?"

"I don't think the word distressed accurately describes the state of my mind. I think a better word would be lost." Anne looked at the silver cross resting on Gertrude's chest and said, "If it wasn't for the cross you are wearing, I would have said that I am in the wrong place. None of what I heard today could have been framed into what I had read in the Bible."

"I know," Gertrude replied compassionately. "It is a bit too much to comprehend in the beginning, but believe me it will make your adaptation to this paradise a lot faster and easier."

"Are there other paradises?" Anne enquired.

"Yes, many."

"I'd rather not ask any more questions," Anne replied quickly, "so as to avoid a load more informationthat I will have to deal with."

Gertrude smiled gently saying, "Give it some time. Knowledge always finds us when we are ready for it."

"I don't think I was ever ready for such a turn of events."

"Before physical death no one does, and you are no exception. I am sure that your classmates are all as lost as you are. Bartholomew is a very old and wise soul, and I personally asked him to enroll you into one of his classes. He is straightforward and sometimes harsh, but this is the best way to learn."

"I understand," agreed Anne, "Although I have so many questions and no idea of where to start."

"I see," said Gertrude "But before you do that there is a question that I would like to ask you. Would you like another trip to Earth. Another visit to your loved ones?"

Anne jumped like a schoolgirl and exclaimed clapping her hands, "I would love to!"

"Would you like to watch your own funeral?"

"Funeral?" Anne asked cringing her face, "No, definitely not my funeral. To watch a bunch of old men coming back to my home after the ceremony, feeding their faces and filling their bellies with alcohol until they turn blue…I don't think so. I have seen many funerals and know how they go, and I don't expect that mine will be any different."

"Then who would you like to see?"

"My little Rose. I miss her so much."

Gertrude gently took Anne's hand into hers and already familiar with the procedure, Anne closed her eyes.

VISIT

Anne opened her eyes in little Rose's bedroom. It was late in the evening and the child was fast asleep. Anne stepped to her bed and leaned over to have a closer look at the sleeping angel. Her heart became overflowed with love, but pain at the same time. The realization of the fact that she will not be a part of Rose's life and that she will grow into a beautiful lady without her broke Anne's heart. She wanted to hug Rose and land a big kiss on her rosy cheek so invitingly facing her, but under the watchful eye of Gertrude it may become the last visit. Choosing not to disturb Rose's peaceful sleep, Anne looked around to take a last glimpse of her granddaughter's bedroom when she noticed a dark figure standing quietly in a corner. Anne, frightened, glanced at Gertrude not knowing how to react and then her maternal instinct overcame her and thinking that there was an intruder she covered sleeping Rose with her body. Gertrude's smiling eyes calmed her down.

"I would like to introduce you to Rose's guide," Gertrude announced looking at Henry.

Henry stepped forward, respectfully nodding his head. He introduced himself and without waiting for Anne's response said, "Don't worry, I know who you are."

"By the way," Gertrude spoke to Anne, "Henry is the one who helped me to locate you in your grandparents' farmhouse."

"Thank you, sir," Anne said with deep gratitude in her voice, unsure of how to address this man.

"I am glad to have been of help," answered Henry, and facing Gertrude he added, "Although someone has a strange way of showing appreciation!"

"I know, and I am sorry that I left you behind, but you must understand that I was so preoccupied with Anne's safe passage that I had no thoughts of anything else." apologized Gertrude.

"I do understand," said Henry, "but can I count on you now?"

"Why are you so adamant to come to our reality anyway?" Gertrude asked.

"The very same Planner who appointed you as Anne's guide advised me to follow you to your reality."

"Our way of living is very different to yours. Our realms are more organized, or should I say, more structured compared to the ones you know. This is why I don't see you there with us. Besides, if you leave this physical reality who is going to take care of this angel and Croton who seems to be already on a moral decline?" Gertrude commented.

"You should not worry, as I have recently discovered the amazing ability to be in several places at the same time, so I don't see me being a guide being an obstacle to this quest. Prior to your visit to this room I was in my reality, and besides, I have set for myself a list of priorities with Rose and Croton right at the top."

"Good for you, Henry," answered Gertrude, "but for now allow me to keep the door into our world closed to you. Although one thing that I will promise you…"

Henry looked at Gertrude with eyes filled with hope.

"I will speak to Thales and find out who exactly he meant for you to meet. Our realms are filled with many old and wise souls. If it is in my power, I will assist you with this matter. You have my word."

Henry nodded his head in a sign of gratitude and respect.

While they were conversing, Anne kept watching Rose, trying to memorize her face to take with her in the form of pleasant memories to reflect upon later, in a time of serenity in her own little world framed with the wall of her tiny one roomed house. Unconsciously Anne joined her palms and began to pray.

"Please, dear Lord, please take care of my little Rose as I will not be around to do that. Allow her to grow up into a beautiful young lady who I already know will one day make me proud. Thank you for allowing me to be a part of her life. Although the time together was short, it was so sweet, when I could hold her in my arms and kiss her."

On finishing her prayer, she instinctively leaned over and kissed Rose's cheek. Disturbed by this act, Rose woke up and began to cry. Anne jumped back with the realization of what she had just done and looked at Gertrude with horror in her eyes.

"What have I done?" Anne cried out in despair.

"Don't worry," Gertrude rushed to calm Anne down. "Just don't ever do that again. Children are very sensitive to our presence and can be easily frightened."

"I think we should go back." Anne reached out her hands to Gertrude.

"I will see to your request," Gertrude said to Henry, and by holding Anne's hands transported them back to the schoolyard, right to the spot where their journey back had begun.

"It seems as though we had never left this place," noticed Anne.

"A day on Earth is only minute here."

Anne cast her eyes around, "I am still having a hard time comprehending all of this beauty surrounding us. Is this real or some kind of illusion, or perhaps a dream from which I will soon wake up into oblivion. Nature cannot be so irresistibly beautiful."

"You are forgetting where you are, dear Anne. You are in paradise. The place where each soul living on Earth dreams of ending up one day. If it was ordinary, it would not have been called paradise, and answering your question, this is not an illusion as it does not exist by your ability to perceive it. It is all real and now you are a part of this reality. You can touch the palm trees, the beach sand, and even the water and the ocean and you will be able to feel it."

"How can I feel it if I have no body?"

"It is true, you have no physical body armed with all five senses, but you have an emotional body which has more senses than a physical body can ever have."

"I am not following you," Anne said.

"Without getting too deep into the technicality of it, I will try to explain." Gertrude leaned over and filled her hand with beach sand, letting it slowly slip through her fingers. Anne copied her.

"What do you feel?" Gertrude asked.

"Nothing special, just sand like any other on Earth," answered Anne.

"Now the question is, how can you feel the texture of the sand without nerve receptors on your fingers, or a neural sensory system transmitting signals to your brain informing it about objects in your hand?"

"Yes, that's what I want to know," Anne said.

"Memories of the physical world are deeply ingrained into our souls, and whatever you feel in touching this sand is nothing but a memory. Simply, you feel it because you remember how it feels."

Anne let the sand slide through her fingers and blowing the remnants left on her palm she questioned Gertrude, "What do you feel?"

“Do you want to know what I feel when I touch the sand?”

“Yes, I am interested.”

“Do you really want to know?”

After some hesitation, feeling underwater stones, Anne replied, “Yes, I want to know.”

“Okay, then be patient because there is no simple explanation to it. I don’t feel the sand, I read the sand.”

“What?” asked Anne in surprise.

“Yes, you heard me right. I can tell you more. I can hear its thoughts.”

“I didn’t know that sand can think?”

“Sand, like anything else, is energy, and energy is nothing else but consciousness. Different to our level of consciousness, but still consciousness. Each grain of sand has a memory of its own, but together they sound like a divine symphony. When I touch sand, I become sand. I am tapping into its soul and am able to hear all that it has to share.”

Utterly confused Anne asked, “What is it that sand has to share?”

Gertrude closed her eyes and in Anne’s mind strange images appeared blended with unfamiliar emotions and sensations. Suddenly Anne knew that she was a shell at the bottom of the ocean. Then she began to disintegrate into pieces soon to become sand. Then she became a part of this big family of tiny grains who in their multitude united to hold mighty oceans. She felt the waves upon her skin so gently rolling her around. She felt a storm and the crazy dance inflicted by the swirling waters. She felt the heat of the burning sun and the calmness of the night highlighted by moonlight. Gertrude opened her eyes and looked at Anne, frozen.

“So?” asked Gertrude.

“This is crazy. How you can live with such a gift. My already overwhelmed mind is about to explode.”

“I agree, it was a bit too much. But at least you had a glimpse into the true essence of creation.

Everything that has ever sprung into existence has a mind of its own. Different from ours, but it does.”

“To be honest I wouldn’t say it is different from my mind…I felt it all.”

Gertrude smiled, and taking Anne’s hands into her’s said, “We were reading sand through our emotions and as a result we personalized it. In reality, sand has no emotions nor feelings. All it has is the memories of its existence, and that is what we perceived from our perspective.”

"I see now," Anne said adding, "I guess all of this is a bit complicated for my inexperienced mind to absorb and digest. So, I will take each new thing as its comes without forcing it."

"Good thinking. Most of all try to enjoy your time here, because like anything else in this universe it is temporary, bowing down to its majesty, change, the one and only certainty of creation."

"Change?" asked Anne.

"Yes, change. No matter where you are, here or down on Earth, everything is bound to change. This is one of the many universal laws set by God."

"You mean Jesus Christ?" Anne corrected.

"All that, and Universal Laws in particular you will study in school," Gertrude answered avoiding Anne's direct question.

As Gertrude finished her sentence Anne heard ringing bells. "It seems that I need to get back to my classroom." She hugged Gertrude saying sincerely, "I hope to see you after class."

"You will," promised Gertrude.

AKEANA

Vanishing into the sound of the bells, Anne appeared at her desk next to Maria. Before they had a chance to exchange one word, an aged, but still quite attractive lady appeared in the doorway. She gracefully walked to the teacher's desk and turned to face the students. A strange wave of deep, loving emotion traveled throughout the entire auditorium, touching each and everyone's highest pitch, resonating with the most sensitive string of their souls. She filled the entire room with her presence, spreading extreme comfort and a most welcoming tenderness. Involuntarily, the students moved to the edge of their chairs just to be an inch closer to her, to the source of her congenial vibration. She wore a long blue dress that covered her entire body, only leaving exposed her head and her elegant hands. She had long dark brown hair that was pulled to the back, and covered with a semi-transparent silky fabric that hardly touched her hair, seemingly hovering above her head. Her elongated, olive-skinned face had unusually big, light brown eyes accentuated by long eyelashes. Those eyes were the main cause of her gravitational force. Her big, long straight nose did not spoil the entire picture, but rather added uniqueness to frame. Ready to introduce herself, she smiled to expose a set of pearly white teeth, adding further irresistible charm to the face which was impossible to tear your eyes away from. "Hello everyone. My name is Akeana. Welcome to this world, and in particular to my class."

No one made a sound, nor any movement. The class was completely silent, in a state of deep trance.

"You have already met with one of our counselors, brother Bartholomew, whose sole purpose was to help you to understand and make sense of the spiritual realm that you have become a part of. He will teach you how to safely navigate a multitude of non-physical worlds created by God, all integral to the paradise that we are a part of. In short, he will fill you with light, where light stands for knowledge. While my purpose is to fill your hearts with love. Love that you were so desperately searching for on Earth, and every time that you thought you had it, it slipped away like morning mist, so vivid, but still ungraspable. I step into your life not only to remind you how to love, or how to be loved in return, but also to become love itself, because that is what you are."

The class was snapping out of the hypnotic state that she had somehow managed to place them just by entering the room and began to listen to what she had to say.

"Why is it so important?" Anne heard a voice ask from the back row.

"Love is the first and most important component, or should I say, ingredient of this and any other God created existence."

"And what is the second?" asked the same voice from behind.

"The second is light. Nothing can come into existence without these two constituents. Light stands for knowledge and love for creation. Further, nothing ever created can last without these two. What you should know as well is that everything in the universe, be it in physical or spiritual realms, is in constant balance. What is more important to understand is that that equilibrium is achieved as the result of counterbalancing forces. Darkness, that stands for ignorance, counterbalances light. Anger is counterbalanced by forgiveness. Sin by righteousness…"

"And what is counterbalancing love?" came the voice again from the back.

"Love has no opposing force. Love is the purpose, means, and cause of all that is in existence."

"What about destruction? If love is creation, then destruction would be its opposite," a girl at the front asked.

The word destruction immediately brought memories back to Anne from her recent past that she had completely forgotten. Just before leaving her physical body, she had vivid dreams of a city completely destroyed by earthquakes. Demolished buildings, with terrified people running around. She saw herself covered in gray ash…she quickly shook off the remnants of the past, convincing herself that it was just a nightmare of her dying brain.

"Destruction, my dear ones, can happen through love, and as an act of love," Akeana continued, "You may not agree with me now, but later you will understand the meaning of these words."

The class fell quiet trying to make sense of this information.

"If it wasn't for God's love neither me, nor you, would be here, and this paradise would not have been necessary. That is why it is so important to see the unconditional love that we are all blessed with by our Father, to understand it and to allow yourself to feel it. To grasp within your soul the magnitude of this love, and to know that no matter what, all of you are not only worthy of love, but also that you are loved unconditionally regardless of anything that you have done in the past. If you were not worthy of forgiveness you could never be here."

Rapture of optimism rippled through the class, and Akeana kept going, "All of you toward the end of your physical life, by some miracles were awakened. Awakened from the slumber placed upon you by the glee and false joy that the physical world provides. Trapping you, and deceiving you into the sweetness of possession, the pleasure of owning and controlling. Controlling the uncontrollable, grasping the ungraspable, and eventually the non-essential. After a time here, you will realize that no physical object is worthy of attachment. It makes me sad to see so many famous artist's works hidden in vaults. I call it 'imprisoned' love. You must understand that love is free and cannot survive in captivity. Love has to be free in order to spread its essence into the hearts of souls newly arriving in the human world. To make that world better and turn it from a hostile environment into one where all can live in peace, and acceptance of one another."

The class was quiet, with each to their own thoughts, judging and measuring their past lives against the values raised by Akeana.

"So, admire love but do not try to possess it. The energy of love is so strong that it will burn your inexperienced heart and will enslave your still developing mind."

While listening to Akeana, Anne had the strong impulse to get back home to undo all that she had recreated.

"So, I have a question for you. What one thing would you like to change in your past life if you had the opportunity?"

One by one the students expressed their regrets, and along with that the pain that they had carried over with them into the world of spirit. From what Anne was hearing, most regrets centerd around insufficient time spent with family and loved ones. Some said that they completely missed out on quality time with their children while they were small. Others regreted misplaced values of what they wanted to have and what they really needed. Some spoke of their overrated personal ego obstructing their path to happiness. There were so many more regrets.

"What about the happiest moments of your past lives? Did you bring some of those with you, too? You don't have to answer, I already know. They still involve your loved ones, and I know these moments were not as many as they could have been."

"May I ask something?" Anne asked raising her hand.

"Of course, please," answered Akeana.

"If it wasn't for the extra money we managed to save back home, we most certainly would not have had many of those happy moments. I mean, vacations spent with the family."

"You are right, dear Anne, money gave you financial freedom and independence, but the question is how did you make that money? Trust me for saying that back on Earth each human knows the difference between honestly earned or directly, or indirectly, stolen money. Unfortunately, most choose to suppress the inner voice of righteousness whispered by spirit guides, or sometimes by their own consciousness. In conclusion, money is not the enemy, and by sending you back to Earth you will always be provided with enough to accomplish your mission, but when along the way you chose to have more than you need, and develop an unhealthy appetite, then you will complicate not only your life, but also the lives of your loved ones forcing them to act against their conscience, and eventually to commit sin."

Anne quietly sat down regretting that she had asked the question. Akeana had struck a most sensitive and painful string in her heart resonating with the blame that she had to take for pushing Raymond to become the man of her dreams.

Another of the students raised a question, "You mentioned something earlier about a mission. Do we have a specific mission while we are on Earth?"

"Yes, without exception all incarnations on Earth are purposeful and deeply meaningful. Generally, we go to Earth to gain knowledge and experience. Whilst most are there to learn, some are there to teach. I don't want to go deeper into this subject as this knowledge will be revealed to you in time."

"What time?" asked the same voice.

"The time of going back to Earth?

"What if I don't want to go?"

"When you reach that point in your life here, you will ask us to send you back and it will be the most sensible thing to do."

Akeana delivered the last sentence with utmost certainty leaving space to the subject to be further entertained. She smiled, returning to her normal gentleness saying, "Allow me to end this lesson, one of many to come, and I will see you soon." And with that Akeana gracefully left the classroom.

REGRETS

Anne's priority was to get back to her house and get rid of all that had suddenly become non-essential. On arriving back home Anne felt jailed by her own creation. Her first and strongest urge was to wipe out the vases on top of the dining table, but before doing that she picked one up to have a better look. On close observation she noticed the intricate artwork by the ancient Chinese artisan was all hazy and blurry. The once irresistibly ornate blue on white masterpiece now looked like a worthless, poor imitation of something that she had once adored. Anne released her grip and the porcelain vessel slipped into destruction. Shattered pieces of white and blue flew apart as though realizing that they did not belong together. Then Anne looked at the second vase and closed her eyes. When she reopened them, the tabletop was free of clutter. Next was the chandelier, overpowering in its weight. Having dealt with that, Anne stepped out into the backyard, restoring it to its original simplistic beauty. From there she emptied the wall of the cheap reproductions she had managed to plaster them with. Soon she found herself back in front of the dining room suite and for the last time she swiped her hand over the tabletop to feel its texture and checking for the presence of dust saying, "Damn it, it would have been so much easier to maintain you here." She closed her eyes and the white table with four wooden chairs reclaimed their rightful place. The last, and most massive piece of her creation waited patiently for its turn. Anne stood back, leaned against the table, and cast her eyes on its beauty and perfection.

"Everything was made exactly the way I wanted it." She stepped forward and from left to right opened wide all of the cupboard doors and drawers scanning their contents. Satisfied, she sat on a chair and facing the kitchen said, "Gertrude."

Instantly two short knocks at her entrance door announced Gertrude's arrival. Anne proudly invited her in.

"This is an improvement!" Gertrude exclaimed, satisfied with the scene that greeted her. "What about the kitchen?"

"I thought we could have one last cup of coffee together before erasing it."

"You know that we can have coffee without the kitchen?"

"But like this it feels more homely."

"Okay," agreed Gertrude getting comfortable on the most uncomfortable chair.

While Anne was busy boiling water and gathering coffee and sugar from the cupboards, Gertrude thought, *"It's amazing how the human mind can manifest the physical reality in the finest details. Boiling water, steaming coffee…All the results of Anne's repetitive habits from her past life."*

Once Gertrude had taken a sip Anne asked, "Do you like my coffee?

"It is the best I have ever tasted," Gertrude answered, despite being completely unfamiliar with the taste of such a drink that had become such an important part of human experience only in the last 400 years.

Satisfied with Gertrude's answer Anne closed her eyes and with a heavy heart said goodbye to her favorite creation.

"Don't you feel liberated?" Gertrude asked.

"It will take some time before I get used to such an ascetic style of living, but I guess it is all for a reason."

"And what do you think that is?" asked Gertrude.

"Do not have it unless you really need it?" said Anne searching Gertrude's eyes for validation.

"Yes, you are absolutely right, my dear. As you embrace this simple truth your life will become less complicated and as a result more manageable. Simply put, it is possible to live life much happier with much less. One of my favorite philosophers who lived on Earth used to say, 'If you realize that you have enough, you are truly rich'."

"That's absolutely true," Anne replied. "Back home I used to compete with 'friends' who had more than me, trying to buy something more exquisite, something that none of them could ever have, and of course to brag about it. Now I see how foolish I was. Especially here where none of that matters."

"Let me cheer you up," Gertrude said cheerfully trying to redirect the train of Anne's thoughts. "What type of activity would you like to participate in?"

"It depends on what my choices are," Anne answered cautiously.

"The sky's the limit."

"Okay," said Anne and after giving it some thought she replied, "I always liked to sing but never had a voice to match my good ear for music."

"I see," said Gertrude, "This can be easily arranged."

"Really?"

"Yes, we have a beautiful choir who from time to time perform for the residents of this realm."

"Are they good?" Anne asked nervously.

"They are excellent."

"Then they will definitely reject me."

"Don't be so pessimistic. Let us try and see what happens."

"Okay," Anne said cautiously putting her hand in Gertrude's.

They momentarily stepped into a large room framed with white walls and paved with red mahogany wooden parquet flooring. The first thing that Anne noticed was a large grand piano in the middle of the room with a lady seated behind it. She graciously stood up to greet the newly arrived guests.

"Hello, Sister Beatrice," Gertrude said. "Thank you for seeing us in such short notice." Referring to Anne she continued, "This is Anne who would like to join your choir, if you don't mind."

Anne blushed and modestly lowered her head.

Sister Beatrice was a tall lady in her mid-forties, dressed in a long black dress that reached down to the floor. She was the most striking teacher that Anne had met so far. Surprisingly, the dress was a cocktail dress, tightly hugging her curveless slim figure, emphasizing her commitment to her chosen profession. Her blonde hair, pale face, thin lips, and piercing blue eyes left no doubt of her dedication to music, and in particular, running the choir.

"Welcome to your audition," Beatrice invited Anne to stand next to the piano.

"Audition?" Anne exclaimed confused.

"Yes, my dear. To begin with we need to establish your vocal abilities."

"This is so sudden, and I don't think I am ready," Anne mumbled in distress looking at Gertrude with big eyes.

"Don't worry, no one is ever ready," Beatrice comforted her, "I just need to determine the range that you will be comfortable to sing in. Next you will become a member of our choir. By the way, some of our members recently departed back to Earth and we have openings to be filled."

"Whoa, whoa!" Anne exclaimed, "Not so fast. I think we are getting ahead of ourselves. I have never sung professionally. I cannot read music at all, and I have no voice." She stumbled and then announced, "I think I am in the wrong place."

Beatrice took Anne's hand in hers and facing Gertrude said, "I will let you know once we are done."

Gertrude nodded her head and without saying anything vanished into thin air.

Sister Beatrice led Anne to the piano, taking a seat in front of the keys. One look at the perfect formation of the white and black soldiers lined up next to each other ready to strike the tense strings raised Anne's anxiety to the next level.

"Just relax and sing a note," Beatrice said calmly as she struck on of the white keys.

Anne instinctively filled her non-existing lungs with air and vocalized the note. It came out so clear and unexpectedly loud that she quickly covered her mouth with her hand.

"Good," said Beatrice, "Now, try this one," as she struck another key.

Anne easily conquered that, too. Beatrice began to climb higher and higher up the bars and to Anne's amazement she followed effortlessly.

Beatrice stopped, commenting, "You have good hearing."

"What about my voice though? I cannot believe the sound that I can produce. Isn't it amazing!"

"My dear Anne, your voice is the last of my concerns, all souls have beautiful voices. The ability to hear and reproduce notes is most important and from what I hear you are quite good at this, and I gladly welcome you into our choir."

Overwhelmed, Anne expressed her gratitude for the opportunity, and saying goodbye, walked out of the door into a long corridor.

Gertrude was already there. "So, how did it go?"

"Brilliant. You can congratulate the newest member of the choir."

"Wonderful," said Gertrude, "I had no doubts. Now tell me what else you would like to study, or perhaps some sporting activity you'd like to participate in?"

"Definitely no sports for me, although there is one thing that I would love to learn."

"Just name it."

"Dancing. It was one of my dreams to master ballroom dancing, but I never had the talent to give it a try."

"That can be fixed," said Gertrude, grabbing Anne's hand and pulling her into the long corridor.

RELUCTANT MEETING

Greatly disappointed with Gertrude's unwillingness to assist, Henry returned to his beach house. He walked to the edge of the water, and with his feet sinking into the wet sand, he crossed his arms over his chest. The promised venture that has again been paraded in front of his nose still remained intangible. So desirable, but still unreachable. Although Croton's shady work affairs were keeping him quite engaged, and growing-up Rose was a handful, Henry couldn't get out of his system the promised meeting with a "great soul". Opportunity of such an experience were lately rare and highly anticipated since being promised. Gertrude's complete silence was draining the last drops of Henry's patience and although Thales advised him to find his own way into Gertrude's reality, he was left with no option but to disturb Thales himself. Henry returned to the house and closed his eyes and solely concentrated on the Planner, hoping that his call for help would be answered.

"Yes?" Henry heard the unmistakably deep timbre of Thales' voice.

"I would like a word with you if that's possible," Hery cautiously asked.

"Face to face?"

"Yes please," insisted Henry.

Suddenly there appeared a softly glowing light in the middle of the room, soon materializing into the Greek philosopher. Standing as still as a stone, Henry patiently waited for Thales' vibrational decline to reach its completion.

"What is the urgency?" Thales asked emotionlessly.

"Sorry for disturbing you, but there is a matter that I would like to address, hoping for your advice and possibly assistance."

"I am listening," said Thales still standing in the pose of a erect Greek statue.

"Would you like a seat?" Henry asked politely.

“I do understand the practice of humans to sit down for important conversations, but allow me to decline.”

“Okay,” Henry agreed, sensing Thales’ reluctance to engage in an extended conversation. “I would like to talk to you about Croton,” Henry began.

“Oh?” Thales reacted in surprise. “I thought it would be about something else.”

“No, Croton,” Henry stipulated anticipating that the reason why he really wanted to meet would be blown out of the water abruptly.

“I am listening,” Thales replied with an easing of the tension in his attitude.

Henry took a deep sigh before exposing the wound inflicted by Croton that was worsening continuously.

“I can see Croton rolling down a hill and cannot do anything about it.”

“Be specific please.”

“He is taking bribes and allowing the unallowable.”

“It was predictable,” Thales answered shortly.

“And you as the Planner have no problems with that?”

“I don’t think you entirely understand my role in this game. I am a game creator, conductor behind the scenes. Each descended soul is exposed to various degrees of temptations and greed is one of them. Do I expect Croton to act differently? No. Do I care? No. Once a soul becomes a human, they begin to act as a human, and inevitably pay the cost.”

“What do you mean by paying the cost?” Henry asked in alarm.

“You know, every action has an equal and opposite reaction. But you should not worry about that. He will learn his lesson soon.”

“You are scaring me, Thales. What have you planned for my poor boy?”

“I didn’t. He has done it all by himself, and to himself. All I have to do is orchestrate the scenario of that opposite reaction.”

” Will you share that with me?”

“Hhhmmmm…probably not. You will have to wait and see and react accordingly. After all, Croton’s descent is also a test for you. Besides, you should not bother yourself with these matters, leave them to me. The sole purpose of his visit to Earth was to find his ‘one and only’, the one he can spend eternity with. The one without whom his entire existence would become meaningless. The rest is an inevitable byproduct.”

To ask the question that suddenly popped into his mind Henry considered may be too personal, but he could not resist.

"Forgive me for asking, but did you find your 'one and only'?"

Thales lowered his head, smiling for the first time, and with a heavy irony in his voice answered, "As a matter of fact I did. Or to be exact, I am."

"I am not following you," Henry said confused.

"It is hard to explain, and I am not sure if you will be able to grasp the entirety of it."

"Entirety of what?" asked Henry.

Thales looked into Henry's eyes, smiling again saying, "Maybe sitting down isn't such a bad idea after all."

Placing himself at the top of the table he offered Henry to take a seat in front of him. Henry lowered himself into a chair not knowing what to expect from such a great and powerful soul. A soul that with one spark of his mind is able to create the destiny of descended humans. A soul who could undoubtedly be perceived as a God by those whose futures were dependent on the flow of his thought. His judgement of what is best for them as they go on with their lives completely unaware of the hand ready to pull strings at any given moment. Suddenly Henry realized that he was sitting in front of a demi-God, who had not only unbounded power over humans, but also over him and all those who he loved and cared for.

"So, you want to know if I found my true love?"

"Yes," Henry confirmed cautiously.

"Why do you think we Planners try so adamantly to help souls experience love to its fullest extent? Triggering the spark of dormant emotions in their hearts into a burning fire. Why love? Why is it so important?"

"Why?" Henry repeated simply.

Thales stood up from his chair saying, "Look."

In front of Henry's eyes Thales began a transformation and a second later he faced the most beautiful Greek goddess. He couldn't take his eyes off her slim figure and irresistibly attractive face. A white tunic barely covered her exposed shoulders and firm breasts. Confused, Henry did not know how to react to this suddenly arrived guest and just observed her motionlessly.

"How do you like my 'better half'"?" said the goddess.

"Thales?" exclaimed Henry pushing himself backward in his

chair.

"Don't be afraid, it is still me."

"Will you please go back to your normal self."

"Why?" asked the goddess.

"I will feel more comfortable."

"If you insist," she replied, transforming herself back into the old man so familiar to Henry.

"What was that?" asked Henry breathing heavily.

"It was my one and only that is now an integral part of me."

"Like a two in one?" carefully asked Henry.

"You can say that, but I warn you that it will not be easy to understand."

"Please explain."

"Long ago I met her on Earth in a pre-recorded historical time. We had many incarnations, or should I say trans-migrations of our souls into many physical bodies until we understood that we cannot exist without each other. Then we become spirit guides to other souls, just like you and Rose. Timelessly separated and reunited again with a stronger force of love each time. Then…"

"Then?" Henry asked impatiently.

"Then a miracle happened. We became one."

"Just like that?" Henry asked incredulously.

"Yes. It's like we grew into each other, becoming one inseparable consciousness. One complete being.

A being able to feel and understand male and female consciousness equally. Earth is a reality of extreme diversities, and the only force able to manage opposites is love. There is no force of attraction greater than love itself. Paradoxically the further apart opposites are, the stronger is their attracting force."

"So, following your logic, by merging into each other two opposites should stop being opposites. They become one. In other words, they reach a point of absolute balance. But then, the attracting force of love will cease to exist." Henry fell quiet, uncertain in his conclusions, and then asked, "Are we looking for love just to lose it?"

"Not exactly, but you have grasped the concept. This is what the ascension of souls is all about. Love brings souls together, completes them, giving them the opportunity to access higher realms of consciousness. We call it universal consciousness, and this is, my friend, a state of mind when you will know everything you need to know without knowing anything."

"You lost me again. This does not make any sense."

"Allow me to explain. In the state of mind that you have now, to learn something new you have to experience it or to study it. But what is the definition of study? It simply means learning through the experience of others, or their logical assumptions. When you reach the level of universal consciousness you don't need to study anything, as the entire collective universal knowledge becomes available to you. And I am not talking only about the collective knowledge of humanity, but all other knowledge in existence."

Thales fell quiet allowing Henry to swallow this big pill without harming himself.

Digesting it, Henry asked, "Can you grasp God's knowledge?"

"I cannot," Thales answered smiling sadly.

"Why not?"

"Compared to the supreme Creator's vast capacity, my vessel is miniscule."

"What do you mean"

"Can you pour the ocean into a cup?"

"No."

"Well, that is the answer to your question."

"If you are comparing the level of your awareness with a cup, where do you place me?"

"That's for you to decide," answered Thales.

This was the first time that Henry has had the opportunity to converse with a Planner and to learn something from him. Maybe not entirely understood, but still being exposed to vaster knowledge which one day would definitely become his reality.

Indicating the end of the meeting, but before leaving Thales said, "I will see what I can do about the matter that you really wanted to talk about."

His last words echoed around the room as he vanished. Henry moved to the sofa to reflect upon what was just unveiled to him.

"If what he was saying is true, one day Rose and I will become one. No." Henry rejected the thought shaking his entire body, that's weird. I don't want to lose Rose by melting into each other. I look forward to our reunions regardless of the time of separation. Distance holds in itself the sweetness of anticipation, while time validates the strength of your love."

Suddenly Henry realized that this constant motion of engagement and disengagement with the object of your love keeps the fire of love alive. Placing loving souls together in a confined compartment with nothing to do or to strive for, the fire of love will be extinguished, burning them out. Love likes turmoil and obstacles. Love thrives in suspense bartered with the hope of imminent possession. Conquered love loses its height. Some are able to dwell in it, but some throw themselves in search of a new summit.

"I knew you would not get it," Henry heard Thales' voice.

Henry smiled and stood up pronouncing loudly, "One day, one day."

SEARCH FOR THE HOLY BIBLE

While Anne, closely guided by Gertrude, was exploring the reality she found herself in, and absorbing all that was there to learn, and to have fun with, Henry could not stop thinking about the passage into the world of Christians. Although he was once invited by his father into the so-called church-city and had a wonderful time catching up and exploring the Christian reality, still deep inside he knew that this one that he was so adamant to gain access to, was not quite the same. This one was tightly guarded by its inhabitants from curious wanderers such as Henry considered himself. The fact that he couldn't get what he desired made him even more impatient, raising the level of his determination to possess this forbidden fruit no matter what.

Suddenly a great idea popped into his mind. "Bible," Henry said loudly, and sinking deeply into his sofa, he closed his eyes. When he reopened them, a black leather covered book with the inscription "Holy Bible" embossed in gold across its front was placed right in front of him. Henry reached for the book, carefully holding it in his hands as a golden ticket into the promised land and opened it's crisp pages. To his complete disappointment he couldn't read a word. The pages were filled with print exactly as he expected it would be, but they were unreadable. The lines were blurred and sentences meaningless.

Henry closed the book, looked at it, and placed it back on the coffee table. "Fiasco all over again."

After some thought, he realized that this is exactly how he found the Bible while on Earth. He never actually read it in his teen years finding himself in church, just passing over the verses following the congregation without paying any attention to their meaning. Then he remembered that when a bit older he tried to read it on his own, but after a few verses he lost his concentration and completely missed out on the essence of what he had read. "Okay," he said to himself, "now it's all making sense. Let's try another approach." He remembered a book containing the New Testament that Anne read so desperately just before her passing into the world of spirit. In the next moment he transferred himself into Anne's bedroom. Since her crossing-over he had not returned. Everything was still exactly the way it used to be. Raymond did not want to change anything, keeping everything just the way Anne wanted it. The wound was still too fresh.

After a quick glance around the room, the book's location was established. Henry quickly walked to the bedside table placed on Anne's side of the bed, and tried to pick it up, but disappointment found him again. "Damn it," Henry cursed as his fingers passed right through the book. "Non-physical body in a physical world—what the hell was I thinking!" Downhearted again Henry searched another avenue to the golden nugget that managed to slip from his hands again. A chain of logical exclusions funneled his attention to the one and only place where the entire collection of mankind's knowledge dwelled in anticipation of thirsty seekers. "Library, of course, the library, how could I forget it!" exclaimed Henry.

A second later he was walking into the reading hall. His chair, as though promise by the librarian, was patiently waiting for him, or rather calling him. Between them appeared a short figure wearing funny looking wooden-framed spectacles. The one who many times before had come to his rescue when it was needed. Henry saw him as a devoted guardian of the past. The one who was holding the keys to the past lives of each and every soul. Everything was carefully stored until someone chooses to disturb their peace.

"I wasn't expecting you back," said Aaron pleasantly surprised. "How can I be of help?"

"There is a book that I would like to get my hands on please," Henry asked politely.

"And what book might that be?"

Without further ado, Henry answered "The Bible."

"Oh, that's unexpected. Why the Bible? You don't strike me as someone interested in Bible studies."

"You're right, dear Aaron, but there is a reality that I would like to get into, and the way I see it, the only obstacle in my way is my own ignorance."

"I see…" said Aaron. "Which Bible exactly would you like to study?"

"I don't know…how many are there?" asked Henry in surprise.

"If I take you to the rows of shelves occupied by the multitude of Bibles that exist you will not see the end of them. To begin with, I'd like to know which of the two testaments you are interested in…new or old?"

"Definitely new. It is Christ that I am mostly interested in. His teachings, and particularly his life."

"Still, you will need to be more specific. I do have here every testimony ever written about Jesus over a timespan of almost 2000 years."

"Okay," said Henry, understanding Aaron's predicament. "Then please give me the most common version of the New Testament. The one that most of the physical world reads today."

"Let me choose for you," Aaron said disappearing between columns supporting high arches.

Henry took a seat and took a long slow look around. There were some souls deeply engaged in their reading, but no one familiar to him. Before Henry had time to settle Aaron returned with a thin brochure-like book in his hand.

"What is this?" Henry asked in surprise.

"This is four gospels written by Mark, Mathew, John, and Luke. This is the most common version." "Yes, but I thought there would be much more to it than that."

"Read this, and if you choose to learn more about Christ, I will get you other testaments. The ones that did not make it into the canonized Bible."

"Okay," said Henry ready to take the book from Aaron.

"Would you like to watch or read it?"

"To read please," Henry replied.

Aaron handed the book to Henry and disappeared.

Streaming through the pages Henry recognized text familiar from his past. One by one the old stories and parables surfaced into his memory, long forgotten in the attic of his childhood, like a fairy tale of a perfect man who once lived on Earth, one who died for little Henry to free him of all his sins. Sometime later Henry was finished all four testaments, and still deeply unsatisfied, sat back in his chair. Aaron, who was watching him from the far side of the reading hall, wondering what this man was up to now, chose to approach him.

"Is there something wrong?" he asked noticing Henry's dissatisfaction.

"Nothing is wrong, but I have a feeling that there is more to Christ's character."

"What do you mean?"

"In all four gospels Jesus spoke in a similar way, and forgive me for saying this, it seems quite unnatural."

Aaron crossed his arms across his chest, taking the role of a patient listener.

"I don't know, maybe what I am saying is sacrilegious, but he was a man and lived amongst others. There is no information about his youth, nor how he came to the ideas of love and forgiveness. Who were his teachers and mentors? And forgive me for saying, I am not buying all these stories about the miracles he performed."

"Are you saying the picture is too perfect?" Aaron probed.

"I would say, too legendary or maybe mythical. Such a great soul should surely have had more to say to his disciples since he was proclaiming himself the one and only Son of God. Which, to be honest I am having a hard time believing."

Aaron smiled, and lowering his head said, "There were many more testaments that never made it into the Bible. I can bring them to you if you wish."

"Yes, please," asked Henry.

A second later Henry was facing a pile of at least fifty manuscripts written on papyrus in unknown languages.

"What is all this?" he asked, confused.

"All the gospels and testaments which were written about Christ in the 2000 years after his death."

"Are you kidding me? How am I going to read all of these? Don't you have English copies?"

"Nope."

"Why not? Isn't this supposed to be a universal library?"

"We don't have them because none of these writings were ever translated into any other language. Most of them were destroyed before they had a chance to see daylight."

I see," said downed Henry.

"Maybe I can help you in this matter?" asked a young lady sitting at a desk not far from them.

Henry looked at the benevolent volunteer who so willingly offered to assist and couldn't believe his eyes.

"Gertrude?"

"Yes, my dear friend," answered the voice, and face to go with it, that Henry most desired.

Henry immediately excused himself, saying to Aaron, "I think help was sent to me by the Creator himself!" and he hurriedly approached Gertrude's desk.

"Hi, what are you doing here?"

"Same as you, searching for truth."

"What truth?"

Gertrude handed him the book that she had been studying. Glancing through it, Henry realized that it was about Anne's recent physical life.

"Why Christ?" Gertrude asked.

Henry looked straight into her eyes saying, "The life of a man who was, and is still worshipped by so many is worthy of study, don't you agree?"

"I do, and how have your studies gone?"

"Not that well."

"Why?"

"There is almost no information about him. And any other writings that could have shed light on his character and his teachings are in languages unfamiliar to me. Some of them are in Arabic, some in ancient Greek, some in Latin, even ancient Egyptian. Perhaps you can help me?"

"Just maybe," Gertrude smiled.

"Will you translate them for me?" Henry asked.

"I can offer you an even better deal."

"Like what?" Henry asked suspiciously, but still excited.

"What would you say if I arranged a meeting with HIM?"

"With whom?"

"With Christ himself."

As she said that she looked deeply into Henry's eyes to determine the impact of the pronounced name.

"Are you serious? Did I hear you right? Are you offering to set up a meeting with Jesus Christ himself?"

"Yes. Yes, I am," Gertrude announced proudly.

Henry lowered his head in respect saying, "I would be eternally grateful to you."

Gertrude smiled widely like a happy parent seeing their child receiving their most wanted gift.

"Before I show you to him, I need to brief you first."

"I am all ears," said overjoyed Henry.

"Look," started Gertrude. "He is a very high vibrational energy, way above the frequencies that we are able to handle."

"Let me guess, you are going to raise the level of my vibration?"

"No. I am not. I have to ask him to lower his in order for you to perceive him as the human he once was."

"Got it," replied Henry.

"If you notice during the meeting that he is reluctant to answer your questions, please do not insist."

"I understand," agreed Henry.

"And remember, this is not going to be a buddy-buddy talk, so be prepared with your questions in advance."

"Okay can I ask you a question?"

"Yes, you may."

"Why now?"

"What do you mean?" Gertrude asked in surprise.

"Why did you choose to let me into your world now?"

"First of all, it was at Thales' request, but that would not have been enough. Secondly, it was your attempt to find his true identity and his true teachings. I wouldn't help you just to satisfy your curiosity. I do not want to be embarrassed presenting somebody who has no depth, or to the subject they are seeking to understand. Above all, I am sure that you know that knowledge finds only those who are in pursuit of it."

"Got it. I will not embarrass you, That I can promise you."

Gertrude stretched both of her hands toward Henry expecting him to grab them. Instead, Henry stood back, hesitant and a bit frightened.

"Are we leaving right now?" he asked nervously.

"Isn't that what you wanted after all this time?"

"Yes…But…"

"Don't worry, you will be all right," she said grabbing both of his hands.

CHRIST

Henry opened his eyes standing beside Gertrude at the bottom of a hill. The surroundings had hardly any vegetation. A couple of bushes were dotted around, leaning over to the ground with tiny dark leaves forming their silhouettes. Scattered rocks were abundant, all of various sizes. The entire landscape was draped in different shades of golden brown with no shine, nor glory to it. It seemed as though the entire land had suffered a longevity of constant exposure to the harsh summer sun.

"If I had a physical body," Henry thought to himself, *"I would probably feel extreme heat radiating from the ground and the very source of that heat—the sun."* Henry looked up but found no trace of it in the sky, only a blue infinity with no sign of any clouds. Henry looked at Gertrude and asked, "What now?"

"Now, you walk," she replied, pointing at a narrow pathway worn down by continuous travelers. It led up the hill in a serpentine shape, disappearing beyond the silhouette of its projection. From what Henry could see and judge, it stretched almost a mile into the distance.

"I have to leave you now," Gertrude advised as she rewarded him with a gaze filled with compassion.

"Thank you," Henry answered as Gertrude vanished from sight.

Left alone, Henry looked up at the hill and chose to transfer himself right to the top of it, hoping that the one who was waiting for him would be there. But nothing happened. He had never had a problem with transformation before. It seemed as though someone had switched off the most common function of souls in the spiritual realms.

"You have to walk," Henry heard Gertrude's voice clear and loud, "and I will meet you on your way back."

From his first step toward the hill Henry felt the long-forgotten force of gravity. Each step demanded of him increasingly greater effort. By the time he was close to the top of the hill, Henry was exhausted, with his legs barely holding him up. But the summit was near and the hope that on top of the hill he will find the one he had been in search of for such a long time boosted his morale and determination. A few more steps and he made it to the top, only to discover another one, a lot higher than the one he had just conquered. The unforgiving serpentine pathway called him to keep climbing. "I hope that this will be the last one," Henry said as he took a step forward. The sudden realization that his body was heating up caught him completely unaware. At the halfway point he felt perspiration on his forehead. The first drop of sweat slid down to the tip of his nose and flew down to the thirsty ground. Closer to the summit the heat became unbearable. Henry stopped for a moment and looked up in search of the sun but could not see it. He could find no other explanation for the rise in temperature.

"Am I back on Earth in a physical body?" Henry asked loudly, but received no answer. He checked the boring landscape surrounding him, then looked down the hill, and satisfied with his progress commented, "Not bad. Not bad at all."

By the time he reached the top of the second hill his shirt was completely wet, and he could hardly breath. The lungs that reminded Henry of their existence could hardly cope with the rising supply of hot air and their incapability to cool the blood rushing through them. The scenery that revealed itself at the top was predictable. There was another hill higher than the previous two and the damn pathway still like an endless snake, slithering up between boulders and bushes which now wore nothing but long thorns. Unable to stand any longer, Henry collapsed onto a rock, and removed his wet shirt, slamming it on the ground saying, "I hope this is worth it."

By now his long forgotten five senses had returned to him, and together they were screaming for help. He was so thirsty and would have given anything for a glass of cold water. "I can't quit now. I am going to reach the top. No pain will stop me," he stated boldly through tightly clenched teeth and pushing himself up set his mind and exhausted body to new heights. Each step raised the pain in his body to new levels. The path became narrower due to the bigger rocks in its way. In some places Henry had to squeeze between them, suffering their intensely projecting heat. The breathing space between each formation of boulders was seeded with thorny bushes. Halfway to the summit Henry stopped. He leaned against a large flat stone to support the weight of his unbearably heavy body and then looked at his legs. The trendy trousers chosen for him by Helen when he first arrived in the spiritual realm were unrecognizable. They were sliced by the thorns into strips of fabric covered in dust mixed with blood. Henry checked his bleeding wounds by touching them, and a sharp pain caused him to pull his hand away, with a final test using the tip of his tongue on his bloodied finger left no doubts. "Yup, it looks like blood, and it tastes like blood." Then he checked the soles of his shoes to see that they had developed sizeable holes through which his skinless flesh was visible, with blood just about to seep through. His dried-up lips covered in dead skin were on the verge of cracking. With great difficulty to overcome the pain, Henry opened his mouth to say, "Where the hell am I?" Then he lowered his head whispering, "Will it be too much to ask for a glass of water please?" But his words fell on ears unwilling to answer or help him in any way.

Henry looked up the hill and noticed that close to the summit his ascension would turn into rock climbing. Sizing up the energy and strength left in him compared to the distance he still needed to cover, plus the injuries he had already sustained, Henry fell to his knees. His entire body felt on fire. Doubts about his chosen path began to creep into his mind and feed the rising sprouts of regret. Regrets that he had ever listened to Thales, and for being so stupidly stubborn in the pursuit of enlightenment that had turned into torture. While on his knees Henry looked back to check the distance that he had covered, and suddenly noticed down below where he started his journey a beautiful green valley splashed with a multitude of colors of blooming flowers, and fruitful trees touching the ground with the laden branches. Among all that nature, self-expression was playfully running down the valley as a sparkling, clear stream of water nourishing the land on its way with the gift of life and boundless abundance. "Eden," whispered Henry.

His first impulse was to run down the hill, even to roll down to the precious water and to throw himself into it and spend eternity in it. Henry motionlessly watched the unveiled scenery with wild blinks of light reflecting off the water's surface playfully called him to indulge in the sweetness of the carefree life that he had just left down below.

He lowered his head, looking at the dead and dusty ground beneath his feet, placing his palms upon it he clenched his fists filling them with dirt and rocks and throwing his arms wide apart as though on a crucifix he looked up at the summit and shouted, "Whoever you are up there, you had better be worth of all this!"

With the last of his strength Henry stood up, unclenched his fists and began again his climb to the unknown with only the promise of more pain ahead. About an hour later he faced a steep and almost vertical cliff, approximately thirty feet in height made entirely of obsidian, which was actually volcanic glass. The way it was formed puzzled Henry the most. There were some places where he could hook his hands and place his feet to pull himself up the rock face, but they were all as sharp as broken glass. To get a strong grip without cutting himself was hard to imagine.

"I came all this way, and you are not going to stop me," Henry addressed the black wall, placing his hand on the edge of the sharp rock. Where he was expecting to get the strength to climb the wall he had no idea, but he was certain of one thing, he was going to get to the top no matter what, and no physical pain could stop him. He placed his right foot onto a small platform and launched himself up to grab the next available ledge. Step by step he moved upward. The higher he got, the ledges became smaller and sharper. Henry was bleeding from multiple cuts, and his shoes were full of blood. He stopped for a moment noticing his reflection in the polished black wall and couldn't recognize himself. There was no trace of the good-looking young man who sometime ago chose to commit himself to this quest. The face of an aged and exhausted man stared back at him. Henry, covered in dust appeared completely gray. Wrinkles handsomely plastered his face, with the only recognizable feature being his eyes filled with determination and everlasting will. Pain by pain he drew closer to the summit. Blood running down his sleeves no longer bothered him. One more push and he would reach his destination. But his hands full of blood and completely numb suddenly slipped. An inch away from the long suffered and so desirable target, Henry lost his balance and was about to freefall right to the bottom of the cliff. His attempt to hold onto the wall with his left hand failed, and the weight of his body in alliance with gravity was too great to be balanced. Henry looked down anticipating his freefall, then cast his sight up one last time with the dying hope of a miracle to happen, bracing himself for imminent painful impact. Suddenly, a strong hand grabbed his wrist and with enormous force pulled him up.

MEETING

Henry found himself standing on the edge of the glass wall facing a man wearing a white cloak with a hood covering his face. Without saying a word, the savior offered Henry to step away from the fringe and take a seat on a rock worn by time into a concave shape. Hardly standing Henry dragged his worn and tired body, overcoming the pain, and lowered himself onto the rock. His throat was a dessert itself and his lips were stuck together by dried blood.

With the last of his strength Henry whispered, "Thank you, thank you for saving me."

The cloaked stranger offered him a jar made from clay. Henry took it in his shaky hands and with the first touch to his lips realized that it was the coolest and most refreshing water he had ever tasted. The life-giving liquid ran down his throat reaching his parched insides. When the jar was empty, he handed it back saying, "I haven't tasted water since I died."

The stranger, without saying anything, nor revealing his identity, bent his knees taking Henry's right foot into his hands. He removed Henry's shoe and covered his naked foot with his palm, pausing for a moment. When he released the foot it was free from wounds, completely healed. He then repeated this action with the left foot. Long awaited relief traveled up Henry's body delivering healing, and with that, great comfort. The stranger then took Henry's hands into his, turning them palms up. Only now Henry realized how badly lacerated they were. Remaining incognito, the stranger lowered his head and kissed Henry's palms, one by one, delivering instant healing and repose.

Although Henry did not feel so comfortable with the stranger's way of healing, the relief and comfort provided was so great that he couldn't resist. When his body was completely restored from exhaustion and physical damage Henry asked, "Who are you? Please reveal yourself."

The man in the cloak lifted his hands to slowly remove his hood exposing his face and identity.

Henry was facing a man in his thirties, with light brown curly hair and a beard a shade darker that pleasantly framed his face. His nose slightly elongated and a bit pointy protruded from his face. His eyes remained downcast. Beneath the long white coat Henry could see brown leather sandals, covered in dust, loosely hugging his feet.

"I think that you will be more comfortable in this," the stranger said, offering Henry a neatly folded light brown coat with sandals placed on top of it.

Still not seeing his eyes, Henry accepted the gift, cast away his useless old clothes, and dressed himself into the stye of biblical times.

Only when Henry stood in front of his savior, did the stranger lift his eyes to look at him from toes to head. When their eyes met, Henry realized who he was facing.

"Feel more comfortable now?" the savior asked.

Henry wanted to say, "Yes, thank you, and thank you for saving me," and much more… but he couldn't. A big lump was stuck in his throat preventing him from saying anything, and somehow immobilized him. From the moment that he looked into the stranger's eyes he became paralyzed. He tried to swallow the stubborn lump, but instead it grew until it occupied his entire chest. Henry began to run out of breath, and an irregular heartbeat caused his chest to tremble. When his first tear drops broke through the long overdue relief was delivered. His entire body convulsed, as though crying from the inside out. Every part of his soul was weeping like no grown-up should. Unable to control himself, Henry chose not to resist letting it all out, all that was there to be spilled. Henry could not move his gaze from the stranger's eyes, blue like the deepest ocean. They captured Henry's soul into their depths, and he could not move from their most pleasant captivity. To him, this felt similar to the experience he had when visiting the cradle of souls standing in front of the bright orange "soul-creator" wall. While that wall was calling him but at the same time keeping him at a distance so as not to contaminate it, these eyes were inviting him unconditionally, lovingly, and completely free of judgement. The magnitude of his presence was so overwhelming that it was almost impossible to endure.

Giving Henry time to recuperate, the savior spoke, "Do you feel better now?"

With great difficulty Henry pulled himself together and answered, "Yes sir, thank you. I feel much better and thank you for rescuing me."

"You're welcome," gently smiled the savior, "I believe you wanted to meet me?"

"Yes indeed," Henry answered indecisively, "I don't know where to start, and most of all I don't know how to address you."

"Jesus will do," said the savior simply.

"Yes, sir Jesus," Henry began.

"Just Jesus," corrected the savior.

"I presume that we are in your reality," Henry started cautiously.

"One of them."

"It feels as though I am back on Earth, all of my senses are back, and I feel alive again."

Jesus watched Henry quietly in anticipation of a question.

Realizing this, Henry asked, "Why is this so?"

"Most of me is down on Earth and I prefer it this way, so as not to become detached from this most." Trying to make sense of what he had just heard, Henry said, "I am sorry, but I don't get it."

"I feel that it will be unfair to those who are suffering down there in my name to indulge in a pain-free existence here."

"Now I understand," Henry said falling quiet.

Sensing Henry's apprehension Jesus said, "You can ask me any questions. If the answer is known to me you will have it. Besides, I knew what I was signing up for when I agreed to meet you."

"Please understand my predicament. Jesus himself sitting in front of me with me in the role of interrogator…this is so weird."

"I understand," said the savior, "Let me help you. I have been through this countless times, and the questions remain the same. While I knew the role I took upon myself when choosing to become Christ, which by the way is the Greek word for 'Anointed One', or 'Chosen One.' The one who was chosen to deliver a message, having nothing to do with the tool of my execution as many still believe." He fell quiet in anticipation of Henry's questions.

Henry braced himself and spilled out the question that had been bothering him the most for quite some time, "Do you consider yourself a God?"

Jesus laughed loudly answering, "I have never said that."

"Okay. Are you the only son of God?"

"Only as you are, no less, no more."

"But…"

"I know what the Bible says," Christ interrupted him. "You should know that I did not write the Bible. All the gospels were written by those who never knew me, saw me, or heard my teachings. All that I stand for, and so adamantly believe in was twisted and institutionalized into a religion, into a tool to control people's minds, suppress their will through fear of imminent punishment for committed sins. The criteria of sin were not set by me, and I have never built a church, starting my preaching in synagogues and then later outside in nature. If you ask me, nature is the purest place to worship and pray to God. Churches are man-made structures, while nature is created by God himself. Being outdoors, standing barefoot on the ground humans connect with two beginnings at the same time."

"What do you mean by two beginnings?"

"The two main forces of all physical creation. The first is Mother Earth, and the second is our Eternal Father. Earth is the creator and sustainer of the human body, while our Father is the creator of souls occupying those bodies."

"I see," said Henry knowing that another question was in order. "May I ask how this all begins? And what is your role in it?"

"Are you questioning the first chapter of the Old Testament?"

"Yes, actually, I am. To me the way that Genesis presents the beginning of life seems too simple, even naïve. Although, I do understand it was good enough for those living 3000 years ago, but now…" Henry fell quite hoping that his question was not conveyed in a disrespectful manner.

Jesus smiled and answered, "Let me explain to you the beginning of all as I explained it to my disciples, although I do not like the word disciples as they were all my friends, and still are. Anyway, unfortunately none of what I am going to share with you now found its way into the Bible."

Henry tried to make himself comfortable on his rock so that he could absorb all that this great soul had to convey. He knew that this was a once in a lifetime opportunity that would never be repeated again. What made it even more valuable was how hard it had been to get here, with all the suffering he had endured so that he could hear him and hopefully to know him, even if it is not in his entirety.

"So, listen my brother," Christ said.

Henry felt flattered to be called brother by Christ himself. *"Who in their right mind would believe me if I told them this."*

He quickly chased these thoughts away so as not to be distracted, and Christ began.

"Once the decision was made to build this school, with that decision being made by a great 'Visionary' who masterminded the entire project to its tiniest details. Builders were called upon to begin with the construction, and to bring it to life. They arrived with all the necessary equipment and the power needed, and when the walls were up, carpenters were invited to install the roof and add in the doors and windows. Plasterers followed them to cover the bricks to a smooth finish, and then painters and many other professionals to bring the project to completion. When the school was executed to perfection the great 'Visionary' stepped in to check the quality of the work, and above all to ensure that there were no hazards for the children who were to attend it. Satisfied, he sent messages to nearby villages and cities to bring their children to the new school that he had built. While parents were making their decision he found a principal for his school, a beautiful lady named Gaia, who benevolently agreed to take good care of the school and all the students whose parents would agree to enroll them."

"One by one, cautiously, people appeared at the doorsteps of the newly opened school to begin their studies. To begin with, they came from nearby villages and then the cities. Soon the school made a great name for itself as a place where kids could learn almost everything they needed to know for their age—both good and bad. When its reputation was well established, parents from neighboring countries began to show up. What was most important were the conditions for entry into the school that were put in place by the great 'Visionary.' This condition applied to the parents…they could bring their children in the morning and take them back in the evening, but while they were in the school they had to stay and watch them without any interference, no matter what the lessons they had to learn."

At this point Jesus fell silent to observe Henry's ability to follow his parable.

Noticing Jesus's hesitation Henry said, "Let me guess, a day in the school was equal to one human life?"

"Exactly," replied Jesus unable to hide his satisfaction. "And you were one of the teachers?"

"No, I was just a substitute?"

"A substitute?" Henry asked in surprise.

"Yes, my brother. From the time of the school's foundation a pantheon of great teachers was invited to lead classes."

"So, what happened to them?"

"They served their purpose. No matter how good you are as a teacher there is only so much you can give. The kids had to evolve."

"Then what happened?" Henry asked impatiently.

"Then I and many others like me were invited by the great 'Visionary' to replace those strong and very powerful God-like teachers to deliver a message of love and forgiveness."

"I see," said Henry, and after some thought asked, "Wasn't your message too revolutionary for that school? Or should I say, for that barbaric time?"

"Apparently it was, and that is the main reason our message was so distorted."

"Doesn't this upset you?"

Jesus laughed loudly for the first time and answered, "Nothing of what happened or is now happening on Earth could ever upset me."

"Even the fact that humans commit such atrocities in your name?"

"You must see the root of the problem, to try and understand the cause of such behaviors. Once you do, only then will you be able to forgive and accept humans with all that is good and bad."

"Are you saying that there is no punishment for the crimes that humans commit in these spiritual realities? Or should I say, in the Christians heaven?" Looking around Henry added, "Although this can hardly be called heaven!"

"You are judging a book by its cover. This is one of my realities that I visit when peace and seclusion is needed. Or when I have the opportunity to have an intellectual conversation with those who want to learn, and hopefully to understand, my past and my present. Now about heaven for Christians," smiled Jesus. "Most of the souls who reside in my realms are quite comfortable and fully engaged in educational processes and many recreational activities. When it comes to punishment," Jesus said on a serious note, "it works the same way here as it does in all other realms. No one can punish you worse than you can punish yourself. You above all are familiar with this concept. So, if souls can forgive themselves for all that they have done on Earth, they have my forgiveness unconditionally."

"What about the sins they have committed and the imminent punishment that follows, as preached for the last 2000 years to those who believed and followed your teachings?"

"Let me be short on this. From the parent's point of view

misbehavior is the nature of children. But what most see as misbehavior, I see as an opportunity to learn. After all, the best lessons are learned in the worst circumstances. Do you agree?"

"Yes, I do. But what I am hearing contradicts everything we have been told about you." Henry held his head in his hands saying, "The longer I converse with you more questions surface in my mind."

"Isn't that the reason why you are here?"

"Yes, but do you have so much time for me. I don't want to take advantage of your kindness, nor hospitality."

"Not at all, we have all the time in the universe." Christ smiled placing his hand on Henry's knee. "You, my brother, can ask any questions, and if I know the answers, they will be yours."

"Thank you," Henry said and continued with his interrogation. "Is there a definition for sin?"

"No, it varies from soul to soul, depending on their level of development."

"Is there some kind of common denominator?"

"It is…'If your actions do not hurt nor cause harm to any other soul physically or mentally, then you can say that your actions are righteous'. But you can argue that doctors cause pain to heal their patients."

"Yes," agreed Henry.

"To harm for the sake of healing is a righteous act. Besides, inside each human dwells their own inner judge, and most of the time that judgement is the best indicator, but as you know, not many are listening."

Henry nodded his head in agreement, and then unexpectedly popped another question, "Did you really die on the cross? You know there a lot of controversies out there."

"I know my brother and believe me when I say it was a grand finale to my life on earth."

JUDAS

"Can you elaborate on that please?" Henry asked.

"Before I took the body that you are looking at, and chose to become Christ, I knew how it would all end. My decent to Earth was a conscious decision, although like any other human, once born I did not remember what I had agreed to. But closer to the time of my death it was revealed to me."

"What was revealed?"

"My way of exiting from the physical reality."

"So, you knew what kind of death was waiting for you and you did nothing to escape?"

"I couldn't. They knew the whereabouts of my family and I couldn't risk them being arrested and tortured just to find me."

"What about Judas? Didn't he betray you? Could you ever forgive him?"

"Judas was and still is one of my most devoted disciples."

"Am I missing something? What about the thirty pieces of silver?"

Christ laughed loudly, "The story depicted in the gospels are only partially true. What Judas did was at my request, and it took a long time to convince him to do it."

"What about his suicide? Is that true?"

"Let me share with you what really happened," Christ said and in front of Henry's eyes pictures began to appear in 3D, an event of ancient history.

He saw a man arguing with four others who seemed to be accusing him of some deeds. Henry couldn't understand their language, but one of them, presumably Judas, was trying to prove his innocence. Eventually the argument became heated, ending up in a short physical fight with one of the disciples, after which Judas stormed out, disappearing into the night. The next scene was of two men standing on the outskirts of a village. Henry could hardly see them with the only source of light being the full moon above their heads. One of them was familiar to him from the earlier scene, and the other a Jewish Rabbi. After a short exchange of words, the Rabbi pulled out from his inner pocket a leather bag, offering it to the man in front of him. Despite the lack of light, Henry could see the facial expression of the one supposedly being paid. Disbelief and adamant rejection in receiving payment was the emotion so clearly visible to Henry, despite it happening in the distant past. The protruded hand hung in the air and unable to find a receiving one, released the leather sack to hit the ground with a clang of the coins within. The Rabbi turned around and left with misunderstanding and deep disappointment portrayed on his face. The other man stood motionless, with eyes staring into the darkness expressing emptiness and disbelief about what had just unfolded. Rejected and trashed, he untied a rope around his waist and threw it over a nearby tree branch. Fastening one end and making a loop in the other placing it around his neck.

"The rest you know," said Jesus as he made the pictures disappear into thin air.

"Couldn't you help him?" Henry asked, deeply touched.

"No, but I was the first to greet him on this side."

In total disbelief Henry asked, "He went into history books as a symbol of treachery. That is so unfair and unjust."

"As I said before, all the gospels were written by those who weren't even born when these events happened. But what upsets me most is that the entire nation, my nation, stagnated because Judas was portrayed as a traitor and the guilty party in my execution. Condemning many generations of Jews to carry the birthmark of a 'God-killer'."

"This is so unjust," said Henry.

"You must remember my brother, that today's Bible, especially the New Testament, were forged and institutionalized into organized religion by the Roman Emperor, Constantine, who couldn't stand his own nation carrying the blame as the guilty party in my execution."

"Now it makes sense," said Henry.

"You can see now how history and the true facts have been twisted to mislead and disorientate the majority to condemn the minority."

"Yes, I do. To be honest I was not much of a believer back on earth…no offence," said Henry biting his tongue.

"None taken, brother, nor was I."

Henry looked at Christ who was laughing, "Sorry, but this feels weird. I am sitting in from of the creator of the biggest religion on Earth who says he is not a believer!"

"It was not my intention. All I signed up for was to be God's messenger, but I guess He had bigger plans for me."

"So, from day one you knew your life purpose?"

"Not exactly. It took a while before I realized it. Although, from a young age I felt different from those around me."

"Different how?" asked Henry.

"I was always hungry for knowledge. At the age of five I learned how to read, and since then the Torah became my obsession."

"What is the Torah?" Henry asked.

"It is the Old Testament in the Bible."

"And you could understand it at such a young age?"

"It took time and a lot of explanation from the wise teachers that I was honored to meet, for me to really understand the complexity of the texts. I was a quick learner and the intricacy of it only added fuel to the fire of knowledge burning in me. When I was done with the Torah, I began to study unwritten wisdom passed on from Rabbi to Rabbi verbally. By the age of twelve I had enough knowledge to teach others, in other words, to preach. In my teens I had conquered Latin and Greek, two of the most important languages of that time. Since Judea was part of the Roman empire, which was most of the civilized world, I had the privilege to be exposed to other teachings."

"What do you mean?" asked Henry.

"By grasping the essence of Judaism, I came to the realization that there had to be more to learn. In short, my vessel of knowledge was not fulfilled and I had capacity to take in more."

"I know the feeling," agreed Henry.

ALEXANDRIA

"Although the Roman regime was oppressive upon their conquered nations, they still allowed the defeated to practice their own religions and follow their traditions. There were no borders like there are now, and people could travel freely if they wished. In those days travelers could always find shelter in the villages they passed through. Before reaching sixteen I asked my parents to allow me to go."

"Go where?" Henry asked surprised.

"From a young age I had heard about a magnificent place. A place that had the capacity to hold the entire knowledge and wisdom gathered by the civilized world since ancient times. It was an inner call for me to reach that heaven and satisfy my thirst for knowledge."

"Are you talking of the Royal Library of Alexandria?" asked Henry.

"Yes, the Great Library of Alexandria. Every scholar dreamt, at least once, to set foot into the halls of the greatest repository of human mind achievements of all time. Repository of the brightest intellectuals who had ever lived on Earth, and left trails of their once achievements in various forms of writings."

"How did you get there?" Henry asked impatiently.

"Where there is a strong will, a way appears. It was predestined. From village to village, from city to city, I laid my path to Egypt. In those days it was unsafe to travel with money, and the only way to pay for shelter and food was to perform manual labor. To secure place in a barn on the hay next to the livestock."

"How long did it take you to get to Alexandria?"

"Almost a month. Nazareth was at the north of Israel, called then, Galilee."

"What!" Henry exclaimed. "Weren't you born in Bethlehem?"

"I was," Christ answered, satisfied with Henry's awareness.

"I was small when my family chose to move to Nazareth. It was a better place for my father, with greater demand for his skills. Anyway, a month later I was standing in front of the long cherished destination, full of hope and great anticipation. Unfortunately, not everyone could gain access to its halls. Firstly, it wasn't free, and secondly you had to display some level of knowledge and intellect to be granted entry to the most sacred scriptures. So, to get in I had to find work and a place to stay. To cut a long story short, it wasn't easy. I was paying for food and a roof over my head with manual labor, and with the bit of money earned I gained access to the heaven of ultimate knowledge. I could have stayed there indefinitely, but every night I was chased by guards to come back the next day."

While Jesus was telling the stories of his life, Henry could see muted scenes of this biblical time transferred to him by Christ to simplify the task of visualization.

"I became such a frequent visitor that the librarians stopped charging me entrance and years later offered me a job. Besides being a place of storage of ancient scrolls, it was also a great educational center where one could study history, astronomy, philosophy, natural science, medicine, mathematics, you name it. I attended almost every class led by the greatest teachers of those days. Years later I became a teacher myself and began to earn a decent salary."

"What subjects were your favorites?"

"Ancient Greek philosophy, and later I developed a great interest in Eastern religions, although they could hardly be called religions, but rather philosophies or ways of living. I came across translations of Hinduism and Buddhism. I cannot say that I agreed with what I read, but they opened me up to the message that I was meant to deliver to my own nation. I found that studying various ways of thinking broadened my understanding and opened paths to greater knowledge. So, after years and years I expanded my consciousness through studying the opinions of others to form my own. I realized that the process of learning serves to awaken our inner knowledge, the one that you originally came with, the one that you are supposed to share."

"Why couldn't you download this knowledge, or the message, directly from the One who sent you to Earth?" Henry asked.

"That would have been easier, but unfortunately things do not work that way. As you know, the human brain is limited in its ability to process large volumes of information and can be easily damaged. The only way to avoid this damage is to stretch it gradually."

"What do you mean by stretching it?"

"I mean exposing it to larger volumes of knowledge moderately. Then it becomes more alert, more awakened to various types of knowledge, sometimes polar opposite to your certainties. Then…"

"Then what?" asked Henry.

"The miracles happen."

As Jesus pronounced those words he looked up in a display of respect and gratitude for whatever it was that he had received from above.

"My Father chose to let me have it."

"Have what?"

"The message. It became so clear and undoubtedly true. So bright in its clarity that it left no question in my mind that it was time to return home to the place where I had begun my journey, a journey of awakening to the truth, to my Father's truth."

"Forgive me please, but I am not following you. When you say my 'Father', who exactly are you referring to?" asked Henry boldly.

"A great visionary. The one who created all. The one whose energy in the form of consciousness was used to create all that has come into existence, be it in the physical or spiritual worlds."

"So, how do you describe your relationship with this great visionary, or should I say, with God himself?"

"Same as you. Part of his energy in the form of consciousness."

"I do understand that," Henry kept on drilling, "But how big is your energy in Him compared to other souls?

"If you really want to know, you could say that if he is the entire body of water on the planet Earth, I would be a glass of water, and most who surrounded me on Earth would be drops."

"Thank you for your honesty. I have one more question to ask if you don't mind?"

"I know," answered Christ, "and you will regret it if you don't."

"You lived a life as any other human, it will be strange not to assume that a woman would have crossed your path to awaken love in you."

"You are right, I tasted women, and not only once, with my heart being broken many times. One could not teach love without knowing or being in love. Love is in the core of our souls and passionately waits to be awakened. It takes a multiple of lifetimes on Earth to find 'that one' who you will stay with forever. But it was not my purpose and a bond with a woman could have altered my chosen path."

"I am puzzled now," said Henry. "Why do you expect celibacy from priests, while the taste of women, like you said, is known by your flesh."

"I did not create priesthood and did not ask them to be celibate. To ask such a thing is to go against the laws of nature. Abstention from the call of nature can bring deficiencies of any kind. This strange request was made much later by the founders of the Christian faith. Maintaining celibacy for them was an easy task, as they were all old and indifferent to the charms of the opposite gender."

"I see," said Henry, "My curiosity is satisfied, and sorry for interrupting you."

"As I was saying, I realized that the time to head back home had arrived, and without further ado, I packed my bags. I had a strong urge to share the knowledge I had gathered in the thirteen years of intensive learning and teaching at the same time."

"Did you know what was waiting for you back home?" Henry asked impatiently.

"You mean my execution?"

"Yes."

"No, not at that time. I was excited to see my family and old friends, but most of all the opportunity to share the wisdom. But my excitement was not long lived."

"Why?" Henry asked.

"Don't take me wrong, but I came to the realization that my knowledge was too advanced for those who soon surrounded me. I had to assess the level of their perception, establish a foundation to start sharing the information upon which I could build a structure, which today has become a superstructure!" Christ proudly exclaimed, "But I guess you are more interested in the past."

"For now, yes, but I have lots of questions and some major disagreements with what is happening in Christianity today."

"I know. We will get there," answered Jesus, pleasantly smiling,

"What puzzles me, is there in any truth in the miracles that the gospels claim you performed?"

"Being in Egypt I spent a lot of time studying medicine and natural science and different healing techniques. I discovered that I had an amazing ability that no one around me had."

"What was it?" asked Henry.

"I was able to generate an enormous source of energy concentrated in my hands when I wanted to heal someone. In the beginning I could not understand the origin of it, but later I realized that it was Father's way of helping me to gain the trust of my future followers. I guess, an extraordinary message could not be delivered by an ordinary man. Besides, the Egyptians were advanced healers themselves, the knowledge gained combined with my God-given powers enabled me to become a very advanced healer."

"Okay, but what about the miracles?" Henry insisted.

"Like I said, I was a healer, not a magician as the gospels presented me, dragging into the Bible the image of a God-like man later to be placed on a same podium with the supreme creator."

"I see," said Henry, noticing Jesus's dissatisfaction and unwillingness to elaborate further on the subject.

A moment later Jesus continued, "Very soon I realized that the seeds that I had cautiously sown about soul's transmigration from one body into another were falling onto infertile ground. Besides, it could have caused a loss of listeners and probably disciples, too. Simplicity became key."

Christ fell quiet, immersed into the events of years past, further from those recorded in history by humans and closer to the version still vibrant in him.

"What about baptizing?" Henry asked carefully, inviting Christ back to the present.

"What you call baptizing today had a completely different meaning in those times. It wasn't invented by John the Baptist. The practice of purification of the body and soul through water was undertaken long before John. Also, you have to take into consideration the times we were living in. Frequent showers that humans take today was not an option then. A complete body wash was quite a big event and to see it as a chance to wash away old sins was not a new perspective. What was important was that the person had to repent their sins before being submerged in the water. By admitting their sins and asking for forgiveness, they emerged as a new purified soul. You above all should know that the acknowledgement of shortcomings delivers peace of mind from self-forgiveness."

"Since you mentioned it, I have a question."

"Fire away."

"Is it right to baptize newborns if the purpose of the act is repentance, then what do newly arrived souls have to repent?"

"I must agree with you. The act loses its symbolism and very meaning, and it ceases to serve the purpose that it was originally designed for, plus baptizing was an act of acceptance of religion and its philosophies which needed to be a conscious decision by those in the search of faith."

RETURN HOME

"Since I have cleared that up, I would like to get back to the time of my return home. As I said, I was met with disappointment. Nobody was interested in the transmigration of souls that I was so captivated by. Unfortunately, I realized that the whole idea of having another physical life on Earth was too complicated for them. All they wanted to know was how to ease their suffering and find happiness in the country which was under the suppressive rule of the Roman empire. Many times the Jews tried to rebel, with each new failure followed by harsher punishments. While most were expecting a die-hard revolutionary to show them the way to freedom from this most hated regime, I came with the message of love and forgiveness. Many rejected me, while strangely enough, women were the most attentive listeners, convincing their husbands to listen to what I had to say."

"I can imagine how difficult it was to preach love and forgiveness at a time of war," said Henry.

"I know you can, because you lived in that time."

Henry raised his eyebrows in complete shock. "I don't think so."

"Did you forget about the slave girl in the house of a wealthy Roman? The one who was chained to the wall and butchered and whipped to death. A girl with the name Aurelia?"

"Oh my, I had completely forgotten about her," said Henry with his mind drifting back in time. A moment later he said, "Some memories are best erased."

"We have all been victims and witnesses to terrible events which only humans are capable of orchestrating. Nevertheless, it was you who chose to dig up your past and now must live with that knowledge. For that I applaud you."

"I live with regret for doing that."

"You shouldn't. A revealed and relived past brings clarity to the present. After all, isn't that why we are digging into my past now?"

Henry smiled and nodded his head in agreement.

"So, you know firsthand what it is to be a slave, and there were many of them in Judea, and across the entire Roman empire. My words about a pain-free life after death placed hope into their tortured hearts and souls beyond my expectations. Recognition of finiteness of the current state of existence gave them strength not only to accept the fact of being enslaved to the end of their lives, but also eliminated the fear of death. Death, which was stalking them around each corner, became a most welcome liberator. The vanished fear of death made them bolder, and I can say happier, also. Many were shocked when I explained that 'if anyone slaps you on the right cheek, turn your other one to them'."

"Did you really say that?" asked Henry.

"Yes, I did," Christ announced proudly.

"It still puzzles me."

"So also for those hearing it for the first time. Replacing 'an eye for an eye, and a tooth for a tooth' with no resistance to an oppressor sounds shocking 'till these days."

"To be honest I thought that those words were placed in the Bible a lot later through the hands of Romans to keep the conquered nations obedient."

"No, I said that, and I will explain why, but to do that I will speak to you through the mind of my Father," and as he said that he closed his eyes.

Not entirely understanding what Christ just said, Henry became tense, leaning backward just in case.

When Christ opened his eyes there was another man looking at Henry. The eyes and face were the same, but his facial hair was now white. Instinctively Henry crossed himself placing both hands on his chest.

"Don't be surprised, it is still me, just in the form of higher consciousness."

Henry, feeling completely numb, just nodded his head.

"I have been observing the development of humanity on Earth since its creation. It was all fun at the beginning, but then it became too violent because of continuous warfare that did not give humans the chance to complete a full lifecycle. What I mean is, to experience childhood, parenting, and grandparenting, especially the male population of souls that came back to the world of spirit before having the chance to produce offspring. The world became male dominated, cruel, and hungry for blood. The ambitions of the ruling elite to conquer and possess more transformed humans into merciless, revengeful, and brutal beings. Human life lost its value and I had to do something about it."

Henry was listening attentively, afraid to move a muscle.

"So, I called upon my son to become Christ, a message bearer of love, empathy, and forgiveness."

"Your son?" Henry asked, hardly moving his lips.

"Yes, as any other human on Earth who are my sons and daughters. They are all an integral part of me and my consciousness…each and every soul at their own personal stage of development. The difference between the majority of souls living on earth 2000 years ago and Christ, is that Christ was created by me a lot earlier, and as a result, he knows more of me and is better aligned with me." The Father closed his eyes and leaned back.

A moment he reopened them, and Henry was again facing his savior. Henry took a deep breath, and freeing his lungs of air he felt relieved of a tremendous weight that had mounted him so suddenly and unexpectedly.

"Who was that?" Henry asked, still puzzled.

"It was a tiny part of our Father's consciousness reaching you through me."

"All this is confusing and bit scary. Next time please, your words will be enough for me," pleaded Henry not ready to face the Father again.

"So, as you see, I came to change the world, or to be exact, the way it was evolving. You probably already know that to change the world all you need to do is change the way the majority thinks."

"Sorry to interrupt you, but the way I see it, you tried to give them knowledge, but instead they received faith."

"Yes."

"And you are okay with that?"

"Of course, my brother. Untimely knowledge could have been easily dismissed due to the receivers being not yet ready. But in the form of faith it could be firmly rooted into their minds, to be explained and understood many years later."

"How much later?"

"Time is irrelevant. The number of lives lived on earth is most important."

"Two thousand years have gone by, but the world has not change much and humans are still at each others' throats."

"I know my brother, but believe me when I say the world today is no comparison to that which I lived in. Two thousand years seems a lot, but it is nothing compared to the distance that humanity on this planet still has to travel. The world is constantly changing, not at the speed that we would wish for, but it is changing."

"Okay," said Henry, "that's the future, but my hunger to know more about your past is not yet satisfied."

"What do you still want to know?"

"Some say that you didn't die on the cross and lived happily ever after, if you know what I men."

"I do," answered Christ with his face lighting up with a most genuine smile. "Many would have wished it was so, and am talking about on both sides, those who believed in me and those who didn't. Humans always prefer a happy ending to the most horrifying stories, having a hard time believing that despite all of the pain and suffering I lived to see another day. If I didn't die on that cross, no one would know about me today, and my message would have gone unnoticed. Crucifixion as a way of death was the highlight of my once-lived physical life."

"Forgive me for interrupting, but I have to ask, did you really go to the cross so that the sins of those who believe in you would be forgiven, so that they could directly ascend to heaven?"

After a short pause Jesus answered, "Indirectly, yes." "To me that is absolute nonsense. So, 2000 years ago you freed all Christians of their sins, sins that they still had to commit, just like that! Do whatever you like, just believe in me and you will get a shortcut to heaven." After saying these last words Henry bit his tongue, suddenly remembering who he was talking to.

"It's all right, don't worry. I see that this has been boiling in you and was waiting for the right time and the right person to be spilled out. You are not the first, and definitely not the last, to ask me this very same question. Unable to explain myself to those on Earth, at least here I have the opportunity to do it. Your curiosity and questions raised bring me nothing but joy." Christ smiled, "Now, about the purpose and meaning of my death. Isn't it ironic that unless one gives up their life for what they truly believe, no one will believe them."

"Are you saying that you gave up your life just to land your message?" Henry interrupted.

"Yes, my faith, and faith of my Father, were so strong that I chose the most horrifying death for the sake of the truth that I had to deliver. Who would have believed in me and my teachings if I had betrayed my Father's trust to save my life. So, yes, I died on the cross and at the very same moment I was visited by my guides, although in those days we called them angels, who three days later guided me to the doorways of my newly forming kingdom."

"Before we get to that part," Henry interrupted again, "why did it take three days? Also, I am dying to hear, and to also understand, how you explain the disappearance of your remains from the tomb. The reason why I am asking this is because the idea of you rising into the spiritual realm in a physical body does not make any sense."

"Of course not, I did not rise in a physical form. Like any other soul, I left my body behind. In my case, hanging on a cross. The destiny of my body after my death was out of my control."

"If I remember correctly, according to the gospels, Mary didn't find your corpse in the tomb where they had left you to rest a day earlier."

"It is true. My body was stolen and placed into another abandoned tomb in the middle of the night."

"What!" exclaimed Henry. Shocked to his core he added, "Who and why?"

"I know it will be hard to believe, but it was done by my own disciples. I will not share names, but it was so. The answer to your question, why, is quite simple. They couldn't stand being mocked as followers of the wrong Messiah."

"I'm not getting it?"

"The whole idea of a soul leaving the body for the next existence was too complicated to explain to those who challenged my teachings. In comparison, an empty tomb would be easily explained and could stand as undoubted proof of my divinity. Lived once, died, and risen into his Father's kingdom… no further explanation was needed."

Henry covered his mouth with his hand in utter disbelief, unable to say anything. Scenes of this fraud were playing in front of his eyes. The conspiracy committed by this bunch of followers to prove their own worthiness shook Henry to his core. "How could they? And how could you forgive such an act of betrayal?"

Christ smiled and said, "You are considering only one side… allow me to show you the other."

"This one can overcome a hundred other sides…there is no

forgiveness for what they did."

"Be patient," Christ said lovingly.

Henry sat back, interested to hear how Christ was going to justify such an unjust act.

"If you remember, I said earlier, that three days later I departed to the spiritual realms that had been prepared for me."

"Yes, I remember," confirmed Henry.

"The plan for my body's reburial was masterminded by my disciples before my execution."

"Why didn't you confront them?" asked Henry.

Jesus placed his index finger across his lips indicating that Henry should be patient and keep quiet.

"First of all, at the time it was only a hazy idea. Secondly, I was incarcerated by Marcus Pontius Pilate and had no contact with them. Only after the exit of my soul from my tortured body, I realized that their hazy plan was going to become a harsh reality. With the permission of my Father, I delayed my exit from the physical world to bear witness to their plans. While I was still questioning the integrity of their intentions, only once it happened, or should I say, when they relocated my body on the outskirts of the old cemetery, did I realize the greatness of such an act."

"What!" Henry spluttered, unable to keep quiet any longer.

"Yes, you heard me right. In the very same day when they gathered again at my tomb, I revealed myself in the most possible semi-physical form and let them know of my awareness of the previous night's actions."

"And?"

"And we made a covenant not to be broken, to be sealed 'til the end of their lives. Not one soul should learn of their act. The rest you know. The 'miracle' of my resurrection and further appearance were skillfully used to convince nonbelievers in the truth of my divine origin. They all kept their promise, paying dearly for their silence. All except Peter were tortured to death, later to be welcomed into the spiritual reality created by me for them. You are familiar with the procedure," Jesus motioned to Henry, "Croton did the same for you."

"And this should be the beginning of your newly formed kingdom," stated Henry.

"Yes, it was, and my deepest gratitude goes to Paul. The one who became the most dedicated missionary in the promotion of my message."

"If I remember correctly, he was once a persecutor of Christians?"

"Yes, he was, but later I had to reveal myself to him, turning Paul into my strongest ally. The one who channeled messages from me, writing them down through the prism of his perceptions. Honestly, no one expected the magnitude of exposure and the depth of devotion to my teachings that we had to manage. The seeds of love and forgiveness fell into fertile ground and began to flourish. The idea of enslaved souls gaining their freedom after death raised a great deal of hope. Long-lost happiness found its way back into their minds, eliminating their fear of death. Some of my followers saw death as the only way to escape the horrible realities of their lives."

"And you had to live up to these expectations set by yourself."

"That's right."

"From what I understood," said Henry, "one should be careful of attracting followers or disciples on Earth."

"Absolutely right, and this is not about how certain you are in what you are preaching, it is about generating an enormous weight of responsibility thereafter. If someone dies with your name on their lips, you had better be ready not only to meet those souls on this side, but also to accommodate them in comfort. As you know, only a few true teachers managed to survive the test of time."

"Like?" Henry asked to establish Christs point of view about other teachers.

"Like those who, until now, most of humanity pray to and in return receive answers to their prayers."

"So, you are saying that answering prayers is an eternal task for you."

"Maybe not all are answered, but I assure you that all have been heard. The bottom line is…one's ability to answer prayers is the only validation of your true power, which becomes the foundation of faith one will chose to create and lead."

"Is this the secret of Christianity's popularity these days?"

Christ smiled and said, "Not only. Spirit guides appointed by me, or the Planners, are very attentive to their duties, following each step of the souls they guide, providing full support in the accomplishment of the tasks chosen for their reincarnated selves until their last days on Earth, and especially beyond death. They must form a strong bond with the souls they guide, and those ties can be broken only if one of them outgrows the other."

"I noticed that when observing Gertrude's behavior with Anne. She acted as a loving mother, not leaving Anne's side until the end of her physical life, and then desperately looking for her when she was lost."

"By the way, one of the reasons that you are sitting in front of me was your benevolent participation in her search."

"I have to admit that it wasn't so benevolent," Henry said shamefully, "I was trying to get to you."

"That is the second reason that you are here now."

"Are they still together?" Henry asked.

"Their bond has grown stronger than ever," answered Christ, then adding, "In contrary to yours."

"To mine?"

"Yes, look where you are, and where are the souls supposedly being guided by you?"

Henry wanted to argue such accusation of being an unfit guide, but realized that since stepping into Christ's reality he had completely lost contact with little Rose and Croton. His immediate attempt to re-establish the connection so easily achieved before was a failure.

"You cannot reach them from here," said Christ, "but you should not worry as this meeting was arranged by Thales and he assured me that your absence would be covered."

"Covered by who?"

"It doesn't matter, but if you wish we can take a break and you will be able to find me again in this exact spot."

After giving some thought and weighing the pros and cons of this suggestion, Henry said, "If my task is covered, I would like to stay, if you don't mind."

"Stay as long as you wish. I see that your hunger is not yet satisfied, and it will be only my pleasure to assist you." He looked inquisitively into Henry's eyes saying, "After what you went through to get to me I owe you 'big time'."

Henry leaned forward boldly and fired his next question. "You said that you love humanity unconditionally, no matter how badly they screw up."

"Screw up?"

"I mean misbehave, or sin."

"Yes, I do," answered Christ.

"Does this apply only to those who believe in you, or to the entire humanity?"

"I think the answer to this question is self-explanatory. The connection has to be mutual."

"So you love unconditionally only those who truly believe in you?"

"I would say those who need me. Those who praise in my name and expect miracles to happen."

"And you make so-called 'miracles' happen for them?"

"Hmmm, I create conditions."

"Conditions?" asked Henry.

"If someone rigorously prays to be rich, I will create opportunities for them to earn money. Whether they will use that opportunity or not will be up to them."

"What if it goes against the tasks that they chose to learn while on Earth?"

"Any lesson is a good lesson. If a soul cannot have enough and wants more, so be it. At the end there will be more lessons to be learned."

"And will they have your unconditional love and forgiveness?"

"Yes," confirmed Christ.

"What if they do horrible things?"

"Those who truly believe in me cannot do horrible things."

"I would like to argue that. Right through the history of humanity people have killed and tortured others in your name."

"Using my name to pursue one's own personal agendas does not make one a follower of mine. I taught love and forgiveness."

"So, what happens to those who commit atrocities using your name?"

"Laws and regulations set by my Father to sustain this school and to ensure the growth of its students' consciousness are irrevocable. As in any other reality, once a soul crosses over into the world of spirit it has to experience all that they put others through. Be it physical pain or emotional suffering. This is the best and only way to teach souls their lessons. Although some lessons will be enforced during their stay on Earth, but if the student is too stubborn to understand and change their behavior, imminent punishment will be waiting for them on this side."

"What about love and forgiveness?"

"Those souls will have my unconditional love and forgiveness because I know why they act one way or another. I can always justify their actions and therefore forgive them. But the laws set by my Father will always prevail in the form of self-punishment for all that they have done, and in this regard I am powerless. All that I can do is step aside and when the time comes provide them with comfort."

"And when would that time be?"

"When the lessons are learned, and balance is restored."

"It sounds like an eye for an eye from the Old Testament," Henry said.

"Yes, unfortunately it does," Christ sighed deeply. "But there is a good side to all this. The souls that survive these lessons intact will never hurt other souls on their next returns to Earth. They become gentle, tolerant, and forgiving human beings, trying by all means to avoid conflict, so as to not create new punishable debts."

"So what do you see as the ultimate sin?" Henry asked.

"I would say ones that are committed consciously."

Henry was confused and asked Christ to explain.

"When you knowingly do something that you know you should not do, is enough to qualify it as a sin."

"In other words, listen to your conscience," mumbled Henry.

"Yes," Christ confirmed.

After a short pause to reflect upon what he had just heard, Henry asked, "I think now will be a good time to ask about being burned in the eternal fire that has frightened us from a young age."

"I have heard this one countless times and was hoping that you would not ask."

"Sorry to disappoint you."

"It's okay, I don't mind. Although, let me ask you a question in return. When you need to forbid your child from doing something that could hurt them, what will be the most effective method of prevention?"

"I think to avoid long explanations would be to frighten them."

"Thank you!" exclaimed Christ. "That is why back in time, the founders of Christianity chose to use it to create fear to forbid."

"I see," said Henry with a sigh of relief. "To be honest, at the back of my mind I had doubts. What if it really exists here?"

"You mean the way theologians keep describing it? Underworld with furnaces of eternal fire with the Devil in charge."

"I know, silly of me," Henry smiled awkwardly.

Then Christ became serious, gazing straight into Henry's eyes with such intensity that Henry felt cold shivers rushing up his spine. The extended pause made Henry feel extremely uncomfortable. There was no trace left of the kind and lovingly warm energy that had been seeping from the eyes of his savior.

Henry chose to break off the gaze saying, "Please do not scare me."

"Do you want to see it? Christ asked dead seriously.

"No!" Henry answered abruptly, noticing how quickly fear had begun to inhabit his entirety, chaining his heart tightly and raising regrets for ever asking the question about hell.

Christ unexpectedly placed his hand on Henry's shoulder and said, "Follow me, my brother."

INFERNO

An enormous force pulled Henry down. The dusty and thirsty land beneath his feet gave up its strength and Henry found himself free-falling. For some time, he plunged through thick clouds impenetrable to his sight, but a minute later everything cleared and he came to the realization that he was plummeting down toward a blue planet. A few seconds later he saw the outlines of continents surrounded by blue oceans. It was undoubtedly Earth. The speed that he had gained was enormous, and the realization of his imminent impact froze his mind and heart. With the last strength left in him, Henry braced himself for the horrifying collision, and tightly clenched his teeth and squeezed his eyes shut. But the expected did not occur and he kept descending, but now with deceleration until he came to a complete halt. Henry opened his eyes in an underground chamber facing Christ who was standing with his back to a massive wooden door, heavily encased in a wrought iron frame that looked impenetrable. Two sizeable burning jars attached to the wall on either side of the door filled the underground cavity with a hard, chilling glow. Henry could hardly see Christ's face due to the source of light being behind him. Despite the poor light, the excitement on his face was hard to miss.

"Ready?" asked Christ.

"Ready for what?" Henry asked fearfully.

Stepping aside to clear a passage for Henry to proceed, Christ pointed to the heavy door, and leaning a bit forward pompously said, "To visit hell!"

For the split second that Henry had before the heavy doors were to expose what they were hiding, he closed his eyes tightly shut. He concentrated his entire will on his own reality in an attempt to escape the pending nightmare. The only safe haven he was left with, the place where nobody could have disturbed him without his consent.

"Home. Home. Home," Henry repeated tirelessly, cursing his curiosity, and repentant of the burning desire to take this journey. The last drop of hope evaporated when he reopened his eyes still facing that damned door.

Blinks of light lit up Christ's perfect profile, who paused briefly giving Henry space to come to terms with his present reality, and to bring his attention back to the present moment. He looked at Henry and compassionately said, "I know that you want to escape this realm and would give anything to rather be in your own, but trust me when I say that you need this. You need to know and understand all about this place. It will only benefit you."

Henry looked at Christ filled with fear and asked, "Shall I be afraid?"

Christ stepped forward and embracing him warmly said, "Not next to me, my brother."

Henry hugged him in return placing his cheek against Christ's. He felt the silkiness of his hair and the warmth of his face. A feeling of absolute calmness entered his mind and heart, leaving no place for fear to dwell.

"Ready?" Christ asked again.

"Now I am." Henry announced confidently.

Christ turned around, and by applying the entire weight of his body pushed the heavy doors open. Unwillingly they gave up, filling the underground chamber with the highly irritating sound of squealing hinges. Immediately, through the opening crack, Henry could feel burning heat which began to rush out exuberantly to swallow the uninvited guests who dared to disturb the seals of Hades.

When the doors had swung to their fullest extent it became harder to confront the open mouth of the inferno. Ignoring the burning heat, Christ stepped in, inviting Henry to follow. Being afraid of being left behind, Henry hurried to stay close behind his savior.

"You can walk next to me," Christ invited.

As Henry stepped forward next to Christ he stumbled into the horrifying reality. The reality that he had only heard of, never believed in, and used to mock those who entertained the very idea of its existence. Henry walked beside Christ along a narrow passage just wide enough for two. On either side of the poorly paved pathway built of uneven rocks, were steep drops of at least sixty-five feet in depth, and that was the place where all of the drama, so vividly described in the countless testimonies of the greatest minds who once lived on Earth, were explicitly exhibiting the authenticity of their words. The passage that they were traveling on served as a divider between the left and right sides of a humongous cave, the size of which was impossible to establish due to the disappearance of the path as it twisted and turned into the darkness. The walls of the cave curved upward to its dome high above them, which was decorated with pointed crystals, resembling sharp swords waiting to plunge down onto their chosen victims. Dancing flashes of orange absorbed by the crystals only to be released with high intensity, adding horrifying beauty to the hungry bellies of the burning furnaces below. Any soul finding itself on this passage would find itself in the perfect position to observe the unveiling scenery on either side of the winding road.

"The burning furnaces of eternal fire," Henry thought to himself observing openings in the ground with blazing flames down below. Next to the furnaces Henry could see figures with long sticks in their hands busy keeping the fires alive. The effort applied by them was quite remarkable and hard to miss. Henry couldn't identify the gender of the workers, nor if they were human or not. They were blurry and sketchy in their appearance.

Henry wanted to ask Christ about their origin, but foreseeing Henry's question Christ said, "Leave them."

A while later the path took a sharp turn to the right and in front of Henry a new interior appeared, head spinning in its magnitude and breathtaking in its presence. They came to the edge of a huge opening seemingly dug into the middle of the planet Earth. To establish the dimension of this underground lacuna was an impossible task due to the opposite side fading into the distance. In the center of this spectacular underground world stood an isolated formation that was hard to identify from where Henry was standing. The significance of it in relation to this reality was obvious and undeniable.

Christ cast a quick glance at Henry and with unbridled excitement said, "One day you will thank me for this. For now try to keep up," and confidently stepped toward the center.

After only a few feet of walking Henry froze, unable to move any further due to the discovery he made. He immediately lowered himself, placing his hands on the ground in an attempt to stabilize himself in the face of the scenery that had appeared. They were still standing on the bumpy pathway, but now it formed a bridge that connected the center of this realm to its perimeter. The fact that it was so narrow and high above the spectacularly long drop did not concern Henry. What was at the bottom of it raised an enormous fear in him that weakened his knees. The drop to the depths measured at least three hundred feet and ended in hot boiling lava. A spiraling multi-level structure, resembling an upside-down cone, funneled around the edge of the cavity into the lava. The main source of light struggling to overcome the total darkness was the radiant red surface of the lava, which was covered with swirling mists of white vapor. Seconds later, once he adjusted his vision, Henry saw isolated burning flames randomly placed on each level of the spiraling floors within the cone. Sudden moans ending with human screams reached Henry's ears leaving no doubt as to where he was.

Embarrassed by his mental instability, Henry looked up at Christ who was still standing and stood up from his knees.

"Sorry, this came unexpectedly," Henry said pointing down.

"Are you afraid of dying?" Christ asked.

Henry kept quiet expressing his readiness to proceed. Staying next to Christ, but half a step behind, Henry tried to keep his balance and his eyes off the horrifying reality down below. Despite the height and narrowness of the bridge, it was quite stable providing firm support to the two figures walking toward the floating islands, the silhouette of which was gradually revealing itself. Being preoccupied with what was ahead, Henry did not notice that the walkway that they were on was disintegrating behind them. Big boulders that were firmly attached beneath their feet were falling apart and tumbling down into the inferno as the two figures passed over them. Approximately halfway to their target Henry looked back and the scenery broke his heart and with that all the hopes of returning back the same way. He added a tempo to his pace trying to keep close to Christ.

"That's right," nodded Christ laughing. "While walking in hell, keep moving."

"If we were on the way out, I would have agreed, but we are moving right into the heart of it."

"Be positive, my brother. Great discoveries lie ahead of you. The time will come when you will thank me for this."

"If I live through it, I will."

"Have no fear, my brother. Freedom can be found only on the

other side of conquered fear. Isn't it what you all want?"

"Freedom from what? Freedom from who? And who do you mean by all?" asked Henry in an attempt to clarify Christ's references.

"He will explain it to you," Christ said, pointing in the direction that they were moving.

THE HOST

The elevated level of suspense reached Henry's brim and was about to spill over. Each step took him closer to something which, most likely, any soul would have given anything to not face, or even be close to. The collapsing passage behind, and the steady steps of Christ, were leaving him with not much choice. For the moment, Henry felt trapped in a situation where his free will was utterly compromised. He had no say as to his near future. Trying to embrace the inevitability of the upcoming events, Henry convinced himself that this was going to be for his own good, and that it was going to be just another reality that he was going to go through, soon to be placed into a remote box in his memory bank. But for now, his heart was flooded with anxiety beyond his ability to control. Fear was rapidly expanding in his chest as they got closer to the target chosen by Christ. Henry was breaking into a cold sweat and resistance was mounting to the upcoming meeting.

What looked at first to be a dark spot with a hazy outline, revealed itself as a huge throne made entirely of black crystals. Their curved sharp ends in various lengths joined together as a Japanese fan at the back of the throne. Short, thicker crystals created a seat which formed the foundation of the throne, firmly erected into the floating island. Moving a bit closer, Henry could see a figure lounging on the throne. Dressed all in black it was difficult to distinguish his features from the throne. Once they got to sixty feet away, the figure in black rose up from his seat and approached his guests. Henry slowed down to allow Christ to step forward and face the master of this underworld reality.

Contrary to Henry's expectations, the figure wore a classy black suit immaculately tailored to his frame. Beneath the buttoned up waistcoat, he wore a crisp white shirt, and the knot of a silky red tie revealed itself to complete the picture of unequivocal style. His face was unusually pale and well-manicured. A pointed, short black beard further emphasised the color of his skin. His long, curly black hair framed his elongated face, giving it utmost elegance. His black eyes, with unusually long eye lashes, were proportionally placed on either side of his straight nose completing the image of this very attractive man, who in different circumstances would be hard to resist by any gender. Henry had a good idea of who he was facing, and the pretentious mask of a gentleman was not going to fool him.

The approaching figures of Christ and the man in black stopped about six feet apart and firmly greeted each other. They nodded their heads and placed their right hands across their chests. The man in black was the first to speak.

"Welcome to my humble abode. What did I do to deserve a visit from such a prestigious guest?"

His words were pronounced with a most pleasant timbre of voice and a wide smile plastered across his face.

Christ smiled back warmly saying, "I have come with a friend who would like to learn about, as you called it, your 'humble abode'."

Shifting his eyes to Henry, the master of the chamber said, "Your friend is my friend," and gesturing with his right hand he invited Henry to step forward. "It will be my pleasure to assist him within the scope of my ability."

Henry hesitantly stepped forward and glancing at Christ asked, "Are you leaving?"

"Yes, I have to. Be still and open minded. I will meet you when you are done."

On saying that, Christ expressed his gratitude to the owner of the place and withdrew.

As they stood alone, the man in black moved closer to Henry and attentively gazed into his eyes.

"Have no fear, Henry, see this as another opportunity to broaden your vision and the level of your consciousness. After all, you are one of those souls who prefer to study realms not only horizontally, but vertically as well. Hell, unfortunately, is an integral part of all newly formed physical realities such as Earth, along with their inhabitants. Denying its existence makes the picture of creation incomplete."

Gaining a bit more courage and confidence from the way in which the man in black spoke to him, Henry said, "It's hard to study something that we all try to escape."

"That is because of a lack of awareness of this place's origin and its very purpose."

"Before you enlighten me in this matter," Henry respectfully addressed his host, "may I please ask how to address you?"

"Of all of the most unpleasant names that humanity has awarded me, I prefer to be called Hades, God of the underworld. This is how the ancient Greeks called me."

"Were there other titles before that?"

"No, just Hades."

"So where do we go from here?" asked Henry with a deep sigh.

"To start with, I would like to show you around. To give you a short excursion into the world of humans misachievements and self-punishment. A world of mastered skills in planting fear into the hearts of those who trust."

"I am not sure that I understand your reference?" said Henry a bit confused.

Hades sighed deeply saying, "Please follow me and you will soon understand."

The floating platform that they were standing on was about 150 feet in diameter with nothing on it but Hades' throne. Hades led the way toward the edge of the island, with Henry following, expecting another freefall, this time straight into flames of hell itself. But unexpectedly a narrow staircase unfurled itself right down to the edge of the boiling lava. Hades began the descent with Henry one step behind. Henry couldn't help noticing a deep sadness, perhaps even pain, that was overshadowing Hades' soul. Overall, he was nothing like what Henry expected him to be. Not on the outside and especially not on his inside. It was hard to imagine that this well-spoken, well-mannered, and deeply sympathetic soul was in charge of hell.

Hades stopped for a moment and looking at Henry asked, "Disappointed?"

Used to having souls read his mind, Henry said, "I think a better choice of words would be surprised."

"I hope in a good way," said Hades, continuing to descend into the depths of the deepest deep.

Observing the multi-level structure spiralling down, Henry asked, "How many floors are there?"

"As you can see, one level slides into the next, creating a constant decline, but generally there are seven," Hades answered, adding a moment later, "Although it can vary according to humanity's development."

"Is it getting less or more?"

"Less," answered Hades.

When the outline of the first level became clearly visible Henry could not resist to remark, "It is reminding me of an ordinary motel corridor."

The first floor was the widest in the cone. It was neatly balustraded with an ancient dark gray stone banister. It seemed as though it was purposefully placed to prevent someone from accidently falling to the level below that was smaller in diameter, and protruding slightly further toward the center. The same applied to every level below in this colossal cavity. The banister framed a six foot wide corridor on one side, and a black wall on the other. Dark wooden doors lined up, one next to the other, hard to notice at first glance. They were cut into the black wall, similarly unattractively in their appearance.

"What is behind these doors?" Henry asked.

"Prison cells," answered Hades.

"Do they have inmates?"

"Most do."

"Did you incarcerate them?"

"No, they did," answered Hades.

"Are you saying the doors are not locked?"

"Yes, that is exactly what I am saying. Every resident is free to walk out, not only from these doors, but from this place as well."

"I guess then that they are not ready."

"Yes, I call them self-condemned souls."

Hades stopped, looked at one of the tightly closed doors, and with a heavy heart said, "Most of them are old souls. Souls with an exaggerated level of self-judgement. Souls who have convinced themselves that they have committed terrible sins and deserve nothing but punishment."

"I've heard about this place, and learned how difficult it is to free them from their own perceptions of right and wrong."

"And you know who should be blamed for this!"

"I presume society," answered Henry.

"The biggest blame in this lies on the shoulders of organized religion."

"Are you talking about Christianity?" Henry asked.

"Christianity, too. This reality is nothing but an extension of religious doctrination."

"Are you saying that the true master of this place is Jesus Christ himself?"

"The answer to this question is not simple and requires an excursion back into the past, to the time of the birth and formation of Christianity and Christ himself as a God."

"Sorry for the interruption," Henry jumped in, "but I specifically asked him, and his answer was that he is not a God. Besides, he always refers to his Father above him."

Hades smiled ironically saying, "If people on Earth begin to see you as a God, pray with your name on their lips, and expect miracles to happen through you, whether or not you want it, you become a God. And let me tell you, to me he is a God. I have never known someone so attentively, lovingly, and selflessly devoting themselves to their duties. His kingdom is growing by the hour, and him along with it."

"Now I have to ask probably the most common question. What is his formula, or recipe of success?"

Hades gave some thought to this question, and after a short pause he said, "In one word, love."

"Love?" asked Henry.

"Yes. If by any chance while being a human you consciously find a place in your heart for him, Christ will shower you with love from head to toe. You will feel loved beyond your wildest imagination. Many lonely souls trapped in a human body deprived of that magnificent feeling once experienced, cannot get enough of it. This is the reason why today's churches on Earth are filled with congregations craving that love. Christ speaks through pastors and preachers in their language, and what is important, at the same level as the congregation. Above all, he fills those churches with love, compassion, and unconditional forgiveness, warmly welcoming everyone into his arms. Ancient churches, opulent in their appearance and magnitude, are giving up their congregations to newly built and aesthetically simple ones with no attributes of Christianity at all. Just four walls and rows and rows of chairs. From mighty unreachable heights where churches used to dwell in the past, there is no trace. They have learned to speak to their congregations in a language that they can understand and relate to. Once high and almighty priests become simple preachers trying to help their fellow humans to find their way out of the mess that they created for themselves. Preachers who speak in their language, who have also been in the same mess, or even in a worse situation, finding in themselves enough willpower not only to rise and overcome their demons, but also to become teachers of others as well. Let me share with you a small secret, those are Christ's favorites, and they have his full support."

"This all makes so much sense," said Henry stepping in.

"I have seen some of those churches filled to capacity. The attendance is absolutely crazy, with a staggering number of souls being attracted to them despite the scams that happen in some of these institutions."

"Unfortunately those preachers are vulnerable to temptation, just like any other human, and it is understandable and forgivable."

"Wow! How?" Henry protested.

"For 2000 years Christianity cultivated perfect priests. Flawless humans being an example for others to follow. Free of sins, completely detached from the real world. Well educated theologians which can memorize the most important verses from the Bible. In short 'saints'. In reality, people want to hear from sinners like themselves, and Christ speaks through these preachers, finding his way into the hearts of ordinary humans."

Hades stopped his speech, giving Henry time to grasp the magnitude of Christ.

Henry looked around and said, "Judging by the size of this place and the darkness of the lower levels, the inhabitants will not free themselves to walk out."

"Yes, you are right," Hades nodded sadly. "The deeper you are placed, the bigger your sins, Bigger sins, harsher punishment."

"So where in all of this is the love and forgiveness so adamantly preached by Christ?"

"I am pretty sure that by the end of this journey you will have the answer to your question."

DESCENT

They were descending at the same time as they were talking on their way to the second level of this strange "hotel".

"Dear Henry," Hades explained, "This place has an ancient history of existence, as long as humanity's time on Earth. Hell, by definition, is a creation of human imagination. You know how it works. Any crazy idea fed with enough energy will manifest into reality. For thousands upon thousands of Earth years the ruling elite constrained obedient souls through fear, the best and most effective method to manipulate human minds. The place we are in now has been through multiple transformations. The harsher the living conditions on Earth, the more horrifying this realty was, but now as you can see it is more 'civilized'."

"As above, so below," commented Henry.

"Precisely."

"I get it," said Henry.

"This place represents and stands as a token of humanity's collective perception of good and bad, and as a result this is the ultimate place for the punishment of wrong doers."

"What I do not understand is what is Christ's role in all of this?"

"Okay, let me tell you this much, followers of his teaching are the biggest contributors of souls to this place. Frightened and lost they need his guidance to be freed from their own perceptions of righteousness and sin."

"Does he do this personally?"

"If appointed guides are unable to help, then he will definitely step in. Besides, there are souls residing right in the very end of this structure, waiting for his verdict," Hades said pointing to the bottom of the gigantic cavity.

"Verdict?" asked Henry.

"Yes, his final decision to save or destroy them."

"Destroying doesn't sound like something that Christ would

do."

"Sometimes the destruction of souls is the only, and most merciful way of saving them from themselves."

Noticing Henry's confusion Hades said, "Once we get to the bottom you will understand."

Arriving at the second level, "Who is incarcerated behind these walls?" asked Henry.

"Similar to those who reside one level above. Self-incarceration following their realization of the impact of their actions."

Henry noticed that the setup here was similar to the one above, but that the number of doors was a lot less.

He asked, "Does the wider distance between doors mean that the holding cells are bigger in size?"

"Good observation. Behind these doors are not confined spaces, but rather realities on their own. By the way, you have been in one of them not long ago."

Henry reacted in surprise.

"The battlefield," Hades reminded him, "The one that you visited with Soccy. Remember?"

"Oh yes, how could I forget. It was so real and frightening. A terrible place to be for any soul."

"Agreed," Hades confirmed.

"So, behind these doors are warriors who cannot find their way to freedom?"

"Not only. I would say behind these doors are those innocent young souls who naively believed that their actions served a good cause. Some of them saw themselves as liberators of nations, or revolutionaries who committed everything they had and took with them many innocent lives for a higher cause. In short, those who were skilfully manipulated by stronger minds in service their selfish agendas to dominate or possess things that they were not entitled to."

"There is another question coming to mind," said Henry. "How do souls end up here if they were so certain that their actions were justified? I know for a fact that most of them died in battle by other soldiers just like them."

"What are you trying to say?" Hades asked, confused by the question.

"I do not find much of a reason for them to be here. Besides, death on a battlefield is so sudden, most of them don't even realize that they have been killed. In the end it is just soldier against soldier, and I don't see any injustice in their actions."

"I see now," said Hades. "Behind these doors are mostly soldiers who took the lives of civilians. Women and innocent children. Martyrs who blow themselves up trusting the words of their spiritual teachers. Those who saw no value in the human lives that they took, with pulling their triggers as easy as cutting a loaf of bread."

Henry stopped walking for a moment, fixing his attention on one of the doors. Hades stopped as well.

"Do you want to visit one of them?"

"I am gravitating toward one of them," said Henry, pointing to a door distressed by time and the elements.

"You must be brave to do that!"

"Still, I am interested."

"I have to warn you, once you step in, their reality may become your reality, and you may have to go through and experience all that they are."

"I know that, but then I have you, almighty Hades, by my side. Besides, I know Jesus himself personally. So, what do I have to be frightened of?" Henry said jokingly.

"Once you are inside, you are on your own," Hades warned. "The door that you are looking at, and the reality that it holds behind it, has no connection to Christ. Anti-Christ would be a short description of the resident of this cell."

"Still," Henry insisted.

"Be my guest," said Hades.

As he fixated his attention on the door chosen by Henry, a new pathway formed leading them to their new destination.

When they stood outside the door, Hades looked at Henry and asked, "Why do you want to do this? Most visitors to this place prefer to be observers."

"To be in hell and not to have a taste of it would not be me."

As Henry said those words, he placed his hand on the black door knob, but before he had a chance to turn it Hades placed his hand over Henry's.

"Just before you enter, I would like to warn you, you need to be prepared for any turn of events, as they might be very unpleasant." Hades gently squeezed Henry's hand and for the last time asked, "Are you certain about this?"

"Maybe this is my chance to help a lost soul to find the light."

Hades placed his right hand on Henry's shoulder saying, "Your quest is noble, but please do not have high hopes, and remember, whoever is inside of this cell is quite aware of their whereabouts, but can't see a way out."

“Thank you,” Henry said, and by turning the knob pushed the heavy door in.

Inside, absolute darkness ruled. Even the orange/red blinks of light on the outside could not find their way into this confinement. The place seemed to have been made to not only trap souls, but the light, also. Henry closed the door behind him and concentrated his attention on his surroundings. A while later the interior began to reveal itself. Previously hardly separable shades of black surrendered their grip, and suddenly a pale light appeared from nowhere, unmasking the shape of the room and its contents. What amazed Henry the most was that the source of this light was his own body. He had begun to radiate a soft glow, enough to conquer the unwilling dingy black. Slowly he could distinguish the walls of the room, the ceiling, and the concrete floor that he was standing on. The room was about twelve feet by twelve feet with a low ceiling just high enough for Henry to stand under at full height. The corners of the cell were still covered in darkness, and as Henry chose to observe them the intensity of his glow increased, revealing the horrifying reality that he had just stepped into.

SUBSTITUTION

Thales knew that he couldn't entirely rely on Henry with respect to being Croton's guide. Croton was too dear to his heart to be brushed off into the hands of an amateur newcomer, unfit for his duties. When Thales proposed Henry to be Croton's guide to find his one and only, he was mostly counting on Rose, and she did not let him down. But when Croton grew older, he was in need of Henry's guidance, or at least his presence. Being well known amongst Planners as a man of drastic measures, Thales strategically chose to lock Henry in the Earth realm by sending Rose back to Earth. He was hoping that once separated, Henry would not leave Rose's side until her return to the world of spirit. At the same time, this would keep him close to Croton, having the opportunity to keep his eyes on both of them. Besides, Rose was such a well-behaved child that Henry would have enough time to concentrate his attentions on Croton, and to keep him away from shady deals, because he was inclined to get involved in such even in his previous lifetimes on Earth. His high status, and the respect of society that he was so accustomed to, would have been impossible to achieve without a considerable amount of money. The country that Croton was born in did not offer much opportunity for legal enrichment, leaving him with no option but to break the law and drown himself up to his ears in the swamp of corruption. Unfortunately, his so carefully orchestrated and flawlessly executed plan had backfired. Even little Rose could not capture Henry's free spirit and his unquenchable appetite for knowledge. By giving his approval and assistance for him to meet Christ, Thales knew that this adventure could trap Henry for quite some time. This length of time was impossible to predict even for this great Planner. Knowing Christ's personality, the magnitude of his presence, and the amount of love he could project, left no doubt that Henry would be most welcomed, and there will be no doors locked to him in Christ's kingdom. Being aware of all these facts, and having no suitable guide to replace Henry, Thales still encouraged him to follow Gertrude. He had to stick with the "supreme code of Planners" that stipulated that they had to provide conditions for soul's growth by all means. Taking into consideration all pros and cons, Thales chose to step into Croton's life before things could get out of hand. The accelerating decline of Croton's morals could have destroyed his relationship with Gaya, and this was not Thales' intent.

"I have to put an end to this," Thales thought to himself.

After a short meeting with his superior, Thales secured permission to substitute for Henry as Croton's guide. After all, no one knew him better than Thales, and his intervention into the flow of Croton's life could spare him taking another life to accomplish his chosen tasks.

"Drastic measures have to be taken," Thales said to himself as he stepped into Croton's world.

Such strong words vocalized by any Planner, addressed to any human, could have meant nothing but upcoming trouble. Trouble of a major scale. In a scale that qualifies to be called a major event, where the worst scenario was known only to the Planner himself, but not it's finale due to the unpredictability of human behavior when deep emotions are awakened.

Thales found Croton in his office submerged deeply into the blueprints of a new building. A nine-story block of residential apartments ready to be handed over to their owners. As Thales stepped in he noticed a "Punisher" dressed all in black, standing at Croton's left hand, observing his train of thoughts. On noticing Thales' presence, he stepped forward and respectfully greeted him.

Thales slightly nodded his head in return and asked, "Still the same?"

"Yes, my Lord," answered the Punisher, and looking at Croton added, "Finding the short cuts made by builders and profiting from them."

Thales cringed his face in dissatisfaction and asked, "What about Gaya?"

"We have no business with her."

"I see," said Thales. He slowly walked around Croton's desk until he stood at his back and said, "I will take charge from here."

The Punisher bowed his head saying, "As you wish, my Lord. Before I leave, I must say that he deserves to be in hell."

"I will be the judge of that," answered Thales, and by nodding his head let the Punisher know that it was time for him to leave.

The Punisher bowed again and disappeared.

Thales never liked Punishers, but the importance of their role in the healthy development of humanity was an undeniable fact. He always said, “Humans should know that no one is above the laws of creation, and once disturbed, balance has to be restored”, and this is what the Punishers were doing. Long before Thales advised Croton to take another life as a human, he designed for him a beautiful life tree, one that he was absolutely certain was one of his best creations. He left most of the branches long, signifying a long life, but some of them he cut short, which meant only one thing…an abrupt exit…death at a young age. Knowing Croton’s weaknesses from the chain of previous lives on Earth, Thales chose to leave some options open that he could manipulate later. Depending on how Croton’s character developed and how he behaved in harsh circumstances in a place filled with temptations and low moral standards.

CONFLICT

At 5pm Croton packed away the blueprints that he had so meticulously been studying, and ten minutes later he was driving home on a street seeded on either side with majestic tall buildings, resembling a line of stern-faced soldiers on a parade ground. Every time he rode through those streets his heart filled with pride knowing that his inputs, even though small, contributed toward their existence. If it wasn't for his precious signature, none of the current residents would have had the opportunity to become happy owners of their own living spaces. This fact fed Croton's ego, leaving no space for doubts, but only disappointment at helping total strangers who would never know of his existence, nor the job that he had done for them.

Submerged in these random thoughts Croton arrived home and parked his car in the ground-level parking. The unusually designed building that he lived in was constructed for elite residents, and if it wasn't for his father's, Raymond's, intervention, this young family would never have had the opportunity to own such a prestigious apartment. A few moments later and Croton was standing at the entrance to his home. All this time Thales was following him, and his thoughts, so that he could grasp the depth of his character. A glimpse back in time to assess the extent of Croton's development left Thales deeply unsatisfied, but most of his interest lay in the development of his relationship with Gaya, the gentle and caring soul that Thales personally chose to partner with Croton in this physical life. He knew that these two souls belonged together and the tiny hope that one human life on Earth would be enough to merge them into one still smouldered in his heart.

Croton inserted his key into the door and cautiously stepped into the apartment. No one was there to welcome him home from work.

"Anyone home?" Croton tossed the question into the air

hoping to find a responder.

Gaya reluctantly stepped out from the kitchen. leaned against the door frame and said, “This is uncommon for you.”

“How so?”

“To see you back from work at this early,” answered Gaya hostilely.

“You know me, my love, I always come back home.”

“I know you do, but the question is at what time?”

“It is only 5:45,” Croton said innocently pointing to his wristwatch.

“What about yesterday, and the day before, and many days before that? Our poor child has forgotten what her father looks like.”

Croton reached into his back pocket to retrieve a wad of bank notes and offer them to Gaya saying, “Maybe this will sweeten my bitter wife!”

Gaya looked at the wad contemptuously, saying irritably, “I don’t need your goddamned money, especially when I know the price tag attached to them.”

“This is very unfair,” protested Croton, “I work hard, you know, to provide for my family. I want you and Rose to have everything of the very best.”

“All I want is you,” said Gaya holding back tears. “No, I do not want you. I hate you. I want my husband back. The one that I fell in love with. The one who couldn’t wait to come home to me. The one who actually noticed my presence in the house.”

“I am sorry,” Croton stepped in, “But it is hard to read you. You kept on complaining when we had no money, and now you are complaining because I am making money. Unfortunately, getting together with colleagues after work is a part of my job, and I cannot say no to them. I have to fit in.”

“To fit in with your partners in crime!”

“Please stop it,” Croton shouted loudly.

“I will not. I have kept quiet long enough and now I will say it all.”

Croton braced himself for another portion of fresh accusations.

“Your so-called gatherings are nothing but an excuse to get drunk and discuss your shady deals. And you know why alcohol is an essential part of these assemblyies…?”

“Enlighten me,” sarcastically threw Croton.

“Because you have to drown your conscience in the bottom of the vodka glass before taking another sin upon your soul.”

Croton listened quietly without further interruption, letting

Gaya run out of steam, and then to step in with his counter argument.

"Yes," Gaya kept going, "You know that this money is dirty and one day we will all have to pay the price. Let me tell you now, the payment will be heavy, mark my words."

"Are you finished?"

"No. I'm just getting warmed up. There is more for you to listen to. Rose is already three and she has begun to ask questions that I don't have answers for. She hardly ever sees you. I do not know what to tell her when she asks, 'When will Daddy be home?' Even when you are home, most of the time you are drunk, too tired, or asleep. And I am not mentioning my own needs as a young woman still."

Those words were the last drop into the overflowed glass of Croton's patience. He threw the wad of money on the floor and stormed out of the apartment, slamming the door into Gaya's face.

"Yes, sure, go away. Run from the problems instead of facing them. Go to your 'friends' and God knows where else you go. I will not be surprised if one day I find out about a mistress in your life."

As she said these last words, Gaya kicked the money under the chair, and hardly suppressing tears ran into her bedroom to wet a pillow, which had not yet dried from her previous visit.

What he had just witnesses upset Thales immensely. The life that he had so carefully planned for Gaya and Croton was falling apart, and dragging with it the beautiful future that he had paved for them. A quick excursion back in time to grasp the entirety of Croton's descent as a father, husband, and human left no doubt in Thales' mind that now was the time to step in and interfere in the flow of upcoming events.

"I think the time for Plan B has arrived," said Thales, leaving the world of humans with their weaknesses and deceptions to add another twist into the already complicated life of Gaya and Croton.

BACK TO INFERNO

As Henry managed to increase his luminescence, a pair of frightened eyes looking directly at him pierced the darkness. A second later he grasped the entire picture, which was heart breaking and chilling at the same time. Henry found a frightened woman dressed all in black, shoved by herself into a corner of the cell in an attempt to be invisible to the uninvited guest. All Henry could see was her dark brown eyes with long eyelashes framed by the black fabric that covered the rest of her body. Judging by her outfit Henry concluded that she was Muslim. The first question that surfaced in his mind was, *"What is a Muslim woman doing in a Christian hell?"*

Once her hiding place was uncovered, the woman spoke. "Did I hurt you, too?"

Not knowing what the woman was referring to, Henry said, "No, you did not."

"Oh, thank God," the woman exhaled with great relief.

Her next question caught Henry completely off-guard.

"Are you an angel come to save me?"

Henry momentarily juggled with his answer, either yes or no. To say yes would probably help him to assist this woman, but on the other hand a lie may backfire in a most unexpected way.

"No," answered Henry, " I am not an angel."

Noticing her disappointment he rushed to say, "But I am here to help you."

"Do you even know what I have done?" asked the woman in black.

"I was hoping that you will tell me."

She took a deep sigh, lowered her eyes and with a heavy weight in her voice said, "Go away. Nobody can help me. There is no forgiveness for what I have done."

"What did you do? Share with me. I know I can help," said Henry hoping to win her trust.

She raised her head, gazed into Henry's eyes, paused, and then lowered her head again saying hopelessly, "How can you help someone who wants to die in a place where there is no death? How can you help someone who wants to fall into an unconscious slumber and to wake up with no memories of the past in a place where you cannot sleep, and your past becomes your infinite present."

On saying these last words, she dropped her head between knees. For the moment Henry stumbled with no trace left of the confidence he had had on entering the cell. He was lost for words. He realized the truth in her statement and his inability to change anything in how things were. He wanted to turn around and leave, accepting his incapacity to help this poor Muslim girl. A girl who was trapped in this horrible place with her irreversible past. But some unseen force stopped him. He lowered himself to her level to take a second go.

Henry crouched on his knees, the way a Muslim man would have done during Namaz "prayers" and addressed the girl.

"What is your name?" he asked.

"Nazia," whispered the girl.

"Is there any special meaning to your name?" Henry asked genuinely interested.

She looked at Henry, and with deep sadness in her eyes smiled and said, "It means proud."

"That is a beautiful name," Henry said trying to cheer her up.

She hid her face again saying, "I hold no pride in what I have done."

Henry's first impulse was to ask, "What the hell have you done and let me see if I can help you", but the fear of being unable to understand due to his ignorance in the matters of Islamic culture and religion, he paused. A quick review into his memory bank revealed nothing but the names of Allah and the prophet Mohammed. He was completely unaware of their teachings, and he had an overall negativity toward the entire religion and its followers implanted into his mind at a young age while he was still in his physical body.

He hesitantly reached his hand to the girl saying, "Allow me to see you."

The girl looked at him and asked, "Are you sure?"

"Yes, honor me please."

Nazia retrieved her hand from the pile of loose black fabric and cautiously placed it on top of Henry's offered palm. She looked straight into his eyes and her story began.

REVENGE

The momentarily dark room that they were in disappeared and a bright light painfully penetrated Henry's vision. Instinctively he covered his face, but then quickly removed his hand to allow a small portion of the sun's glare to welcome him into Nazia's past. Henry found himself standing in the middle of a busy road filled with people, cars, motorbikes, and bicycles. At first, he found it difficult to adjust to this drastic change of scenery, but then judging by the style of clothing worn and the familiar brands of cars on the road, he realized that he was in a vibrant Eastern city. Even though the cars were familiar to him, they were old worn-out models. The complete absence of any rules and regulations and the chaotic movement of the vehicles and inhabitants of this city created a great deal of dissonance in Henry's mind, who was used to an orderly behavior and organized flow of traffic. The people and funny looking bikes and cars tried to avoid each other in their course leaving no vacant spaces.

After a while of observation Henry realized that there actually was order in the seeming disorder. He stood motionless allowing everyone to find their way around him. For the moment, the surroundings became irrelevant, being replaced by the indecisiveness of the age-old question "to do, or not to do". Henry felt his body begin to pump adrenaline into his brain affecting his ability to think rationally. His thoughts became disorganized, scattered, and meaningless in search of the answer. Henry observed himself in a shop window and the image he saw was expected…he was the woman in the black dress. "It could not be any different, I had to be in her body", Henry admitted sadly. Accepting the fact of his present situation, Henry realized that the answer to the dilemma in Nazia's mind had been found, and she was on the move.

She was rapidly making her way through the multitude of people dressed in all shades of earthy colors. Soon Henry realized that his breath was not flowing the way it usually should, something was definitely obstructing the supply of oxygen. He touched his face saying, "Niqab." He could not recall the origin of the name for this women's dress where only the eyes are visible. Regardless, he was moving forward inside her body in search of something important. Something significant that was going to define the purpose of her search. A couple of blocks later, breathing heavily due to the fabric across his face and the uncomfortably tight underwear across his waist, Henry stood in front of a Christian church. It was built of white marble, but the stone had lost its purity from the foundation up due to pollution and human waste. After a short observation of his surroundings, Henry, in Nazia's body, looked up at the entrance. Heavy wooden double doors stood invitingly open winning over the last remnants of Nazia's indecisiveness. Involuntarily she tried to fix the tight corset around her waist to make it more comfortable. Finally, having made up her mind, she ascended the worn marble stairs to the inviting entrance.

"Why is she going into a Christian church?" Henry asked himself, momentarily disconnecting from Nazia. "What could she have done to bring herself to such a state of mind where self-forgiveness is not an option."

A second later Henry stepped back into Nazia's body, but now everything was different. The bond between their states of consciousness became so strong that he completely lost his identity and grew into hers. With each step her heartbeat got faster, clouding her mind and vision. At the heavy doors she stopped and leaned against the door frame and took a couple of deep breaths to calm herself down and concentrate her mind on the task ahead.

An unknown Arabic man appeared in front of her, looking at her with eyes filled with love and tenderness. Nazia's chest became inflamed with hate and the uncontrollable urge for revenge. Whatever she had committed herself to suddenly became so clear and undoubtedly righteous.

With a whisper on her lips, "I'm coming to you, my love," she firmly stepped into the church.

The church was filled to its capacity, and unable to find vacant seats, some members of the congregation were standing along the walls. The priest at the pulpit was mumbling verses from the Bible. In a split second she had taken everything in and had moved into the main aisle. Next, Nazia closed her eyes so as not to see the faces of those who noticed her and placed her hand under her dress where the uncomfortable corset was still embracing her slim body. The well rehearsed motion to perfection made it easy for her index finger to locate a cool metal ring and with a loud, "Allahu Akbar", she pulled the ring.

An enormous force threw Henry out of Nazia's body and the unbearably loud explosion blocked his hearing and vision at the same time. When the dust had settled, and Henry regained his senses, a horrifying picture slowly revealed itself. Unable to observe the results of Nazia's act Henry immediately pulled his hands back, disconnecting the lifeline between their minds.

Henry was still sitting on the floor of the dark room in front of Nazia. His breathing was heavy, and his eyes were wide open, filled with horror and staring directly at Nazia.

"Still adamant to help?" Nazia asked calmly.

Lost for words and in the depth of her atrocious act, Henry stood up, and excusing himself, walked out of the door. Hades was there waiting for his reappearance, anticipating Henry's retreat.

"So?" asked Hades sensing confusion and disorientation in Henry's behavior.

Henry closed the door behind him and leaned against it.

"Are you all right?" Hades asked indifferently.

Henry cast his eyes upward beyond the confinements of the place he was in, saying, "How can One forgive her?"

Knowing exactly to whom those words were addressed, Hades said, "He can forgive her. The question is can she forgive herself?"

On saying these words Hades placed his right hand on Henry's shoulder, inviting him to step away from the door and the troubles that it was holding behind it.

"Come, let's go. You have tried."

But, for some unknown reason Henry objected saying, "I am not done yet."

"Do you wish to go back?"

"Yes," Henry confirmed adamantly.

"Come on, my friend, let's go. This is not your fight. You are not responsible for her actions. Don't make it your problem. She is exactly where she belongs."

"Like I said, I am not through yet," Henry insisted.

Hades took a deep sigh and said, "So you want to save her soul from the depths of hell?" Hades asked with an ironic smile.

"Yes I do," answered Henry.

Hades looked directly into Henry's eyes and with a chilling voice said, "Sorry, my friend, you failed. You pulled out at the most important time. At the very time when you were supposed to witness the result of her act. You failed her," repeated Hades. His last words echoed through the corridors, returning in a condemning and accusational tone.

"What do you mean?"

"If you really want to ease her pain, you have to share it with her. You have to take some of the weight that she carries upon your shoulders. To go through what she went through. To feel what she felt. To see what she saw. Without that, it is all nonsense and empty words filled with pretentious bravery and show of chivalry."

Without saying a word, Henry turned around and stepped back into Nazia's cell.

"You're back!" Henry heard as he stepped in.

"Yes I am."

"Where did you go?"

"I just walked out of the door," Henry said, confused by such a seemingly obvious question. "Didn't you see me walking in and out of the room?"

"No. All I saw was you here and then suddenly you disappeared. And you are back again." The she fell quiet before adding, "And that is what matters."

"I see," said Henry, realizing that the poor girl cannot see a door, and with that, the exit from her personal nightmare.

He sat back down on the floor offering her both of his hands. Nazia gently placed her palms in his, and Henry closed his eyes.

The hall of the once majestic church was unrecognizable. Settled dust unveiled the magnitude of destruction and the scale of human tragedy. Lifeless bodies around the epicenter of the explosion and previous rows of well organized benches, were all piled up on top of each other. In a split second, perfection had become destruction, hope into despair, and life into death. The air was filled with moans and pleas for help. Henry tried to avoid looking at the mutilated corpses, afraid of carrying such gruesome images with him for eternity.

Suddenly Henry felt the presence of another soul standing next to him. Hades, in his immaculate black suit, was also witnessing the tragedy.

"Do you mind if I join you?" he asked.

"No, not at all. I am actually glad that you are here…but how did you get here?" asked confused Henry.

"This is still my reality," answered smiling, Hades.

"How many?" asked Henry without moving his eyes from the scene.

"Thirty souls left their bodies instantaneously. Another five later in hospital. Over fifty ended up with various degrees of injuries."

"There is no excuse for what she has done," Henry said helplessly observing the suffering of the wounded. His heart was overflowing with anger toward Nazia, and sorrow toward those who survived this tragedy.

"Had enough of human reality? Or should I say, irrational stupidity? Can we go now?"

Henry continued to observe the surroundings, capturing into his memory, and into his soul, the pain of each survivor.

"Why?" he asked a moment later.

Hades raised his right hand and the entire scene froze. "Are you asking about Nazia's motives?"

"Yes. How can someone in their right mind do something like this. To take the lives of innocent people as well as her own… why?"

"I guess then you want to stay," said Hades since his offer to leave was left unanswered. Hades sighed deeply and said, "Why don't you direct those questions to Nazia herself and let's see what she will answer."

"Okay. One more thing I'd like to know," asked Henry.

"And what is that?"

"What happened to her?"

Hades raised his eyebrows saying, "Isn't it obvious?"

"I know what happened to her body. I am more interested in the journey of her released soul. Where did she go?"

"She was immediately pulled into the reality that she vibrationally belongs to. You know the drill."

"I know the procedure. It is the details that I am interested in. If I am not mistaken, she should expect to be in heaven as reward for her bravery."

"Yes, you are right. She saw herself as a Jihadist—a warrior of Allah against non-believers."

"I guess that would be all non-Muslims?" asked Henry.

"Absolutely right," confirmed Hades.

"Honestly, I am dying to see what kind of reality she is pulled into."

"I can help you with that, but first you have to step out of Nazia's cell, remember you are still sitting there."

"Oh yes," Henry suddenly realized, and pulling his hands back he reappeared in Nazia's confinement.

"Why did you do that?" Henry threw the question at Nazia

as he faced her.

Nazia looked at him hopelessly and said, "I was blinded by anger and revenge."

"But…this is so stupid and cruel. To cut short your own life and the lives of others. Causing enormous pain and emotional suffering, not only to those who were in the church, but to their relatives, also."

Nazia immediately pulled herself back into the dark corner covering her face with her hands.

"What, now you are pulling away from me!"

"No, it's just too painful."

Henry realized that he had touched an exposed nerve.

"Why," whispered Henry compassionately.

"I had to meet them one by one. All of the family members of those who I have killed."

Henry was confused and asked for clarity, "Are you saying that you had to meet, not the souls of those you killed, but instead their relatives?"

"Yes. Though to meet was probably the wrong choice of words. I meant to say that I felt all that they felt by losing their loved ones. One by one I stepped into their lives, witnessed their pain, their hopelessness, and their hate. Yes, hate toward the Jihadist who had taken their husbands, wives, children, and parents from them. Ripped them out of their lives… Eventually I began to hate myself. There was a time that I wanted to kill myself, just to fall into an unconscious sleep and never wake up again. But as you know, one cannot do that here."

Henry kept quiet letting Nazia's cry for help settle, and then said, "Part of me feels sorry for you, but the other part…"

"I know what you feel. I feel the same way, except there is no sorrow left for myself, just hate. One big repulsive hatred of what is left of me."

They sat quietly for a while until Henry broke the silence, "Did you meet the souls of those who you killed?"

"No, not personally. Only through their relatives. It might sound strange, but I learned to love them."

"To love them?" Henry asked uncertainly.

"I know it seems weird. Before my actions I had only one love in my life, my husband…"

"What happened to him?" Henry interrupted.

"He was killed by a Christian mob."

"I see, and you were obviously looking for revenge."

"Yes, I had learned to hate Christians, and everything that

they stand for and believe in."

"But surely this should not be enough to orchestrate such an act of mass murder?"

"Imam, of the local community Mosque, helped to redirect my anger."

"Is that the name of the man who gave you the explosive devise?"

"No, Imam means spiritual leader, teacher."

"I seeeeee…"

"Please, at least you do not judge me. I was naive, gullible, and hateful. I truely believed that it was the only way to have my revenge. Plus, there was a bonus."

"Bonus?" asked surprised Henry.

"Yes, they told me that I would go to heaven and finally see my beloved husband again."

"And, did you?" asked Henry.

"None of what Imam promised became reality. Actually, everything was the opposite of my expectations."

"So, you still haven't seen him?"

"Hassan? No, I haven't. I have learned that he is in Jannah (heaven). A place where I cannot gain access because of what I have done."

"Do you realize where you actually are?" Henry asked.

"Yes, I do. I am in Christian hell, and I deserve to be here."

Henry got up from his knees and politely said, "Let me leave you for now."

"Will you be back?" Nazia asked with eyes filled with hope.

"I promise I will return. There is something I need to find out first," he said as he walked out of her cell.

Hades was waiting for his exit, leaning against the balustrade with his arms across his chest.

Henry closed the door behind him and addressed Hades, "Please walk me through what happened to her when she departed the physical world."

"Be my guest," Hades said placing his hand on Henry's shoulder.

PROMISED JANNAH

Henry found himself standing in a mosque beautifully decorated with colorful mosaics. The floors were draped with Persian carpets, impressive in their size and intricacy of their design. High walls framed by columns were crowned with a dome encrusted with intricate golden mosaic of complex geometrical patterns. At the center of the dome, at its highest point, was a hexagonal opening through which an intense stream of light rushed down to the floor, creating a bright spot of light on the carpets below.

Henry, standing next to Hades, fixated his eyes on the spot in expectation of something to happen. The rising suspense of a soul deserving to claim the spot charged the air around it, ready to manifest itself into the expected object. The anticipation did not disappoint, with the spot transforming itself into a woman dressed in black. Henry couldn't see her face, but a glimpse at Hades' face confirmed his suspicions.

Nazia appeared, looking confused and frightened. The explosion which should have ripped her body apart, causing excruciating pain, seemed to have no effect. Everything happened instantaneously and she had no chance to adjust herself to this altered reality. All she could remember was the ring that she pulled out from one of the many grenades attached to her waist…but the outcome of her actions remained unknown to her due to the immediate change of location. She closed her eyes in a Christian church and opened them in a Mosque, standing all alone right in the middle of it.

"I guess she cannot see us?" Henry asked.

"No," confirmed Hades.

Done with her observation of her new surroundings Nazia looked up at the source of light showering her from head to toes.

"What now?" Henry asked impatiently.

"Wait and you will see," replied Hades

As he finished his sentence a small rectangular door appeared in the wall that Nazia was facing. One after another, three figures dressed in long white robes walked in. They sat next to each other with legs crossed on a raised podium, also covered with Persian carpets. They were wearing white Kufis (prayer hat) covering their gray hair. All three had snow white beards of different lengths, which highlighted the olive skin of their deeply etched faces. At first they looked similar to each other, but at closer observation their differences became clear and hard to miss, not only in their appearance, but in age as well. The one in the middle appeared a lot older than the other two. Getting comfortable, he bent forward to pick up a large book that was in front of him, placing it in his lap.

"This is strange. These judges look nothing like those who judged me," Henry thought to himself, with the explanation to be revealed later.

All this time Nazia waited patiently to be addressed by the elders.

The one in the middle began to flick through the pages of the large book, and when done with the reading he spoke to Nazia, "Salaam Alaikum, my child."

"Wa Alaikum Assalam," Nazia replied respectfully, slightly bending forward.

Done with the formal greetings, the man in the middle returned his attention to the book, completely ignoring the girl for quite some time.

Unable to stay quiet any longer under the weight of silence and the uncertainty of her future Nazia spoke, "Please tell me that I am in paradise."

The panel of judges kept quiet ignoring her question, and seemingly her presence, too. The man in the middle kept going through the pages, inviting the others when its pages attracted his attention. After quite some time in total silence he finally turned his attention to the girl in the spotlight.

"So, you want to know if you are in paradise?"

"Yes please," answered Nazia.

"No, not yet," the judge in the middle pronounced slowly.

"Am I on trial?"

"Yes, my dear child," answered the man to the left of Nazia. "We have to see what will be the best way to help you to rectify all that you have done."

The condemning tone of his voice and his references left Nazia confused and bewildered.

"Will someone please tell me what is going on here, and where am I. Is this a bad dream? Am I dead? If I am, why am I not in paradise with my husband?" Nazia shouted out in despair.

The panel of judges sat motionless through her questions, giving her time to calm herself. Then the one in the middle spoke, "Will you please reveal your face."

After a bit of hesitation Nazia removed her niqab, unveiling her entire face and her long black hair that reached down to her waist.

From where Henry was standing, he could only see her profile, though to observe her face was his wish from the moment that he stepped into her cell. Henry looked at Hades seeking permission. Hades nodded his head and Henry stepped closer to Nazia to stand right in front of her. Finally, he could complete the picture that had puzzled him since first meeting her. The removed cover revealed the rarity of her beauty. What struck Henry the most were her eyes. He had seen them before, but now, combined with the rest of her features they took on a new meaning. Henry saw absolute innocence seeping through them, with his perception probably being influenced by his realization of her age. Completely lost, and now uncertain in the righteousness of her act, she faced her judges with the smouldering hope that this would all turn for the better. She was barely eighteen, and even heavily applied mascara did not add age to her youth. Her small nose with a slight hump resembled a tiny bird, with her eyebrows as its widely spread wings. Her lips filled with sensitivity were irresistibly attractive in their purity. Her overall appearance made Henry forget for the moment the atrocity that she had just committed, and to see her for who she was, and probably still is, despite the place they were in and the given circumstances.

With his curiosity completely satisfied, Henry returned to his place next to Hades where he had the best angle of observation and would not miss the words coming from the judges, nor her emotional responses.

"So," spoke the judge in the middle, "You want to know where you are."

"Yes please," pleaded Nazia.

"You, my child, are on trial."

"From what I remember, trials are for those who have committed crimes. I have done nothing wrong. I was following the will of Allah."

"Yes, my child," spoke the judge on her right. "We do understand your motives and we see your justification, but there is much more to the situation that you can imagine."

"Like what?" Nazia asked loudly, expressing her anger to the unfairness of what she was witnessing, and was a part of. "I was taught by Imam, and directed by faithful Muslim brothers to do what Allah expects of me."

"And, if I may ask, what was that?" enquired the judge in the middle.

"To kill non-believers," Nazia answered with confidence.

Her words echoed around the Mosque walls returning to her much louder, raising fear in her mind, and the spontaneous realization of the horror that her act caused. She took a couple of steps back in an attempt to increase the distance between her and those who were about to condemn her, but strangely enough she could not move an inch from the spot.

"Are you trying to escape?" asked the judge on the left.

"No," Nazia answered softly as she realized the inevitability of what was to come.

"There is no escaping the outcome of your deeds, and that is the will of Allah. Everyone should be rewarded accordingly. In other words, for every action, there is a reaction to be faced.

"Something tells me that what you are saying is not positive in my case," Nazia mumbled hardly moving her lips.

"Didn't you think that Allah, the creator of all humanity, would somehow be against the idea of his children killing each other?"

The sudden realization of the truth of his words struck Nazia's soul like a bolt of lightning, followed by the thunder of enormous fear. She could see how mistaken she had been, and the kind of punishment she could be dealt. Nazia fell to her knees, bent forward until her forehead touched the carpet, and pleaded for forgiveness. Horrifying Suras from the holy Koran of the punishments one may receive if going against the will of Allah surfaced in her mind, plunging her deeper into uncontrollable dread.

"Please stand up," asked the judge in the middle. "We are not your jurors and certainly not your judges. The purpose of this meeting is not to glorify nor condemn your act."

"Then, why am I here?" asked Nazia with a bolder voice. "Please let me go to heaven to see Hassan, my beloved husband, to whom I stayed faithful and devoted."

"You will meet him when the time is right."

"And when will that be?"

"When you will be ready."

“I am ready now,” Nazia said, raising her voice.

With a deep sigh, the judge in the middle said, “There are consequences for our actions. Consequences that we have to face. Do you understand?”

“No, I don’t”

“You have to face the result of your actions.”

“Youwant me to see what the explosion did to those in the church?”

“Exactly.”

“Why are you punishing me?”

“We are not punishing you, nor judging you. As I said, this is the will of Allah, laws established by the Creator himself, and we are not entitled to break, nor change them. As I said, each action has a reaction. You, by your will, triggered action, now you have to face the reaction.”

Hearing their dialogue, Henry suddenly came to the realization that there was something missing in all this, or to be exact, someone.

He faced Hades with a question, “Why is she all alone in this?” “What do you mean?” asked Hades.

“I mean, where is her spirit guide. Why is he or she not present?”

“Oh, of course, she had one.”

“And, what happened?”

“She failed her task, too.”

“You are confusing me.”

“You see Henry, as you already know, take you for example, spirit guides are not perfect, sometimes instead of influencing those that they are taking care of to abstain from certain things, they themselves get deeply involved, dragging them down.”

“I’m not following you?”

“It appears that her guide had her own score to settle with the Christian faith.”

“No!” exclaimed Henry.

“Don’t worry, she has been taken care of.”

“How?”

“She is getting ready to be sent back to Earth to a beautiful family of a pastor, deeply devoted to his faith, and in the near future who will become a preacher of a Christian community.”

“Today you mentor and tomorrow you are a student again,” mumbled Henry.

“Exactly,” Hades confirmed. “We are all in an eternal process of learning and personal purification.”

"So, there is no one to accompany her?"

"No," said Hades.

Henry heard Nazia's voice again, "So, what is out there for me?" she asked.

"Purification," answered the man in the middle. "You have stained your soul with the blood of innocents. All the pain that you have caused others you have to experience yourself."

Nazia lowered her head in anticipation of her upcoming pain and suffering.

"Are you going to send me to hell?" she whispered.

"We are not here to send you anywhere. If there is a judge of your short-lived life on Earth, it will be you."

Nazia lifted her head with a tiny spark of hope in her eyes.

"Do not be deceived my child," the man in the middle continued. "No one can punish us harsher than we can ourselves."

In a desperate attempt to stay afloat Nazia tried to grab at a last straw, adamant to convince these judges otherwise, she fell to her knees and screamed, "But they were all Christians!"

The judges smiled sadly, and instantly changed their appearance. Their white robes turned pitch black with a distinguished white collar at their throats, and they looked like typical Catholic priests.

Nazia jumped up covering her face with her hands saying, "Am I in a nightmare? What the hell is this? Am I going to be judged by a bunch of Christian priests?"

"Look at us," said the man in the middle. "We are still the same. All we did was just change our outfits."

"What kind of sick game is this?" screamed Nazia.

"Please calm down my child," said the man on the right. "We would like to emphasize to you that there is no difference between his children in the eyes of the Creator. All that you perceive of segregation is just different outfits for the soul."

"Are you saying that there is no difference between Muslims and Christians?"

"Not in God's eyes."

Hades raised his right hand to freeze the scene, and facing Henry asked, "Is your curiosity satisfied?"

Henry kept quiet, not having an answer to the question. What Nazia had to face next was predictable. But a feeling of unfinished business dwelt in his mind, preventing him from closing the door of this chapter of this learning opportunity.

He looked at Hades and said, "I don't know, will it be too much to ask, but I have a request."

"I am listening," said Hades.

"May I have a short break. There is someone I would like to visit first."

Hades smiled and said, "Somehow, I know who it is that you would like to visit, but before letting you leave my kingdom we have to get back to reality. Not to lose track of time, but above all, to separate past from present."

With that he lowered his right hand, and they appeared again in Nazia's solitary cell. Henry leaned against the door and Hades posed a question, "What exactly are you trying to achieve by visiting HIM?"

"You know, I am her last hope."

"After all that you have seen you still want to help her?"

"Somebody has to."

"Why you?"

"That is question with no sensible answer."

"You are free to leave," said Hades turning around to face the staircase leading to the floating island where his throne stood.

"I'm not saying goodbye," said Henry.

"I know," answered Hades.

Henry closed his eyes, and with each fiber of his soul visualized the MAN. The man who changed the course of the world's history with his short visit. The man who ceased being just a man. The one who captured the minds of millions with his simple truth.

PLEA

Nothing could have prepared Henry for what he had to face. He was standing in front of countless rows of people, and the first impression he had was that they were all watching him. The shock he was to experience was imminent and unavoidable. Henry was literally facing thousands of people sitting right in front of him, in what felt like an amphitheater. At first he thought a miscommunication had happened and that he had been transported to an ancient Roman arena…but soon everything became clear. He was in a modern time, and in a modern stadium, which only confirmed his fears that he was in the wrong time and the wrong place.

In that very moment he felt someone's hand landing on his shoulder with the words, "Don't worry, you are in the right place."

Henry looked to his side to find Christ himself looking forward at the ocean of faces, various in their appearance, but extremely tense in their unity.

"Don't you love it?" Christ asked still looking forward.

Being uncertain as to what exactly Christ was referring to, Henry looked back and realized that they were standing on the edge of a green field while a football match was in progress right behind them.

"What exactly do you mean, Lord?" Henry asked cautiously.

"Look at these faces, at the excitement."

Still puzzled, Henry looked back again at the players tirelessly chasing a ball saying, "Forgive me Sire for saying this, but I think the real excitement is right behind us."

"That's where you are wrong, my brother. What you are referring to is the cause of the excitement. True, unveiled emotions are right in front of you."

Then Christ lifted his right hand with his index finger pointing straight up to the sky, and froze in expectation of something great about to happen.

"Watch them," instructed Christ, "One more second…"

He kept his eyes on the spectators and demanded the same from Henry. Henry, puzzled, froze, in that moment of time.

Then Christ said, "Now!"

The entire stadium jumped to their feet and an unimaginably load roar erupted like a tidal wave cascading down to the field, filling the humongous stadium to its capacity.

"Look, look at them!" Christ said excitedly. "Look at how happy they are. Feel the energy of their emotional explosion. Sense the freedom and absence of self-control in this moment of absolute unity."

Henry turned around and realized that the home team had scored a goal.

Once the emotions had settled down, Christ looked at Henry for the first time and said, "Truly freedom of self-expression brings one an enormous sense of happiness."

"I guess you are right Sire," agreed Henry.

"You wanted to see me?" asked Christ momentarily changing the subject and focussing his attention on Henry.

"Yes, Lord, I was hoping that we could…" Henry stumbled, trying to express himself but his words were failing him.

"I see," said Christ, and touching Henry on the shoulder said, "Follow me."

Henry closed his eyes, surrendering himself to the will of Christ, knowing that it would lead only to light, knowledge, and hopefully to his peace of mind. Peace that could only be reached through an undistorted view of the world, your place in it, and especially your purpose. Once understood, one can find temporary relief, only for a short-lived moment before life presents new elevated obstacles to test your soul in all kinds of virtues.

Henry delayed opening his eyes to extend the experience of the touch of this godly soul's hand upon his shoulder that had filled his heart with delirious happiness.

"You can look now," Henry heard Christ's voice next to him.

Henry carefully opened his eyes and stood astonished, mesmerized by what he saw. He was standing in the middle of a massive cathedral, decorated to its fullest. Expansive not only in its magnitude, but its beauty as well. Henry felt small and insignificant in comparison with the flight of fantasy of the visionary architects from the past. Those artists from the Renaissance period who had designed and built such a wonder for generations of humans to indulge and spirits to endure.

"Where are we?" asked Henry looking around.

"St. Peters Basilica in the Vatican City."

"I have heard a lot about it, but have never had a chance to visit it."

"Now you do, dear friend," said Christ observing the strong light right above them showering down through the opening in the summit of the dome.

After some time of thorough observation of all the beauty surrounding him, Henry said, "To be honest this is the setup I was expecting to find you in the first place, not in a dessert, and especially not in a football stadium!"

"So, you think this is the place where I belong?"

"Since all of this was built to glorify your teachings and…"

"You wanted to say…me!"

"Yup."

"That's where you are wrong, my brother. None of this was built to glorify me, nor my teachings. This is a monument to humanity itself."

"I'm not getting it?" said Henry puzzled.

"All of this," Christ spread his arms wide apart to include the whole place, "is the brightest illustration of the genius of the human mind, but also their ability to create."

"But all of this was erected in your name," insisted Henry.

"First of all, it was named after one of my disciples," smiled Christ, "And secondly, it stands as a beacon of human ambition, the strive for power, domination, and glorification of themselves, ego, but definitely not of me."

Henry lowered his head at the sad realization in the truth of Christ's words.

"There's nothing to be upset, nor disappointed about," Christ said cheerfully.

"No?"

"No, you have to see the bigger picture. The sole purpose of sending souls to this planet is for them to learn, to learn as much as possible. Every new day presents them with opportunities to discover something new, be it about the planet, about each other, and hopefully about themselves. Don't forget that the ability to create is embedded into the very core of the soul. Exercising their creativity brings nothing but happiness and bliss."

"It's hard to disagree with that."

Then, Christ became serious and said, "But you are not here for a lecture on humans' ability to create."

After a moment of silence he continued, "I am listening."

After a short hesitation Henry chose to spill it all out. "Do you believe that each lesson is taught through punishment?"

Christ smiled and gestured that Henry should take a seat on one of the many pews. "I see where you are going with this question, so it is best that we are seated."

Once seated, Henry looked at the front to see a crucifix directly opposite him.

Noticing Henry's stare Christ asked, "What does it mean to you?"

"I would say…punishment," answered Henry.

"So, what did I learn through that punishment?" probed Christ.

"It's made you…God."

"I will pretend not to hear that…but you will get your answer. Punishment does not teach us lessons."

"Then, what does?"

Christ looked deeply into Henry's eyes and clearly articulated, "Fear of punishment. Punishment makes one resist and resent, whilst fear makes one cautious and self-aware so as to avoid punishment. I believe that you are not here for a philosophical debate and there is something more specific that you want to ask me…or am I mistaken?"

Henry sighed deeply and said, "No, you are not. There is something, or should I say someone, that I am deeply concerned about."

"I'm listening," said Christ.

"There is a Muslim girl with the name Nazia which committed a terrible crime. Don't get me wrong, please, I do believe that there is probably no excuse for what she has done, but….I still would like to ask you to help her. Show her mercy, and with that, a way out of the hell she is in now."

"I am afraid that I cannot help her," answered Christ, lowering his head, with his golden wavy hair covering his face from Henry's sight.

"That's it?" Henry asked, deeply disappointed. "Aren't you God?" he continued with a raised voice.

"I am God to those who believe that I am. She obviously does not see me as such."

"Are you saying that the only way for you to help her would be through her conversion to Christianity?"

"If you will, yes. To receive someone's help you need to believe in them. Without her belief I am incapable of helping her."

"I see," Henry said with his eyes lighting up with a tiny spark of hope.

"What do you see, my friend?"

"I see that I need to get back and convince her to become a Christian."

Christ laughed sadly as he said, "Don't be naïve my friend. Her faith is strong. Yes, she is in pain now, but don't be fooled. Deep in her heart she still believes that her act was just and all that she is going through is unjust."

"So, how can I help her?" Henry said in despair.

"That is for you to figure out. Where there is a will, there is a way. You have to find a way my friend. I can see that your will is strong and your heart pure. I wish nothing more than for her to come out of the place that she is in now. I know that she has suffered enough, but I am not the solution, nor her savior."

"Then who is?" Henry asked.

Christ gazed at Henry, and placing his right hand on Henry's chest said, "You are."

"Me?" Henry exclaimed in genuine surprise. "What do I know? I am just a lost soul in search of phantoms, bouncing from one reality to another, gathering useless knowledge far away from my loved ones…what do I know?"

Withdrawing his hand, Christ commented, "You are judging yourself too harshly. There is no such thing as useless knowledge, and you know that very well. All you need to do is to believe in yourself, and in the power of love." Christ paused for a moment and then continued, "By the way, what is your stance on love these days?"

Henry clenched his fist and replied, "All whom I loved have been ripped away from my heart. My lovely wife, who I hardly tasted in the world of spirit, is now a three-year-old child again back on Earth, unaware of my existence and the love that we once shared. My mentor, Croton, is her father, which brings me nothing but great disappointment. Once a highly respected figure in my life, he has become a corrupt official and an unfit father. Will I ever have him back the way he was remains a question with no answer. So, you want to know where I stand on love…I will answer with one word…nowhere."

Christ smiled gently at him, saying, "No heart can remain 'nowhere' with respect to love…it would stop beating." He placed a hand on Henry's shoulder and leaning forward whispered into Henry's ear, "Your question has been answered and you can return now."

Before Henry had a chance to ask Christ to clarify his words, he appeared back in Nazia dark and gloomy cell. In a place where even the brightest ray of light would certainly have been distinguished before it could touch any object. The unusual inner glow of Henry's body was the only source of light in this dungeon of guilt and self-pity.

"You're back!" exclaimed Nazia filled with hope and anticipation. "I knew that you wouldn't leave me here all by myself."

Henry kneeled in front of her, and taking her hand in his said, "I didn't come back to stay with you. I came to take you out of this place."

Nazia pulled her hands away and retreated away from him, "No."

"Why not?" Henry asked surprise.

"There is no way out of this place. This is my punishment. I know it and I have to…"

"You do not have to be here. You have suffered enough," Henry said with a raised voice.

Nazia stood up and took a step toward Henry saying boldly, "You know nothing about me."

"Then why don't you tell me."

After giving some thought to his invitation she leaned over Henry and whispered into his ear. "No, I am safe here." Having said that she looked around the room afraid that someone may be listening.

Henry stood up tall and compassionately asked, "Are you afraid of someone?"

"Yes, I am."

"Who?"

"Those who betrayed me, sentencing me to this Christian hell. I was a devoted Muslim and submitted myself to the will of Allah. And this is what I get as a result. Do you know what I fear?"

"What?" asked Henry.

"I am afraid that next they will arrange meetings with those whom I killed in the church. If I managed to survive the blast, that means they did, too. It was painful enough to meet their relatives, and I am afraid that in my current state of mind I will not survive another test. I am already losing my mind."

"I know what you went through, although I cannot say that I felt what you felt, and yes, you are right…I do not know you, but one thing that I know for definite is that I want to, and I can help you. I do not know yet how, but it feels predestined to happen. All I need from you is to believe in what I believe."

Nazia was looking straight into Henry's eyes and shaking her head from side to side in utter disbelief. Ignoring her reaction Henry said, "To begin with, I would like you to see the real me."

In front of Nazia's eyes Henry began his transformation into an elderly man as he was before crossing over into the world of spirit.

Terrified, Nazia stepped back crying, "What kind of sorcery is this?"

"This is not sorcery, Nazia. This is my appearance at the time of my death on Earth and rebirth into the world of spirit."

Coming to terms with Henry's new look, Nazia sadly said, "For sure your rebirth was nothing like mine."

"It is true, I died in the hospital with a heart attack, but I would like to share with you the story of my life and love. Of course, only if you allow me."

Henry held his hands out to Nazia hoping that she would place hers into his palms. Hesitantly she accepted his offer and closed her eyes.

Deep inside Henry knew that to gain someone's trust you had to become vulnerable. You have to let them into your life with no boundaries, dropping your guard in hope that you won't be judged. While holding Nazia's hands in his, Henry closed his eyes and let Nazia into his personal love story. He held nothing back. Right from the moment of separation from his own body, separation from Rose, and his beloved daughter. Henry allowed her to see everything that he went through in the world of spirit, the pain he felt seeing his wife with another man, his conscious decision to set her free to find happiness again. Then followed scenes of Rose's accident and their happy reunion.

On that positive note he chose to stop the transmission and retrieved his hands saying, "You know me now. Allow me to know you."

Nazia now looked at Henry differently, despite her face still being covered in black fabric, Henry saw deep compassion in her and for the first-time signs of trust.

"Do you mind if I call you Uncle?"

"I would be honored," Henry agreed.

"What would you like to know beyond what you already know?"

"To begin with, will you please remove your niqab?" Henry asked knowing that if she did that would be an ultimate acknowledgement of her trust.

Without any hesitation Nazia lifted her hands and removed

the cover.

"You are so beautiful, my child," Henry said stepping into the role of uncle.

She fluttered her eyelashes, pleased with the compliment, "May I ask you something?"

"Anything, my child."

"All those beautiful places that you have shown me…"

"Yes…?"

"Do they really exist here?"

"They are not only in existence, but waiting for you. There is a universe of love and wisdom lined up with anticipation of meeting with you. Impatiently waiting to share with you their unimaginable beauty. Indescribable combinations of shapes, colors, and sounds."

Henry stopped talking for a moment taking her hand saying, "Heaven is out there beyond these walls, waiting to welcome you if you would only choose to trust me."

"Will you take me there?" Nazia asked with eyes wide open.

"It will be my pleasure."

Visualizing his and Rose's reality, knowing that only there he will have everything under control, the way he wants it. After all, it was his own realm where the laws of physics were set by him to satisfy his and Rose's needs. He pictured his beautiful beachfront, turquoise water, and the palm trees gently leaning over the waves. His visualizations were so clear that happiness shone through this face. A moment later he opened his eyes ready to inhale the fresh ocean breeze that he had missed so much, but instead he found himself still standing in front of Nazia with her eyes closed in her same confinement in hell.

"This is strange," Henry said in absolute disbelief.

"What happened?" asked frightened Nazia.

"It didn't work."

"I knew that they will not let me out of this place so easily."

Then covering her face in absolute horror, she exclaimed, "You are probably stuck here, too!"

"No, this cannot be. I will get to the bottom of this," Henry said as he walked out of the cell.

As the door closed behind him, Henry faced the long flight of stairs reaching up in front of him, suspended above the hungry throat of boiling lava. He looked up and with a deep sigh took the first step.

BACK TO ANNE

Time in the Christian paradise had lost its meaning for Anne. The time between her arrival up to now was hard for her to estimate. The space between then and now was occupied with many different types of activities which were mostly about two things, education and recreation. Numerous lessons of life orientation, the history of humanity, science, philosophy, and many more interesting subjects were buffered with music, singing, painting, and visits to theaters for concerts of artists once famous on Earth. Reunions with long forgotten friends and making new ones. Events followed one after each other, leaving Anne with little time to spend in her tiny personal space that had been given to her by Gertrude…her friend and savior who she had hardly had a chance to see lately. During her short breaks between activities, Anne tried to track the time of her presence in this most amazing place, the place where all her wishes had come true. It seemed like it was only yesterday that she had got rid of all unnecessary goods that she had managed to clutter her space with. Her strongest and most favorite subjects were singing and playing the piano. They were coming to her so naturally and effortlessly, leaving no doubts in her mind that if an opportunity were to present itself for her to be born back to Earth, she would definitely choose a family with a piano in the house, and parents with good singing voices so that she could inherit the singing genes.

Once in a break between classes, when Anne was carelessly laughing and discussing with a classmate one of the lecturer's strange habits, she saw Gertrude out of the corner of her eye, standing on the edge of the school courtyard and lovingly watching her. Anne excused herself and ran to Gertrude to find a warm hug in the arms of her most devoted friend.

"So how are you, my dear Anne?" Gertrude asked, still holding her hands.

"Look, I have so much to tell you, but overall, I am happy.' She looked into Gertrude's eyes and continued, "Thank you for not giving up on me. I am eternally grateful to you."

She kissed the back of Gertrude's hand, and in return, Gertrude kissed her forehead saying, "You do not have to thank me. Thank yourself for opening your mind and soul to Christ's teachings. For allowing his light into your heart, and for trying to help your family members to become a part of it, too."

"Yes, but it seems that I failed. If you ask me, what is the one thing I wanted most I would say when the time arrives, to see members of my family here with me in this most beautiful place of the entire universe."

"Do you miss them?" Gertrude asked.

"Immensely, but I do understand the necessity of the fact that they have to go on with their lives without my interference." Anne went quiet, drawn into memories of her recent past. "You know who I miss the most?"

"Probably little Rose?" Gertrude guessed.

"Absolutely right. I miss her the most and would give anything to have a glimpse of her."

"You do not have to give up anything. I can arrange a meeting," offered Gertrude.

'That would be the best gift ever!" Anne clapped her hands like a preschool girl.

Anne's excitement made it difficult for Gertrude to disclose the reason for her visit.

Once her excitement had settled down Anne asked, "When are we leaving?"

"Before we leave for Earth there is something that I'd like to talk to you about."

Noticing the change in Gertrude's voice Anne asked, "Is there something wrong with my family?"

"Let us sit down so that I can share the reason for my visit."

"I knew it, my family is in trouble. Tell me, what have they done now? Is it Croton or Raymond?"

"Calm down, Anne. There is nothing wrong with them," Gertrude said, inviting Anne to take a seat in one of the benches facing the ocean.

Anne hurried to seat herself on the bench and once Gertrude was also seated, she said, "Do not spare me. Tell me the truth, no matter how bad it is. I can handle it."

Gertrude placed her hand over Anne's and with a genuinely loving voice said, "This is not about Raymond or Croton."

"Then who is it about?"

Gertrude took a deep sigh and spoke, "Honestly, I don't know."

Anne made a surprised face, and then Gertrude continued, "Let me tell you the whole story. I have been approached by Planners and asked to accompany you back to Earth, to your family, but…on a specific date and hour."

"So, this is not bad?" said Anne recovering from her initial panic.

"Please bear with me," asked Gertrude.

Anne covered her mouth with her hand to help herself to keep quiet.

"As I said, Planners called me in to ask me to take you down to Earth, and on my plea 'why?', they didn't give me any specific answers. Just asked me to honor their request."

"That's strange?" said Anne, "I would like to be prepared."

"I know, dear Anne, so would I, but you cannot argue with Planners, neither deny their request."

"Why? Will they punish you?"

"No, my dear, no one punishes us guides. It's just through thousands of years experience that you realize that Planners are never mistaken, and their decisions are always mutually beneficial for both us guides, and the souls who we guide."

"What if you disobey?"

"Someone else will step in to replace me."

"I see," said Anne, and after some thought added, "If there is one thing that I've learned since being here, it is that despite of temporary difficulties or obstacles, or even so-called tragedies, everything works out in the end to serve a bigger purpose. A purpose that we cannot see, and as a result to understand in that particular moment."

"Are you saying that no matter what the Planners have prepared for you and your family to go through, you are ready to face it?"

After a short hesitation, Anne answered, "Yes, I am."

"Then, let our journey begin," Gertrude said, asking Anne to close her eyes.

DEVASTATION

When Anne reopened her eyes, she found herself in her son's apartment, right in the middle of the living room.

"Stop it, Rose!" Anne heard Gaya's voice, "It's time to go. We are going to be late."

Anne followed Gaya's voice to find her in the bedroom trying to dress playful Rose.

Gertrude followed Anne, alert and vigilant to any sudden change of events. Deep inside she knew that something major was about to happen in the life of this family, but what exactly remained a mystery. Despite the secrecy and the Planners attempt to veil upcoming events, Gertrude noticed strange and long forgotten havoc amongst spirit guides, plus she couldn't help but notice the newly appeared large area of housing right next to the place where Anne's single-room house was situated.

"Come on, Rose, we must hurry. We are going to be late for Daddy's return from work. I still have to cook his favorite dish."

Gaya looked through the window into the pewter gray winter sky, and placing her right hand on her tummy gently whispered, "And I have wonderful news for him."

Anne looked at Gertrude standing next to her and said, "I am dying to hug my little Rose. I miss her so much. Look how much she has grown. I have missed out on her best years."

"You can look at her, but do not get any closer," Gertrude warned.

"I understand," Anne agreed, crouching down to have a better look at her one and only grandchild.

Finally getting hold of a bouncing Rose, Gaya began to dress her for the cold December afternoon.

Suddenly a realization came upon Anne, "Wait, what date is it?"

"Who cares," answered Gertrude keeping her eyes on Gaya and Rose.

Anne remembered the electronic calendar that Gaya had in her kitchen and quickly left the bedroom and a minute later came back with her eyes wide open.

"What do you see?" asked Gertrude.

"Today is the 7th of December."

"So what?"

"It is Raymond, my husband's, birthday. Can you believe it."

"Happy Birthday," Gertrude said with no emotion.

"Do you think that is the reason for us being here?" Anne asked naively.

"I highly doubt that your husband's birthday would create such unrest in the spiritual realms."

"Anyway," Anne said disappointed, "at least I will be present at his birthday celebration."

"Allow me to not share your excitement, dear Anne. It is almost 11:30."

"So what?' asked Anne.

"Whatever we have to be exposed to will happen at 11:45."

"How do you know that?" Anne asked plunging into the depths of rising anxiety.

"Right after the meeting with the Planners I came across Gaya's guide, Lita. She happened to be better informed. Not about the event itself, but rather about the time of its occurrence."

"I see," said Anne, and a bit later she asked, "Why is she not here? Her presence will probably be a great help and support for Gaya."

"Who says I am not here?' calmly pronounced Lita as she stepped forward in her striking beauty, proudly carrying herself, remaining cool and indifferent to the rising anxieties in both Gertrude and Anne's hearts.

"Thank God you are here," Gertrude said with great relief in her voice.

Surprised by Lita's appearance, Anne forgot about all norms of etiquette and couldn't take her eyes off her. Since she crossed over into the world of spirits, Anne had never encountered such a rare beauty combined with such strong presence. Noticing Anne's piercing fixation, Lita smiled with the corner of her mouth and introduced herself, and Anne reciprocated, "I am Anne, Gaya's mother-in-law."

"I know who you are," Lita answered unemotionally.

Her tone made Anne snap back and relive her past life with Gaya to see if she had done something to deserve such cold treatment from her guide. After announcing her presence, Lita left as though she had never been there. Ignoring Lita's act, Gertrude, being unusually alert, followed each and every step of little Rose, warning Anne to be ready for any turn of events.

"Stop it, Gertrude, you are scaring me. Can you at least tell me what to expect?" complained Anne.

"The worst!" Gertrude replied abruptly.

Anne looked around in search of anything that could be of immediate danger, and relieved that nothing obvious presented itself, she shrugged her shoulders, puzzled by Gertrude's behavior. She stepped to the window to see if jeopardy could approach from outside. Not finding anything unusual she was about to turn around when she suddenly noticed abnormal behavior by the animals on the street. A large stray dog, that had been peacefully sleeping on the pavement suddenly jumped up for no reason and crossed the street in a hurry, disappearing around the corner. She also noticed two cats who had jumped down from the ground floor balcony of a nearby apartment, easily conquering the high fence of the neighboring house to disappear into its yard. Next was a flock of birds spontaneously erupting from their roof, seemingly frightened by an invisible predator.

Without taking her eyes from the street Anne said, "Actually, the animals outside are behaving very strangely."

As she said these words she heard Gaya's loud scream. Turning around she saw Gaya grabbing semi-dressed Rose and run out of her bedroom. Not knowing how to react to what just happened Anne simply followed Gertrude who seemed to know what to do. Gaya immediately opened the entrance door, quickly scooped up confused and frightened Rose and stood firmly in the opening. In the sudden havoc, Anne didn't notice how the entire contents of the room had come alive. The bed slid to the side, the mirror on top of the dressing table was sent into involuntary tremble, the doors of the wardrobes exposed their contents. When all of the motion came to a standstill, only the crystal chandelier swinging from side to side stood as a strong reminder of the powerful disturbance.

"Earthquake!" Anne screamed and braced herself for a second tremor, familiar with this geographical event that so frequently visited her town when she was in her physical body.

A few moments later came the second tremor, a lot stronger than the first one. Anne saw the books that were previously well organized on shelves literally flying to the floor. Priceless China tea set, gifted by her to the young couple at their wedding, turning into a pile of meaningless rubble.

Gaya was still standing in the door frame, holding little Rose in one hand and pushing herself firmly against the doorway with the other. This second tremor lasted approximately five seconds, and when all of the loose items in the apartment had found rest on the floor, and the havoc had settled, Gaya released her grip and let out a deep sigh of relief. Through the entire duration of the earthquake Lita and Gertrude stood of either side of Gaya, joining their hands around the terrified mother and her crying child. Their eyes were closed in a meditative state of mind, providing love and comfort in the given circumstances. The next turn of events was beyond anyone's' prediction.

Gaya, with Rose still in her arms, was suddenly thrown airborne together with the entire contents of the flat and everything in front of Anne's eyes crumbled. Floors, one after the other, plunged down to Earth, leaving Anne suspended in midair, and looking down at what once was the roof of a six story apartment building. Instantly it had become a sarcophagus of concrete rubble, which only seconds ago was a safe haven for many families to reside, live, and flourish. A thick cloud composed of cement dust moved like a tidal wave, rushing away from the epicenter of the disturbance, blocked Anne's vision and the entire surroundings, disguising the magnitude of the tragedy. Once the thick dust cloud reached her height, Anne instinctively covered her face to avoid being suffocated.

When the dust had settled Anne looked around in absolute disbelief at what she had just witnessed. Refusing to believe what had just happened, Anne softly called Gertrude's name. Not receiving any answer, she then screamed, "Gertrude!"

Communication was shattered just like the building in which she had been standing a minute ago. Anne carefully lowered her non-physical body to the building's roof, kneeling in the realization of the horror screaming, "Noooo," covering her face with her hands. She leaned forward until her head touched the surface of the roof now completely covered by gray powder.

"Noooo," she kept screaming as the realization of the pain that her son will experience losing his beloved wife and daughter simultaneously.

She felt the pain of her husband, Raymond, receiving such a terrible gift on his birthday…that his granddaughter and daughter-in-law were no more. Waves of uncontrollable emotions pounded her soul rendering her unconscious, unable to bare such torture. With her eyes closed she fell onto her side, tranquil and motionless.

REVELATION

Looking up at the suspended staircase, Henry anticipated a long and physically tiring ascent like it had been on his quest to reach Christ, but he was pleasantly surprised when he realized how easily, and effortlessly, he was conquering the pathway leading to his island destination. Each new step delivered more weightlessness and relief. Relief from the heavy burden that had landed on his shoulders from the moment that he had stepped into this kingdom. The kingdom of darkness and emotional suffering. The kingdom of pain and regrets for all that had been done in the past, and most probably all that wasn't.

This relief was accompanied by a strong hope to find an escape from the tormented existence of the poor Muslim girl who had done the unfixable, not knowing any better. When Henry finally took the last step, he appeared on the surface of the island creation composed of black crystals. A few more steps and he was raised from the depths of hell, standing in front of the jagged crystal throne with its possessor peacefully resting with his eyes closed. For a moment Henry thought that Hades was in a deep trance and had not noticed his reappearance, but then the ruler of the underworld spoke, dispersing the illusion that he could be temporarily detached from his own realm.

"Please have a seat," Hades invited without opening his eyes, pointing at a perfectly shaped cube made from naturally formed crystals.

It wasn't entirely black, with veins of white conveying a glimpse of hope to those who landed upon it. Henry sat on the block and gazed at the still peacefully lounging Hades. Henry was about to speak when Hades raised his hand in a request for silence. Henry kept quiet and pulled back, waiting for permission to speak. Becoming bored, Henry began to observe the surroundings. He looked up and admired the dome made from an unimaginable volume of crystals, all different in size and growing so close together, collectively pointing to the center of the island. Suddenly Henry noticed a spark of hardly breathing light flashing within one of the crystals hanging right above him. Shifting his attention to the one next to it he noticed a similar effect, and soon he realized they each held a tiny source of light planted within them, occasionally sprouting into life and then dimming into darkness again.

Before Henry could come to any conclusions Hades spoke, “They are alive.”

Not knowing what Hades was referring to Henry asked, “Who is alive?”

“The crystals. They are alive and continuously at work.”

Confused, Henry asked, “What kind of work? To me they are just hanging out there looking pretty.”

‘’That’s where you are wrong my friend. The entire inner core of Earth is composed of various types of crystals each with a specific purpose.”

“What purpose do crystals serve?” Henry asked in surprise.

“To register and memorize all the events of the past and present which momentarily becomes the past.

They are an integral part of the universal library, holding all that there is to know about Earth.”

“Are you saying that each crystal is like a memory bank?”

“Yes.”

Henry looked up again asking, “Does one of them belong to Nazia?”

“Yes.”

“That explains why they are all so black.”

Hades smiled and opening his eyes for the first time answered, “Exactly.”

Henry was about to reveal to Hades the reason for his visit, but the King of the underworld rose from his throne inviting him to take a walk with him.

“I know what you were about to ask, I see your motives and urge to help a lost soul. In other circumstances but this one I would have probably let you take her to wherever you think would be helpful for her recovery, but…” Hades stopped, looked at Henry, carefully articulating his next words, “But not yet.”

“Why not?” Henry protested. “Give me a chance to show her another world, other realities and I promise you that if this does not work and she remains stubborn in her beliefs, I will personally deliver her back to her cell.”

“You are so naïve, my friend,” Hades laughed rowdily. “If

by showing a better lifestyle or ways of living we could change the mentality of souls, then none of them would still be here. You must understand and accept the fact that all the residents of this realm were not born yesterday. In other words, their present situation is the result multiple life failures."

"Life failures?" asked Henry.

"Precisely. You heard me correctly. Life after life, they keep falling into the same worn out deep pit, and the cause of their failures is the rejection of the most fundamental law of existence."

"Which is?" asked Henry.

"Live and let live. In the case of your new friend, it was her inability to stop a series of waves once triggered by someone who committed a murder. Waves of revenge and unforgiveness rippling through the entire planet since the dawn of humanity, timelessly poisoning their hearts with a sense of false justice. They always choose to take the law into their hands, ignoring universal laws, and as a result, ending up in this hell hole. Humans are blind and their spiritual leaders are blinder."

Hades' tone of voice and rising anger made Henry back away a bit, after all, Hades was the last person Henry wanted to upset. Hades lowered his head and fell silent. Henry sensed deep pain in his words caused by his inability to change the paradigm of human behavior, as well as their unwillingness to lose the crystalized pattern of false virtues. The presence of emotions, such as empathy and compassion, were the last things that Henry expected to discover in the heart of the underworld's ruler.

With the last dying flame of hope to convince Hades to change his stance on Nazia's case he asked, "So, what about Nazia, may I have her soul?"

Hades looked straight into Henry's eyes and spoke, "I have a firm request coming from the Planners to return you to Earth, so Nazia has to wait."

Like a gust of wind, endless thoughts rushed through Henry's mind bringing with them numerous possible causes for why Thales would have requested his return to the surface.

"It must be something of great urgency to pull me out of a journey advised and approved by him," Henry said, still shuffling possible reasons through his mind.

"Please do not waste time," Hades advised.

"I am ready," said Henry, adding, "But I would like to come back, with your permission of course."

"You will," said Hades placing a hand on Henry's shoulder.

BACK TO CROTON

Henry was transported by Hades straight to the place where Thales was waiting for him, being Croton's office. On seeing Thales, Henry respectfully bowed his head and greeted him the way Thales is accustomed to.

Seeing Croton at his desk peacefully submerged into paperwork Henry said, "I hope this is an emergency."

Thales smiled and answered, "Why else would I pull you out of hell.' And with those words Thales faced Croton and fell quiet.

Having run out of valid reasons for his presence in the room and this time Henry asked, "Why are we here?"

"Shush!" Thales said, and pointing at Croton whispered, "Watch him."

These were the last words that he heard from the old Greek before his evanescence. Left alone with Croton, completely clueless and deeply disappointed, Henry moved closer to Croton's desk and fixed his attention on the technical documents in front of him. Unable to see anything worthy of his attention, Henry stepped back into the middle of the room and looked around in anticipation of seeing something which had so far managed to escape his attention. In that very moment he noticed that the room, unprovoked, came to life. In a split second each and every object in the office was violently displaced. A heavy mahogany filing cabinet was tossed to the side like a toy.

Croton grabbed his desk with both hands to stabilize himself, and a second later he was running down the corridor shouting, "Earthquake!", urging everyone to evacuate the building. The next violent shake found Croton outside on the pavement. Barely managing to stand straight, he moved further away from all surrounding structures. Henry followed each of Croton's steps, confused with no idea of how to behave, or how to protect Croton from possible danger. The next events were completely unexpected by both of them. Suddenly everyone jumped up as though by someone's command, falling back down to the ground. All of this was accompanied by a tremendous sound that echoed through the entire city, to be followed by a cloud of dust that rushed toward them. Soon the entire street and all that was on it was plunged into darkness. Still lying on the ground and afraid to move, Croton waited for the cloud to settle to discover that there was not one of the tall buildings that managed to survive the violent knock generated and delivered from the core of Mother Earth.

The only structure that remained intact was a 100-year-old double story building, expropriated by the government after the revolution from some rich family. Having recovered a bit, Croton stood up and dusted himself down, unable to digest the magnitude of the catastrophe that surrounded him. He rubbed his eyes hoping to make it all go away. The confused and fearful faces of his disorientated staff made him pull himself together and advise them to go home and check on their families. Based on his observation and assessment of the surrounding damage, Croton concluded that his apartment block should have been able to survive this violent tremor. Due to its lower height and the fact that it was built for the ruling elite, and there was no way that any construction company would have taken any shortcuts that would have compromised its strength. Calmed by this conclusion of his reasonings, Croton decided to check on Gaya and Rose anyway. He wanted to get to his car parked behind the office building, but found it smashed by a nearby lamp post.

"Damn it," said Croton, "I will deal with this later."

Stepping back into the street he realized that the car would not have been much use anyway because all of the streets were covered by the rubble of collapsed buildings, so he chose to walk back to his home. One hundred yards later the magnitude of the devastation and the associated human tragedy struck Croton's mind. When he saw people running aimlessly around collapsed buildings in a state of panic screaming for help, Croton sped up his steps. A moment later he was running toward all that had gave meaning to his existence. Passing nearby apartment blocks not long ago allowed by him to be occupied, and seeing them turned into mountains of crushed concrete, Croton recalled all the violations that compromised the strength of those buildings that he chose to ignore.

"No, this can't have happened," he kept denying as he saw flames blazing through in search of oxygen becoming full blown fires.

"Burst gas pipes," Croton noted to himself.

The rising shouts of pleas by survivors for help, he stopped paying attention, having only one aim, to get to his loved ones and ensure their safety.

Henry, shadowing Croton, was observing the surroundings as well, because he could see a lot more to assess the impact of the tragedy. He saw guides taking care of newly released souls on their way out from the all physical into the infinite spiritual. The comfort and peace so suddenly received in contrast to the pain of separation felt by those who were destined to survive and mourn. It seemed as though Earth had shaken off all that was not hers. All that was mounted upon her body by mortal humans to satisfy their needs in search of comfort in their impermanent state of existence.

Each newly reached street deepened Croton's awareness of the scale of the unthinkable and rising uncertainty in the safety of Rose and Gaya. Seeing five-story buildings, some still standing, most half devasted, his heart plummeted into his stomach and the question, "What if?" began to choke the supply of blood to his brain.

"What if the last 6th floor on top of their apartment block was unplanned and added in a way so familiar to him?"

The realization of this possibility made him run faster, jumping over obstacles ignoring the surrounding drama, and struggling to breathe. Finally appearing at the straight stretch of street leading to his home at the end where Gaya and Rose would be waiting for him. Luckily the street was clear and soon Croton stood in front of his building… In front of what once was the place where he belonged...what once was his castle of safety with two loving hearts always expecting his return. Now, it was no more.

Turned into faceless rubble were his crushed hopes of finding his Gaya and Rose alive. Not wasting a second, he ran toward the hill climbing to the place where he presumed the remains of his apartment would be. Holding onto tiny hope that Gaya and Rose could have survived in a "pocket of life", cavities formed by upright pillars that managed to survive and carry the weight of semi-demolished bulkheads. From outside the collapsed building it resembled a pyramid where sides of it were composed of floors and ceilings smashed into each other like a multi-layered cake. Inside the pyramid, a still structurally strong staircase stood tall, at least up to the 2nd floor where someone may have had a chance. Croton knew this possibility and that knowledge filled him with the strength to dig through the rubble with his bare hands to free his family. From time to time he stopped to listen for signs of life, but then again tossed to the side boulders of concrete armed with twisted reinforcing metal bars, turning his hands into a bloody mess. A while later he stopped, realizing his powerlessness against the force of nature and the destruction it caused. Croton laid down on the rubble, exhausted and crushed by the weight of the sarcophagus that so successfully managed to trap souls in and out of its concrete walls. After a few minutes with regained strength and the will to fight destiny itself, Croton stood up and led by tiny hope that Gaya may not have been at home when all this happened, he walked down the concrete hill keeping his eyes on the road. Anticipation of their appearance at any minute, safe and unharmed, filled the tiny space remaining in his heart, making him stand in the road searching the vanishing horizon. So many men came past him, rushing to save their families from their horrible entrapment, but the absence of Gaya with little Rose buried the light within the closing in darkness. His hopes melted with the dying daylight bringing him everlasting pain, taking with it all whom he loved and cared for.

So many fathers with their sons, like a tiny group of ants, were aimlessly still digging through the concrete without tools or any hope or help from others, just driven by the wish to free their loved ones. Each with prayers on their minds and lips to reach the Creator, who just might by a miracle hear them, and hopefully forgive them for all that they have done, which by now began to surface in their corrupted minds.

Before the sun found its final rest, Croton's father Raymond had arrived. He passionately hugged his only son, the hope to find him still alive had vanished from his mind upon seeing the scale of the destruction.

"Are you okay, my boy?" Raymond asked seeing traces of dark red dried blood stains mixed with dust on his hands and body that were exposed through holes in his clothes.

"I have lost them Dad," said Croton breaking into tears for the first time. Like a walled lake would find its freedom, they flew to salt his father's shoulder.

"To lose a wife and daughter in a single act…what could be harder to withstand? To find the will to stay and live instead of ending all together." Henry heard the Planner's voice.

He turned around to find the face indifferent to the drama.

"Was it you who planned all of this?" Henry asked referring to the scene filled to its brim with misery and pain.

"Not all, just a tiny part of it…concerning Croton and his

Gaya. The train was already on its way, and to miss the opportunity to jump on the wagon would have been reckless, don't you think? Besides, if my memory serves me correctly, you wanted Rose. She's yours for now. Don't waste any time, she is back in the safety of your world. Leave Croton, he is mine. I will make him feel the depth of love through loss that had so suddenly invaded his tiny world of illusionary comfort."

"You broke his heart and probably his will to fight and live. You crushed his soul like the buildings right behind him..."

"It seems that you didn't hear what I said! I said that Rose is back. Your prayers have been answered. Go and welcome her. Deliver comfort. She will be lost without guidance."

"I heard you well," replied Henry. "I feel as though I have been ripped apart in an instant. My boy is tormented, turned to dust, and you are asking me to leave his side. To chase my own happiness and to betray my son."

"He is not your son, and the stamina he carries is well designed to take the blow that I have just delivered. Go to your Rose. No one but you can help her back to the life that she once so willingly surrendered to play the role, or should I say, to be an instrument of pain that I surgically inflicted."

Henry cast his eyes over the scene of ultimate destruction, and the son so tenderly embraced by his father in the hope to ease his pain by sharing the weight of loss amongst them.

"Look after him," Henry said, "And please be kind. Not many can recover seeing this, to lose both his wife and daughter in an instant."

"Leave them to me. Once Rose is settled safely at home, return to us to see the fiasco of this drama, although the end to it remains unknown to all participants."

Henry nodded his head agreeing with Thales' proposal, but mostly in acceptance of his might in molding the destinies of all those who he loved so dearly. Saying "Rose", Henry closed his eyes departing from the hell created on earth by powers unknown to him.

REUNION

Leaving Earth to all its troubles, Henry chose to get back home where he presumed Rose would be waiting for him. Thales' casual advise, "Get back to Rose", left no doubt in his mind that Rose would be back in their shared reality and couldn't wait to see him. As usual, Henry transported himself into the middle of their living room. Looking around not finding Rose, Henry assumed that she had gone out, probably to visit the white sandy beach abandoned by them for such a long time. The palm trees leaning over the turquoise waters of the sea were patiently waiting to envelop their creators into its entirety, and hopefully into the warm, velvety waters.

Henry stood halfway to the edge of the sea and looked around to locate his Rose, but as far as his vision could see she was nowhere to be found.

"Rose, Rose," Henry called out hoping that she would hear him and come out from wherever she was hiding. *"Maybe she is at the cascading pools,"* Henry said to himself, and as he decided to go back to the house he stumbled, closed his eyes and concentrated his thoughts to reach his one and only.

The intensity of his inner call was so great, that regardless of the distance Rose should be able to hear him, even if she was on a remote corner of the universe. But there was no reply. Henry stood lost, feeling abandoned in the middle of the white sand paradise, trying to find reasons for Rose's absence. He knew that Thales would not mislead him just to get him away from Croton and all the tragedy he was about to experience. The way that Thales insisted on his departure left no doubts in Henry's mind that his return to Croton would be imminent. Suddenly a horrifying revelation came to him...deep anxiety flooded his heart and mind. Like a sack of lead it dropped onto the sand in the realization of the fact that Rose could be still in the state of mind she had just left the physical world. This knowledge shattered his world into tiny pieces with no hope of being reassembled. The very fact that his lovely Rose could stand in front of him in the shape of a three-year-old child made him cover his face with the palms of his hands and scream in despair, “Nooooo!”

After some time he came to terms with the reality that he had to face, Henry stood up and walked back to the house. He went to find little Rose in one of the bedrooms where she was most probably sleeping, completely unaware of his existence. Carefully opening each bedroom door, one by one, he still didn’t find the girl who gave him some small hope that perhaps he had been mistaken, and that Rose was waiting for him somewhere else.

“But where?” Henry asked himself.

Attempts to locate Thales failed, as probably he was helping Croton to ease his grief. Henry dropped onto the sofa with the question timelessly on his lips, “Where are you?”

Usually in such situations, the librarian was his next choice, but this time Henry chose not to bother Aaron, and rather solve this puzzle by himself. A minute later he asked, “What if she is where I saw her last?” and without wasting any more time Henry transported himself into the preparation chamber.

As always it was filled with souls getting ready to be sent to Earth. Looking around Henry tried to locate amongst the thousands of doors the one that had separated them, but he couldn’t. They were located so close to each other, and all so similar in appearance, that Henry chose to wait for her at their usual place, at the same table, at the same cafeteria. Passing in front of him full of excitement newbies getting ready to face a human lifetime of constant tests made him dizzy, and leaning back in his chair he closed his eyes to escape the frenzy.

As though awakened from an infinite slumber, Rose slowly regained her sight. Three nurses were standing at her side and tenderly observing her arrival.

One of them leaned over gently asking, “Are you okay, my dear?”

‘Yes, I am,” Rose replied immediately, surprised thinking ‘why shouldn’t she?’

“You can get out of your bed,” said the nurse standing next to her, offering her hand.

Rose accepted the offer and effortlessly stood up, feeling slightly disorientated. She continued to hold the nurse's hand to take a step toward the door of the ward.

As she regained her confidence, she freed her hand and facing the nurses asked, "Am I free to go?"

"Do you know where to?" asked one of the nurses.

"Yes, to my husband," answered Rose.

"Do you have any memories of the past?" asked a nurse.

Rose looked around, holding her temples in both hands in an attempt to refresh her memory and then said, "I remember walking into this ward to be transferred to Earth…"

"That's right. Anything else?"

"Then I woke up," said Rose.

"Can you recall any memories in between?" insisted the curious nurse.

Rose closed her eyes to recover her memories, but nothing surfaced to her mind.

"I'm not sure that you will be satisfied, but it feels like I just fell asleep and woke up with not much to add."

"That's right," said the nurse, "You are free to leave. Your husband is waiting outside this door to greet you back into his life."

The door opened wide and Rose, feeling nauseous and confused, stepped into the preparation chamber, into the noisy world of hustle and bustle created by the souls ready to start their new lives from scratch. Unable to locate Henry at the exit, Rose went to the cafeteria and soon she was standing right in front of him.

"Couldn't you have waited for me at the door?" Henry heard the voice that was so dear to him and missed for such a long time.

He opened his eyes, stood up, and stepping forward carefully hugged Rose as if he was embracing a fragile artifact which could have shattered with any sudden movement.

Rose was confused by Henry's silence and the intensity of love that he conveyed with a single touch. Placing her hands around his waist she simply asked, "You're acting as though I have been lost?"

Realizing the fact that Rose was unaware of the time she had spent on Earth and her tragic exit, he only pressed her tighter into her chest afraid of once more losing her.

"You've been lost to me," Henry whispered allowing tears of

happiness to be a witness of his joy.

Rose gently pulled back and looking straight into Henry's wet eyes asked, "What did I miss?"

"Not much my love. Four years of our common life."

"What do you mean?" exclaimed bewildered Rose.

Henry tenderly took her hands into his and deeply sighed saying, "Let's go home."

DISCLOSURE

Henry transported them into the wonder of the cascading pools, created by Croton in his backyard to welcome him into the world of spirits.

"Please have a seat, my dear," Henry gestured to Rose.

Rose lowered herself onto a flat rock that was harmoniously chained with others like it to frame the upper level of the shallow waters, emerging from nowhere, cascading down to the lower levels, and disappearing into the sands of their common reality. Rose was clueless and confused by her husband's words.

Henry sat near her on the well-maintained grass, placing his hands on her knees, squeezing them tightly together as though chaining them, and said, "Not in a million years."

Rose dipped one hand into the peaceful water and the other ran through Henry's hair, and then tenderly so as not to disturb the serenity of the moment she asked, "Speak to me, my love. What do you mean by that? You mentioned earlier four years which seems that I am completely unaware of."

Without taking his eyes from the vanishing horizon, Henry said, "Between your exit and entrance through the doors of the preparation chamber you were on Earth in the body of a baby girl who had a loving mother, Gaya, and Croton was your father. Does this disclosure ring any bells?"

Rose froze for a moment and closed her eyes, and as though observing a movie, she watched the life of a toddler spread into segmented pieces. Rose witnessed the time of the baby's birth, some scenes of carefree existence surrounded by toys and loving parents…

"I was a girl. Yes, I remember now." Rose whispered as if awakening from a timeless slumber. I remember the faces of my parents, and the love that they showered me with from head to toe, accompanied by a thousand kisses."

Rose paused momentarily and then continued, "I also

remember scary nights alone in bed, and then the comforting embrace of my mom…"

"Do you remember me?" Henry asked interrupting Rose's journey into her recent past.

"No, I don't remember you there."

"No wonder," Henry said disappointed.

"Are you saying that all the time that I spent on Earth as a little girl…"

"I was a witness of your absence from my life. What can I say…it wasn't easy."

"Sorry for the pain that I caused you," Rose replied, stumbling for a moment. The word "pain" brought back some memories, still blurry, but increasingly alarming.

"Wait a minute," said Rose as she stood up and gently pushed Henry to the side. "I just remembered something."

She stepped away, placed her hands on her temples and concentrated the entire energy of her soul to recall her exit from the human world. Suddenly she looked at Henry with horror in her eyes and almost screamed in absolute despair, "Mommy! What happened to my mother?"

Henry sighed deeply before pronouncing the words capable of breaking the most tested hearts, "She didn't make it," Henry said, stepping closer to embrace her, but Rose stepped away to fully recall the emerging order of events.

"Wait a minute, what happened to my father? Where did my mother go? They are probably in a lot of pain, to lose a child so young. I have to check on them," demanded the loving daughter.

"We just got home my love. I haven't had enough time with you yet. Your long-awaited presence here next to me still burns a hole in my craving soul."

"Once my heart is settled, we will have it all, but for now, please, take me to my parents. I won't be able to do it on my own. You know the place. I beg you, please. Take me at least to one of them." Rose cried out grabbing Henry's hands.

Filled by Rose's pain Henry said, "I will be able to locate your father, but I do not advise you to see him now, as he is in a lot of pain."

"Please take me to him now," Rose begged.

Henry squeezed her hands and with a heavy heart foreseeing a troubled future, he transported them to the land of humans, showered with sadness and boundless sorrow.

Croton was on Henry's mind, and they appeared right beside him.

Rose cautiously stepped in front of him to see the face of her mourning father. He was completely covered in dust. Dirt, crystalized with tears, surrounded his eyes, and his forehead was smeared by the sleeve of his jacket that had been ripped into shreds.

Rose gazed deeply into his eyes and surprised her husband by saying, "What happened to you, my son?"

Croton was in front of her, the one she nurtured as her own, from the time of his arrival in the sinful world, until the time he chose to be a father. A strange mixture of emotions in the shape of love, both as Croton's daughter and his guide, filled her heart and ripped it in half. Soon the emotions took their path and Rose faced Croton, now as a loving mother crushed by the pain that she had caused him as his daughter.

"You should not have brought her here!" Henry heard Thales' rebuke.

"I didn't want to. She insisted to see and say farewell to the one who was her father."

"I know her reasons!" shouted Thales angrily. "I need Rose to visit Gaya, and to comfort her after such a tragic exit."

On seeing Thales standing next to Henry, conversing casually, seemingly unaffected by the tragedy imposed by him, Rose was unable to control her anger and walked straight up to him boldly stating, "I hope you are satisfied!"

Thales gently smiled, accepting Rose's attack, especially the nonverbalized ones, and calmly answered, "The path to awakening is always harsh. For those who want to smell the flowers, a tiny poke from a thorn should be no obstacle."

"A tiny poke!" Rose said loudly. "You call this a tiny poke. The annihilation of an entire city. Thousands of souls ascending in the nick of time, condemning many more to mourn the deaths of their loved ones."

"Don't blame the entire devastation on me," answered Thales. "I saw an opportunity and took it. What, if not emotional turmoil, can strengthen the barely breathing flame of love?"

Seeing Rose's uncontrollable frustration, Henry stepped to her whispering in her ear, "You must remember who you are talking to."

Rose managed to contain the growing fire, realizing the Godly power of this seemingly simple man. She stepped back and respectfully asked for forgiveness.

"It's quite all right, my child," Thales said, deeply satisfied. "To witness this and be emotionally detached is an enormous task for newly recruited guides. You keep forgetting that death is a simple transformation and also an important lesson for those who remain alive. For now, I suggest that you leave all of this behind. Forget about Croton, I will help your husband to ease the approaching weight of tests and expected terms to be presented to our Croton. Can he withstand the emotional destruction, or will he break like a branch beneath the heavy weight of the fruits it carries."

Hearing Thales' words Henry jumped in, "Please be merciful on Croton. He won't withstand another blow."

Ignoring Henry's plea for kindness, Thales looked at Rose and said, "Are you forgetting someone?"

"Who?" asked Rose.

"Your mother, Gaya. Although Lita is taking care of her, she needs your presence. The pain that she is experiencing now at losing her only child is a lot stronger than separation from her husband."

"What should I do?" asked Rose. "My current appearance will confuse her."

"You'll find a way to ease her pain. A true mother will always recognize her child, regardless of the shell of her appearance."

On saying these last words, the old Greek stretched out his hand and gently touched Rose on her shoulder.

"Goodbye, my love, I will see you when you are done," Henry said to his wife as she evaporated from sight.

WITHDRAWAL

Lita, Gaya's guide, being familiar with the procedure of a soul's sudden exist into the spiritual realm, stood firmly besides Gaya. She knew the exact time and scenario of Gaya's death with a child in her arms. She had no concerns about the inevitable drama. Her target was the mother standing in the doorway. The destiny of the child was also known to her in advance, with her exit being predestined and so no assistance was required. Although Gaya's stepping into the world of spirit remained problematic due to the unpredictability of the young mother's reaction.

When the sudden devastating knock from the Earth's core left everyone to hang in mid-air before plunging to their final death, Lita stepped forward, placing her arms around Gaya's waist and locked their heads together. When Gaya's Earthly body, with child in arms, flew to certain death, her soul, like a glove, slipped from the owner's hand, left suspended in the air like floating angels head-to-head above all physical destruction. A moment later, mind to mind they gently flew to heaven. Without leaving anything to chance, experienced Lita did not allow the frightened mom to witness any drama. With the power of her mind, she placed her Gaya into an unconscious state, a sleep from which she would be awakened from in heaven, in a place of comfort and manifested pleasant dreams.

Gaya opened her eyes to face the most beautiful garden. Flowers that she'd never seen before were thoughtfully coordinated by color, to be admired and impressed by those who choose to witness their beauty and inhale their exquisite blooming scent. The surroundings were plunged in colors that Gaya had not witnessed before. It seemed that her vision had been unveiled to the true identity of nature, so bright, and yet tastefully composed to touch and melt the most awakened of hearts in appreciation of creators of such a symphony of floral life.

Gaya stood in the middle of a narrow pathway, and not to

explore this beautiful garden, not to discover all that it had to offer was beyond her nature. She cautiously stepped forward toward the sound of music that was soothing and compelled her to find the source and owner of the garden. She stumbled upon this garden not by her own will. A few more steps and Gaya came across a pond of crystal-clear water, playfully reflecting the world confined into the tiny heaven which could only exist in vivid dreams.

She looked around, pinched her arm, and realizing the absence of feeling she said, "I am definitely dreaming. Only in dreams can things be this perfect. I would love to stay in such a place forever."

"You may if you just wish it," Gaya heard a voice invading her calmness.

She looked around frightened and confused, but no one came forward to identify themselves.

"Who are you?" Gaya whispered cautiously.

"My name is Lita, and I am standing right in front of you."

Gaya stepped back with her fear subsiding, softly squinting her eyes to see a silhouette at first, and then the figure of a strange, unearthly beauty of a woman looking tenderly and kindly at her.

"Are you the owner of this garden?" asked Gaya, unable to move her eyes from the perfection standing in front of her.

"Yes, dear Gaya, you are in my world. But if you wish to stay forever, you are more than welcome. Be my guest."

"I can't," said Gaya, frightened again.

"Why?" asked Lita.

"No one can stay in dreams forever. All of this will vanish when I wake up."

"So, you think that all of this is nothing but a dream, and that I am a figment of your imagination?" asked Lita still showering Gaya with tenderness and love.

"I don't see any other explanation for how I am here."

Lita gently took Gaya's hand in hers and asked her to sit with her on a nearby bench. Without letting go of her hand, she kept looking at Gaya, like a mother with a child who was about to be hurt. With pain in her heart and the crashing weight of feelings Lita said, "This is not a dream, my dear Gaya, and this reality is yours."

"No, this cannot be," cried Gaya pulling her hands free.

"Do you remember how you got here?" asked Lita inflicting a tiny cut.

"I was with Rose, my tiny daughter. It was my husband's

father's birthday, and we were getting ready to..."

She stopped clenching her fists tightly to face the approaching agony, reliving the final moments of her life she froze in the moment of reflected past. The distraught mother slid off the bench onto her knees placing her arms as if holding a child, looking at Lita with insanity in her eyes and screamed in agony, "Where is my child? She was right here in my arms..."

Casting her eyes from side to side she asked Lita, "Did you see my little girl. I lost her on my way to you."

"Please calm down, you didn't lose your child. I am sure that she is somewhere close to us. You need to settle down first, to come to terms with the changes that have occurred in your life and to hopefully understand why you are here and who I am," said Lita delivering her final blow. Inflicting a deeper cut into Gaya's heart to be healed later when the bleeding stopped.

Gaya stood up, looked at the peaceful water in the pond, and under the weight of crushing facts whispered, "Did I die?"

Being an experienced guide and knowing that there is no easy way to break the news, Lita stood up and facing Gaya said, "Yes."

Still looking far away, right through Lita, with tears running down her cheeks, Gaya said, "I was so young. My life had just begun. It was so short. I didn't have the chance to live. This is so unfair. What did I do to deserve such a brutal execution?"

Lita took both of Gaya's hands saying optimistically, "As you can see, you are not dead and neither did Rose suffer the earthquake. She is well and safely back in the place where she came to you from."

"Your words are confusing," said Gaya. "She came from me, and I demand to see my child. I want to hold her in my arms. I want to pamper her and give her all my love. Where are you holding her? Please be my guide and lead me to my daughter."

Grasping Gaya's unwillingness to give up, Lita offered, "Let me see what I can do. If there is a tiny chance I will bring your daughter here, but not for long. Besides, don't be surprised to find her changed, or maybe all grown up."

Saying this she vanished completely from Gaya's sight.

RECAP

Once Rose had departed to attend to her mother Gaya, to help her to find her footing, peace, and rest in a whole new world into which she suddenly appeared, Henry moved back to Earth and addressed Thales, "Please bring me into the picture, what did I miss while I went to welcome Rose home?' How is Croton dealing with his loss?"

"Three days have passed since your departure. As you can see, the hill of a building is now a lot lower thanks to a single excavator that Raymond managed to persuade to change course by flashing money at the driver."

"Any luck?" asked Henry.

"Only from the upper floor they managed to retrieve a family of four, alive, a mother and three daughters."

"What about the rest?"

"The rest of the humans have found their final rest, freeing their souls into the spiritual realms," stated the man who was the tool in a bigger game.

In the game of punishment of those who had to stay behind to judge themselves, or even mighty God. To stay alive and pick themselves up again from scratch and hopefully to find answers to the most important question of their life…"What did I do to violate the Creator's laws and deserve such a heartless retribution?"

"Have they recovered Gaya's body?" Henry asked.

"Yes, they were found lying one on top of the other."

Suppressing a rising wave of eye watering emotions Henry asked, "Has Croton seen them?"

"Yes."

"That image will be hard to irradicate from the memory of a loving husband and father of little Rose," said Henry with a single sigh, expressing sorrow for his "son" and long reassigned, but dearly missed mentor. "Where are their bodies now?"

"In the mortuary, where they belong. Although most of the recovered bodies have been buried already without wasting time, hoping to avoid the possibility of plague."

As Thales ended his speech, Raymond stepped into the scene, approaching Croton from behind, he placed his hand on his dusty shoulder.

"I don't know how to break this news to you my son," he said extracting the words like teeth by a dentist.

"Just spill it out Dad. You can't kill one who is already dead."

"The results of the autopsy of Gaya's body have been made available…"

"And?" asked Croton. "Was she terminally ill and death would have found her sooner or later, or perhaps something was wrong with my daughter?"

"No, my son. I thought that you should know this…she was pregnant with your son."

Saying these last words Raymond burst into tears, burying his face in Croton's shoulder and fighting the pain that clenched his entire self. Croton didn't move a muscle. He stood like a statue staring at the horizon where hopes and dreams once flourished, but had now come to an end, and were completely banished from his future without a trace. As if someone with a mighty hand had dropped a blanket of darkness to disguise the light from one who innocently thought he had found steadiness and comfort. This tiny world created by a husband with a humble wife and lovely daughter. This island of happiness and bliss fell to pieces in an instant, leaving him lost, unwanted, and unambitious.

This news was the deciding fall of the scale, tilting the arms to a nonrecoverable state and without hesitation Croton said, "Thank you, Father, for your assistance in relieving the pain of my decision."

"What decision son?" asked Raymond concerned for his only son.

"Go and rest, you look so tired. We have both been through what no one ever should be forced to deal with…yes, and one more thing, I am really sorry about your grandson that you so badly wanted to embrace. But, if you ask me why all of this found you and me, I'll answer…Mom was right. Out of shady deeds of the past will always bite us on the ass."

"Stop placing blame upon your shoulders," said Raymond, worried for his son. "Just look around and grasp the magnitude and depth of this disaster, it's not only us, but the entire nation who are mourning the loss of their loved ones, and you say Mom was right? If there is a God like she was saying, all loving and forgiving, then how in a normal state of mind could he permit such a profoundly evil act? No, don't tell me that He is somewhere up there watching us. But, if he is, I curse him from the depth of my tormented heart for taking all whom I have come to love."

Raymond's last words were addressed to the pewter skies filled with snow and ready to discharge their contents. A few flakes were already dancing in the air, warning of the approaching frosty night. Raymond left, leaving Croton to his own quest, to deal with his loss under the watchful eyes of Henry, his guide, who had lost his footing, time, and space, with that part of him wanting to remain with Croton and the other to reconnect with Rose.

"I have to leave you now," Thales said, "He is all yours. There is no Rose to back you up. Please don't forget that his destiny is in your hands, and so is yours in his. You have a night and probably tomorrow to hold him back and hopefully prevent the plan that is rapidly growing in his fragmented mind."

"What plan?" asked Henry in alarm.

"You'll find out soon enough," replied Thales, leaving on their own two souls completely lost on either side of this harsh existence.

Night approached silently, inviting to this place of broken hearts and structures, the chill of inescapable frost waiting to decorate the entire scene. To freeze to death all that had managed to escape the destruction in a desperate strive for life. The life that had lost its purpose in the eyes of poor Croton.

Unable to feel the cold, but sensing its approach, Henry moved closer to the frozen Croton and whispered in his ear, "You are going to freeze to death. Find shelter now before it is too late."

As though awakened by Henry's words, Croton slipped deeper into his jacket, exposing to the harsh climate only his eyes and nose. Then he looked again at what was once the center of his world, where the dear two lives were blooming, but the sudden turn of terrible events left him to face the sarcophagus of buildings once standing tall. Soon, followed by his devoted guide, having failed utterly all tasks of being a husband and protector to his child, Croton took the path up the hill again, hoping to find some evidence of his past which may have survived in the concrete mess, evidence that could warm his heart chilled in the fist of ruthless winter. He climbed slowly up to the flattened top of the hill left empty by the excavator that had moved away in desperate search to find survivors elsewhere. A moment later Croton found himself standing in the remnants of his own living room, on a section of the floor covered in Persian carpets. He knelt to free the carpet from the rocks, leaned to his side, and slowly lay down with the desire to freeze to death before the new dawn touched the surface of the earth.

Seeing Croton's plan to end it all in sleep, Henry sat down next to him and found himself in scary thoughts, "Why not? This could be an easy exit from such a nightmare. This could be his ticket to freedom, not only for poor Croton, but also for myself. Without Croton being here no force in the universe could tie me to this place, to this city forsaken by the Gods where life has turned into death by a single flick of a switch turned by an undetected finger. I hate this place," said Henry, surprising himself with such a confession. "I miss my Rose. I miss all that which is detached from the misery of this soulless place, designed for the suffering of poor humans. To die in sleep…what a relief. It cannot be seen as suicide…and maybe…I can have my mentor back, my devoted guide that I lost once to his stupid quest to find his one and only, but instead he lost it all, what he was so adamantly seeking. Go on, my friend. Fall into sleep and I will wait for your arrival on the side of happiness and joy, where Gaya and your little Rose will welcome you into peace and comfort."

Unknown of the upcoming act, Henry stood next to Croton so that when the moment comes for his soul to leave his unconscious body he would step to grasp and lift his friend up to the world of spirits.

INTERRUPTION

"Not so fast!" Henry heard a woman's voice so frightfully familiar. The one he left in the past with the utmost hope to never see again in the future.

"Tatiana?" Doubting his vision, Henry asked. "Why are you here? Don't you see that he is done? Just let him leave in peace," Henry pleaded, foreseeing nothing good coming from the Tempter's sudden visit.

"You know, my dear Henry, these things are beyond our will. I have been sent to my duties."

"And what are they?"

"To keep him safe and warm until morning," Tatiana said pointing at sleeping Croton, and then without further hesitation she covered Croton with her entire body.

A moment later, the life that was about to check-out from a frozen corpse stepped back into Croton's body, inviting back steady breathing, color to his face, and pleasant dreams to be dispersed with the arrival of morning. Completely lost and puzzled, Henry lay down next to them, not understanding the purpose for saving Croton's life. He chose to wait until morning to witness the bigger plan, the plan that by someone's will he was undoubtedly excluded. With the gentle touch of the rising sun, he checked on Croton, still enveloped by the Tempters body, in a tranquil sleep ignorant of the ordeal that has been orchestrated just for him to be experience in the approaching day.

Sensing Henry's movement Tatiana gently moved away from Croton, stood up to face Henry and said, "My job is done. He is all yours again."

"What was the purpose of your actions? His soul was almost free. You brought him back to life. I wish I could thank you for your act, but all you've done is extend his torture."

"I know," Tatiana replied, self-satisfied. "You didn't think that Croton could leave this place without paying the price for all of the sins that he has committed?"

"He has paid the price, he has lost his wife and daughter. He lost it all. There is no greater punishment. Why didn't you let him leave this world in peace?"

Tatiana smiled and stepping closer, right into Henry's comfort zone, softly whispering into his ear, "You should know once Croton crosses the line between two worlds, he will find all that he has lost in an instant. But before that can happen, he has a karmic debt to cover."

In front of Henry's eyes scenes played of Croton's shady deals, the result of which were the crumbled buildings that became the graves for many lives, emphasizing the insatiability of human greed in the desire for more possessions.

"I see," said Henry, acknowledging the awakened Croton.

Dissatisfaction with the fact that he was still alive was hard to miss by Henry and Tatiana. He stood up slowly and watched the rising sun, seeing it as a sentence for another day in hell. He looked around searching for something meaningful in memory of those who ripped his heart into tiny pieces, leaving for a place where he just failed to visit. The blink of awakening sun reflecting off the surface of a smooth, white surface attracted Croton's attention. Gaya's pearl necklace that he gave her as a birthday gift was hiding in a dusty corner. Croton knelt and picked it up, dusted it off, and pressed it against his lips. He sensed her dear presence and the scent of skin concealed in the essence of the tiny beads.

Completely absorbed by Croton's act, Henry failed to notice Tatiana's quiet disappearance. She slipped away just as she appeared, unnoticeable like vapor exhaled by a man in the freezing cold. Left alone with Croton and forced to act like a caring guide, Henry focused on Croton's mind. He tried to hear Croton's thoughts and hopefully to understand his own role in the soon to unfold human drama.

Suddenly he heard a voice, not of the man in front of him, but rather the voice of his mighty friend that could reach him irrespective of the distance, time, and place.

Doubting his own hearing, Henry moved closer to a man with the beads so tightly squeezed against his lips, then he heard him say, "I have lost it all. There is no meaning left to life, to breath. All that I loved has perished in this rubble, and purpose of my life is buried underneath it all. How can I live with the nasty worm of guilt living in my mind and eating me alive? All that I could, but never did…all whom I loved, left unattended…if I could only bring those days back, I would spend them at Gaya's side. To touch her, look into her eyes, to know her better…oh, there was so much to know. She was a cup filled with love and I am a fool who failed to drink it to the bottom. All that I had was a sip, not even a taste, and most of her was left still unblemished."

Croton cast his eyes to the winter sun awakened from slumber and walked down the concrete hill, right to the dead-end of the street. Before disaster struck this city there was a barrier preventing curious observers from accidental fall off a dramatic cliff. The depth of the gorge measured 100 yards with a mighty river at its bed. Due to the earthquake the barrier was gone, probably lying at the bottom of the gorge, exposing the end of the road to unsuspecting drivers to find their end at the bottom of the rocky bed. A few more steps and Croton was standing right on the edge. Having a phobia of heights avoidance of this place, and especially this spot, was a priority for Croton, but now… something had changed. He had lost his fear. Standing at the edge and looking up into the cloudy sky it felt so right.

Henry's worst nightmares slowly regained their shape, turning into a ferocious creature, the one that waited for its prey right at the gates of hell, where the victim would not only be Croton, but his guide as well, if suicide was choice for an early exit.

Henry heard again, "I wanted to grow old with you, my Gaya, to embrace old age together, to be surrounded by the love of our children and hopefully their children, too, and then, and only then, when time and age will force us to face our death together. Two bodies cuddled into one to slip away into the darkness. But… those dreams are shattered like this world. You couldn't wait. You were impatient always and in this rush for an early exit you took my daughter, and my son as well. So, most of me is gone. What is left behind is just a ghost, and a ghost as you know does not belong with the living. My purpose is served," Croton said spreading his arms apart like a bird preparing to launch into the sky.

"No!" Henry screamed into Croton's ear, "Don't even think about it!"

Scenes from the hell from where he had just emerged paraded in front of him. He saw his friend and mentor trapped in dark confinement with lost and self-condemning souls.

"Not yet," Henry heard the Tempters voice.

"Tatiana, I thought your business with us was done?"

"Not yet, my friend. There is a final brush stroke left."

"What is that supposed to mean?"

"Realization of the truth and the part he played in the city's demolition."

"It was a natural disaster," Henry screamed into Tatiana's face.

"You can believe all what you want, but the truth is brutal and definitely hard to be faced."

Ignoring Henry, Tatiana stepped into Croton's space and closed her eyes, transmitting pictures from the recent past. As if awakened to an unknown truth, Croton stepped back from the frightening edge. He grabbed his head and slowly sat down on the frozen earth. Henry could see how pitilessly Tatiana was battering Croton's weakened mind with images of him accepting bribes.

"My mom was right," Henry heard Croton's words. "I lived in sin. Because of me so many people found their final resting place buried beneath what they believe to be the safest place. Their houses became their burial stones, because of me and my insatiable love of money. The loss of Gaya, Rose, and our unborn boy is the price that I had to pay. Hell, if it exists somewhere, is definitely where I belong," said Croton, inhaling his chest with cold crispy air, screaming on the top of his lungs, "God knows I tried. I don't expect forgiveness. If hell is what You want me to embrace, then I am yours."

Before those words were echoed in the gorge, Croton stood up and stepped right to the edge. Foreseeing the aim of Tatiana's task and sensing Croton reaching the apogee of his decision, Henry stepped between them like a wall and pushed Tatiana into the gorge to free his friend from such entrapment. Tatiana's eyes, filled with compassion, met with Henry's for one last time. There was no anger, nor resentment. She was aware of the pain her act would cause the guide and the guided by him soul.

As she plunged to Earth, she simply said, "Apologies, my friend."

Ignoring the Tempters final words Henry turned back to check on Croton, but he was gone, and the spot where he had been standing was empty. Confused, Henry looked down to look at the bottom of the gorge.

"Oh no, what have I done!" Henry shouted in despair, holding his head in his hands and falling to his knees.

A moment later Henry tried to overcome emotions, looked around in a desperate search for Thales, or someone who could help, but the universe was quiet, leaving him alone to deal with Croton's liberated soul, wherever it may have been transferred. He descended right to the bottom of the gorge with a tiny hope to find his mentor standing next to the battered body of a boy.

"What if he's back the way I met him? Wearing a white tunic as he always did. I will give him a hug and lead him to the place where we spent our entire life together. To the place that remained empty without him at my side."

Reflecting on those times Henry realized that all his troubles began right at the time when Croton took a leap of life to find his true love. The aftermath was a roller-coaster. To Henry's great displeasure he did not find a confused and lost newly departed soul next to Croton's lifeless body.

"Goodbye, my friend," said Henry to the corpse that once served as a cage to its soul. To a soul who chose to leave this god forsaken land, to all its troubles and eternal strain, which incarnated souls had to experience. The last tie attaching Henry to Earth was hacked by Croton's desperate act, thereby granting freedom to them both. But he was wrong.

Henry turned his back on the gruesome scene, casting his eyes up to the unfriendly sky.

"I'm coming back," he said, "to rest in the arms of my beloved Rose and hopefully in the company of my devoted friend."

But he was utterly mistaken. There was no Rose, and no Croton to salute him on his return.

"Rose is probably still busy with her mother, Gaya." He said to himself. "But what about Croton? I must be wrong in my assumptions. I am comparing him to Rose, who stepped straight back into what was left unfinished. What if…what if he is lost in a different dimension? After all, it wasn't death of natural causes, but a suicidal act."

This last thought made Henry sit down to gather his thoughts.

"No, this cannot be right. Could he be in hell?"

"Where else?" Henry heard Thales' invasion. "All suicides are destined to descend to the place that they see themselves belonging right at the end of their intolerable life."

Henry recalled Croton's final words which were definitely addressed to God, "If hell is what You want me to embrace, then I am yours."

Henry, with a heavy heart, looked at Thales, who lately it seemed like he could not escape.

"If my memory serves me right, you said that Croton's safe, and all those shady deals that he was involved with would not affect his future life. You said that his target was to find his better half. What happened? Why is there a change of plans?" Henry asked.

"First of all, his final words were probably addressed to God, and it was not the heaven that he envisioned. Hell was on Croton's mind before he set himself to freedom."

"Are you saying that his self-judgement at the final moments of his life created a path straight to Hades' kingdom?"

"That's right. He basically condemned himself into a tiny cell."

"Well…I have unfinished business there anyway," Henry said, remembering Nazia.

"Before you do," said Thales, "just remember that Croton is no prisoner of hell. To free him from the burden that he placed upon himself should be your priority."

With these last words the old Greek fell silent, allowing the moment to settle for a more important message to be conveyed.

"By freeing him you will get your own freedom and comfort in the arms of Rose."

"Regardless, I will free my friend," said Henry, ready to descend, but then he stopped and looked deeply into the Greek's eyes and asked, "Is there a chance for me to have my friend back in the spiritual realms the way I had him back in time?"

Thales smiled and answered, "Where there is a will, there is a way." These were the final words from the Planner.

RESCUE MISSION

Croton cast his eyes to the sky in search of answers to the question that so many humans came across in search of a remedy to stop the intolerable present, either to leave behind all that was hurting by crossing the line and ending their destiny for an unfathomable future, or to simply stay and fight. But, to fight for what and whom? There was no enemy to face with his only rival being himself. Can he forget his wife and daughter. To shadow the memories of the past and find a replacement for his Gaya?

"No, I cannot," said Croton to himself.

Then he inhaled all the oxygen he could to have enough to last him to the end and looking up at the skies he shouted, "God knows I have tried. I don't expect forgiveness. If hell is what You want me to embrace, then I am yours."

Next, he felt the sensation of utter freedom. The upcoming impact with Earth was of no concern to Croton. He had a second more to exist and it was filled with bliss and a tiny hope, like a blink of light on a weathering horizon, that Gaya and his little Rose were waiting to welcome him into a different, but perfect world, where pain and suffering did not exist.

He closed his eyes before the horrendous crash, leaving natures gravity to do its work. But impact with Earth did not occur. He simply penetrated through the crust into a corridor of gloomy darkness, into the unknown which certainly was not death. Strange images on the walls of the channel that he was in rushed all around him. Scenes from his recent past filled his heart with hatred toward his own actions, where the word forgiveness could no longer be. All that was perceived in the past as doubts became certainties of his immoral act, where piles of documents highlighted with his own initials flashed into his face were cause for his deep remorse. His accelerating fall became unbearable emotion comprised of fear, panic, and regrets. Croton closed his eyes to stop the painful visions. He clenched his entire body in anticipation of a crash, presuming that by chance, instead of hitting ground he had fallen into an endless hole that would come to an end where he could find his own ending. Suddenly he realized that motion had stopped. He was no longer in a weightless fall, and the anticipated crash did not occur. Without opening his eyes, he realized that he was sitting on something wet and mushy. Choosing to observe his surroundings he concluded that his eyes were never closed and the place he ended up in was plunged in darkness. No source of light could find its way through a door or window to help him to assess the place. The smell of dampness was overwhelming, and only the echo of water drops seeping through the ceiling helped him to assess the restrictions of his confinement.

Croton stood up carefully to check the perimeter of his entrapment, realizing that the room he was in measured about sixteen foot by sixteen foot. Lost into reasons of how he could survive such a tremendous fall and end up in such a dump made him find the center of the room and lower himself back onto the mushy substance.

“Where the hell am I?” Croton asked hoping to find some reasonable answer.

Left alone to plan his next steps to rescue Croton from hell, Henry came to a dilemma. To disturb Christ and beg him for help, or to descend straight to Hades. The second choice was a longer shot, but in his judgement seemed to be the right one. One thing that Henry had learned for definite in these realms was that presumed shortcuts eventually would backfire, and not in a pretty way.

“So, Hades it is,” he said loudly, closing his eyes.

“You are back so soon?” Henry heard Hades’ voice before reopening his eyes.

“Yes, I had to.”

“Is this still about the Muslim girl?”

“No, I have a friend who ended his life and as result may be here.”

Hades smiled sadly saying, “Give me some clarity on this. You have come to rescue a soul who you are supposed to guide? To keep him safe from harm, and above all prevent his early exit?”

“Yes,” admitted Henry. “But the way you put it feels like you are condemning me.”

“Don’t you?”

“I saw his tree of life and many branches were extremely short, which I presumed indicated an early exit.”

"Let us see," said Hades, and in the middle of the floating island appeared Croton's tree of life standing taller than Henry. Right between them firmly rooted in the crystal soil.

"I see," said Hades after thorough observation. "You were right. It seems like suicide was the Planner's vision to trigger dormant, powerful emotions." After a moment Hades added, "Yup, love was the purpose for his decent to Earth."

"You are right," said Henry.

"And?" asked Hades.

"He found it, but then he lost her in a horrible event."

Hades signed deeply saying, "The Planners really know how to push the right buttons, but most importantly, when to push them."

"Why do they do that?' Henry asked.

"The way I see it, the purpose of their acts is to create a perfect being, or should I say, to help each soul to their perfection. Although perfection is something one can never achieve. In short, they push us to find our best selves by forcing us into emotional turmoil."

"So, what about Croton, do you know his place?"

"With the recent cataclysmic events, I have had so many souls arriving lately, but to accelerate our search, share with me his image."

A second later Hades asked surprised, "A Roman senator?"

"Oh, I am sorry, this image of my friend has been embedded in my head."

Henry placed both hands on his temples and sent to Hades images of Croton standing on the edge of the cliff.

Without any hesitation Hades said, "He is on level four."

"Why four? He should be on level one," protested Henry.

"The location of souls in hell is not my prerogative. They find their own way to my forsaken kingdom all by themselves."

"I guess they are pulled to the level according to their soul's vibration."

"Not only that, also the deeds of their past are a deciding factor. Simply, bigger sins lead to a deeper placement."

"I still remember levels one and two, but what about three and four? Who do you keep in those confinements?"

"Please remember, dear Henry, I do not keep them in those cells. Neither are they prisoners of mine. The doors are all wide open. All they have to do is to forgive themselves."

"Can we go ahead. I am dying to see Croton?"

"Be my guest," said Hades walking to the edge of the floating island.

Henry followed him, spontaneously planning his argumentative speech to convince his dear friend to release himself from the heavy burden. The long stretch of suspended staircase appeared in front of them.

While passing the second level Henry asked, "The Muslim girl, Nazia, is she still in her cell?"

"Where else can she be?" Hades answered.

At level three Henry addressed him again, "What type of souls are attracted to this level?"

"Here I have souls who choose to play with forces of darkness. Those who extracted income by manipulating humans through their weakness. Those who were helping souls on Earth to ease their lives through magic. Casting spells and curses on others to line their pockets, greed, and ego. But, as you know, the universal laws prevails and what we cast on others will always find its way to us."

"I see. Then what about the fourth level?" Henry asked.

"The fourth is allocated to corrupt officials," smiled Hades, "If this was a physical and not a spiritual realm, I would say that we are running out of space on this level," Hades continued with irony seeping through his voice.

A moment later they stopped in front a door behind which Henry presumed was Croton.

"You know the rules, keep it short and leave the room before it grabs you. You are stepping into another being's world."

Placing a hand on Henry's shoulder, Hades compassionately said, "Good luck my friend, you will be needing it."

He turned around, took a step back, stopped and said, "To be a spirit guide is a heavy burden, but good luck to get into the heads of foolish humans."

Left one on one with his upcoming task, Henry looked around, noticing many other guides appearing in front of various doors on the level he was on, and walking through their designated doors to reach those whom they were guiding on Earth. It seemed as though they were familiar with the drill, and the help of Hades was not required. Observing them, Henry felt small and inexperienced. Croton's future was in his hands, but they were shaky and insecure. Henry leaned his forehead on the door with his palms on either side. Behind that door, in total isolation, his friend was trapped. The friend who had saved his ass so many times, who had been entirely devoted to the task of rejoining him and Rose when they were timelessly separated.

"What am I afraid of?" Henry asked himself. *"I have seen it all and I am well prepared to step inside and tackle the task in the nick of time, to free my friend from Hades' shackle that he has chained himself in self-condemnation."*

Affirming his own strength, without further hesitation Henry placed his hand on the handle of the wooden door which was separating the past from the future.

REUNION OF MOTHER AND CHILD

Thales' soft touch on Rose's shoulder took her away from the horrifying Earthly realm where life and death were tied into each other, where the line between them became so easily traversed. Rose gained her vision back in a well maintained and charming garden where each single plant had been thoughtfully arranged to convey calmness and the utmost sense of balance. A narrow path made from tiny pebbles led Rose to a beautiful gazebo composed entirely with blooming bougainvillea and placed beside a creek. Rose knew that the object of her attraction was waiting there patiently for her arrival, but who it was remained a mystery until the moment she placed her foot into the flowery hut.

"Oh Lita!" Rose exclaimed, "Thank God it is you and not Gaya. I would not know how to face her and as a result would make matters worse. I am afraid that my normal look will scare her, and the appearance of little Rose I don't remember."

"Hello, my dear," Lita said wrapping her arms around anxious Rose. "It is so nice having you back in your spirit body. Please, take a seat and we will figure out a way to help poor Gaya."

"Where is she?" Rose asked as she sat down. "Is she all right? Did she experience any pain when the building fell apart?"

"No, my dear, she is well and did not feel a thing. She was instantly withdrawn from her body. To feel the pain and suffering of approaching death was not her task."

"What was my poor mother's task?" Rose asked compassionately, regaining her feeling for the mother who gave her life and love together.

"She went to Earth to find her other half. Once found, to fall in love. Once in love…to lose him in a tragic act, and to enhance the strength of her emotions."

"And, what about me?" Rose asked. "Why was I punished by the Planners? What was my crime to be so heartlessly removed from the man I had come to spend eternity with?"

"Think about it, dear Rose. The time spent by you on Earth went undetected by your present self."

"Yes, you may be right, but Henry, on the other hand, spent a lifetime without me being present at his side"

"I feel your pain," said Lita. "To be a spirit guide is a harder task than to just be human. The sacrifices we have to make to keep the school of Earth intact and safe for the souls to visit and ascend."

"I understand," Rose said sadly. "Besides, it was solely my decision, and no one should be blamed."

"I am so glad you said those words. But, what about Gaya. Would you still like to face your mother?"

"Of course I do. But how should I present myself. I'm afraid that my current look won't be much help. Unfortunately, I am unable to recall the physical appearance of little Rose."

"Please trust me in this matter. I have faced such a task more than once. One thing you should remember is that love, once finding a path to our soul, will harbor there forever. Your appearance will not mislead, fill with grief and pain, the long-suffered heart of your mother."

"I will take your word for it," said Rose, and standing up from the bench showed her commitment to the task filled with uncertainties and possible dismay.

She followed Lita to the banks of a peaceful lake to meet with the mother that she could not remember. Approaching the bench that Gaya was sitting on, Lita gestured to Rose to stay behind and show herself a bit later when called.

Lita's appearance made poor Gaya jump up in anticipation of a reunion with her child, but Lita was alone, and a cloud of disappointment shadowed her mind.

"Did you find my daughter?" Gaya asked.

"Yes, I did."

"Then, where is she? I can't wait to hug my little Rose," said Gaya in an attempt to grab an undetectable thread of hope."

"Here she is," Lita announced loudly inviting Rose to step forward.

Rose appeared, cautiously revealing herself from her hiding place, confused and unbalanced she stood in front of Gaya in her full height. Exposed, and anticipating to disappoint all who placed their hopes upon her shoulders, she confronted Gaya in her final stage of transformation from the human world into the world of spirit.

Gaya froze for a moment and looked intensely at Rose,

placing everyone into a state of contemplation. An enlightenment visited her, and she smiled with happy tears falling from her eyes, and she stepped to Rose and gently hugged her saying, "You survived, my child."

Rose, feeling lost for a moment, hugged her back, which triggered waves of love that showered her from head to toe, submerging her into the memories of the tiny girl. Non-present emotional abundance appeared momentarily and was immediately fulfilled by the strength of love that Rose found in the arms of her loving mother. Rose pulled her tight, placing her head on Gaya's shoulder and whispered, "I missed you Mommy."

In joyous victory Lita pulled back, allowing the reunion between mother and daughter to be privately enjoyed, still remaining close but undetected, she observed them, surprised. "How can love, ignoring time, distance, and appearance, attract two loving souls back together just to fulfill the void of separation."

Next to each other and hand in hand, mother and daughter walked through the garden of their dreams, taking turns to share their stories. Gaya shared memories of little Rose, and Rose shared her life before she became her daughter. The moment Rose mentioned Croton's name Gaya stopped as though rooted to the spot. Horror covered her entire face.

"How could I forget him?"

"Who?" asked Rose.

"My husband. Where is he? Did he survive the earthquake? Is he alive? I totally forgot about him. How could I?"

"Calm down, Mother," the daughter said, "He is all right and safe. I saw him the day after the earthquake. He was unharmed, but certainly emotionally shattered."

"Of course, he would be. He lost both his wife and daughter in an instant. I am so worried, he could lose his mind. No man can take such a devastating knock and stay intact."

She looked at Rose and pleaded, "I know this might be foolish of me to ask, but is there a way to tell him that we are still alive?"

Rose smiled and answered gently, "You know, my Mother, there is not. The pain of loss will slowly subside revealing other paths for him to take, recuperate, and hopefully move on."

"Is there a chance for me to see him now?" Gaya asked.

"Not now, Mother. His pain is still strong and your presence, even in non-physical appearance, will add more ache."

Cautiously, Lita, still hidden, chose to intervene, to redirect her dear Gaya's thoughts of Croton and the danger they may hold.

"Sorry for the interruption," Lita said addressing Gaya. "I

hope your reunion went well, and that your peace of mind has been delivered."

"How can I find peace when Croton's mental health is at stake?" said Gaya.

"Why don't we ask our dear Rose to check on him?" suggested Lita.

Rose looked perplexedly at Lita, "If things are still the way I remember, your husband, Henry, is Croton's guide, or did something change?" Lita asked, hinting that Rose should leave the scene.

"Yes, you are right," Rose replied, "I will check with him about Croton, and in an instant will be back."

The very moment Rose vanished Gaya yelled in horror. "Oh, dear God, what happened to my daughter?"

"Don't worry, dear Gaya," Lita replied seeing Gaya's shock, "This is the normal way of travel in these realms."

"Realm?"

"Yes, the reality that you have become a part of by crossing into the world of spirit."

"This is crazy," Gaya said disarmed. "It feels like I am losing my marbles. This is too much and so unreal. I feel like I am dreaming, and the imminent finale of this dream will soon approach, delivering relief in the comfort of my bed."

"I am sorry, Gaya," said Lita, "This is not a dream, and you cannot step into the past. This is your present now and the faster you get used to it, the easier your adaptation will proceed. I feel your pain and the crushing weight of the changed conditions, but to explore your current state of life and ways of adaptation will require your full concentration."

"Forgive me, dear Lita," Gaya said, "My mind is now with my husband."

"I know that, but you shouldn't worry. Rose will take care of your husband. Rose's husband, Henry, happens to be Croton's guide."

"My Rose is married?" Gaya exclaimed.

"Oh God," Lita sighed deeply, realizing that the time for explanation had arrived and further procrastination would only cause more harm.

"Let's walk," said Lita, "And I will tell you everything that you need to know."

She led Gaya to the pathway along the shore of the lake. Then she extended her elbow expecting Gaya to link arms and walk along like sisters.

A few steps later Gaya checked out her attire and said, "Thank God that I am dressed for the occasion. If only the earthquake had happened an hour earlier, I would have ended up here in my pajamas."

Lita laughed loudly and said, "I am so glad you haven't lost your sense of humor."

Then she stopped, looked deep into Gaya's eyes and asked, "Who do you think I am?"

Without hesitation Gaya answered, "You are the owner of this place."

"But who am I to you?" insisted Lita.

"You must be some kind of angel," answered Gaya.

"Why 'kind of'?" laughed Lita.

"I don't see any wings on your back."

"So, you assume that I am a wingless angel?"

"Yes," Gaya nodded.

"No, I am not an angel, I am just your spirit guide."

"What is that?" enquired Gaya.

Over the next hour, while they explored the beautiful gardens laced around the crystal-clear lake, Lita briefly explained Gaya's current state of existence, the reality she was now in, and how things worked in the spiritual realms. When she was pretty much done with her lecture and answering Gaya's many questions, they came across a double-story white house with a terracotta tiled roof facing the lake.

"This must be your house," Gaya commented, "It is so beautiful."

"Do you like it?" asked Lita.

"How can you not love it. If you ask me, I would say that this is how I imagine paradise would look."

"I know, my dear Gaya," Lita answered adding, "Would you like to step in?"

"Of course I would," Gaya answered impatiently, adamant to check Lita's taste in the décor of the house's interior.

A few more steps and they were standing on the steps of the snowy white house. Lita pushed open the dark blue door, inviting Gaya to step in. To Gaya's utter disappointment the house was completely empty of furniture, and any décor for that matter. Just clean white walls…an empty shell of a house.

Gaya walked to the center of the entrance hall covered with parquet flooring, and spreading her arms wide asked, "Where is all the furniture?"

"It will be up to you to fill this house with furniture and

breathe life into these walls, just the way you would like it," answered Lita.

Confused, Gaya looked around and said, "You want me to choose the furniture for your house?"

Lita stood in front of Gaya saying, "This is not my house, and neither is this reality."

"Then who does all of this belong to?"

"It's all yours."

"Mine?" asked Gaya more confused.

"Yes, my dear. This is your welcoming gift. I have created all of this for you and am immensely glad that you like it. Now it is up to you to decorate it," Lita said unable to hide her excitement.

Gaya stepped closer to Lita and hugged her saying, "Thank you, but I don't know where to start."

"Don't worry. It is quite easy. All you have to do is just imagine the pieces of furniture that you would like to have. Why don't we start in the lounge?" Lita invited, leading Gaya into a spacious empty room filled with light from tall windows that looked out onto the lake.

"Just like that?"

"Just like that," said Lita, and by clicking her fingers she created a cozy three-seater leather couch right in the middle of the room.

"Wow!" exclaimed Gaya jumping in surprise, completely mesmerized by the magic act she had just witnessed. She stepped closer to Lita's creation and carefully touched it.

"It feels real!"

"What did you expect?" said Lita pretending to be offended.

"I thought it would be an illusion."

"You are not too far off from the truth, my dear Gaya. This is a place where the border between illusion and reality is hard to distinguish."

"But…this can be very confusing."

"Sometimes it is, but soon you will be used to it, and your stay in the transitional realms will become as natural as was your stay on Earth."

Gaya walked around the newly created sofa, gently stroking its surface. "It really does feel real," Gaya concluded, adding, "Should we move it against a wall?"

"If that's what you want to do, be my guest."

Gaya bent over and tried to push the sofa, and failing to move it an inch, "It is so heavy," complained Gaya.

Lita laughed and with a light touch of her finger she moved

the couch against the wall.

"How did you do that?" exclaimed Gaya.

"It's quite easy. The difference in our approach to the task is that you presumed that the couch would be heavy and that you would be unable to move it. Basically, you set yourself up for failure. In contrast, I imagined that it is as light as feather and could be moved with a gentle push of my finger. Now, you try it again."

Gaya closed her eyes, and placing her hand on the back of the couch effortlessly moved it forward.

"It worked!" exclaimed Gaya excitedly.

"Of course it did. Just like everything in this reality of yours. Objects will adapt the characteristic that you will reward them with."

"May I create something?" Gaya asked.

"Be my guest."

Gaya closed her eyes again and in the middle of the room appeared a colorful Persian carpet. When she reopened her eyes she screamed in delight, and bending over she touched the surface of the carpet and said, "Exactly the way I wanted it."

"I am glad you have mastered the act of creation of objects. Now you can breathe life onto the walls of your house, too, and I will see you later."

"Are you leaving me?" asked Gaya alarmed.

"You have nothing to worry about in this realm. Nothing can happen here against your will."

Trying to postpone Lita's exit, Gaya asked, "What is upstairs?" as she pointed to the wooden stairs.

"Just two bedrooms," Lita answered casually.

"Can we see them?"

"Sure."

Gaya walked upstairs followed by Lita and entered one of the bedrooms.

"This is the master bedroom," said Lita.

She left Gaya's welcome gift unfinished on purpose. To recreate it like the home she had on Earth would have been too risky, permanently reminding her of the past and the pain attached to it. So, she left it for Gaya to choose the interior for her new place of residence. The door to the balcony was standing wide open, and Gaya, without moving her eyes from the horizon, walked out onto the terracotta balcony.

A moment later she asked, "What is beyond the lake and the surrounding gardens?"

"Whatever your heart desires," answered Lita.

"A range of mountains would be nice," said Gaya, and in front of Lita's eyes appeared a large range of snow-capped mountains framing Gaya's entire reality.

"Do you feel safer now?" Lita asked.

"Yes, I do," answered Gaya, and then added, "You can go now. I have lots of work to do."

"Call me if you need help," said Lita.

"How do I do that? I don't see any phones around here."

Lita smiled saying, "One thought of me will be enough."

"I see," said Gaya, and stepping closer to Lita, she gave her a warm hug saying, "Thank you for saving me and my daughter. I am in eternal debt to you."

Stepping back, she added, "Also, thank you for taking care of me while I was on Earth. I still don't know what is my connection to you, besides the obvious one, but I know it is there in my past life, I can feel it."

"When the time is right you will remember," answered Lita, and waving goodbye left Gaya's bedroom, and with that the reality that she had so lovingly created for her loved one.

SEARCH

Leaving Gaya's newly created reality and promising her to check on Croton, Rose went home. She was hoping to find Henry and through him learn about Croton's current state of being, but the house was empty. The search for him on the beachfront ended in disappointment, so was her visit to the back yard. He was nowhere to be found. She sat down on one of the well-polished rocks at the cascading pools and placed her palms on her temples. Numerous calls to Henry were left unanswered.

"Maybe he is with Croton on Earth," thought Rose. She closed her eyes again and concentrated her attention on Croton. Usually just a light hint of the soul guided by her was enough for her to appear next to him, regardless of where he was. Reopening her eyes Rose realized that she was still in her own reality.

"Something is not right," she stated. "How bad things must be down there for none of them to respond."

Without wasting another second, she envisioned herself standing in front of the once standing six-story building, now turned into rubble, hoping to find Croton by it and Henry somewhere nearby, but no transformation into the physical world happened. It felt as though she was stuck in her own reality, or to be exact, imprisoned in her own house. All the doors leading to the physical world were shuttered closed, leaving her distressed and unpleasantly surprised.

"What now?" Rose asked herself utterly confused.

Her desperate call for Thales sank into oblivion, too.

"What the hell!" Rose exclaimed to the universe and went back inside the house to plan her next move in her attempt to get back to Earth, or else to penetrate the brick wall that appeared so suddenly and go to her loved ones. Reaching the dining room, Rose sat at the head of the table, placing her hands on the table, stretched wide apart, and strummed her nails on the surface. She shuffled in her mind all of the characters that she had encountered in the spiritual realms, wondering who could assist her. Suddenly, from the depths of her memory a figure surfaced who had briefly appeared in her past, leaving a deep impact upon her. The figure who could be identified as highly evolved, but his depth of wisdom still remained untested by Rose.

"Timekeeper!" loudly called Rose hoping to meet with the old and odd-looking man.

"Yes, my child," Rose heard his voice behind her.

Jumping up from her chair and spinning around she stood face to face with the Timekeeper.

He stepped back respectfully and asked, "You wished to see me?"

"Yes," Rose answered desperately. "I didn't know who else to address my cry for help."

"I see that you are quite distressed, my child. What seems to be the problem?"

Rose took a deep sigh and said, "I don't know where to start."

The Timekeeper smiled, and joining his palms together over his flat tummy and said, "Why don't we sit down to begin with, and then you can tell me all that I need to know."

Rose invited him to take the seat at the head of the table, but her offer was kindly declined, and he took a seat at the side. Rose placed herself right in front of him.

"You were saying…" the Timekeeper started the conversation.

"Do you remember the reality where we met?" asked Rose.

"How could I forget, I created it for Henry, although you on the other hand was an unexpected guest."

"Yes, good," answered Rose. "So, everything happened exactly as you visualized it. The city fell into ruins…"

While Rose was struggling to find a short-cut through the long story, she found herself entangled, the Timekeeper closed his eyes and quietly slipped into a sleeping mode. A few sentences later Rose fell quiet to check if the old man was still listening.

"Timekeeper?" Rose asked quietly and gently touched the sleeve of his robe.

He opened his eyes and smiling tenderly said, "The answer to your question is simple. None of them are in the physical world. That is why your access to Earth was denied."

"What? But that is impossible."

"Nothing in this universe is impossible, my child."

After giving thought to what the Timekeeper had just said, Rosc asked, "Are you suggesting that Croton is dead?"

"Not Croton himself, just his body. It has served its purpose and has been shoved aside."

"Okay, but how did that happen? I saw him after the earthquake, and he was unharmed."

The Timekeeper's smiling face adapted to one of sadness, "He killed himself."

"Killed himself!" shouted Rose in utter disbelief.

"Yes, my dear, he simply jumped off the cliff."

"No…no…please God…this is not good. I have heard what happens to suicides."

Rose stood up and began walking anxiously up and down the room.

"Now it all makes sense. All my ties as a guide to the physical world have been abruptly hacked,"

She stopped in the sudden realization, "My poor boy, what did you go through to commit suicide?"

A minute later she stated firmly, "Where is he? I have to be next to him."

"You don't have to worry about him," the Timekeeper said calmly. "The matter has been taken care of."

"By whom?" Rose demanded loudly, wondering who has taken her rightful place.

"By Henry."

"Henry?"

"Yes, as far as I remember he is also Croton's guide."

"Yes, he is," answered Rose.

Settled with the changed circumstances, Rose asked, "Can I see them?"

"I'm sorry, but you certainly cannot."

"Why?"

The Timekeeper sighed deeply saying, "I have to let you in on a secret. Why a secret…because it is not mine, but I think it will help you to calm down."

Rose sat back in her chair in front of the Timekeeper, afraid that another blow thrown by the old man would be better taken sitting down.

"Although Croton choosing your husband as a guide for himself may have seemed to be short-sighted move, but he knew the possible outcome of his visit to Earth, so trust me on this, your husband is the right soul to be next to Croton now."

"Are you suggesting that Croton knew about his life on Earth from the beginning?"

"In broad strokes, yes."

Rose put her head in her hands and with sudden enlightenment mumbled, "So, all of this was just a charade."

"No. No, my child. All this was and still is real. The life that Croton took on Earth was real. Your motherly love for him was real. His love for Gaya is real. Everything. Every single thing was real."

The Timekeeper was quiet for a moment and then added, "Croton wanted to help you and Henry to ascend to the next level of your internal journey as a soul, and at the same time to bear witness to his newborn love. How can you call all of that a charade?"

"I didn't know what else to think. I am confused and overwhelmed with all the revelations you have dumped on me."

The Timekeeper smiled saying, "You can handle it."

"Is there anything else I should know?" Rose asked rhetorically.

"Oh yes, one more thing."

"What?" Rose asked cautiously.

"Just the tiny detail in addition to what I said earlier. Henry and Croton are now in hell."

Rose's jaw dropped and her face became a mask of absolute horror.

"What!" she screamed.

"Please don't worry," the Timekeeper said hurriedly trying to calm her down. "Hell by definition is not a real thing, at least for them."

"Are you deliberately confusing me?" Rose protested.

"Look, things down there are not that simple."

"Maybe that is why they call it hell," said Rose.

"Perhaps," agreed the Timekeeper, "But please be patient. They will be all right. Trust me, I know this."

"When?" Rose asked suddenly.

"What do you mean?"

"When can I see my husband."

"Unfortunately, dear child I cannot reveal to you the timing of events, but a good outcome I can definitely see."

Rose dropped back in her chair and exhaled with relief.

"Thank you for all of the disclosure that you piled on me, and at the same time relieved me of their weight. Thank you for your visit, and kind words filled with hope regarding our future."

"You are welcome, my child. Give them some time and you will meet again," said the Timekeeper and nodding his head he turned into the vapor of a misty cloud.

Left alone, Rose stood discontented, more knowledgeable

than before, but still trapped in her own reality.

"Maybe I can go back to my mother, Gaya, to help her organize her new reality. But, on the other hand, what am I going to tell her about Croton's well-being? No, I'd rather stay where I am, and make some changes to my own reality."

She glanced around saying, "I'm tired of this constancy. I think it is time to bring some change into this world of ours, and when Henry is back with Croton next to him, I will have something to brag about," said Rose as she rolled up her sleeves.

THE MEETING

Before stepping into Croton's cell, Henry visualized a room resembling the one that he found Nazia in. Instead of the darkness diluted with the stench of dampness, he was invited in by warm sunlight. For some reason Henry chose to knock on the half open door and ask permission to enter. Then he opened the door to its fullest and stood facing the room filled with daylight. He took a few seconds before managing to adapt his vision to the unexpected.

"Am I in the right place?" Henry asked himself, and just in case he looked back at where he came from, uncertain that he was still in a place that no soul in their right state of mind would willingly descend to.

He stepped deeper into the room, closing the door behind him. A few more steps and Henry noticed another door, probably leading to the next room. Although the interior of room felt familiar to him, only on reaching the white double door leading to the next room did Henry realize where he was. It was an exact replica of Croton's office. A second later he saw the man himself, at his work desk, submerged in a pile of blueprints. Scattered all over the floor, official documents created a scene of dissonance and despair, reflecting the state of the man behind the desk. Croton was intently studying the blueprints and from time to time with broad strokes of red marker he wrote the same word over and over again. Stepping closer Henry was able to read the word… REJECT…REJECT…REJECT. The same word was dominating the documents that had found their way onto the floor.

With his head sunk into the paperwork, Croton did not notice Henry's entry. Trying to attract Croton's attention Henry coughed. Croton immediately dropped the red pen and looked at Henry, cautiously observing the intruder's attire.

Croton smiled sadly saying, "Oh, you have finally arrived. I was hoping to fix everything before your visit."

Confused, Henry stepped closer to Croton's desk and in a voice filled with hope he asked, "Do you know who I am?"

"Aren't you the one who collects sinister souls to burn them on the stake?"

Heavy disappointment landed on Henry's shoulders with the realization of the long road that he had to cover to convince Croton to step back into the light.

"Do you think I am Satan?" Henry asked sadly.

"Yes, or probably one of his family."

Henry sighed deeply and sat down on one of the chairs placed near the wall to gather his thoughts.

"To try and convince Croton otherwise would be premature, and a desperate act destined for failure," Henry thought to himself, *"I have to gain his trust first."*

"Sorry for the disturbance, you were busy doing something before I stepped in," Henry said to Croton, "If I may ask, what is it that you were busy with?"

"Do you really want to know?" Croton replied bravely.

Croton's cockiness, considering the fact that he was presumably talking to the devil himself, pleasantly surprised Henry.

"At least his spirit seems to be still intact," and after a small pause Henry answered, "Yes, I do."

"Okay," Croton began his story. "To begin with I appeared in a kind of dungeon, dark damp, gloomy place in complete isolation…"

"Sorry for interrupting," Henry stepped in, "Are you aware of what happened to you before that?"

"Yes."

"And?"

"I died," answered Croton.

"Or to be exact, you killed yourself," Henry corrected him.

"Does it really matter?"

"If it didn't matter, then you wouldn't be here," mumbled Henry.

"Sorry?" Croton asked unable to hear Henry's last words.

"Hhhmmm, nothing," Henry answered, asking Croton to proceed with his story.

"Yes. As I was saying, I ended up in a kind of jail cell. I would say it was about sixteen feet by sixteen feet. A complete disaster. An unbelievable black hole."

"You sound surprised, after what you have done, what did you expect?"

"I know that what I have done was wrong, and I deserve to be punished with whatever you think I should get. I see it and I will not try to justify my actions…but…"

Croton fell quiet, and then in the next moment his face lit up, ignited by the spark in his eyes. For that one brief moment Henry saw in this young man his long missed Roman senator.

"I think, maybe I am wrong, but I am almost certain that I managed to find a loophole in the system."

"What system?" Henry asked surprised.

"I mean in the system you have created here."

"Do you even know where you are?" Henry said raising his voice.

"Of course I do," answered Croton.

"And?"

"I am in hell."

"Then what the hell are you talking about…that you have found a loophole?" Henry angrily paraphrased.

"Please, hear me out." pleaded Croton.

"Okay," submitted Henry.

"Sitting alone in the dark I analyzed the last couple of years of my life. I was employed by the government to run a legal department for Civil Construction."

"Yes," Henry said.

Interrupting himself Croton said, "Why do I have the feeling that you already know what I am about to say?"

"Maybe because I do."

"I bet you don't know how I found a way to fix it all."

"To fix it all?" questioned Henry.

"Yes, my wish to fix all that I failed to do back on Earth was so strong that I managed to step back in time."

"Back in time?"

"Yes, to a time before the earthquake. I realized that if I can undo all of the unlawful deeds that I did in the past, I can… maybe I can save my family, and maybe…just maybe I will get the chance to see them again unharmed."

In an attempt to hide the approaching wave of tears Croton grabbed his red pen and pulled another blueprint in front of him to fix the unfixable. Watching Croton, Henry came to the realization that he had become the witness of a strange phenomenon. Croton had managed to create a new reality inside another reality, and not just in any reality, but in hell itself. Croton's will to undo the past was so strong that he had managed to recreate his entire office in the gloomy dungeon. Then the age-old question, to tell and cause pain, or not to tell, cast over Henry's mind.

"Sooner or later, he has to find out," Henry thought to himself. *"The delay will only make matters worse."* Self-convinced due to the inevitability of his act, Henry stood up and stepped in front of Croton. Croton looked straight into his eyes and in that very moment Henry's heart fell to the floor. If he had had any blood running through his veins it would have been pulled down from his face leaving him pale and lifeless. Suddenly Henry recalled a similar scene that occurred almost 2000 years ago in ancient Rome, where he was a perpetrator and Croton a mighty Roman senator. Just as before, Henry was about to cause him pain, with the only difference being that in the past he was about to plunge a cold blade into Croton's heart to take his life, and now he was about to cause pain to bring him back to life.

With deep sorrow depicted in his voice, Henry said, "Stop it Croton, you cannot change the past. What was done cannot be undone."

"What are you saying?" asked frightened Croton.

"I am saying that you are not in the past, and all of this is just an illusion created by your desperation."

Croton dropped the red pen onto the table and stepped back. "Are you saying that I am still in hell?"

"Yes, my dear friend. I know how confusing this can be, especially for someone who just arrived from the physical world, but…"

Henry stopped, realizing that he had lost Croton's attention, as he had quietly gone back into himself, and the entire office evaporated into thin air in front of Henry's eyes, inviting in its place complete darkness to be partially challenged by Henry's inner glow.

Leaning against the damp prison wall and observing Henry's sudden luminosity Croton asked, "Who are you?"

"You are not going to believe me," said Henry.

"Try me."

"For now, I am your guide, but in a recent past, you were my savior and mentor. You were all that I had in the world of spirit."

"You are right. It's not only hard to believe, but even harder to understand. Let us start with the first part, you said that you are my guide?"

"Yes, I am."

"What does that mean?"

"It means that before taking another life on Earth, you asked me to become your spirit guide, to help you to navigate safely in the world of humans, and when the time came, to guide you back home."

"I see," said Croton, adding a moment later, "According to how everything turned out, you weren't very good at any of your duties."

Croton's last words sounded to Henry like a verdict delivered by a Roman senator whose character was beginning to show sparks of life in the body of the young man standing in front of him. Henry's face went red not knowing how to answer such a direct accusation. He just mumbled, "I tried my best…"

"I see," Croton said calmly, "Don't worry, I am not going to blame you for the way things turned out. It was my decision, and I will accept the outcome."

"What outcome?" asked Henry.

"I committed sins, I know it. Because of me many innocent people died last night." He lowered his eyes adding, "Sure, this deserves a great punishment."

"And what will that be?" asked concerned Henry.

"To be burned in an eternal fire," whispered Croton.

Henry stepped closer and looking deep into Croton's eyes said, "Aren't you going to ask me to help you to escape the eternal fires?"

"No," Croton stated firmly, "I deserve it."

"One lifetime on Earth did not change you at all," Henry thought to himself. *"Still so full of pride and honor. Still brave and fearless, ready to embrace eternal pain because he believes he deserves it."*

Henry sighed deeply, searching for a correct angle to deliver a penetrating punch to destroy the defence of this self-condemning young man.

"You do realize that even if you didn't approve those projects, they would have still come to life with all of their deficiencies."

"I know, but it was still me who approved them, and quietly agreed to accept those faulty buildings."

"Okay," said Henry finding Croton's defence too strong, or his argument too weak, to shake Croton's fortifications. "What if I tell you that the sole reason for your visit to Earth was to find your one and only?"

"What are you talking about?"

"I'm talking about Gaya," Henry said raising his voice.

"She is dead!" Croton shouted into Henry's face, "She died with my unborn boy and my beautiful daughter. They are all dead because of me. Don't you see that? I have been punished by God!"

Croton's voiced echoed off the walls delivering an even stronger impact upon Henry, unveiling the horrifying depth of Croton's tragedy.

"So, do not tell me that I am innocent. The eternal fire is the least that I deserve."

"What if I tell you that Gaya and Rose are safe and pretty much alive," said Henry in a desperate attempt to squeeze a single ray of light into the kingdom of Croton's darkness.

Croton smiled sadly saying, "I dragged their bodies out of the rubble with my bare hands, so don't tell me that they are not dead. The only remission that I have is the hope that they died instantly and did not suffer a slow death."

Suddenly Henry realized that he had a chance to deliver a final winning blow,

"Didn't it cross your mind that your inability to die, or to perish into oblivion after such a long fall into the bottom of the gorge, will apply to Gaya and Rose, too?"

"What are you implying?"

"You are alive still, right?"

"Yes..."

"So, shouldn't they be, too?"

Croton fell quiet stepping back into his thoughts. After a few moments of consideration of Henry's argument he asked, "Are you saying that they are alive?"

"Yes," Henry lit up victoriously, although Croton's next question puzzled him.

"Can I see them?" Croton asked suspiciously.

"Yes...eventually you will, but..."

"What's that supposed to mean?" Croton asked unpleasantly surprised.

"The only obstacle separating you from your family is..."

"What? What is the obstacle?" Croton said raising his voice.

"The only obstacle is you."

"Me?"

"Yes. Or should I say your inability to see the bigger picture."

"Bigger picture? What are you talking about?"

"Yes, bigger picture. And if you will allow me to explain, and yourself to listen, you will probably understand your current state of existent and the way out of it.'

"I am listening," Croton replied simply. He leaned against the wall, closed his eyes in a desperate effort to relax.

Croton dropped his defences, wondering what this strangely glowing creature in human form had to say.

Henry's next act surprised even himself. He stepped up to Croton and slapped him across the face. Such uncalled-for behavior from someone claiming themselves to be a guardian angel shook Croton to his core.

Covering his cheek with the palm of his hand to ease the pain, Croton shouted, "What the hell!"

Henry, absolutely unphased by Croton's reaction and words, calmly asked, "Did you feel that?"

"Are you crazy. Of course I did."

"Concentrate on my question please," Henry insisted. "Did you really feel pain?"

Croton rubbed his cheek and surprisingly admitted, "Not really!"

"Exactly!" Henry said excitedly, "You didn't feel the pain. Do you wonder why?"

"Why?" asked Croton.

"Because you do not have a body."

Croton looked at his hands, touched himself in various places, and concluded, "I do have a body, although it feels a bit numb."

"That's right. It is numb because you do not have a nervous system to send signals to your brain to confirm your senses. In other words, all you are left with is emotions."

Henry knew that he had managed to grab Croton's attention, and all that was left was to patiently undo the entangled rope of Croton's world in hell that had shut out the world of spirit, even those whom he loved so dearly. Bit by bit, Henry was conquering Croton's defences, exposing him to the truth once delivered to him by Croton on a silver platter. Croton was listening quietly without saying a word, giving Henry the opportunity to navigate his message not only into Croton's mind, but to his heart as well. Henry didn't have the slightest idea where he was going with all this. His only aim was to get Croton out of his deep emotional hellhole, back to the light.

The plan of action was completely void compared to the structured chain of events that Croton had prepared for him when Henry crossed into the world of spirit after having a heart attack.

When Henry ran out of words, Croton asked, "Are you saying that I am not guilty for the death of so many citizens?"

"No," Henry confirmed.

"And that they were going to die anyway because there was a bigger plan?"

"Yes."

"And the fact that I took my own life has nothing to do with the fact that I am standing here in hell now?"

"No, I didn't say that. You are here because you assumed that you belong here."

"So, am I free to leave?"

"Yes."

Croton stood, feeling lost for a moment, and then asked, "Where do I go from here?"

Henry suddenly realized that he did not have an answer to that question. Various paths of possible exit were tangled in his mind leading him nowhere, and in that very moment the entire cell filled with an intense light. It seemed as though the light had struck the darkness leaving nowhere for it to hide, and the source of that light was the figure of the man appearing right at the center of the tiny confinement. In an automatic reflex Croton and Henry stepped away from the invading visitor, covering their eyes. A few moments later, adapting to the luminosity of the newly arrived guest, Henry looked at him.

"Thales!" he exclaimed.

"Who else?" answered the old Greek, "Were you expecting someone else?" laughed the Planner.

"In truth, I wasn't expecting anyone," answered Henry, "Although I must admit that your presence is very welcome and as always in the nick of time. Honestly, I thought you had forgotten about us. I tried to reach you but…"

Croton observed the old man dressed as an ancient Greek, trying to make sense of what was happening in his tiny cell. Thales stood quietly anticipating his formal introduction.

Henry stepped forward saying, "Please meet your old friend, once a guide, and now the Planner of the physical life that you have just checked out from."

Croton, still mesmerized by Thales' appearance, completely missed Henry's introduction, and recovering from his sensorial shock asked, "Excuse me, but who are you exactly?"

Thales answered proudly, "I am the one who planned your last stay on Earth."

"This is getting more interesting," said Croton, and realizing something important continued, "Oh, so you are the one who got me into this mess!"

"Hmmm, you can put it that way, although I would rephrase it. I am the one who helped you to the next level of your soul's ascension." Turning his head toward Henry and almost whispering, "By the way, that applies to you, too."

"What is that supposed to mean?" Croton asked, unimpressed.

Thales faced Croton, raised his right hand placing it on Croton's shoulder. Croton's first reaction was to step back, but then he allowed Thales to touch him, thinking that the old man with so much light would not cause him any harm.

Landing his hand on Croton's shoulder, Thales smiled tenderly saying, "Allow me to introduce you to the real you."

Croton looked at Henry in confusion and closed his eyes in confirmation of his consent to Thales' offer. Thales closed his eyes, and a second later Henry was left alone standing in the dank dark place where no one would want to remain a second longer.

But strangely, Henry was not in a hurry to leave. He had unfinished business in this kingdom created by human weaknesses materialized into a reality of darkness., into a reality of souls condemning themselves to be tenants through the choices they made while on Earth, be it willingly or otherwise. Henry firmly pushed the door open and stepped out of Croton's cell, which had lost its purpose without its resident, although Henry knew that it would not stand vacant for long.

SPRING OF WISDOM

Henry stood leaning against the balustrade separating him from the free fall into the boiling lava. Above him, just two levels above, was Nazia serving her sentence. The Muslim girl who managed to touch Henry's heart in the most mysterious way. Below him were another three levels of hell with its residents whom he had no idea about and wasn't sure if he wanted to. His inability to help Nazia to free herself from her prison of religious beliefs had left Henry with the bitter taste of disappointment. He was free to leave this underground world, and with that, all the memories attached to it, but he couldn't. A pulsating beacon with the name Nazia was hammering his mind and consciousness with an increasing rate. He turned around, placed his hands on the rail, and looked up in search of the soul who could help him to rescue the poor girl from her own prejudice. Suddenly four words boldly invaded his thoughts… "Savior of Lost Souls."

"Christ," said Henry, and he placed his palms on his temples, closed his eyes, and began say Christ's name repeatedly as a mantra with the hope of being heard and invited by the one who in his mind was undoubtedly God.

The one who was elevated to such a status by 2000 years of human belief in his powers to help and his ability to deliver upon the prayers of his followers. After a while Henry gave up in his attempt to contact Christ, opening his eyes, thinking that it was presumptuous of him to expect an audience at such short notice. On opening his eyes expecting to face the belly of the beast filled with the pain and sorrow of some innocent, and some not so innocent souls, but instead a blinding ray of light pierced his vision delivering the hope that his desperate call had indeed been heard.

Henry found himself standing in the middle of a big yard facing a white double story building which could be compared to some kind of palace, or to be exact, a bad replica of one. In the center there was an impressive entrance made of white marble stairs leading to imposing double doors encrusted with stained glass. A multitude of tall columns dressed the façade of the building, allowing rows of windows to find their place in-between them. The main building was flanked by left and right wings attached to either side, protruding their arms to circle the courtyard. The wings seemed more like a continuous chain of warehouses judging by the size of the doors making up the entire façade.

Turning around, Henry found a magnificent fountain placed right in the middle of the neatly paved yard. The fountain's basin was circular, mounted with a huge globe of Earth in its center. Seven angels were place on its perimeter with golden horns at their lips completing their ensemble. Through their horns, powerful streams of water were shooting up toward the north pole of the globe and running down into the basin, seemingly washing Earth to its cleanest. The meaning of this composition was quite obvious, although its execution was regrettably poor, leaving an aftertaste of uncertainty, not only in the designing abilities of the one who made the fountain, but also in the taste of the one who ordered, it as well.

Henry looked around expecting to find Christ, but it seemed that he was not in any hurry to show himself, rather allowing Henry time to acquaint himself with this tasteless reality. A sudden change in Henry's outfit, from funky modern into a robe and sandals, left no doubt in his mind that Christ was about to appear.

"So, what do you think?" Christ asked, standing next to Henry and facing the building.

Henry stepped back, and facing Christ bowed respectfully saying, "Thank you for seeing me and blessing me with your presence."

"Stop it," said Christ, paying no attention to Henry's words.

Henry looked up at the structure, and then said, "Honestly?"

"Yes."

"Not the best."

Satisfied with his answer, Christ said, "I thought as much."

Then he directed his gaze to Henry causing him to lower his eyes.

"Shall we meet the owner of this reality?" Christ asked excitedly.

"Sure," answered Henry, choosing to delay his request about Nazia to be raised when the time was right.

Christ stepped boldly toward the entrance, and Henry followed him a step behind. Before they reached the marble steps the double doors were thrown wide open and the owner of the reality appeared in the doorway. He was dressed in a gray striped, immaculately tailored suit with black shiny shoes, white shirt, and a silky blue tie. The tie pin was hard to miss, impressive in its size and the clarity of the diamond embedded within it.

The host almost flew down the stairs to kneel in front of Christ, reached for his hand and passionately pressed it against his lips.

Christ allowed the act and a moment later said, "Rise my son."

The host stood up slowly, hesitantly releasing Christ's hand, although remaining slightly bent over at the waist. He then greeted Henry, not sure how to address the young man next to Christ and just nodded his head. Henry answered in the same manner.

Facing Christ the host said, "I knew that the day would come when you will call me, but to see you in my humble abode was beyond my wildest expectations."

Christ gazed over the building and said, "Come on…that would not be my choice of words that I would have used to describe your realm!"

The host bowed even lower saying, "Thank you for allowing me to have an exact replica of my house on Earth."

"You are welcome," said Christ. "Aren't you going to invite us in?"

"Of course I will," replied the host, stepping aside and gesturing to the guests to enter.

"Lead the way," commanded Christ.

While the host stepped forward Henry used the opportunity to ask Christ, "Who is he?"

"One of my soldiers," Christ answered.

Unable to grasp Christ's reference, Henry followed them into the mansion. The interior was dressed to impress newcomers, leaving no doubts as to the owner's financial status and his belonging to a highest step on the social ladder.

The house was tastefully decorated, with no corner managing to escape the touch of the skilful decorator. Each item of artwork, and piece of furniture was crafted to perfection and placed exactly where they should be. All of this made Henry feel that he had stepped into a museum, rather than into a house.

"Would you like to sit in the living room or at the dinner table?" asked the over-accommodating host, who seemed to be stuck in his bent over posture.

"The table," answered Christ, placing himself in the middle of the huge twelve-seater table. He invited the host to sit directly opposite him, gesturing Henry to sit at his right.

Once all participants had taken their places, Christ placed his elbows on the table and clasped his palms together. The host and Henry patiently waited for Christ to ease the crushing weight of silence.

Unable to wait any longer, the host asked anxiously, "Is this my judgement day?"

Motionless, Christ continued to stare into his eyes. There was no condemnation, nor approval depicted on his face, rather calmness and contentment of a man in absolute control of the situation.

Unable to read Christ's intent, the host disrupted the silence again, "All that I have done on Earth…I did it for you, my Lord. I praise you, your teachings, and your visions. I healed the sick in your name. I dedicated my life to glorify you, my Lord."

With each sentence, the host's voice became increasingly strenuous and desperate for Christ's approval., but Christ remained silent and motionless.

"I built churches in your name, my Lord. I was generous to your followers. I woke up each morning and went to bed with your name on my lips, my Lord."

Running out of accolades and still seemingly failing to impress Christ, the host fell quiet and lowered his head to face his own reflection in the highly polished tabletop. Again, a rising dense energy began to fill the room, leaving Henry wondering where Christ was leading this meeting with his absolute indifference to all that the host had to say. Next, as the host lifted his head, Henry noticed tears and his face expressing nothing but remorse in the sudden realization of the truth, with unwanted memories hidden deep at the back of his mind waiting to be awakened and faced, now finally finding their time. The host silently stood up from his chair, walked around the table to kneel in front of Christ.

He bent over and grabbing hold of Christ's foot began to passionately kiss his sandals, saying in-between, "Please forgive me. I got lost on my way to you. I was tempted by Satan and couldn't resist. I have done things that I shouldn't."

Unable to move Christ, the host placed his forehead on the thick Persian carpet, wetting it with his tears, and through his sobs pleading for forgiveness.

Finally, Christ stood up. Pushing back his chair he leaned

over to help the host up to his feet.

"Get up off your knees, my son," Christ said tenderly. "I am not the one who must forgive you. You have my love and with that, forgiveness with no conditions attached."

"Thank you, thank you, my Lord," the host repeated whilst kissing Christ's hand.

The Messiah retrieved his hand saying, "You have a beautiful home, please give me a tour. I, and my dear friend, Henry, would like that very much."

"Please, please, be my guest," the host said excitedly, sensing that the worst was over, and protruding his left hand invited the guests to explore.

Without hesitation Christ took the lead. It seemed that he knew exactly where he was going, with Henry and the host just following him.

Soon Christ stopped in front of a white wooden door, and pointing at it asked the host, "What is behind this door?"

A bit confused and lost for words, the host answered, "Forgive me, Sire, but I don't know. This door was not here back home."

"Open it," Christ commanded.

"I have tried before, but it seems to be locked."

"Try now," Christ invited.

The host grabbed the golden handle and pushed it down, cautiously stepped forward and froze in the doorway. From where Henry was standing, he could see the host face, but not the contents of the mysterious room, though the grimace distorting the hosts face assured Henry that whatever was in that room was horrifying in its nature.

THE ROOM

“Please enter,” Christ invited the shaken host.

Unable to take his eyes away from whatever he had become a witness, the host cautiously stepped in, leaving just enough space for Christ and Henry to squeeze themselves in, between the host and the door frame., Nothing could prepare Henry for what he saw. It was a big room with a double volume ceiling filled halfway with white envelopes. Ordinary envelopes, with no stamps and without any writing on them. Millions and millions of envelopes just dumped in the room. What surprised Henry most was the fact that they had all been unsealed, or to be exact, they were ripped open to get to their contents. Impatiently, Henry stepped forward and picked up one of the envelopes from the floor and checked what was inside. A neatly folded sheet of white paper was resting inside. He carefully retrieved it and looked up at Christ, and at his silent approval he unfolded the letter. There was a short message written in cursive. Just a glimpse at the neatly written sentences made Henry realize how much care and effort the epistler had applied to their writing.

“Read it,” Christ commanded.

“Dear Pastor,” Henry began uncertainly.

“Louder please,” Christ insisted.

“Dear Pastor, I beg you to mention my daughter’s name in your prayers. Let our dear Lord, Jesus Christ, hear my voice in a prayer for my only child. I have been from pillar to post to find healing of her sickness, but it was all in vain. No doctor on Earth can help her. My only hope is upon our Lord Jesus and your everlasting compassion. Therefore, I am giving a humble contribution toward your prayers. Her name is Liya, and she is five. Since her vaccination I have lost my perfectly healthy child. If this is not enough, I will get more. May God bless you for all the good that you have done and are doing for your congregation. Thank you in advance, Dusty Meyer.”

Done with the reading Henry checked inside the envelope expecting to find money, but it was empty.

Christ took the letter from Henry handing it to the host asking, "Did you read this letter?"

The host lowered his head and stood quietly.

"Did you read this letter?" Christ asked again.

"No," mumbled the host.

"Although you did not hesitate to take the money?"

The host, still with eyes cast to the floor covered with envelopes said, "I couldn't possibly read them all."

"Then why did you keep accepting them?" Christ asked calmly.

The host stood quietly.

"Let me help you," suggested Christ. "Greed is the key word here."

"I wanted to help them all," protested the host. "I even hired assistants to deal with the letters, but they just kept coming and coming."

"And money along with them," added Christ.

Running out of justification, the host said, "All my life I was glorifying you, my Lord and preaching your words to bring the best out of people."

"And for that I am grateful to you. And this mansion that you are living in is my gift to you for your work, but…"

"There is always a but…" the host admitted sadly.

"Yes, my friend, by taking money from members of your congregation you sealed a deal between them, you, and me. I held my end of the bargain and answered all pleas addressed to me in this ocean of envelopes. You on the other hand failed to do your part."

Silence invaded the room and froze in anticipation of being dispersed, but such an occurrence was halted. The host went deep into his memories of the past, disrupting his shameful deeds, like a strobe light come to life, exposing numerous events so conveniently forgotten by the recipient. A moment later the silence was disturbed.

"I am guilty, Lord," admitted the host and kneeling in front of Christ he spread his arms apart resembling a crucifix. "Forgive me Lord, I have sinned unknowingly. I did so. Please don't sentence me to hell. Instead forgive your lamb, my shepherd, for getting lost in the woods."

Christ smiled ironically and said, "Get up my 'lamb', you are forgiven. My love for the human race is eternal. Souls dressed in flesh, so feeble against temptations, to punish them for being weak is not my intent."

The host, filled with hope, stood up and joining his palms together whispered, "Thank you, thank you, dear Lord."

"Not so fast," Christ dropped a rock on the glassy surface of the calmest water, creating ripples of dismay.

Suddenly Henry remembered what he went through to get to Christ. To earn his presence, to hear his voice and words at once. So, to be visited by Christ you should be someone either extremely good or bad. Which one the host was, was not difficult to determine.

"As I said, you have remission on my behalf, although there are established rules set by my Father, and they are above my will."

Confused by Christ's remarks, the host said, "I am lost, my Lord."

"Don't be. I will give you the opportunity to rectify your flaws, and earn your humble place in my substantial kingdom."

"Give me a chance," pleaded the host.

"You see this mountain of unwanted letters?"

"Yes, my Lord."

"You have to read them one by one."

"I'll do it gladly…"

"Wait, don't rush," Christ interrupted. "Each letter contains a range of deep emotions, and they will capture your mind the way that they affected me. I hope your task is clear, and you will leave this place once the final letter is read."

"As you wish, my Lord," the host replied anxiously.

"I suggest that you start with the letter picked up by Henry," offered Christ.

The host took the page from Henry's hand and magic happened. He found himself facing a little girl. The room filled with letters disappeared, replaced by a poorly decorated tiny bedroom, lit with a barely breathing globe hanging hopelessly from the ceiling and crying for attention. Henry saw the host sitting on the edge of the single bed, looking at the child lying in a wooden cot. The health deficiency that the child suffered from was evident, though her face… It seemed like a tiny ray of sunlight was stuck on her face, once accidently landed. A strong current of unfamiliar emotions captivated the host's heart once he realized that he was the mother of the child. Like Christ suggested, the host found himself out of himself in the arms of strange emotions. The most overpowering was love for the child, but hovering satellites of darkness in the shape of pain, regret, and powerlessness to change the fact that the child was partially paralyzed left him in despair, and worst of all, was the fact that he was the only one to be blamed for the child's sickness. The host saw a day when the child was perfectly healthy, and then the days after the vaccination that were the beginning of the end.

Distressed, he stood up, walked to the old chest of drawers and retrieved two one-hundred dollar notes. He placed them into an envelope, regardless of the fact that they were needed to last them to the end of the week. Then he sat at the table and began to write the very same letter that the host held in his hands. Done with writing, he sealed the envelop knowing that in the morning he would hand it to the pastor, to the one who's voice stood closer to God, and was the only hope sealed with the donation will find the ONE to whom it was addressed. Realization of the fact that he was simultaneously residing in two bodies, placed the host in a strange predicament. He was addressing the letter to himself, filled with desperation and hope, assured of the fact that he would totally ignore its presence. Accustomed to the procedure, the host knew that the letter would be lost with thousands of others in the hands of his assistants who will retrieve the two-hundred dollars, and tossing the letters into a dustbin to meet its destiny with others in the furnace at the back of the church. The rise of self-condemning thoughts snapped him back from the gloomy scene of the child in the cot, and him in the body of her mother. The host dropped the letter on the floor as if it was a lit match about to burn his fingers, and looked around to be faced by Christ, but he was gone, along with Henry.

Glimpsing at the mountain of letters and foreseeing the time to be spent to go through each one, and the pain concealing in them, the host angrily spat on the floor pronouncing, "I am not going to do this shit."

He then sharply turned around toward the door to leave behind his past deeds and the endless cries of needy people. He stepped toward relief in the shape of the door to leave the room…but the door was gone. He touched the wall uncertain of his vision, then looked around seeking another exit from this mess. His heart began to pound in his throat making him choke in a desperate state of panic.

"No!" screamed the host falling to his knees.

He was imprisoned in his own mansion. An annoying thought that he would not be leaving this room until the last letter has been read came as a certainty and undeniable fact.

While Christ, with Henry at his side were leaving the lavishes of the pastor's house, Henry heard his desperate call for help.

Unable to keep silent he asked, "Forgive me, Sire, for saying this, but don't you think it is too harsh to lock him up in his own heaven?"

Christ smiled sadly, paused briefly on the porch facing the courtyard, and slowly raised both hands. In an instant all of the roller doors of the garages came to life revealing the treasures hidden in their bellies. From where they were standing, to his right Henry saw many vehicles standing in neat rows. From vintage rarities to the latest models of sports cars, all shiny, polished to their beauty as though never touched before. And to his left he saw hangers containing jets. Wings widely spread apart in anticipation of their owner to fulfil their purpose.

"So?" Christ asked without looking at Henry.

One thing that Henry had learned by now was that Christ was not a man of many words.

"Sad," Henry answered simply.

"As you see, the poor Dusty Meyer's contribution found its place as a tiny part in the satisfaction of our pastor's needs for a lavish life."

On saying these last words Christ stepped away from his promoter's dungeon. Away from the misconception of his words, which led to the glory of a soul who became a pastor to deliver hope and love on his behalf to those most needy. As they moved further away from the house, Henry stopped to have a final look at the place of a humble pastor's dreams turned into his soul's entrapment, when the strangest thing occurred, an event he had never seen before. The entire building, with its contents, including the cars and jets began to crumble into rubble, soon disintegrating into the air, revealing a lovely field with wildflowers of nature. Henry, utterly perplexed, look to Christ for answers. There was no anger, nor dismay on Christ's face, rather contentment with the facts.

"What happened to the preacher?" Henry asked.

"He found the place where he belongs."

"And where is that?"

"You recently emerged from there."

"Did you condemn that poor soul to hell?" Henry raised his voice in utter disbelief.

"I didn't," Jesus answered, "He did it all by himself. Compassion is a quality to be admired, dear friend, but you cannot base your judgement solely on compassion, or else descending souls to the planet will learn no lessons if everything is to be forgiven."

"So, he is in Hades' kingdom now?" Henry asked sadly.

"Yes, trust me in this, ignoring the congregation's letters and their cries for help was not the worst he has done on Earth."

Christ abruptly changed the subject.

"What was the reason for your visit?"

"The Muslim girl. Do you remember her, Sire? I bothered your peace about her earlier."

"I have no peace, my friend," Christ admitted sadly. "Most of humanity expect my answers to their prayers. You be the judge… so, what about the Muslim girl?"

"I heard your words about the dangers of compassion, but still I feel responsible for her release from darkness that she has condemned herself through her reckless act of vengeance."

"There are conditions to her freedom," answered Christ.

"I'll take them all," grasped Henry.

"Wait, hear me out first. They will be hard for her to accept, but necessary to correct her past."

Henry stood quiet to attention.

"She must announce the withdrawal of her faith and readiness to accept another."

"Do you expect her to follow you?"

"No, my friend. You are jumping the gun in the lens of ultimate ambitions. A sudden leap from hot to cold will endanger the essence of her soul. We need to cool her radical perceptions."

"So what do you propose?" Henry asked.

"There is a beautiful religion created by my dear friend, although to my judgement it hardly qualifies as a religion. It is rather the teachings of peace and absolute acceptance. This faith has helped so many souls to find calm and balance within themselves."

"Are you suggesting a reincarnation to a Buddhist country?"

"Why not? It may be convergent."

"I see," Henry said rationalizing Christ's proposal, adding, "Where do you see my role in such a drastic transformation?"

"Your role is simple. Make her believe."

"To believe in what?"

"In her path to freedom through the hardest choice."

Christ slowed his steps and stopped staring directly at Henry. The intensity of Christ's gaze was always hard to take, but this one was beyond. A second later, that seemed like eternity to Henry, the Son of God spoke, "By making the choice to step into her cell in hell you initiated a deep commitment. In other words, you are hooked my friend. Her freedom is now in your hands."

With those words Christ vanished from sight.

Lost and even more uncertain than before he chose to meet with Christ, Henry regreted the day he let his curiosity take charge by stepping into the Muslim girl's confinement.

Then two beginnings caught in battle began to tear his mind apart…one, Rose who finally came back to him and was waiting to be reunited again, and on the other side the poor girl whose any longer time in hell had become his own fault and definite commitment.

"Nazia," Henry said closing his eyes in anticipation of the heavy task ahead.

ATTEMPT

The familiar cell embraced Henry's essence, imposing gloomy thoughts hand in hand with dying wishes. He looked into the corner where the ragged girl usually hid herself. A bit frightened by the sudden visit of an uninvited guest, she pressed herself into the safety of walls, but soon adjusting her vision to Henry's glow, she jumped to give him a hug of unpretentious passion. They stood together quietly embracing, like a statue of a girl who finds her father, reluctant to release her arms in fear of being robbed again of his long-awaited presence. Her head was totally exposed, allowing her dark silky hair to fall onto Henry's hands that were locked around her slender waist.

After a moment she exclaimed, "Don't ever leave me, please. You promised to be back in a moment. It seemed that you had gone for good, and I almost lost all hope."

"I am back, my girl, and this time as the bearer of hope and marvellous news."

"You have found a way to free my soul from hell?"

"Yes, my dear," answered Henry.

Releasing her grip, she stood back revealing her glowing face. Then suddenly, as though remembering something, she fixed her hair and thoroughly dusted her dress and stood ready to be released from the shackles of the hell and constant nightmares that had been haunting her.

"I am ready," Nazir announced.

Offering her hands to Henry, she closed her dark eyes filled with excitement.

"Not so fast, my child," said Henry. "There is a condition to your freedom."

"What condition?" Nazia replied, unpleasantly surprised.

"You have to go back."

"Back to Earth?"

"Yes, my child. You have to take another life."

"Another life?" Nazia asked confused.

"Yes, to be born again as a human, but into a different part of the world. Into another culture with different beliefs to yours."

Nazia stepped further back, going into herself, intensely analyzing Henry's words as a proposal placed on the table.

Henry, being able to penetrate her thoughts, waited patiently for her verdict.

A while later Nazia asked, "What about my husband? Will I ever see him again?"

"You probably will, but only after your return to the world of spirit."

Noticing a flash of fear in Nazia's eyes, Henry rushed to say, "Not this one but, rather one like the one I come from. The one that I am unable to describe due to its unprecedented beauty."

"Do you really think I will have a chance to see my loved ones in heaven?"

"That will all depend on you, although the life on Earth I am offering for you to take will leave you very little chance for faults and especially no major slips on the path which could lead you back to this place."

Nazia looked into Henrys eyes and gently whispered, "I agree."

"You do?" Henry asked, surprised.

"Yes, I said."

"What about your beliefs?"

"They did not help me when I was in need. I guess we can all be mistaken, and sometimes blinded in a time of grief…" Nazia stumbled for a moment and then continued, "It seems I was betrayed. Thrown into hell and forgotten about. Like I said, I will take your offer. What happens next?"

Nazia's sudden, quick submission to such a drastic change caught Henry unprepared. The next step from here was unknown, and the first thought that came to Henry's mind was Christ. The one who seemed to have all of the answers concerning Nazia's future. Caught completely off-guard in a desperate strive to reach almighty Christ, Henry kept sending a cry for help, and a moment later help arrived in the form and shape that shocked, not only the poor girl, but Henry, also, who thought he had seen it all. They both stepped back allowing the intruder to materialize himself and occupy the space he required. Observing the act of slow arrival, Henry knew that the soul who had come to rescue him was not Christ, but on a scale of soul ascension was definitely not far behind.

The cell as lit up in orange which was imposed by the color of his robe. Finished with his appearance, the intruder joined his palms across his chest, and bowing his head he politely greeted Henry and Nazia. They greeted him in a similar manner. The soul was a man in his fifties, with a neatly shaved head and face, with any prominent feature for observers to fix their attention on, except for his almond shaped eyes. His arms were exposed from the shoulders, and the orange fabric, nearly reaching the ground, revealed brown leather sandals.

"Am I in the right place?" the intruder asked, addressing his question to Henry.

"I suppose you are," Henry answered.

Clueless and shocked, Nazia asked, "Are you a Buddhist monk?"

"Yes, I am," proudly announced the intruder.

"Is this your plan?" Nazia asked staring at Henry.

"Yes."

"Buddhist monk!" Nazia said with raised voice.

"Do you want out of this place or not?" Henry asked irritably.

"Sorry for interrupting," the monk stepped in, "May I say something?'

"Yes!" simultaneously answered Henry and Nazia.

"My name is Twan," the monk politely introduced himself. "Before stepping into this cell, I studied your life path on Earth," he said looking at Nazia. "I saw the pain and tragedy that you experienced and put others through. So allow me to help you, that is all that I ask."

On saying these words, the monk stretched his right hand toward Nazia and the left to Henry saying, "If you choose to act on my offer, let us join our hands."

Henry immediately grabbed the monk's hand and tried to get hold of Nazia's. At first, she pulled back, but then after a short hesitation she carefully took Henry's hand and with her left touched the monk's generously offered palm. As contact happened, Henry closed his eyes, trusting his will to the monk, but mostly to avoid any unwanted visuals during the transformation from one reality into the other.

TWAN'S REALITY

Intrusive bright light pierced Henry's eyes through their shuttered eyelids. He cautiously regained his vision. All three were standing in the most beautiful garden of blooming trees. Under the weight of densely arranged pink flowers, branches almost touched the silky green grass below. It seemed as though the flowers were competing for the best spots to showcase their exquisite beauty. Mesmerized, Nazia, who had never witnessed such an exhibition of enchanted nature's beauty, pulled one of the branches to her and leaned forward to smell the flowers.

Noticing her disappointment, Twan explained, "The ones on Earth don't have much fragrance, either, although the beauty of blossoming cherry trees indeed has a hypnotizing effect."

Allowing Nazia time to get used to the reality into which she was taken, Twan said, "Should we go for a walk?"

A neatly laid pathway, paved with irregularly shaped concrete blocks, led into the depths of the blossoming cherry tree forest. The pathway was wide enough for two to walk abreast, so Nazia, accustomed to walking behind the men, stepped back allowing Henry to proceed her, but Twan suggested that she take her place next to him.

Feeling that his mission was complete, and knowing that Nazia was in good hands, and her future in broad terms was predictable, Henry said, "I think that this is a good time for me to leave you together," pretending that he had other urgent matters to attend to.

"If you wish so," said Twan.

Nazia, with great disappointment on her face stepped closer to Henry and questioned, "Do you really have to leave?"

"Yes, I have to....but you will be all right."

She stepped closer, right into his personal space, hugged him tightly saying, "Thank you for all that you have done for me. If it wasn't for you, I would have spent eternity in hell."

She pulled back a bit, looked into his eyes, and landed a long kiss on Henry's cheek. When she stepped back to wave goodbye, Henry noticed tears flooding the eyes of this brave girl. After all, in her own way of thinking, she had done something not many humans would have done. She killed herself to take revenge for the one she loved.

Henry waved goodbye and with Rose's name on his lips, left the Buddhist reality, knowing deep inside that he will never see Nazia again. At least, not in the way he discovered her.

When Henry vanished from sight, Nazia wiped her tears and turned to Twan with a question, "What now?"

"To begin with, let us remove this black fabric," Twan said, pulling at Nazia's niqab.

Being raised as a Muslim, Nazia had a hard time uncovering her face in public, but to expose herself in front of a man was beyond her.

Seeing her hesitation Twan said, "Do it whenever you are ready. For now, let's walk together. I would like to brief you on what we believe in, what we stand for, and how we live."

Nazia quietly nodded her head and stood next to the monk on the winding pathway through the blooming forest.

"Before you do your briefing, please remind me who you are."

"I am Twan," answered the monk.

"Yes, I know that already. But what is your position in this place? What exactly do you do?"

"I am the Planner of your next incarnation."

"What does that mean?"

"It means that I am the one who will help you to find a suitable family to be born to on Earth, and hopefully to have a successful life."

"I see," said Nazia, "So you want to know me better?"

"In some manner of speaking, yes."

"I assume that you know what I have done."

"Yes, I do. But let us not talk about that. To begin with, I would like to show you around, to see if you like it. See if it can become yours. Then you can decide."

"What is there to decide?" Nazia sighed deeply. "Anything is better than the place where I have come from."

They soon came to the shores of a greenish pond, showered with plants that Nazia had never seen before. Big, flat, and round shaped green leaves were crowned with a multitude of solo flowers standing above the water.

Noticing Nazia's curiosity, Twan said, "Lotus. This flower symbolizes our teachings about life on Earth."

"How?" Nazia asked, genuinely interested.

"Do you see how murky this water is?"

"Yes, I can hardly see the bottom of the pond."

"Although it is quite shallow, the Lotus represents all that is good and pure in humans, waiting to emerge from the murky waters to their existence, just as these flowers do."

"Are you saying that there is good in everyone?" "Yes. There is a sleeping Lotus in each incarnating soul waiting to be awakened and to bloom."

"So, what do you think was missing in me that my flower did not bloom?"

Twan stood quiet for a moment, and without taking his eyes from the pond he said, "Tolerance."

"Tolerance?" asked Nazia. "And you know how to become tolerant?"

"Yes. You have to learn to forgive people." "How can you forgive those who have taken from you your most precious loved one?"

Twan's answer shook Nazia's world of culture and beliefs and embedded virtues.

"Those who are able to forgive will not have to lose anyone before their time."

"Are you saying that if I had been able to forgive those who killed my husband, I would never have experienced his loss?"

"That is exactly what I am saying. Unfortunately, being on Earth we see human life as a singular event never to be repeated. But, in reality, each previous life lays the foundations for the next upcoming one, and you should know that this is your opportunity to rectify it."

"To be honest, since ending up in the Christian hell I have learned to see many things differently. I have realized how much pain my act of revenge caused to innocent souls, and maybe their destiny, and probably mine, too, would have been very different if I could only have lived with my loss." Then she sighed deeply saying, "But unfortunately we are where we are."

"I am glad that we are on the same page on the matter of forgiveness. Even Islam teaches that, 'No mercy will be shown to those who show no mercy, and no forgiveness will be given to other who will not forgive others.'"

"That is exactly what happened to me," Nazia admitted. "To

be honest, I have heard that, but I always thought it applied to only Muslims and not unbelievers."

Twan smiled and said, "There are no unbelievers. All people believe in a higher power, and just because their beliefs do not correlate with yours, does not make them unbelievers. After all, belief, or should I say faith, is a very personal thing, and there are no two souls on the planet whose faith, or belief, are exactly the same. We all believe in our own unique ways."

"I see that now," agreed Nazia.

"So, to move forward as a soul, you have to learn to forgive others."

Confused and puzzled by what she had just heard, supposedly from a most advanced soul in this realm, Nazia said, "But I just told you that I have learned my lesson."

Twan, who until now had been staring at the pond, turned to face Nazia, and placing both hands on her tiny, fragile shoulders said, "You have to prove it."

"How am I to do that?" Nazia asked in genuine surprise.

"You have to suffer a bigger loss and must forgive those who are the cause."

"What are you saying?" Nazia raised her voice, and stepping away from the Planner said, "What can be bigger than losing the love of your life? We were just married, and I didn't have the chance to taste married life."

"Much bigger," Twan answered simply.

"You mean my parents?"

"Bigger."

After an intensive search, a grimace of horror appeared on Nazia's face covering it with her hands, she turned around and simply walked away from the Buddhist monk, so as to avoid the answer to her question. The path was long, and she followed it to wherever it may lead. Soon the garden of blossoming trees lost its density, and she appeared in front of a strange wooden structure. It looked like a building with a multi-layered roof, almost reaching the sky. The odd architecture captured her attention and she paused to observe it, but an unusual sound that could hardly qualify as music grabbed her attention. Some undetectable force drew Nazia closer to investigate the inner world of the strange, tall, wooden structure. The doors stood wide open, and a stretch of stairs were calling to be conquered. As she climbed, the unusual sounds became increasingly loud. It seemed as though someone was testing the lower registers of a church organ. Each note began to resonate in her body, triggering her natural inquisitiveness. As she stood at the doorway Nazia saw a humongous golden statue of a man peacefully sitting with closed eyes and crossed legs. The inside was a bit misty, and it took a while before she could discover the source of the noise. There were rows of Buddhist monks dressed as Twan was, sitting in the same posture as the golden statue and creating a deep, low vibrational sound with their throats. It didn't take much for Nazia to realize that she was inside some kind of religious structure, and this was the way that they prayed. No one paid any attention to her appearance, and so she chose to investigate further. Wishing to stay unnoticed she walked along the wall to the most remote corner of the temple, and knelt, preparing herself for namaz (Islamic prayers). She chose to face the wall and forwarded her prayers to Allah. She asked him to save her from this nightmare which had begun the moment she stepped into the Christian church strapped with explosives. The aftermath had become a terrifying endless dream waiting to be over as she was awakened into her physical life where everything made sense. She kept praying for a miracle, hoping that Allah would hear her voice and display his grace and merciful nature toward his devoted believer.

A while later, when she ran out of words of persuasion, Nazia opened her eyes. She was still facing the same wall in the very same temple filled to its brim with strange smell and sounds of senseless praying. Although there was one difference, she found Twan right next to her, kneeling exactly as she was with eyes closed in silent prayer.

Nazia looked at him with one question on her mind, "How can I escape you?"

With eyes still closed Twan answered, "You can always go back to where you came from."

"Back to hell? No, never."

"Then follow me," Twan said, offering her his hand.

Reluctantly Nazia submitted and closed her eyes. The sudden silence made her open her eyes.

HORROR

Bright lights struck her eyes, and she raised her right arm to prevent discomfort, and only a while later was able to observe her whereabouts. She appeared, with Twan next to her, in a long corridor filled with light.

"Where are we?" Nazia asked.

"You will see now."

Twan indicated that Nazia should follow him. Soon she realized that Twan was searching for the right door in the corridor, and once he found it, he pushed it wide open asking Nazia to step in. Once inside she realized that they were standing in an operating room. It was empty of doctors, with the equipment operational and ready at any given moment to come back to life to save some unfortunate human.

"Why are we in a hospital?" Nazia asked, confused.

"You will see now," answered Twan, whose posture indicated expectation of something extraordinary to happen.

In that very moment the double doors leading into the operating room burst open by a violent strike from outside, and with a team of doctors on either side, a hospital bed rolled into the operating room. The events unwound so quickly that Nazia had no chance to see who the patient was. A team of four well trained personnel, each to his duty attaching the patient to the medical equipment and preparing the necessary tools to operate. Nazia, along with Twan, stood by the wall out of the doctors way. In an instant the ward sprung to life with the countless flashing lights ready to support the doctors efforts in a desperate attempt to keep the patient's soul in the confinement of its body. A few moments later and Nazia realized that things were not going the way they should, and the doctors were about to lose their patient. Twenty minutes later everything came to a standstill. The battle was over. Nazia saw the nebulous body of a three-year- old child getting airborne from the operating table and begin its elevation toward the ceiling. Nazia, mesmerized by the scene was afraid to move, not to spoil the beauty of the moment. Tears were rolling down her face, delivering relief to her overwhelmed astral body.

When the doctors covered the child's face with a white sheet and utterly devasted, left the operating room, Twan said, "Let's go."

No questions asked, Nazia followed his lead through the long hospital corridor to find the operating doctor who was about to justify his actions to the parents of the little girl. Crushed by the news, the mother fell to her knees losing consciousness.

Rapidly rising tensions became impossible to withstand, and pleading for mercy Nazia addressed Twan, "Please explain to me…why are we here, and why do I have to witness this drama?"

Unaffected by the occurring events, Twan offered her his hand. Nazia grabbed it as an escape line hoping to be taken away to anywhere else but here. When she reopened her eyes they were back in the garden of blooming trees facing the peaceful pond covered in lilies.

Nazia took a deep breath in a false attempt to fill her non-existent lungs with as much oxygen as she could, and exhaling she said, "Thank you for rescuing me."

"You are welcome, my dear. I just want you to know that you can always count on me, even when I am not around."

"What are you saying? Are you leaving me?" Nazia asked, deeply alarmed.

"Not before I explain what you just witnessed, and what your choices are for your very near future."

"I am listening," whispered Nazia facing Twan, knowing that this was going to be hard to swallow.

Twan turned to face her, placed his hands on her tiny shoulders and gazed into her beautiful dark eyes. "The woman who just fainted in the waiting room in the hospital is going to be you."

"This does not make any sense?"

"I just allowed you a glimpse into the future of your next possible life on Earth."

Nazia stepped back releasing herself from Twan's gentle hold, and with the speed of light began to place loose pieces of the puzzle into one horrifying picture.

"Am I going to lose my three-year-old daughter?"

"Yes," Twan confirmed.

A sudden wave of emotions overwhelmed Nazia's soul with unexpected feelings of love toward the poor child. She gently hugged the invisible baby and placed her head against the child's.

Nazia closed her eyes in a moment of absolute joy delivered by the knowledge of her having a child. Something that she had dreamt about in her past life, but the overcasting future hung like a dark cloud over the longevity of her joy.

Twan, observing Nazia's act, allowed her some time before he spoke,

"And you know what is going to be even harder than losing your child?"

"I am afraid to ask…"

"It's the fact that soon you will find out that the cause of your daughter's death was a doctor's error, and you will have to forgive him and move on with your life."

"I don't think I will be able to do that."

"You will. I am certain of it. The religion you will adopt from a young age will help you not only to learn how to forgive, but also to find reason in your loss as well."

Nazia lowered her head and with a deep sigh said, "I trust you."

"So be it," said Twan inviting Nazia to follow him.

A new and unfamiliar path led them to a small cozy temple.

When they reached the staircase leading to the entrance Twan said, "From here you are on your own, but I want you to know that every step of your future life I will be next to you until we meet again in this very same eternally blooming garden."

Twan joined his palms at his forehead, bowed deeply saying, "Safe journey," and vanished like a vapor into the blooming trees.

Left alone Nazia looked up at the pagoda and began her climb to the entrance, toward the doorway into the world of humans filled with pain and uncertainties, with moments of joy and sorrow. She knew that this was a path to her redemption, and possible forgiveness for all the damage she had done in her past. At the doorway she was warmly welcomed and invited inside by three most beautiful Asian ladies, each dressed in traditional attire splashed with bright, but tastefully selected colors. They bowed gently indicating for Nazia to proceed to a podium placed at the center of the temple's floor. Nazia quietly followed their instructions and stood up in front of a golden statue of a resting Buddha. Beneath her feet was a soft carpet woven with geometrical ornaments that she had never seen before, probably holding deep meaning for the procedure she was about to become a part of. She stood up straight and closed her eyes, submitting her will to whatever was about to happen. The three Asian ladies gracefully stepped forward, circling Nazia by joining their hands.

Her head went into an uncontrollable spin. Her first attempts to gain a clear vision of what was happening failed. Only with great difficulty did she manage to stop the motion and force herself to regain her vision. The only thing she saw were walls of a colorful tube surrounding her, made from a semi-transparent substance. Next was an accelerating descent through the tube. Nazia realized that she was gaining speed and would soon be in a free-fall back into what exactly she could only guess. Twan's last words were still on her mind, reassuring her of her safety. Soon she could not see anything. The walls of the tube had lost their pigmentation, surrendering their beauty to darkness, and the only sound of rushing air was a steady indicator of her long and seemingly endless descent. Suddenly everything fell dead quiet. A moment later she heard a distant voice of a young mother excited by a child's first kick. The feeling of long forgotten bliss reached her, delivering comfort and a sense of belonging. With one effortless push, she arranged herself into the most soothing position and let all memories of the past vanish, never to be sought again.

Her guide, Twan, landed himself in the middle of the quite poor household, walked straight toward the bed where the excited mother kept touching her tummy in desperate attempts to sense movements of her child once again. Soon she closed her eyes, falling into a peaceful sleep next to her husband, completely unaware of the two visitors who had stepped into their lives to deliver a soul to a child that they were so longing for.

THE REUNION

Thales' palm landed on Croton's shoulder along with the word, "Allow me to introduce you to the real you."

Henry's silent approval put Croton at ease. Right in front of him the glowing figure of a strange being from another time, who seemingly came to help him come to the light, suddenly became a blurry shapeless cloud soon to be vaporized completely. This act plunged Croton into pitch black, where Henry's moderate intensity of light also failed. No matter how hard Croton tried to regain his vision, he still faced the impenetrable wall of darkness. Strangely enough it did not place fear in his heart. The escalating motion of rising to the unknown filled his soul with happiness. After all, he was moving up and in his mind no harm could come from ascension.

A while later absolute calm invaded Croton's being, emphasizing the end of the journey. He chose to cautiously gain his vision. A bright light pierced his eyes, and he immediately covered them with his right hand. The presence of light at the end of the silent elevation brought to his heart joy and delight. He was certain that whatever he must face next, it will be better in comparison to where he has come from. His second attempt to gain vision proved to be successful.

He was standing on a crispy, crystal, snowy slope surrounded with white mountains stretching as far as he could see. A sudden gust of wind landed on his chest, nearly forcing him to fall onto his back. He instinctively leaned forward to balance this force of nature. Two steps away Croton saw an old Greek peacefully observing the surroundings and waiting patiently to be noticed.

"Care to join me?" asked the old man, who was definitely not dressed for the occasion.

"Do I have a choice?" asked Croton.

"Hhhmmm, no, not really," Thales replied as he began ascending toward the summit of the mountain.

Croton placed his feet into the footprints left by Thales so as not to sink into the deep snow. When they reached the mountain's crest, Croton stood breathless, both physically and emotionally. Unimaginable in their beauty and dramatism of creation, trying to outdo each other in their attempt to reach the sky, white giants were peacefully sleeping under the thick blanket of crystalized water, with only seldom gusts of wind standing as a witness to their sleeping breath.

Zipping up his leather jacket to his neck, and placing his hands deep into the pockets, Croton asked, "What now?"

"Now we will talk," Thales answered.

"Some spot you chose to talk," sarcastically commented Croton.

"I know, it might seem like not much, but I like it here…there are no distractions."

"I see. So what are we going to talk about?" Croton asked boldly facing Thales.

Thales smiled saying, "You seem so calm and confident."

With a veil of sadness Croton answered, "The worst has happened. I died, lost my family, and with that, all I ever loved. The aftermath is irrelevant."

"Don't you wonder where they are, and if there is the possibility of seeing them again?"

"I thought you would never ask," Croton replied calmly, concealing the rise of emotions to the thought that he might once again see and touch his beloved wife and daughter.

"I can arrange it," Thales stated, curious to see Croton's reaction.

"I will be eternally grateful to you," said Croton, placing his right hand on his chest and bowing his head.

This gesture was so typical of Croton, the Roman senator, that it caused Thales to stumble. To resuscitate the version of Croton was not in Thales' plans. To risk spoiling all that he had worked on for so many Earth years by allowing Croton to recall his past, along with his character, could compromise his love for Gaya. It was just too soon, and Thales chose to forge the metal while it was hot.

He stepped closer, placing his right hand on Croton's shoulder gently asking, "Please close your eyes."

Familiar with the procedure, Croton closed his eyes placing his destiny in Thales' hands. He waited for some time and unable to register any change in his perceptions, opened his eyes. The contrast between what he saw before and what he was facing now was astonishing.

A neatly arranged garden blooming in colors never seen before stood in front of Croton, leaving no doubt that he was no longer on Earth. Thales was nowhere to be seen, and Croton realized that he was on his own. He was standing on a narrow pathway that dived into the depths of the manicured perfect garden. An unexplainable feeling that at the end of this pathway he will find his Gaya filled his heart with excitement. A few cautious steps toward the one he was anxious to see and squeeze tight against his chest soon graduated into a wind-like run. Croton's heart pounded through his entire body in the race to reach his loved one before him. The road led him to the shores of a most beautiful lake surrounded by tall snowy mountains. Almost 100 yards away he noticed a white house with a terracotta roof, placed right on the banks of the lake. Somehow Croton knew that his Gaya was in there waiting for him. In a flash he stood in front of the entrance door, surprised by the speed with which he covered the distance. He placed his right palm on the wooden door, closed his eyes and stood unmoving. He tried to slow his heartbeat and to indulge in the moment between his horrible past and magnificent future.

Three distinct knocks attracted Gaya's attention.

"Who is there?" Gaya asked loudly, puzzled that someone had appeared in her reality without her permission.

Left doubtless, Croton pushed the door open and stepped into the house, cautiously closing the door, to stand in the middle of the large foyer.

"Who is there?" he heard Gaya's voice again.

For some reason he stood curious. He knew that Gaya was on the upper level of the house, and instead of flying up the stairs, Croton stood motionless, facing them deeply concerned to be disappointed in his expectations. A second later he heard the steps of descending Gaya, and then, there she was. Curious to the source of the disturbance she froze halfway down, more beautiful than he could ever remember.

"Croton?"

"Yes, my love," answered her husband emerged from hell, spreading his arms wide apart.

Battling to believe, Gaya flew down the stairs to embrace the one whom she had no hope of seeing for another lifetime. On impact of the two loving hearts, Croton lifted her up from the floor in a spiralling motion. It seemed as though they hadn't seen each other for an eternity. As their lips touched, everything that was before and after converged into one point. Distinct memories of their first and long forgotten kiss of their youth advanced its way, inviting with it emotions lost in the past, leaving them so utterly detached from time and space, and the tragic chain of horrible events that brought them here. When finally, their lips parted, the two souls kept hugging one another in a desperate act, fulfilling the gushing holes created in their hearts by lethal separation.

Suddenly coming back to her senses, Gaya pulled back. She cautiously touched Croton's face.

Sliding her hands along his body, she finally asked, "Are you for real?"

"Yes, I am, my love."

"But how is this possible? You…here? This is defying all that I have learned from Lita. She told me that you weren't harmed when the city crumbed in the earthquake."

Then a revelation crept into her mind. She stepped back, covering her face with her hands and whispered, "No, you didn't…"

"Yes, my love, I did."

"No," whispered Gaya.

"I guess I couldn't stay behind," said Croton smiling.

"Stop joking. I am serious. You can't be standing in front of me unless…"

"Unless I am dead."

"Yes," said Gaya.

"You are right, my love," Croton said seriously. "I couldn't bear the weight of separation. You left and took with you all that I had loved. All that gave me purpose in my life on Earth. Without purpose, life is empty."

"I see your reasons," Gaya answered. "What I would like to know is how your life was ended."

"Do you really want to know?"

"I do, my love, and I am hoping that you didn't end it just to be with us."

"I did," admitted Croton.

"Oh my God. You could have ended up in hell."

"I did, my love. I have paid the price for what I have done."

"You've been to hell!" Gaya exclaimed in horror.

Croton pulled her into his arms saying, "I am out now, and free of the crimes that I have committed."

She pressed her body tightly to his, "One day you will tell me all about what you have been through, but for now we shouldn't stain our reunion with the darkness of the past. You are in heaven now, safe in my arms, and that is all that matters now," said Gaya running her fingers through Croton's hair. "God witnessed that I have missed every inch of you."

As though recovering from shock she exclaimed, "Let's go. I would like to show you our heaven. All that I once wanted I found here. Look at our house, the garden, and lake. Allow me to be your guide."

She almost dragged her husband up the stairs to the bedroom where the stunning view of her once dream, had become reality. They stood on the balcony next to each other with Gaya's head lying on Croton's shoulder, admiring the reality that had been created by thoughtful Lita for them to find impermanent repose, until those having the power over their lives will choose to add a twist to the sudden calm that this poor couple had finally possessed.

"Look at this beauty," Gaya said, "This world belongs to us for as long as we wish. No one can take this heaven from us."

"It's beautiful, my love," said Croton with a shade of sadness in his voice.

"Is something wrong?" asked Gaya.

"There is a question that I am afraid to ask," Croton said facing Gaya.

"Don't be afraid, my love. All fears are behind us, my love."

Croton looked into Gaya's eyes filled with life and hope for the future and carefully asked, "Don't you feel like there is something missing in your life?"

"What do you mean?" replied astonished Gaya, "I have it all, everything that I have always dreamt of, and the final touch to this perfection was your arrival to this world."

"Let me rephrase my question. Don't you see that someone is missing?"

"Who my love?"

"Don't you remember Rose?"

"No, not really," Gaya pretended playfully.

"Rose, our daughter. You have no memory of her?"

"Relax, my love," Gaya laughed. "Of course I do remember our girl."

"And…where is she? Why is she not with you?" asked deeply alarmed Croton.

"You shouldn't worry, my love. Our little Rose is not so little anymore. She is all grown up and living life on her own."

"Damn it. How long was I absent?" Croton asked confused.

"It's not about time, my love. Before she took the role as our daughter on Earth, she was your guide, or should I say your guardian angel."

"I am bewildered, this puzzle is getting bigger."

"Do you want to know a bit more?" Gaya asked.

"What now?"

"Her husband…"

"Is she married?"

"Wait, her husband, Henry, was your secondary guide. In other words, they knew you before you knew yourself on Earth."

Croton shook his head in a desperate attempt to organize the loose pieces of the puzzle, when a sudden sound caught their attention. They turned around to face the Planner. Thales stood peacefully with a humble smile.

"Who are you?" Gaya exclaimed fearfully.

Thales glanced at Croton expecting a proper introduction.

"Be calm, my love, allow me to introduce you to the one who is behind all that we have been through in our last life on Earth."

"What do you mean?" asked clueless Gaya.

"Almighty Thales, Planner of human lives," Croton said, placing his palm over his heart and deeply bowing his head in deep admiration.

"Planner?" Gaya asked.

"Yes, he is the one who rescued me from hell and helped me to find my way to you."

Gaya mimicked Croton's way of greeting, saying, "Thank you, sir, for what you have done. My gratitude has no limitations."

Thales nodded his head in acceptance of Gaya's recognition, and a second later, as if awakening from slumber Gaya said, "May I ask you a question?"

"Oh yes, please do," replied Thales.

"Why? Why was our life on Earth cut so short? We had so much to live for."

Then, referring to Croton she said, "I was expecting our second child, and I was about to surprise you when all hell broke loose."

Seeing tears of despair in Gaya's eyes, Croton embraced her saying, "I know, my love, this was the knowledge that tipped the scale between remaining on Earth and choosing death."

They both looked at Thales with expectation of answers in the shape of reasons why their life was so brutally extinguished.

"All answers to your questions are deeply embedded in your minds. Without the help of guides you won't be able to retrieve the memories of your distant past."

"What do you mean?" asked frightened Gaya.

"Before you chose to take human essence, you both had lives which were disguised from your conscious minds so that you could experience a new one. Those hidden memories can be retrieved, unless you choose for them to remain untouched."

Croton looked at Gaya, "What do you say my love?"

Gaya looked at him perplexed, "What if we discover things in our past which could affect, or maybe ruin, our present?"

"What could be a better way to test your love for one another?" interjected Thales.

"What do you say, my love?" Croton repeated.

"I see that you are adamant to dig up your past," Gaya responded irritably. "What if you find no place for me in there? Or should I say, in your new self? What about me…I will remain alone and unwanted…"

"That will not happen," Thales said firmly.

Gaya was on the verge of asking this ancient man to leave them alone, allowing them time to satisfy the thirst of absence from each other's lives, and afterward to discuss such an important matter, but for some unknown reason Thales kept pushing Croton to commit himself to an act where their newly found bliss could be plunged into a nightmare.

"Can we have some private time?" Gaya asked, whispering into Croton's ear.

"I am afraid that you cannot," Thales insisted. "This has to be done right now."

"What is the rush?" Gaya raised her voice tinged with anger.

"I see your reasons for the attempt to hold your husband back, but you should trust me," urged Thales.

"It's hard to trust someone whose purpose is to play with poor humans' lives."

Thales chose to ignore this direct insult, smiling sadly.

"And why are you so quiet?" Gaya turned her anger toward Croton. "It seems like I am the only one who is fighting for our future."

"I trust this man, my love. I am standing in front of you because of him, and if it wasn't important, he would have not insisted that I see you first."

Gaya pulled back, crossing her arms over her chest, saying submissively, "Do as you wish. My judgement was never a guide to you."

Croton kissed her on the cheek, and facing Thales said, "Do your best."

DOWNLOAD

“Where are we?” asked Croton, observing the place in which he suddenly appeared.

Nothing was unusual in his surroundings. He was standing next to Thales on the shores of the vast body of water, a sea or ocean, although it was unusually calm with hardly any ripples. Beneath his feet was white sand stretching its presence on either side of him.

Croton noticed other souls also facing the water. They were all in pairs, standing apart and engaged in dialogue. The fact that one of them was a mentor was hard to miss. Thales stood quietly, allowing Croton to be done with his observation of the place that he chose to bring him. Although Croton was anxious to learn all about this place, he procrastinated. A dominant feeling that once Thales was done with whatever he had planned, an irreversible avalanche will storm Croton’s life and turn it upside down. This fact was preventing Croton from taking the first step. Instead, he kept studying his surroundings. Turning around he saw a dense wall of forest abruptly standing at the edge of the sand. The entire scenery was nothing but peace and serenity. Absolute harmony entered Croton’s mind frame, inviting with it curious thoughts if this is the calm before the storm. Suddenly, a couple standing not far from them turned around and walked toward the forest. Soon they were swallowed by its density. What amazed him the most was that in the next moment another couple replaced them. Croton looked at Thales without saying a word. Thales indicated toward the forest with his eyes.

Sensing the inevitability of the upcoming event Croton merely said, “After you, sir.”

Thales led the way. Successfully conquering the stretch of sand, Croton noticed a corridor formed by the vegetation leading to the heart of the forest. Following Thales’ steps, Croton dived though the opening. The narrow winding pathway found its end at a wide field plastered with well-maintained grass carpet. It was about thirty yards in diameter. A bright light of unknown source was handsomely showering it, emphasising its importance. As they approached the open field, Thales stopped at the edge and waited for Croton to catch up and stand next to him. Right in the middle of the field Croton noticed a glass cubicle standing alone, that reminded him of a shower stall.

"What is that?" Croton asked.

"Your first impression was correct. It is a shower stall."

"In the middle of a forest?"

"Yes, my friend. And you have to go into it," instructed Thales.

Croton looked at Thales to determine the seriousness of his request.

"I am not joking, so please remove your winter clothing before stepping in."

Suddenly Croton realized that he as still wearing his favorite leather jacket.

"I am surprisingly not hot," Croton said as he removed his jacket, folding it and placing it on the grass. "Now what?" he asked.

"Now, you remove the rest of your clothing."

"Wait a moment. You want me to strip naked without knowing what I am about to face."

"Yes."

"Will you at least give me some idea of what this stall is all about, and what I can expect when I step into it."

Thales took a deep breath and said, "This exercise will help you to recall your true identity."

Croton took a few steps toward the stall to have a better look. Then he stopped, turned around, and asked, "Do I really need to restore my memory? I am quite happy where I am. Do I need to complicate my life?"

Thales stepped closer and placing his hand on Croton's shoulder said, "You are a powerful soul with thousands of Earth years behind you. Knowledge that you have gathered is priceless. Are you willing to waste it all? Besides, you have a great purpose and as you know, life without purpose is meaningless."

Without further hesitation, Croton turned around and stepped forward toward the cubicle to stand right in front of it. There was nothing special about it. Just four thick sheets of glass stuck together to form a shower stall. Croton removed all that was covering his body, and butt-naked, stepped in. The seemingly heavy glass door easily swung open to welcome the knowledge seeker. Croton closed the door and checked for the taps, but there were none to be found. Then he looked up for the showerhead, but instead he saw only the blue sky above. Countless branches of majestic trees embraced each other to form a dense ceiling around the booth, but not above it. Croton knew that whatever was about to shower him had to come down through that opening. Croton crossed his palms to cover his private parts and turned around to see if Thales was still around. The old Greek stood unmoved at the edge of the green field. Their eyes met, and in that very moment a powerful strobe of light hit the booth, originating from somewhere up in the sky, but Croton could not see it, he could only feel it. Golden light invaded the cubicle with such intensity that Croton had to close his eyes so as not to be blinded. In a matter of seconds, he experienced the most unusual bombardment by a tremendous amount of information in the shape of events experienced by his soul from the time of its creation. He felt like a boundless vessel capable to accommodate all that light had to offer. The longevity of the download, Croton could not ascertain, but when the invasion was over and the light vanished as fast as it had appeared, Croton pushed the door open and stepped out of the booth. At his feet he found neatly folded attire and he looked at Thales.

"Didn't you miss it?"

Croton picked up the clothing just to discover his own tunic. He skilfully wrapped it around his body, and said to the approaching Thales, "I am back, my friend."

Thales gave him a warm welcoming hug saying, "I really missed you."

The youngster who has stepped into the shower stall was gone without a trace.

"What now?" asked Croton.

"Now, you are free to do whatever you want. Go wherever your heart desires. See whoever you missed the most."

Croton closed his eyes and taking a deep breath said, "I would like to see my spirit guides."

GATHERING

Since Henry left Nazia with Twan to face her karma, he had predominantly been lazing in his reality. The soothing feeling of accomplishment allowed him to relax and enjoy his own world, his own paradise. Every time that he walked through the forest, he discovered new oasis of tiny heavens which had managed to escape him before.

Rose's frequent in and out trips to visit her mom Gaya, to help her to settle into her new world, gave Henry time alone, and space to miss each other's presence.

As he stepped into the house after a long walk in the forest, Henry found Rose standing in the middle of their living room. She was highly focused and totally indifferent to Henry's arrival.

"Are you okay, my love?" Henry asked stepping closer to hug her.

Completely ignoring his approach, Rose showed no interest to being engaged in conversation.

Henry stumbled for a second, and then asked, "Is something wrong?"

She looked at him and asked in return, "Can't you hear him?"

"Hear who?" Henry asked confused.

"Croton."

In that very same moment, they heard two distinct knocks on their entrance door. They had never experienced this before, and they both stepped back cautiously. Whoever was at the door knocked again. Being the man of the house, Henry stepped forward and pulled the handle, but before the identity of the invited guest was revealed, he retreated. So far, only two souls had the liberty to visit their reality uninvited, Thales and Croton, and they never knocked. One can only imagine their faces when Henry and Rose saw Croton, their mentor and guide, standing in the doorway.

Stepping inside he asked, "Did you miss me?"

"You don't know how much," Henry replied stepping forward to embrace him. It was this energy exchange that Henry had missed the most.

Croton hugged him back and long forgotten emotions overran Henry's soul like an avalanche, bringing tears to his eyes. Above all, it was the forgotten sense of ultimate protection regardless of the tasks that life threw at him that moved him the most.

"You don't know how much I have missed you," Henry whispered.

When the energy exchange was over and balance was restored, Henry stepped aside letting Croton face Rose.

Rose looked deep into Croton's eyes saying, " I don't know who I am looking at. My father or the one I have been taking care of from the moment of your birth on Earth, or my spirit guide and mentor.

"Little bit of all," Croton answered as he gently hugged her.

When they parted Rose asked, "Now I really envy those souls who arrive into the world of spirit without any memories of it."

Croton laughed loudly saying, "Soon things will fall back to the way they were before."

"I doubt it," sighed Rose.

"I am here to help you in that regard," said Croton, inviting them to take a seat at the dinning table.

"It seems as though no time has passed at all," Henry said as he occupied his chair, allowing Croton to sit at the head of the table.

"Well, didn't I tell you it would take no time for us to be back here."

"Yes, you did," agreed Rose while all the troubles they had been through since first meeting Croton rushed through her mind.

"It's all over now," Croton said reading her mind. "Finally, it's all over, my dear ones, and now it is time for me to reveal the purpose of the journey that we all took."

Henry and Rose looked at each other realizing that there was more than they were aware of.

"Wasn't it all about you finding your one and only?" Rose asked puzzled.

"Yes, to find your true love," Henry added.

"And I worked damned hard to make it happen," continued Rose.

"Okay, okay, please calm down," said Croton. "Indeed, it was about finding true love, and I am grateful for the work that you have done, but there was more to my journey to Earth."

"What more?" Rose asked suspiciously, sensing that they had been set up by the one they trusted the most.

Croton sighed deeply as he always used to and said, "My visit to Earth served a much greater purpose than you realize. It wasn't only about me. It was mostly about you."

"Us?" exclaimed Henry.

"Yes, my friend. It was about giving you the opportunity to experience what it is like being a spirit guide. It was about you, Henry, exploring new realms and meeting new souls without me breathing down your neck. It was for you to dive into the depths of hell to save lost souls."

"Wait a minute," Rose cut in. "Are you saying that you went to Earth so that we could experience all that we went through?"

"My dear, Rose," Croton replied, "There is an irrevocable universal law that proclaims, and stipulates, that more advanced souls have to assist younger souls in their ascension."

"Are you saying," Henry stepped in, "that you sacrificed your comforts in this life to help us to grow?"

"Look, it wasn't all bad, I had a bonus."

"What bonus?" simultaneously asked Henry and Rose.

"I had to check out my second half."

"And did you?" Rose asked.

Croton took another deep sigh, saying, "We'll have to wait and see."

"What do you mean?" Rose protested. "Is Gaya not good enough for you anymore?"

"As I said, I will have to see," Croton repeated.

"What is there to see?" Rose insisted.

"I have to see if she will accept the new me. Or should I say, the old part of me, which is most of me, and completely unknown to her."

"I see," said Rose. "I am sure that she will be able to see through you. I mean, I am sure she will be able to find in you the love of her life. The one who she fell in love with…you know what I mean," mumbled Rose.

"The answers to all of those questions can only be found face to face."

"So, what is holding you back?" pushed Rose.

"Since I have told you all that I needed to, we can adjourn this meeting," Croton said standing up.

"Do you need us?" Henry asked.

"No, this one I have to do alone."

With those last words, Croton vanished from sight as though

he'd never been there.

"I would give anything to be present at that meeting," Rose said. "After all, they were my parents."

"I know, my love. I am sure that soon enough we will hear all about it."

Rose stood up and walked to the window facing the sea and said, "I do not have a good feeling about this."

EXPOSED

Croton cautiously stepped into Gaya's reality. He chose to appear in the foyer. Unable to locate Gaya on the ground floor he went upstairs to the master bedroom. There she was, standing on the balcony, leaning against the balustrade, and peacefully observing all that Lita had created for her as a welcome gift, for her to find peace and comfort in this transitional realm.

Croton stood quietly so as not to disturb Gaya's serenity, and to have the chance, one more time, to observe the one that he had spent a short, but such an amazing time with on Earth. Their entire life, like a gust of wind, rushed through his mind, mostly composed of pleasant memories. The love that Croton had managed to find because of her still dwelled in his soul, but it wasn't unconditional. Deep inside Croton knew that from now on it will be up to Gaya to turn the next page of their book of love, or to close it for good.

Suddenly Gaya felt someone's presence and immediately turned around to be confronted by an odd looking man in a white tunic. In defence, she stepped back against the balustrade.

"Who are you?" asked Gaya. "I didn't give you permission."

Croton gently smiled saying, "I don't need one to visit my wife."

Gaya stepped forward uncertainly to gaze into Croton's eyes.

"Is it…" And then a moment later she continued, "It is you. But why?"

"Aren't you happy to see me?" Croton interrupted.

"I don't think I know you."

"We have plenty of time."

"Time for what?"

"To get to know each other all over again," answered Croton.

Gaya stepped backward again, crossing her arms over her chest. Her eyes filled with tears, and her face began to turn red, as it used to when she was upset.

"How convenient for you. You know everything about me, whatever there is to know. And I apparently know nothing about you," Gaya said with an escalating tone of voice. "And tell me, please, where is the man I fell in love with? Where is the one who I chose to grow old with. To have children with, and one day to become a grandparent with? My life was shredded into pieces because someone chose to become a human to provide a lesson to his trainees."

"Who told you that?" Croton asked, unpleasantly surprised.

"It doesn't matter. What I would like to know is what kind of heartless soul could have arranged such a scam? To kill me, my daughter, and my unborn child so that someone can have some practical training."

Gaya's face began to turn purple.

Croton rushed forward to calm her, "It wasn't like that," Croton tried to justify himself.

"Then how was it? Why don't you enlighten me."

Croton wanted to tell Gaya that it wasn't his idea, and that it had all been planned by the Planner. That he, too, was thrown into the deep end without a clear vision of the outcome of that visit to Earth. All he knew was that he was going to find the true love of his life, and his happily ever after. But, instead, he kept quiet, silenced by Gaya's anger and the reasons behind it.

"Did someone cut your tongue?" Gaya threw into Croton's face.

No soul had ever spoken to Croton that way since becoming a spirit guide, although those who had tried, he knew how to teach them their lessons. But now Croton was facing his Gaya. The guilt filled up his heart with doubts that he can ever be forgiven for something he had been compelled to do. Croton raised his eyes to look straight at Gaya. She looked like a compressed spring on the verge of bursting into his face.

"Please calm down, my love. We should talk about all of this. Just give me the chance to explain everything."

"There is nothing to explain. I have made up my mind."

"What are you talking about?"

"I am going back."

Shocked to his core, Croton stumbled backward trying to distance himself from what he had just heard.

"No! You are making a huge mistake," Croton said terrified. "Please tell me you did not agree to another life on Earth."

"I already did," Gaya confirmed angrily.

Croton turned around, walking back into the bedroom to

gather his thoughts. He lowered himself onto the edge of the bed, gesturing to Gaya to sit next to him. She walked over and sat down on the corner of the mattress, distancing herself from the cause of her anger.

"Why did you agree without asking me?"

"Why should I? No one asked for my opinion if I agreed to die so soon in such a horrible event."

"I hear you," Croton said calmly. "Do you realize that accepting this trip to Earth you are signing a lifetime contract?"

"I do. And I will tell you more. I have already chosen the family I will be born into."

"This is crazy," said Croton, lost for words. "What about me? What about my feelings? Did it ever cross your mind…" Croton raised his voice.

"You will be fine. You belong here," sarcastically reflected Gaya.

"But, please, give us a chance and I promise that you will love being here, too."

"Look at me," Gaya said turning to face Croton. "Do I look happy? Did you really think that this perfectly manicured landscape would make me happy?"

"You can change it," Croton jumped in.

"I know, my love, but the problem is that I cannot make it any better than it already is. So, what is the point?"

For the first time Gaya had said "my love", placing hope in Croton's heart, like the last blink of a weathering sunset.

Croton moved closer, taking her hand into his saying, "Please reconsider. There is another universe up here to be discovered, and I can be your guide. If you only wish…" Croton said with a tempting voice.

"I don't want your universe. All I wanted was a normal family, a normal husband, and at least two kids. I wanted to see them grow, and then to raise their children. Was that too much to ask?"

Croton sighed deeply, realizing his inability to fulfill the desires of his one and only. Suddenly he remembered himself, not long ago, persuading Henry to give up on Rose so that she could find happiness on Earth with the architect named Kevin.

A second later he firmly asked, "Who is assisting you? I will be your guide if you must go back."

"I am sorry my love, but I already have a guide."

"Lita," stated Croton.

"Yes."

"I know you can hear me. Please show yourself," Croton called out loudly.

Instantly she stood in front of them. Lita greeted Croton silently by bowing her head. In that single gesture Gaya grasped not only her absolute respect for Croton, but the magnitude of his presence in this world of spirits. Croton stood up from the bed and walked straight out onto the balcony. Lita stepped aside so as not to be crushed by him. He paused in the doorway and then turned around to face them. The light that made its way through the doorway created an unusual aura around Croton's figure, emphasizing his great presence.

Addressing Lita he said, "So, you are taking her back to Earth without my consent!"

"It was her wish, and you weren't around," Lita replied softly.

"I took my own life to be next to her, in case you are wondering why I was late. I literally went through hell to find her."

"With all due respect," answered Lita, "I will refer my words not to you now, but rather to the young man you were on Earth. You didn't take your life to be next to her. You did it out of fear of being alone on Earth with all your loved ones gone, and hell was the last place you expected to find yourself. So please do not blame her for all that you have chosen."

"I see," said Croton staring at the carpet. After a moment of silence he continued, "The way I see it, the stage has been set and the actors are ready."

"That's right," Lita confirmed.

"When?" asked Croton.

"There is no time to waste. The young lady is already pregnant and waiting for her child's first kick."

Croton looked at Gaya, "Forget about me. Aren't you sorry to be leaving all this?" he said spreading his arms wide apart, "For another life on Earth?"

"I do not feel that I belong here," Gaya mumbled.

Croton walked to stand right in front of Gaya, taking her hands into his and helped her up from the bed. Then he turned his head to face Lita who quietly vanished from the scene. Croton looked straight into Gaya's eyes. The intensity of waves penetrating her soul were so great that she had to shut her vision to withstand such a powerful invasion. He then pulled her into his arms, pressing himself against her entire body. She hugged him back. An unfamiliar and most pleasant current of energy misted her mind. She could have remained in this state of bliss forever.

Awhile later she pulled back, and facing Croton she said,

"Let this be a test of the strength of our love. If we belong to one another, no time, nor soul, can separate us. On my return, be at the gate dividing the living from the dead."

"I will, my love," said Croton landing a kiss upon her forehead. "Enjoy your trip. I wish you a safe journey, and above all, that you find all that I was unable to provide."

On saying these last words, broken hearted, Croton chose to leave his wife to the task that she had condemned them both to.

REQUEST

"Home," Croton said to himself, recalling the place that he was once attached to.

The place where memories of the past were put on hold in search of new ones. The reality he considered home for thousands of Earth years. He stepped into his ancient Roman home which once had rejected him by turning into dust and forcing him to adaptation of another human life. He took a walk through the rooms and satisfied with the current state of the house, sat down at the table to gather his thoughts and hopefully to come to terms with Gaya's harsh decision.

"I have to get to the bottom of this mess," Croton said, placing his palms on his temples and asking Thales to emerge.

Without any further ado the Greek appeared at the table.

"What would you like to know, my friend," asked Thales anticipating Croton's quest.

"Was this your plan?" Croton threw the question at his face.

Thales sighed deeply and placing his hands on the table answered, "You know, my friend, that I am not the only Planner in this place."

"I know that, but I would like to know if you were personally involved, or maybe influenced Gaya's decision to return."

"No," Thales answered abruptly.

"I am not getting it," said Croton. "You sent me on a journey to find my missing part, helped me into the world of spirits from hell itself, so that she can ditch me in the dark?"

Thales smiled at Croton's phrasing, "Are you admitting that she broke your heart?"

After a moment of hesitation through tightly shuttered teeth Croton whispered, "Yes."

"You know, my friend, it may seem like the Planners have strings attached to souls, like puppeteers to a doll, but souls have free will and we are able to control them only to a limit. Although, I can also visualize your future, hand in hand with Gaya, enjoying the beauties of the transitional realm, and I know you have a world to show her, but…but this is not about you. I am sorry to say this, you have to respect her wishes, and above all, you have to learn to live with her choice."

Thales was expecting a reaction from his opponent, but there was none. The rising density of silence in the room forced Thales to discharge.

"Just spill it out for God's sake."

"Can I be her guide?" Croton asked.

"Absolutely not," Thales stated abruptly.

"Can I be her secondary guide?" Croton kept pushing.

"No! You must let her go. If she is truly your destiny and future she will find her way back to you again. Consider this as a test for both of you. Your presence will only spoil the authenticity of her experience on Earth."

"Are you suggesting that I would interfere with her love affairs?"

"Yes, you will, and my advice to you is to forget about her for now. You know how short human life is. She will be back in no time."

With these last words, Thales stood up from his chair indicating that he was done talking and about to leave.

"Before you go," rushed Croton, "What should I do now? Any assignments for me?"

"For now just relax. You have had a tough exit."

As Thales disappeared Croton heard, "Although, I will disturb your rest soon."

Croton, who had stood up to say goodbye, sat back into a chair enveloped in a mist of dark anticipation.

INVOLUNTARY CONFESSION

With Croton left to face his destiny with Gaya, Henry asked Rose, "How do you think this is going to go?"

"I think Gaya wants to go back."

"Poor Croton," said Henry hugging Rose from behind while she observed the horizon of their reality.

"Enough about them," Rose said shaking off her troubling thoughts. So, tell me all about you."

"What do you mean?" Henry asked surprised.

"You have been here all alone for almost four Earth years, and don't tell me you spent them like a hermit in the seclusion of our world."

Stumbling from Rose's point-blank request, Henry momentarily recalled memories that he had managed to collect in Rose's absence. And as ill luck would have it, they were all about the adventures he had with Solomea.

Trying to escape these unwanted thoughts Henry rushed to scenes involving Christ and all that he went through with him, but as he was about to speak, Rose interrupted him saying, "Just go one thought back."

"What are you talking about?"

"I just saw an image of a lady who looked like a goddess. Who is she?"

Unpleasantly surprised by Rose's ability to read his mind, Henry pulled back asking, "Are you seeing my thoughts?"

"Yes," answered Rose, also surprised by her ability to do so. "Yes, I actually am," she confirmed.

A revelation of such a scale made Henry choose a trial of visiting images more carefully so as not to disclose the adventures he'd had with Solomea. But as hard as he tried to mask them, the stronger they were re-emerging from the recent past, leaving nothing out. Starting from the moment that he met her, his visit to her personal reality on top of the mountain leading him butt naked into a crystal-clear pool…the harder Henry tried to block those thoughts, the stronger they were haunting him. It seemed as though he was under a spell or tested truth serum. Details of his encounters with Solomea, so comfortably shoved into the dusty corners of his mind, crawled out in such tiny details, leaving even Henry surprised in his ability to recall the experiences of the past to the scale of their emotional extent. Henry realized that he was heading for a calamity, but was unable to shut the wide open flood gates of devastating revelations rumbling down the hill, about to crush the only soul that he cared about in the entire universe. Next, there were scenes when he flew at Solomea's side toward the Buddhist statue, followed by the incredible time with the two gorgeous ladies lying at his side to the point of shattered consciousness in a peak of ultimate rapture. When the reservoir of unwanted memories was empty, Henry, completely drained, lowered himself onto the sofa completely defenceless. Surrendering his future to the judge and persecutor in one, to his Rose, the one he loved most and somehow managed to hurt most.

Rose stood quietly through the entire session with her emotional state only divulged by the tears rolling down her face. She turned around unable to face Henry any longer and by saying, "I need to be alone," she vanished from his sight.

Henry's call for her to come back was swallowed by the room which had suddenly turned into an empty shell that was about to be shut, entrapping Henry into its darkness. He immediately stood up and left Rose's room, returning to his quarters. Heavy feelings of a long forgotten past when he was all alone anxiously waiting for Rose to come back, emerged again. Thoughts that Rose had left him for good, and may never forgive him made themselves comfortable in Henry's mind, forcing him deeper into despair and absolute hopelessness. He fell into the sofa with his hands holding his head. Numerous attempts to reach Rose went unsuccessful. He closed his eyes hoping to shut the door on the involuntary revelations and their horrendous outcome.

Sometime later Henry heard a familiar voice, "It's not going to happen."

Henry opened his eyes to find Croton standing next to him. He sat up sharply at the sight of such a welcome visitor.

"What is not going to happen?"

"It is not going to go away. No matter how hard you try. What has been done cannot be undone."

"Yes," agreed Henry. "You cannot unscramble scrambled eggs."

"Exactly," Croton agreed, lowering himself into one of the occasional chairs.

"I guess we have both been dumped," Henry sighed sadly.

"Yes, my friend."

Henry looked at Croton with a shivering spark of hope.

"Please help me to find her."

"Sorry, but I cannot. Unless she chooses to be found. But you know that. Leave her for now. The wound is still fresh, and she needs some time to digest such a discovery."

"I don't think she will ever forgive me."

"She will. A loving heart will always find a way to forgiveness. Just be patient."

"What about you?" asked Henry. "I believe Gaya broke your heart?"

"Yes, she did," confirmed Croton.

Both sat quietly, each submerged into their own thoughts, until Henry disturbed the silence.

"Somehow, she gained access to my deepest thoughts. I feel as though I have been turned inside out and vigorously scrutinized. She was never like that before."

"That's what happens to us with each visit to Earth. We are getting upgraded."

"Honestly, it was scary. No matter how hard I tried to mask my past, she still read me like an open book. How can you explain that?"

"That's what spiritual growth is all about," exhaled Croton. "Just some advice, don't do anything that you'd need to hide, or be ashamed of your actions."

"Do you think it is possible to live like that?"

"Yes."

"Okay, maybe you can enlighten me. Why couldn't I resist Solomea's temptations?"

Croton smiled saying, "She helped you to explore your deepest and darkest desires. The ones that you kept suppressed, even from yourself. In other words, she helped you to manifest your wishes into reality. Now you have to face the outcome of that."

"I feel used," Henry replied angrily.

"Do not blame her for that. In any moment of you encounter with her you could have stopped it. But instead, you chose to explore further."

After some thought, Henry admitted, Yes, that is true. It would be unfair to blame her. Solomea actually did me a favor, and loneliness is the price that I will have to pay."

"I guess we are back where we started," said Croton with a touch of sadness in his voice.

"What do you mean?" asked Henry.

"Just me and you."

Henry got off the sofa and stood by the dining room table. He grabbed the top of the nearest chair until his knuckles turned white and said, "I will find her."

"Of course you will," said Croton trying to calm Henry down. "But for now I advise that you give her some time to calm her anger."

Releasing the chair, Henry walked up and down the living room, as though it would help him to speed up the time separating him from Rose.

"Will you please stop it! You are making me sick," complained Croton.

Henry stood up, right in front of Croton and said, "Any bright ideas."

"Actually, I have some." Croton threw the bait.

SHOULDER TO CRY ON

"Mother? May I visit you?"

Gaya heard Rose's voice while she stood at the edge of her blue lake. Observing the hardly noticeable ripples, gently swirling over the white pebbles splashed like pearls over black sand. Gaya turned around to warmly welcome her daughter who suddenly remembered her and cared to visit. But her excitement was short-lived. Rose's wet eyes broke Gaya's heart. She instinctively stepped closer and pressed Rose against her chest.

The forgotten feeling of being in the arms of her loving mother overwhelmed Rose even more. The pain of Henry's betrayal reached the limits of Rose's tolerance, spilling over in the form of tears. She cried like a badly hurt little girl, shaking with each wave of painful memories firmly embedded in her mind. Her deeply caring mother kept pressing Rose tightly to her chest, hoping to calm her baby girl down and make her pain vanish.

When the cup of sorrow was dispersed, Rose gently pulled herself back saying, "Thank you, Mother. I feel a lot better now."

Gaya tenderly wiped her tears and asked, "So, tell me now, who dared to hurt my little girl?"

Rose mumbled with her eyes turned to the floor, "Henry."

"I knew it," Gaya raised her voice, and desperately looked around, unsatisfied by what she saw, she created a bench right on the spot.

"Let us sit down, and you can tell me everything," suggested Gaya.

"I see you have mastered the art of creation," Rose said as she lowered herself on the newly crafted bench.

"So, tell me what just happened?"

Rose gazed into her mother's eyes and softly whispered, "He cheated on me, Mother."

Devastated, Gaya slapped her thighs with her hands and looking up exclaimed, "Oh, dear Lord. I knew it. You can never trust a man. Dogs will remain as dogs regardless, on Earth or in heaven. It is their nature, dear child. Not even death can change their nature."

"Okay," said Gaya, trying to gather her thoughts.

"How bad is it?"

"What do you mean?"

"For how long?" asked Gaya.

"I don't know. I just saw her with him, engaged in some kind of disgusting orgy."

"For how long have they been together?' Gaya pushed.

"Mom, I don't know. And why is that so important?"

"If it was just an episode, and he regrets what happened, you must forgive him."

"I cannot," said Rose.

"You have to."

"Look who's talking," Rose served a shot back. "You want me to forgive him the way you forgave your husband?"

"My case is different," retaliated Gaya.

"How different, Mom?" asked Rose.

"Thanks to your father, my life on Earth was a lie. I lost everything that I loved in the blink of an eye, plus, do not compare my tragedy with a bump on your road."

Rose took Gaya's hands into hers saying, "Do you realize that Croton literally went through hell just to be with you?"

"I know that, but…but he is not the same man that I fell in love with and married."

"Maybe you should give him, and yourself, a chance to see through him. I know, sometimes he can be impregnable, but I am certain that the one that you fell in love with is still there, somewhere deep, and if you just wish to reach out you will find what you are looking for. You knew that he is still deeply in love with you and will do anything to hold you back from another trip to Earth. Besides, I am sure that if you just allow yourself to rediscover him, you will fall for him all over again."

Giving Rose's words some thought, Gaya said, "I don't think so. Because of him I feel like someone who took a journey and was expelled right in the middle."

Rose sighed gently and asked, "So, what are you going to do Mom?"

"Thanks to Lita, my guide, I just found out that my baby sister not long ago fell pregnant and is expecting a baby girl. To me that is the best opportunity to stay in the frame of my family, and hopefully to accomplish what I had wished to do before."

"Look Mom, I do not have many memories of my time on Earth, but I assume that you didn't travel much with Dad. Am I right?"

"Not exactly. I traveled with your father within the borders of our country."

"But what about traveling abroad? Seeing other countries?" "No, of course not."

"Why?"

"We were not permitted so as not to be poisoned by the 'smell of rotting capitalizm', as our leaders used to say."

"But, did you ever want to travel?"

"Are you crazy! Of course I did, but it was always something beyond our imagination."

"Let me ask you another question…have you ever been out of this reality?"

"You mean my paradise? No, I haven't."

"What if I tell you that you can see the world without moving a muscle?"

"Sorry, but I am not following you. Besides, we do not belong to the physical world anymore."

"Trust me, the places I would like to take you to are better than the physical world. And maybe then you may change your mind about going back to Earth."

"I am not sure about that, but you can have a shot," said Gaya.

"Do you even know about the existence of cities?"

"No…" answered Gaya confused. "Although I did wonder where everyone else is."

"Did you not ask Lita that question?"

"Once I did, but I didn't get a definite answer."

"I see," Rose said angrily.

Unable to stay invisible and quiet any longer, Lita barged in saying, "I had lots of reasons."

Her sudden appearance nearly gave Gaya a heart attack by being caught off guard.

"Like what?" Rose boldly confronted her.

"I have developed the strange feeling of having been imprisoned," said Gaya.

"No, you weren't," replied Lita. "I explained to you earlier that this is a transitional reality, and no souls will stay here forever. Just be patient and I will get you back to Earth to you family, where you belong."

Noticing a tiny hint of irritation in Lita's voice, Rose said, "May I have a word with you privately?"

“Yes, you may.”

They walked away from the lakeside, leaving Gaya sitting on the bench feeling lost and confused.

“What are you doing?” Lita asked angrily. “Once you take her around, I will not be able to convince her to go back to Earth.”

“What a minute,” Rose retaliated. “Shouldn’t it be her choice? Based on her free will to go back or not? I feel like you have a hidden agenda to trick her into a lifetime imprisonment inside a human body.”

“It’s for her own good. You should know that. She can experience enormous spiritual growth by finally completing a full life cycle on Earth. Something that she couldn’t do the last time. Look at her…she is miserable. Her entire family managed to escape the devastation caused by the earthquake. We can help her to be reunited with them and to find happiness.”

“What about her husband, Croton? He committed suicide just to be with her. You cannot ignore this fact.”

“I know that, but it was her decision to dismiss Croton once she realized that she was nothing but a disposable piece in a much bigger chess game.”

“I hear you,” answered Rose, “But you are the one who played a major role in her interpretation of the facts.”

“Are you saying that I have misled her?”

“I am saying that you directed her thoughts and emotions that suits you.”

“I utterly disagree. I just helped her to have a clear vision.”

Rose stepped back taking a deep breath to calm her rising anger, and then spoke.

“I would like to ask you something sincerely,” said Rose, “But please, if you cannot give me an honest answer, then rather don’t answer at all.”

“Okay,” Lita agreed.

“Do you have another assignment on your hands?”

“What do you mean?”

“Do you have another soul to guide except Gaya?”

Lita looked down and a veil of sadness covered her face.

“I see. You don’t have to answer. If Gaya choses to stay, you will be out of work,” stated Rose.

Lita turned away saying, “It is irrelevant.”

“No, it isn’t, my dear,” Rose said. “I will cut you a deal. Let me take her around, and if she is still adamant to return to Earth, then you can have her.”

“What if I don’t agree?”

"I will expose you to Croton, and the outcome will be very unpredictable."

Lita gazed into Rose's eyes, and before she vanished, she said, "You have a deal."

"What just happened," Gaya asked as she approached.

Rose offered her hands to Gaya with the words, "Come with me Mom."

"To where?"

"You will see. Just close your eyes and trust me," Rose replied joyfully.

ITALY

The first idea that popped into Rose's mind was to take Gaya to Rome, to follow the trail once laid by Henry on her arrival into the world of absolute beauty and perfection. Gaya, who only saw those architectural wonders on a travel channel, was absolutely stunned. Unable to shut her mouth, Gaya stood like a child who for the first time stepped into a candy store.

She asked the most common question all newly arrived souls asked, “Are we back on Earth?”

Arm in arm, they browsed through the famous streets of Rome, showered with all of the imaginable brands of boutiques. Rose kept introducing Gaya to the new world of unprecedented possibilities that she had been unfairly deprived of by Lita.

“Can we go in?” Gaya asked uncertainly.

“Follow me,” Rose invited as she stepped into a clothing store.

Gaya walked through the rows of branded dresses, touching them one by one.

“Do you like them?” Rose asked, following her.

“Oh, they are all so beautiful.”

“Would you like to try some of them on?”

“No,” Gaya declined gently. “I don't think I can afford them,” said Gaya trying to establish the location of price tags.

“Don't bother. You will not find what you are looking for.”

“Why?”

“Everything in this shop, and in any other one is free of charge. By choosing a dress you will be doing a great favor for the designer who created these masterpieces.”

“How is that possible?” Gaya asked removing her hand from the garment.

“Yup, there is no money in this world, and the souls here create things for the fun of it.”

“What about their labor? Isn't that financially covered?”

"No, it is covered by the token of gratitude you can express simply by enjoying their creation."

"I see," said Gaya joyfully grabbing an item from the rail asking, "May I have this one?"

"You may," said Rose leading her to the changing room.

When Gaya stepped out with an unmissable glow on her face, Rose knew that she had found the key to Gaya's lock, and she will keep it and use it until the time comes to pass it to Croton. Shop after shop, boutique after boutique, were explored, leaving almost no store untouched on the famous street named "Via del Corso".

When both carts improvised by Rose for Gaya's use were full, she said, "I'm a bit embarrassed."

"Why?" asked Rose.

"I feel like I came from a remote village and cannot have enough goods."

"It's okay Mom, back home you didn't have access to the works of Italy's best designers."

"It's true, and I cannot hide my joy," exclaimed Gaya jumping up and down like a little girl. "Wait a minute? How are we going to get all of this to my heaven?"

"It's very easy Mom, all you have to do is to imagine these carts standing in your bedroom, and once back you can arrange them as you wish."

"Oh God, I will need more wardrobe space!"

"I am sure that you can solve that problem by yourself."

Clapping her hands Gaya closed her eyes and the carts disappeared in front of Rose.

"Are you enjoying yourself?" Rose asked.

"I have never been happier in my entire life."

"Wait, there is still more to come."

"I don't think you can out do this…an ultimate shopping experience."

"You want to bet!"

"Surprise me," said Gaya placing her hand in Rose's and closed her eyes.

A few seconds later she heard, "You can look now."

They were standing in the middle of a busy street. Most of the passersby were women dressed in all kinds of unimaginable trends of fashion. They were streaming in and out of doors like a colony of ants collecting vital goods.

"Where are we?" asked Gaya in amazement.

"Welcome to the 'Via Monte Napolione' in the city of Milano.

The most important street in the world of design."

"This is mind-blowing!" exclaimed overexcited Gaya, "Me in Milano! This can only happen in a dream."

Facing Rose she asked, "Am I dreaming all of this?"

"No Mom, this is a reality, and if you chose to stay, this could become your reality. You can spend as much time here as you wish, having all that your heart desires. Your future is in your hands, and no one can force you to do otherwise."

Gaya stumbled for a second, but then shook off unpleasant thoughts, saying, "What the hell. Spoil me, my girl."

It would have been hard to determine the mother-daughter time spent together in this ultimate woman's heaven, exploring all that Milano's fashion world could offer. The most memorable for Gaya was her time on "Defile De Mode".

When Gaya's cup of excitement was filled to capacity, Rose said, "There is one more place that I would like to take you before we head for home."

"I don't think there is any available space left in my house, let alone the closet!"

"This one is not about shopping, Mom."

"Then what is it about?"

"You will see," Rose answered mysteriously.

She grabbed Gaya's hand, and already familiar with the procedure, Gaya closed her eyes. A moment later they were standing in a big square in front of a magnificent fountain.

"This is too much!" cried out Gaya.

"Isn't it beautiful," smiled Rose observing the fountain known as "Fountain of Four Rivers", mastered by the famous Bernini.

"Should we grab a coffee?" suggested Rose. "I just happen to know the perfect place."

"With absolute pleasure," answered Gaya, following Rose's lead toward a café. "By the way, where are we?" Gaya asked curiously.

Rose turned around and spreading her arms wide, exclaimed, "Piazza Navona, in the very heart of Rome."

Approaching the café Rose slowed her steps, uncertain if she was in the right place. The gentleman who stepped out from behind the counter and approached them deepened her doubts further. She stumbled for a moment, but his wide welcoming smile as he asked them to have a seat, made her consider the invitation.

"Prego, prego, make yourselves comfortable, dear signoras," insisted the over attentive owner.

Rose looked around noticing some customers indulging in their meals and offered Gaya a seat. Noticing Rose's uncertainty the owner asked, "Is everything all right, signora?"

"Yes…"

"But?" insisted the owner.

"I don't know how long ago I was here last, but there was a different man assisting me and my husband in this very same café. Although, it does look a bit different now…or perhaps I am in the wrong place."

"No signora, you are in the right place. On your last visit, this place was probably run by my dear friend, Renzo. He was temporarily replacing me while I went to Earth with my wife to fish for new memories."

"Yes, you are right. His name was Renzo. So, what happened to him?" asked Rose.

"As I said, he was only temporary, and now I am back and glad to be at your service."

"Wait a minute…are you Mario?"

The owner's face melted into the most charming smile, "Forgive me, signora, but I don't remember you visiting my humble place."

"That's right. My husband was eager to introduce us, but on our visit you were gone."

"Sorry, signora, it makes me very sad to hear that, and if I may ask, who is your husband?"

"Henry," answered Rose.

"Oh dear Madonna, are you Rose?"

"Yes, I am," proudly admitted Rose.

"May I?" Mario asked pointing at the empty chair.

"Please," invited Rose. "Excuse me for being so rude, allow me to introduce my mother, Gaya."

Mario stood up and gracefully kissed Gaya's hand, introducing himself. When the formalities were done, Mario asked, "So, tell me please, I am dying to hear your story."

"Before we get into the story, may we have two cups of your coffee?" asked Rose.

"Mi scuci, signoras," said Mario jumping up from his chair. He rushed behind the counter, but then immediately came back. "Mi scuci, I forgot to ask what type of coffee you and your charming mother will prefer?"

"Two cappuccinos please," said Rose, who then paused to ask Gaya, "Please tell me you have had cappuccino before."

Gaya shamefully admitted that she had heard about it, but

had never tasted it.

"This could be a problem," Mario mumbled.

"What about a black coffee in a small cup?" asked Rose

"Yes, that's what we always had back home," agreed Gaya.

"Bellissimo," said Mario disappearing behind the counter.

"Who is he?" Gaya asked, confused. "I have never met a real Italian in my life."

"Now you have, Mom, and I am certain that you will not be disappointed. Henry always spoke highly of him, calling Mario a love expert."

"Love expert?"

"In a decent sense of the word, of course."

Before Rose finished her sentence Mario was back with three cups of coffee on a round silver plate.

"The third one is for me," Mario said apologetically.

With his customers now served, Mario sat down to hear Rose's story. Noticing the ladies' first sips, he asked, "So, tell me please, how is my coffee?"

"Splendid," answered Rose.

Then they both looked at Gaya in expectation of a compliment, but none came.

"Don't you like it?" asked the disappointed barrister.

"I don't know. My mouth seems a bit numb."

"Is this your first visit to the city?" Mario asked facing Rose.

"Yes," answered Rose.

"I see, don't worry, signora, allow me to assist."

He pulled his chair closer to Gaya causing her a tiny discomfort. Then he said, "Let us try again. Please pick up your cup, signora."

Gaya followed his instruction.

"Now, try to remember the best coffee that you ever had."

"Okay," said Gaya a bit confused.

"Now, have a sip."

With a glimpse of a blush on her cheeks, Gaya touched the brim of the coffee cup and had a sip.

Noticing a smile on her face Mario said, "What about now?"

"Now it is perfect," admitted Gaya with the face of an utterly satisfied customer.

"Belissimo," said Mario moving out of Gaya's personal space. "So, tell me Rose, I am dying to hear your story. After all, this is the reason why I opened this café."

"What would you like to know?" asked Rose.

"Everything. You can start from the time of your departure

from the physical world and your first meeting with Henry."

"Wow! That was so long ago!"

"I know, but being a witness to his struggle, don't you think I deserve to know?"

"You definitely do," said Rose laughing. "So, to begin with, I must say that I didn't die of old age. It was a car accident near the airport terminal where I was planning to change my life on Earth, but instead it delivered me right into Henry's arms, right where I belonged," Rose began with the story of her life. For some odd reason she chose to hold nothing back.

Her entire journey from the moment of her arrival into the transitional realms in the form of words and images found their way out from the depths of Rose's memories. Mario was listening very attentively, not to miss a sentence, image, or scene that Rose chose to share.

Gaya had become a fortunate witness of Rose's life story that she had no knowledge of, and was afraid to move so as not to distract Rose. She was in the process of discovering for herself, the soul who honored her by becoming her daughter. Hearing all that Rose had been through, just to get to the one she loved the most, and then to give it all up to help her and Croton to become parents, shattered Gaya's heart. The sacrifices that Rose had made was beyond her comprehension, and the love she experienced for Rose grew in respect and deep admiration.

While Rose was sharing the story of her life, Gaya thought to herself, *"How come I don't remember anything from my past lives? Or the soul I was before meeting Croton? This is so unfair."*

When Rose's cup was emptied, Mario sat back with a look of utter dissatisfaction depicted on his face. He sighed deeply and said, "I am sorry, dear Rose, but I do not see Henry's fault in this ordeal."

"Yes, sure. One man covers another's dirty trail," retaliated Rose.

"No, this is not about that."

"I see no justification for what he did," said Rose.

"Hear me out please," insisted Mario.

Rose took another sip of her coffee and sat back.

"I know that you feel hurt, broken, and betrayed, but…there is more to Henry's story. I don't know if I can convince you to forgive him for what he has done, but I can definitely help you to understand…"

"I left him for three lousy Earth years, and he immediately jumped into another woman's bed, or to be exact, pool. I can tell you even more…I am sure that there was some kind of orgy, too. Regardless of his attempts to hide it from me, I saw it all. So good luck getting me to understand that."

"I feel your pain Rose, but please, hear me out."

"Okay," Rose backed up.

"Let me ask you a question. Was Henry faithful to you during your last stay on Earth as husband and wife?"

"Hhhmmm...yes…more or less."

"What do you mean?" Mario asked.

"He had a one-night stand with a tramp, but I forgave him long ago."

"So, overall, he was faithful to you."

"Yes, you can say that."

"Good!" exclaimed Mario finding common ground. "What if I told you that male souls are built differently to females, and exploration in any field of physical experiences are a major part of their journey on Earth."

"I know where you are heading with this," Rose interrupted. "In short all men are dogs!"

Mario smiled saying, "I appreciate your conclusion, but don't you think it took a lot for Henry to be faithful to you his entire life? Don't you think that perhaps he had some fantasies that he was not allowed to materialize? In other words, he suppressed his nature so as not to hurt you?"

"Really, you think so?"

"Yes, most men do. The difference is that some act on the core of their nature, whilst others resist it their entire human life."

"Okay, I see," said Rose. "But there is a fault in your theory. He did this not while in his physical body, he did it here in the non-physical. I guess the saying that pigs will find dirt anywhere is true!"

"Prego, signore," Mario pleaded, "Hear me out. What I'm about to say applies to both genders. Any unfulfilled desires or fantasies on Earth will carry through with us into our non-physical existence, even those that are buried deep in our subconscious. Believe me, sooner or later the opportunity to materialize them into reality will present themselves, to act upon, or to pass will be completely up to each individual soul. Although, let me assure you, signore," Mario said blushing, "it is almost impossible to reject a Tempter, especially if she is irresistibly persuasive."

"I have to admit, she did look like an Egyptian goddess, and if I was a man I would have definitely been caught in her web."

"You see," said Mario, "I am so glad that you admitted that.

So please forgive him."

Rose frowned like a child and sat back, crossing her arms over her chest.

"It doesn't mean that he loves you any less, and I am sure that he regrets it deeply. But as you know, one cannot unscramble scrambled eggs. Accepting someone's weaknesses is the first step on the road to forgiveness."

Rose deeply sighed and looked at Gaya, "I completely agree with Mario," said Gaya.

Next Mario directed his attention to Gaya saying, "Now, I would like to give an answer to your question."

"What question?"

"About why you have no memories of your last stay in the spiritual realms."

"Yes, I would really like to know that. I feels unfair that you guys remember everything and I am completely in the dark about my origins."

Mario froze for a moment as though he was downloading information from an unknown source, and then spoke, "Signora, sorry to say, but not many souls are aware of the clause that they agree to before being sent to Earth."

"What clause?" Gaya and Rose asked simultaneously.

"To the life contract."

"I didn't sign any contract," said Rose.

"I mean metaphorically. You can have a condition to remember your last stay in the spiritual realm, or even your previous physical lives upon your return to the transitional realms."

"Why didn't I ask for that?" Gaya enquired.

"Most souls avoid those memories because they are too painful. All they want is a new beginning with a white sheet. Every visit to Earth gives us that opportunity, plus, it allows us on our return to step into a higher vibrational reality, into one that we have never been to before."

"This is very confusing," said Gaya. "Are you saying that I have never been in this realm before?"

"No, you couldn't. The level of your soul's energy, or should I say, the level of your consciousness was not high enough to step into the reality that you are in now."

"I see. So what helped me to climb the ladder?"

"You should ask 'who' helped you."

"Let me guess," stepping in Rose, "Croton?"

"Not only," said Mario.

"Who else?" asked Gaya.

"Your daughter," said Mario pointing at Rose.

Gaya looked gratefully at Rose, placed her hand over Rose's, squeezed it gently and whispered, "Thank you, my dear."

"You're welcome, Mom," Rose replied casually.

"If it wasn't for Rose's sacrifice, Henry would have not been left all by himself for three Earth years, and definitely would have not had the adventure with the Egyptian goddess."

"Now, I feel guilty," admitted Gaya.

"You shouldn't. We all get our share of adventures when visiting Earth," said Rose.

"That is so true," agreed Mario.

"By the way," said Rose. "I remember Henry saying that you were running this café with your wife."

"Yes, that is true," Mario admitted.

"So, where is she? What happened to her?" enquired Rose.

"She is still on Earth," Mario admitted sadly.

"I am sorry, I did not mean to…"

"It's okay, my dear Rose, soon she will join me, although for now I must suck it up and wait."

"Were you visiting Earth together?" Gaya asked.

"Yes, we were husband and wife, and I cannot imagine my life without her in either reality."

"I envy her," said Gaya.

"You shouldn't" answered Mario. "You have the rare opportunity to have what we have, just don't let it pass you by. I know that you feel hurt, and sort of manipulated, but…but I know for sure that Croton loves you, and your departure will be devastating for him. I can see that you love him, too. Give both of yourselves the chance, allow yourself to see his true nature, and I promise you that you will be pleasantly surprised."

"To be honest, already I miss him," Gaya admitted.

"Should I arrange a meeting, sinoras?' Mario jumped in excitedly.

REUNION

"So, how and where are we going to find them?" Henry asked having no doubts of his mentor, the return of whom he had been anxiously waiting for what felt like an eternity.

Croton fell quiet allowing Henry's question to bounce off the barrier of his concentration. Hoping that Croton was busy planning their next move, Henry took a step back.

A minute later Croton asked, "Do you remember Mario?"
"How could I forget him."

"He is back and would like to see us," advised Croton.

"In his café?" exclaimed Henry, unable to hide his excitement.

"Where else?" smiled satisfied Croton.

"Let's go, I can't wait to see him." With these words echoing off the empty shell of his and Rose's reality.

As they approached the café, they were shocked to see Rose and Gaya indulging themselves at the center of Rome, sipping coffee, and casually conversing as though nothing had happened.

As they stood at their spouse's table, Rose said, "Oh, and here they are. The last two faces we wanted to see in this paradise."

"Come on, Rose, we come in peace," Henry stepped in.

Noticing the guests, Mario stood up to greet and welcome his old friends. Hugging Croton and Henry, and after a short enquiry about their current state of well-being, Mario said, "I invited you signores for a reason."

"Which is?" asked Croton meaning business.

"The reason is sitting at that table," Mario said pointing his eyes at the ladies' table, who were acting as though they were ignoring the presence of their husbands.

"Honestly, I don't think that they will let us," said Croton.

"There is nothing to worry about," Mario stated confidently. "Everything is sorted." Then he slipped his hands under Croton and Henry's arms and dragged them to the ladies' table.

"Signoras," said Mario.

Looking unpleasantly interrupted they both looked up at Mario.

"Allow me to introduce you to these two fine gentlemen who you may not have met yet."

"Okay, although the word 'fine' is questionable," answered Rose.

"Please," pleaded Mario. "Give them a chance. You will regret it deeply if you don't."

"Okay, let's see," Rose said begrudgingly.

All this time Gaya was silently looking at Croton, and him at her. It seemed like they saw each other for the first time. Memories of the past began to surface in their minds. Memories of the time when they fell hopelessly in love with each other. Waves of the most powerful emotions swept through their minds, drowning in their depth everything that was between then and now. Croton approached Gaya, and without breaking eye contact, took her hand and gently pulled her to the next available table.

When Henry and Rose were left all by themselves, Rose poked, "Oh, the prodigal son returns!"

"Please forgive me."

"Let's see what you have to say for yourself," Rose poked again like an accomplished swordsman.

Lowering himself into the chair opposite Henry pleaded, "Let's put behind us all that happened in your absence and let's move on with our lives. We have so much to look forward to, instead of digging in my dirty…" Henry lowered his eyes like a child admitting his guilt.

Hardly suppressing her anger, Rose said, "I have a condition."

"I will accept them all."

"You will never see that Egyptian bitch again!"

"I will not," agreed Henry.

"And a second…the time you had with her, I want a better one."

Henry's face melted into a wild smile.

"Let us go home, my love, and I will show you a time that no one has ever seen before."

As he said those last words, Henry cautiously placed his hand over Rose's, fearing rejection.

When Croton turned around to check on Henry and Rose, they were gone.

"It seems as though those two love birds reconciled their differences," Croton said with great relief.

"You do still carry a great deal of responsibility for them, don't you?" said Gaya.

"Yes, I do. It cannot be any other way. They have done so much for me, and for us in particular. Because of them, I found you."

"I see," said Gaya.

"What do you see, my dear Gaya?" asked Croton.

"I just realized that Lita, my guide, had different plans for us. Or should I say, for my future with her."

Croton smiled satisfied, "I am glad you see that."

"Not me, our daughter opened up my eyes. But you shouldn't think that I am cross with Lita. I can see her point of view, as well."

"So, what have you decided, my love?"

The last two words pronounced by Croton were so not like him, but so long hoped to be heard by Gaya, and if there were any doubts in the back of her mind, they had all vanished.

"I choose to give us another chance. I choose to see you," said Gaya looking deeply into Croton's eyes.

"To see me?" asked Croton.

"I mean, all of you. Although I do see in you part of my husband, but it is so tiny compared to the depth that I am facing, and that is a bit frightening."

Croton placed his hands over Gaya's saying, "I will not let you down."

She placed her hands over his asking, "Where do we go from here?"

"Oh, that is easy, let me show you all of who I am."

Gaya pulled back a bit.

"I have seen your reality, or should I say, the one that Lita so lovingly created for you, so now let us explore mine."

"Should I close my eyes?" Gaya asked cautiously.

"Preferably," Croton answered."

A second later Gaya heard, "We've arrived."

Gaya slowly opened her eyes. She was standing next to Croton in the most beautiful blooming garden filled with apple trees.

"Where are we?" Gaya asked.

"You will see now."

As they followed a narrow path, the apple tree garden transformed into an olive tree plantation, and after a few more step Gaya saw, slowly revealing itself, outlines of a white Romanesque house.

When they were standing in front of stairs leading to the

entrance, Gaya asked, impressed, "Is this your house?"

"It was," Croton nodded.

As he led her to the door, Gaya felt as though she had stepped back in time. Room after room, the house unveiled not only its inner world, but Croton's as well.

When they reached the library, Croton paused for a moment in the doorway, and while staring into the room said, "This is my favorite."

"Because of all these books?" Gaya asked.

"No, my dear. Here I met Henry for the first time."

"Oh, was he a Roman senator, too?"

"He was an assassin who came to murder me."

Gaya stepped into the room, walking straight to the desk still stained with blood and said, "It seems like he succeeded."

"Oh yes, he did," answered Croton.

Approaching Gaya from behind, Croton hugged her saying, "You've seen it all, and now there is a question I need to ask."

"Go ahead," whispered Gaya.

"Can all of this ever become yours?"

"Mmm…it might," mysteriously answered Gaya.

"I knew it," said Croton. "Okay, I will buy it. What will it take?"

"There are some changes that I would like to bring to this house."

"You can change all that you want. But please, do not touch the library, nor the exterior of the house."

"Okay," Gaya answered optimistically. "Although the library is a bit creepy, but I guess I can keep its door closed."

Croton smiled as a consensus was reached. A moment later Croton noticed a dark cloud casting over Gaya's mood.

"What now?" he asked.

"What am I going to tell Lita? She has already planned my return to Earth. Oh my God. What about my sister's child. She is pregnant and about to give birth to a baby girl." Gaya held her head in utter panic.

"Stop it, my love, all that is fixable. I have no doubt that Planners have already chosen another soul for your sister's child. Despite all Lita's efforts, your return to Earth was always questionable. So please, calm down. Everything is in order. They always are, and it can be no other way in this realm."

"Thank you. That is a big relief. The last thing I want to is to let Lita down after all that she has done for me."

"You will not, my love. We belong together, and this cannot

be argued."

Gaya stepped forward, right into Croton's space, gave him the most loving embrace, and for the first time landed a kiss upon his lips. Gaya closed her eyes, allowing herself to get the most out of the moment, and she wasn't disappointed. When their lips parted, in a state of sudden enlightenment she said, "It is you!"

"Yes, my love, it's me."

She hugged him again, soaking up all that was her husband in this Roman senator.

"I would like to show you something," said Croton. "The master bedroom."

"I thought the library was the last room to see."

"I kept the best for last," blushed Croton.

She followed him down a long corridor that led them to the opposite wing of the house, until they stood in front of a heavy door.

Gaya said, "Allow me to go in first, and do not enter until I say so."

"Okay," agreed Croton passively.

Gaya placed her hand on the copper doorknob, pushed the door open and carefully stepped inside. A quick glance around the interior made her shut the door behind her with the words, "Were you saying this reality is as much yours as it is mine?"

"Yes, my love," Gaya heard through the door.

After about ten minutes of total silence, that made Croton a bit uneasy, he asked, "Is everything okay?"

A moment later the door opened, and Gaya invited him in. Croton was astonished as he entered.

"So, what do you think?" Gaya asked cautiously.

"Have you recreated the very bedroom we had on Earth?"

"Yes, I did, and I hope you like it. I couldn't stand the idea that there was a time when you were in that bed with your Roman wife."

Croton pulled her to him saying, "I absolutely love it.

The lighting in the room dimmed, Gaya looked at Croton confused and in front of her eyes a transformation happened.

"For one last time," Croton said, revealing the one who she had deeply fallen in love with on Earth.

THE BODY OF WATER

"Where are we?" Rose asked, pleasantly surprised.

She was standing on a beach facing the most amazing sunset.

"We are home, my love," answered Henry.

"But it looks different," said Rose checking the surroundings.

"I took the liberty to make some small alterations, and I hope that you will like it."

Observing a thatched roof gazebo behind them, and two wooden chaise loungers next to each other, covered with orange towels, Rose seductively smiled saying, "This reminds me of a luxury island holiday resort, although the well-built beach boys are missing!"

"Don't push it," said Henry.

Rose laughed loudly saying, "It's absolutely beautiful, my love."

"Wait Rose, there is more to come."

"Okay, surprise me. After such a stressful trip to Earth, all I want is to be spoiled, to leave behind all the bad memories and create new pleasant ones."

"Okay, but you have to trust me on this one."

"After all that I witnessed it will be hard…but anyway…" sadly murmured Rose.

"Please…" Henry pleaded.

"Okay."

"You must do something for me. Something we have never done before."

"You are scaring me. What is it?"

"Will you please remove your clothing."

"What, here?"

"Please."

'Absolutely not," Rose protested. "What if someone steps in?"

"No one can visit without our permission," Henry said to

calm her down.

"Still, I don't think this is a good idea."

"Rose, it is me, your husband, and I have seen you naked before."

"I don't know. I am a bit shy. Let's wait for a deeper dusk. Maybe then I will consider it."

"No. We have to do it now before the sunset is finished."

"Okay," Rose gave in. "Just turn around."

Henry reluctantly agreed.

"Can I turn around now?"

"No, not yet. Please be patient."

"What about now?"

"No!"

"Now?"

"Now you may," whispered Rose.

Henry turned around and stood mesmerized.

Noticing his reaction Rose asked, "No good?" and covered her nakedness with both hands.

"Please," asked Henry. "Allow me to indulge in your absolute beauty."

"Do you like what you see?"

"No, I absolutely love what, and whom, I see," answered Henry.

"I'm not sure if you noticed, but I have done some alterations," Rose admitted shamefully, pointing at her breasts and legs.

"No, I didn't."

"Liar," said Rose.

"I loved you before and I love you now," said Henry, lovingly captivated by her.

"What about you?" Rose asked.

Henry closed his eyes and stood in front of Rose bare naked.

"Not bad," laughed Rose. "What now, brainiac?"

Henry offered her his hand. She softly took it in anticipation of something magical. Something which only a loving heart could offer.

He turned toward the body of water and said, "Now we are going for a swim."

"What? Are you sure about this?"

"Yes, I am. What are you afraid of? Drowning?"

"Hmmm…maybe."

"Don't worry my love, you know it cannot happen."

"I know, but still…"

"Just trust me Rose," said Henry.

When they reached the edge of the water Rose stopped.

"What now?" asked Henry.

"What should I expect?" Rose asked nervously.

"Nothing but pleasure," Henry answered.

Rose cautiously stepped forward allowing an upcoming wave to taste her feet, and immediately pulled back.

"What now?" Henry asked.

"I don't know. It's a bit weird. God knows how long we have owned this reality, but to swim has never crossed my mind."

"Nor mine," agreed Henry. "Still, let us give it a try, although, I have to apologize for never taking you to a fancy tropical island while we were on Earth. Allow this body of water to embrace you. It has been waiting for us since I stepped foot into this reality."

"Okay," said Rose stepping forward again.

When the water reached her waist, she stopped saying, "I just hope you remember that I cannot swim."

"Don't worry, my love, you don't have to. Just keep going."

When the water reached their necks, they both held their breath and submerged themselves with their eyes closed. Henry was first to find comfort and regain his vision. Assured that it was safe, he asked Rose to open her eyes. She did, but for some reason was still holding her breath.

"Just relax my love and act normally."

Hand in hand they stepped into the depths of an unfamiliar reality. Henry, driven by anticipation, and Rose by promised pleasure. The dying sunset was about to deprive them of the only source of light, plunging the underwater world into complete darkness. Suddenly, as if by the wave of magic wand hidden until now, an incredible world revealed itself. They were standing at the center of a most magnificent coral reef, where each tree with its own luminosity of various colors, was serving as hosts to multitude of fish, varied in their sizes. Each had a unique coloring to impress their observers with the most exquisite visual display. Rose couldn't have enough of this private wonder-world beauty, and wanted to explore further and deeper, but Henry gently pulled her back.

"Be still my love, we will have plenty of time for that. For now, be with me."

Rose faced Henry and a moment later their bodies melted into one. The fish miraculously disappeared, and the reef dimmed its luminosity letting two loving hearts to reach possible heights of their rising emotions.

THE DARKENING HORIZON

While Croton and Gaya were walking hand in hand through the well-maintained garden of antiquity, handsomely showered with marble statues, Croton asked, "Should we check on our love birds?"

"I don't think we should do that. Leave them alone. Because of us they have been through hell."

"I know and I feel guilty for putting them through it, but on the other hand, they both had unprecedented opportunities to raise the level of their consciousness, especially Henry."

"Okay," Gaya gave in, anxious to see her daughter one more time. "See if they are available."

A moment later Croton said, "They actually invited us to their place. Shall we?"

"I am dying to see their reality," said Gaya placing her hand into Croton's.

"Wow," exclaimed Gaya standing on the soft white sand facing a breathtaking sunset.

Leaning over the shimmering golden water, tall palms elevated the entire scene to perfection, leaving nothing more to add. While Gaya was indulging in the view that she had never seen before, Croton, who was the mastermind behind the creation of this reality, went to look for the reunited couple.

Four knocks on the door were followed by Henry's loud invitation, "Please enter, my dear friend."

Croton turned around shouting, "Come here, my love, I have found them."

Only then Gaya saw the cozy beach house with its back against a dense forest, and Croton standing on the porch waiting for her. Like a teenager filled with a sudden uplifting energy, she ran toward the house. For the first time feeling happy and incredibly light, not only on her feet, but in her mind as well, she was visiting her own daughter's reality which somehow effortlessly had become well established and happy in her marriage…something that every mother dreams of, to live and witness for their child. As a well-mannered Roman, Croton allowed his wife to enter first, and then he followed.

Rose was first to welcome the guests, saying, "Welcome to our world, Mom."

Gaya threw her arms open wide, inviting Rose for a warm motherly hug.

Once the mother's hunger for the touch of her daughter was satisfied, Croton stepped in with a wild smile asking, "How about a hug for your father?"

For the first time Rose stepped into the senator's space and wrapped her arms around him. Unfamiliar emotions overwhelmed her. Emotions that were hard to describe by one stroke of brush, let alone to paint the entire picture. After a moment she pulled back and invited her parents to enter. Henry, who had distanced himself from Rose's reunion finally stepped forward to ask everyone to go through the corridor to Rose's quarters. The biggest impression on Gaya's mind was the wall of cascading pools.

"Wow. This is so cool," Gaya said. "Ever been inside?"

"Actually, no," Rose answered. "Though, I have to admit, just before you requested to visit us, we had the most amazing swim."

"Please don't tell me that you went into the deep sea!" Gaya exclaimed.

"Actually, I did Mom, and it was amazing."

Henry, with Croton's help, was decorating the table with coffee and improvised alcoholic beverages and could not help but overhear Rose and Gaya's conversation.

"Did you really go for a swim?" asked Croton.

"Oh yes, we did, and I would like to thank you for such an amazing experience. The underwater world was breathtaking."

"Why me?" Croton asked, surprised.

"Isn't this reality your creation?"

"I did create the body of water, but not its depths."

Henry stumbled for a moment and then asked, "If it wasn't you, then who? I didn't create that, and neither did Rose. We definitely are not able to extend our imagination to that extent."

"Look at them," Rose said stepping out from the balcony into the room. "Their imagination was enough to create only coffee and alcohol. What about some food and chocolate for us ladies?"

"Coming right up," said Henry.

When the party was at its highest and the couples enjoying

themselves with lots of memories to share, they heard a knock on the door.

"Shhh," said Rose. "It seems that we have a visitor.

"May I?" Thales asked politely before making himself visible to them all.

A visit by Thales in the middle of a party was never a good sign. The Planner had become for them someone who was most wanted when things were not going well, and most avoidable when everything was in order. Henry and Rose knew this through bitter experience. While Croton asked the old Greek to join the party and have a seat, Henry and Rose froze in anticipation of bad news.

"Please, enjoy your reunion. All I need is a few words with Henry in private."

Henry looked at Rose, and all she saw in his eyes was deep hopelessness.

"Don't worry, my love," Rose said. "Whatever it is, I am with you."

Without saying anything, Henry stood up and followed Thales out of the room.

Thales stood in the middle of the corridor, and turning to Henry said mysteriously, "There is someone who would like to meet you."

"Sounds like a new adventure."

"You can say that."

"Do you mind if I let Rose know?"

"It will only take a minute in her perception of time."

"I see," Henry sighed deeply.

"Nothing to worry about my friend. You will be back in no time."

"Although to me it will probably feel like a lifetime."

"It will be entirely up to you."

"One thing I can say for definite is that I am intrigued, but not excited."

"Why so?" Thales asked.

"Bad experience!"

"I am sorry you feel that way, but this one you cannot escape. All souls reaching a certain level of development must go through this."

"Okay," sighed Henry. "I will buy it," and he closed his eyes.

THE GLASS CUBE

Thales placed both hands on Henry's shoulders saying, "Home."

This destination surprised Henry, but before he could make sense of what he heard, a strong stream of light punched his face in an attempt to penetrate the barrier of his shuttered vision. A few seconds later he heard, "We've arrived."

The intense light was gone, and Henry regained his sight. A quick glimpse assured him that they were inside a glass cube with no doors. Each side of the cube measured approximately thrity feet. Beyond the glass was a milky, cloudy substance. Henry sensed that the cube was floating in some kind of cloud.

"Where are we?" he asked, observing Thales standing peacefully next to him.

"My mission is accomplished," said Thales, "And I must leave you now."

"Wait a minute," Henry protested. "There are no doors to this place. It feels like a trap."

Thales smiled saying, "Be still, son, you can leave this place whenever you wish. Just don't forget to thank me when you get back home."

Utterly stunned and puzzled, Henry nodded his head as a sign of gratitude, and goodbye, at the same time. When Thales disintegrated into the emptiness of the cube, Henry looked around. Finding absolutely nothing to focus his attention on, he walked to one of the glass walls to have a better look outside, hoping that he would have the chance to see something beyond the dense mist. As he approached the glass wall he noticed the silhouette of a human figure approaching him. With each step it became clearer, and when the figure reached the glass wall and they were standing face to face, Henry thought for a moment that he was looking at his own reflection in the glass. But when the man on the other side touched the glass with his index finger,

Henry had no doubts as to the identity of the man beyond the glass. It was not him, but whoever it was bore an astonishing resemblance to him. Involuntarily, Henry placed his index finger against the stranger's and closed his eyes. An unexpected sense of calmness enveloped him, combined with a sense of belonging to the place and to the figure opposite him through the glass wall.

A moment later Henry retrieved his hand asking, "Who are you?"

"I am you," answered his twin.

"What is this? A sick joke? How can you be me? This defies all laws of existence known to me," Henry stated angrily."

"This is not a joke, and I am you, or to be exact, you are part of me."

"You are confusing me," said Henry raising his voice.

"Look," said his twin, and in front of Henry's eyes he transformed his appearance.

To begin with, there were strangely dressed male, and some female, figures. None previously known to Henry, although after the twentieth figure had flashed in front of him, he saw a familiar one. It was a Roman citizen named Titus. The one who had plunged his sword through Croton's heart. Next was the slave girl, Aurelia, raped, falsely accused, and condemned to death. Then followed more unfamiliar faces, and when the transformation came to its end, Henry was standing in front of his older version. The one that he'd had right before the heart attack that had sent him onto this self-discovery journey in the world of spirits.

"What was the meaning of this show?" Henry asked.

"All of those images were you."

"I kind of guessed that. But for some odd reason, you are holding those images of my past lives. Why? If I may ask."

"Those images are mine, too."

"Are you saying that you know more about me than I do?"

"Exactly."

The sudden flash of realization lit up Henry's mind, and after some reasoning Henry asked, "Are you my Creator?"

The man in front of him blinked in confirmation of his identity.

"I see," said Henry. "This is so much to digest. I need a minute please."

His older version stood quietly waiting to be addressed.

A moment later Henry said, "Can I see what you really look like?"

"I am sorry, but I do not have a physical appearance."

"Then, what are you?"

"Energy in the form of consciousness."

"Can I see your entirety? I am sorry for my persistence, but it is important for me."

"I am sorry, too, but it is impossible to do."

"Why?" asked Henry.

"Because you are in me, and this glass cubicle is your only protection."

"Protection from you?"

"No, rather from becoming me."

Henry lowered his head feeling trapped in a humongous maze, uncertain of if he wants to find an exit.

"What will happen if the glass disappears?" asked Henry.

"My knowledge will become your knowledge."

"And mine probably yours?"

"All that you know is already mine. Sorry to say this, but you are an extension of me. All that you have ever experienced I have done through you, too."

"So, I have nothing to give?"

"No, only to gain."

"I see…what exactly am I to gain?"

"Infinite knowledge and boundless wisdom."

"Can you be more specific please?"

"Well, you will become a Creator."

"Creator of what?"

"Look, at the moment I am involved in a most exciting project, which is the creation of a new planet, and soon it will be ready to be introduced to its first inhabitants."

"You mean humans?"

"No, humans will be one of the last species on that planet. We are working on the most basic vegetation, and the world of bacteria capable to survive in the environment of that planet."

"Is it similar to Earth?"

"Not exactly."

"Sounds fantastic," Henry exclaimed suddenly.

"It is fantastic. The process of creation of physical objects, never mind the world, is very emotionally rewarding, and to watch your creation not only survive, but also to thrive as well, is even more rewarding."

"It sounds very exciting, acting like a God, and I am clear how it is rewarding. But there is something that is bothering me."

"Fire away."

"Why did you choose to create me?"

"To study humanity."

"What do you mean? You are the creator of a human soul. What more do you need to know about humanity?"

"Yes, you are right, I created your soul from a tiny part of mine, but you were the first one to incarnate on the planet Earth. Before you, I knew nothing about humans."

"And now?"

"Now I know enough to offer you the chance to return home."

"Do I have a choice?" Henry asked.

"You always have a choice. By setting you into an independent existence, I granted you that privilege, otherwise I would have learned nothing. The explorer has to be free of his creator to deliver untarnished information."

Henry fell quiet again.

"Nothing more to ask?"

"On the contrary, there is so much, and there is more every second. It feels as though I am going to suffocate under the pile of questions."

"Please, calm down and just ask the first question that pops into your mind."

"This was bothering me since I remembered myself." Henry took a deep breath and asked, "Are you a God, and Creator of all?"

The man behind the glass gently smiled and answered. "Neither."

"Then please describe yourself."

"I am the creator of your soul and many others like you."

"How many?" Henry interrupted.

"I will not be able to give you a definite answer."

"Are you saying that you do not know the number of your children?"

"It seems as though you are accusing me of being a bad parent!"

"No, but to my understanding, a father should know each of his kids so as to provide them with good care."

"You said father."

"Aren't you my father? And by the way, who is my mother."

The older version of Henry burst into laughter.

"What is so funny?" Henry asked offended.

"Maybe I made a mistake to assume that the time is right for you to reunite with me."

"You mean that I have not evolved enough?"

"With a question such as that, definitely not!"

"Sorry, I know that energy has no gender identity. I just panicked."

"It's okay, son, but to satisfy your curiosity I will answer. All my creations are doing quite well, all on their own missions. I keep in close contact with all of them."

"How does that work exactly?" Henry probed. "I mean, are you only watching us? Or do you interfere?"

"Both," the host answered shortly.

"I see… My next question is very important to me."

"I am listening."

"Can you oppose our free will?"

The host who, so far, was delivering immediate answers paused for a moment before speaking, "Do you want to know if I can force you to do something against your will?"

"Yes."

"The answer is yes. I can, and I have done so many times."

"I knew it!"

"You must remember that we are one."

"Was it your idea to follow Solomea into her reality, and all that happened after that?"

"Uummm…let's say it was our idea. You can't blame all of your mess-ups on my curiosity!"

"This is crazy," Henry said. "It feels like I am talking to myself."

"In some sense you are."

"Okay," said Henry who was adamantly trying to store in his mind every bit of new information. "Would it be true to say, that every step of my life you were with me?"

"Yes."

"Regardless of it being physical or non-physical?"

"Yes."

"Then, why do I need a spirit guide?"

"Their mission is not only to protect you from harms of the physical world, but also…"

"Also from who?" Henry asked.

"From me."

"From you?" Henry asked in surprise.

"Yes, to be exact from all that I would like to experience through you."

"And that could have endangered my stay on Earth?"

"Yes."

"Are you the one who choose the guides for each trip to Earth?"

"No, that is the Planners job."

"What is your relationship with the Planners?" Henry asked.

"Let's say we cooperate?"

"What does that mean?"

"We choose together what I would like to experience, and as a result to learn."

"Through me?"

"Yes. Don't forget you are me, too."

"To be honest, I feel like a dog who finally realizes who is his real master."

"It's okay, I felt the same way."

"Are you saying that there was a time when you met your Creator?"

"Yes, there was."

"And what did you choose?"

"I am a Creator now. I am all."

"Any regrets?"

"None."

Henry stepped away from the glass wall, placing himself at the center of the cube.

"Are you trying to distance yourself from me?" asked the host.

"I need some time to digest all of this."

"I see. But if you want…"

"What is going to happen to Rose?" Henry interrupted. "If I chose to combine our two energies will I still love her?"

"Yes, but not exclusively," the host replied immediately.

"Please explain."

"In the merger you will own all that I have and all that I am."

"This is crazy," said Henry. "This sounds like suicide. You're asking me to dissolve into you like I never existed."

"I am offering you the chance to become a Creator. To be above all worldly problems, above all fears, and dualities caused by Earth and the transitional realms. I am offering you a way out of the matrix that I placed you into. I am offering you absolute freedom of existence, with your only boundaries being the laws that govern the universe."

And then the host delivered, "You can start to pull strings."

These last words elevated Henry's awareness to the next level.

"Is there someone who is pulling your strings?" asked Henry.

"Probably yes, but I am not aware of it. The level of my freedom prohibits me from entertaining such a question."

"So, you are offering me a chance instead of being a puppet, to become a puppeteer?"

"Yes, I am."

"Tempting. Very Tempting," said Henry.

"What more can you wish for?"

"Indeed. Nothing more…" mumbled Henry. "Do I have to make the decision now?"

"No. You can take all the time you need."

"Let me sleep on your offer."

"By all means," answered the host.

Henry closed his eyes choosing to be reunited with Rose and his closest friends. But when he opened them he found himself still standing in the glass cube.

Disappointed he asked, "Am I a prisoner?"

"Oh no. I cannot imprison myself. It's just that before you leave my body, I must warn you that if you go now, you will have no memory of this meeting."

"Wait a minute. Are you saying that I am not going to remember any of this?"

"That is exactly what I am saying," confirmed the host.

Having a change of mind on leaving the cubicle, Henry asked, "Is this my first time here?"

"Yes, and hopefully your last."

"I don't know," said Henry. "I have to think about it. This is big, you know! Before committing myself to this merger I need to inform Rose first."

"I am sorry. This has to be solely your decision."

"I see. I am afraid, but I will need more information before making such a commitment."

"That is the reason why you are here."

"Then, tell me this. How will my relationship with Rose be affected?"

"We will still love her, but like I stated before, this will not be exclusive."

"I just burnt my fingers and nearly all bridges connecting me and Rose…"

"I know," interrupted the host.

"It seems like you know everything."

"I do."

"Then why do you need me to join you? I don't see a reason for that. I am already part of you. You can easily manipulate me, learn through me, experience all that I experience. So why do you need this merger?"

"Excellent question," said the host. "I will have to give you some history."

Anticipating a long conversation, Henry sat on the floor with his feet crossed like a Buddhist monk.

"Millenia ago I chose to create you as an extension of myself to populate one of the planets in the outskirts of the Milky Way galaxy."

"Why did you do that?" Henry interrupted staying true to his nature.

"I needed to purify myself."

"Excuse me?"

"Before you jump to conclusions, let me explain. As you can see I am composed of energy, with no steady shape."

"You're like a cloud to me."

"That's right. And just like any cloud on Earth, I am mostly white, but also have some darkness in me."

"Let me guess. I was that darkness that you chose to get rid of."

"That's right. And now you are ready to come back."

"In other words, you abandoned me when I was bad, and now you want me back because it will benefit you."

"Please, don't forget, there is no me and you, only us."

"Maybe for you, but not for me," replied Henry.

Sensing Henry's anger the host fell quiet to settle the rising tensions.

"There is something wrong here," Henry said. "I always heard that we must experience love as the highest form of emotion which will draw us closer to God, and now when I finally find her, you ask me to leave her. Where is the logic, or truth in this?"

"The logic is simple. Once you experience love, once it finds its place in your soul, it will stay there forever, and by coming back to us we will learn to love not only Rose, but the entire creation equally. Each atom of your entirety will be filled with love, and only one who is filled with love can contribute to creation."

"I see," said Henry. "There is something else that is bothering me."

"I will be glad to help."

"I have seen judges during Nazia's reading, they looked human…"

"You would like to know why the judges at your hearing looked different?"

"Yes, they looked nothing like humans."

"Because they were not judges. It was a panel of elders from the place of your origin."

"Origin?" asked Henry.

"Yes. It is a planet where you began you reincarnation cycle as a soul independent of me."

"I see," said Henry drawing into himself.

"By the way, there is an easier way to find answers to all your questions."

"I know. To be dispersed into you!"

"Exactly," replied the host.

After some thought, Henry stood up from the floor, standing straight and said, "I have made my decision. I don't know if I can fall in love with the entire creation. But one thing I know for certain is that I love Rose and I want nothing more than to stay with her through thick and thin, through all that human and spiritual life will throw at us. I cannot comment about the future, but that is what I want now, and I hope that you will respect my decision."

The host sighed deeply and with a note of disappointment in his voice said, "Your decision is my decision. You are free to leave."

As Henry was about to close his eyes, the host said, "Before you leave, I would like to present you with a gift."

"Gift?" Henry asked suspiciously.

"Yes, I will allow you to keep the memories of this meeting."

"Why," asked Henry.

"Because I know that you will never be back into us."

"Does this mean that I will never reach the level of Creator?"

"No, it means that you will have to go through rough terrains to get what I have offered you to have effortlessly."

"It's okay," said Henry. "We will forge our bliss hand in hand with Rose, and one day I will stand next to you like equals to remember this moment."

For the first time the host laughed loudly saying, "Son, you will always be my creation and part of me, no matter how much you grow. But one thing I can promise you, that I will do everything in my power to turn your wish into reality."

"Thank you," said Henry, and placing his right hand over his heart and nodding his head, said goodbye.

"Goodbye, son," said the host, and the cube was plunged into darkness.

THE CHOICE

When Henry opened his eyes he was standing in front of Thales in the same long corridor. Just a glimpse into Thales eyes, surrounded by wrinkles, Henry knew that he was aware of his decision.

"What do you say? Good decision?" Henry asked.

"It's your decision and you have to live with it," answered the old Greek.

"I have no doubts," said Henry.

"Good," said Thales, placing his right hand on Henry's shoulder. "From this point on your life will change drastically."

"In what way?" asked Henry.

"You will see. For now, please join your friends before they start worrying."

"Thank you," said Henry nodding his head in deep respect and appreciation.

Once Thales had disappeared, Henry walked back into the room that was filled with laughter and happiness.

"What took you so long?" asked Croton.

"Is everything all right?" asked Rose, alarmed.

"Yes, everything is fine."

"Then where is Thales?" asked Croton.

"He left."

Immediately sensing a change in Henry's mood Rose asked, "Are we up for a new assignment?"

"No, my love," Henry replied, lowering himself into Rose's white leather couch.

"So, what was it all about?" insisted Rose.

"Sometime I will tell you, my love," answered Henry, and in an attempt to redirect the conversation said, "By the way, did I tell you about my meeting with Christ himself?"

"No, you're lying," Rose and Gaya exclaimed simultaneously.

"Did you really meet Christ?" Croton asked.

"Well, yes, I did," bragged Henry.

"Please tell us all about him," Gaya jumped in. "Does he look the way we all think he does? I would give up a lot just to see him. Oh, you are so lucky," she continued.

When the tidal wave of questions stopped, Henry answered, "I wouldn't advise to meet him personally."

"Why?" probed Gaya.

"Just take my word for it."

"Really?" stepped in Rose. "I am interested as well."

"Let's say the path to him is not a bed of roses."

"Is it showered with thorns?" asked Rose.

"Yes, literally."

"Was it at least worth it?" Croton joined in.

"Every step of it," Henry confirmed. "If it wasn't for him, I don't think I would have been able to find you in the depths of hell."

Croton lowered his head saying, "Thank you, my friend, and if by any chance you see him again, please express my deepest gratitude."

"Who knows, maybe one day…have no doubt that I will definitely do so."

"So, I am dying to hear your story," cut in Gaya.

Once Henry was done sharing the most captivating experience he had with Christ, a magical sunset gave its way to mesmerizing dusk.

Croton lifted himself up from the armchair and said, "I think this is a good time for us to leave."

"Oh yes," Gaya agreed apologetically, who would have gladly stayed in her daughter's reality forever.

"We should do this often," suggested Rose, "I am sure that our boys still have a lot of stories up their sleeves which we are dying to hear about."

"Yes, we do," agreed Henry and Croton.

When the guests were gone, Rose faced Henry and asked, "So, tell me, what was that visit all about?"

"What visit?" asked Henry, confused.

"Thales. What does he want now? Can't we enjoy time together? Don't we deserve it, especially after all that he made us go through?"

"Please calm down, Rose. It was actually quite innocent."

"Innocent?" repeated Rose.

"Yes. He wanted me to meet someone."

"Who?" asked Rose suspiciously.

"You're not going to believe it."

"Try me."

"He arranged a meeting with myself."

"What, excuse me?"

"You heard me right. I had a meeting with my bigger self."

"That doesn't make sense. How can you have a bigger self? This is very confusing. If it is bigger than you, how can it be you?"

"To simplify the matter…I just met my Creator." "What? Did you meet God himself?"

"No, Rose. I had a meeting with my source. The one who set my soul into existence, using a tiny part of his soul, God knows how long ago, and now…"

"And now what?"

Henry fell quiet.

"Now what?" Rose pushed raising her voice.

"Now he wants me back."

Rose turned to stone. Motionless she ran possible outcomes through her mind of such an occurrence, and in none of them was a place for her.

"And what did you say?" she asked calmly.

"I refused."

A sigh of relief escaped Rose's lips delivering a temporary sense of comfort.

"Are you sure that was a good call?"

"Yes! Why are you questioning it?"

"Isn't that what you've always wanted? The next level of awareness?"

"Yes but…"

"It seems to me that he offered you the opportunity to become a Creator and you refused him."

"Yes," confirmed Henry.

"Why?"

Henry took Rose's hands into his saying, "I wasn't assured that there would be place for you in that growth, Rose."

"I see," said Rose. "So, you refused to become a Creator because of me?"

"No, Rose. Not because of you. Because of my love for you. I cannot lose you again. I went from pillar to post just to have you back in my life, and now that it has finally happened you expect me to check out because of some silly promotion?"

"Silly! You call that silly? Are you even listening to yourself?"

"Rose, the matter is closed, it is not open for discussion."

Henry abruptly cut her short.

"I just hope you will not regret this decision, and if you do, do not blame me."

Henry looked deep into Rose's eyes and said, "I choose us, my love"

Rose lowered her gaze, sighed deeply and said, "Thank you. I don't know what I would do without you. If I am not with you, I'd rather not be at all. I'd rather stop existing."

Tears filled Rose's eyes finding their way to the corner of her lips. Henry pressed his lips against hers, and Rose heard his voice in her head, *"You have me now. You will have me forever."*

Next, they were standing on her balcony observing the brooding forest. Each new gust of soft wind blew life into its lungs, creating waves disappearing into the horizon.

Without taking her eyes off the forest, Rose commented, "Doesn't it look real?"

"To be honest my love, I cannot say what is real anymore."

"Don't you miss Earth at all?"

"But you just came back."

"I know, but I was just a child and have not much to remember."

"I see, sorry, I forgot. I thought that after what we experienced on Earth, neither of us will decide to go back."

"Maybe, you, but not me. I kind of miss being a mother. Guiding Croton through his stay on Earth gave me that opportunity to experience it all over again. Without it, I feel that I have lost my purpose."

"Please don't tell me that you are craving another trip to Earth!"

Rose shrugged her shoulders.

"Really?"

"You can be my guide," Rose suggested quickly.

"I cannot believe we are having this conversation," Henry protested.

"Or maybe you can come with me, find me wherever I am, and fall in love with me all over again."

"No," Henry refused firmly.

"Please, hear me out," pleaded Rose. "During our last stay on Earth you checked out so early leaving me all by myself. It feels like I did not live up to my potential. I wanted to grow old with you, and hopefully to retire to some kind of tropical island."

"I can easily create that island for you right here," interrupted Henry.

"You know what I mean, love. I want it to be real. I want to feel water when I step into it. I want to smell flowers and feel sand beneath my feet. I miss all the senses that we used to have. In one word, I miss being human."

Henry felt as though a cold hand had reached his heart and started to squeeze it. A shortness of breath in his non-existent lungs pushed him to the edge of a panic attack. He took a couple of deep breaths in an attempt to compose himself and said, "Maybe you forgot all the pain that comes along with those senses. I am not talking only about physical pain which comes with age, but also emotional. Human life is filled with suffering and misery with…"

"Shhh," said Rose covering his mouth with her hand. "Calm down my love. I know it all."

Suddenly realizing something, Henry said, "Don't tell me that you spoke about this with Thales, because he will jump on such an opportunity, like a tiger on prey, and before you know it you will be back on Earth!"

There were no words needed. Judging by Rose's face he knew that she had spoken about it with Thales.

"So, you did," confronted Henry.

"Sorry my love. Before breaking the news to you, I chose to explore our options."

"And?" asked Henry with unmasked sadness.

"He said that he can design a most pleasant life on Earth for us."

"You know that that it is literally impossible. Earth is a reality based on duality, and the struggle of opposites."

"I know."

"It seems that you have made up your mind, and I cannot persuade you otherwise."

Rose kept quiet.

"I have to admit that this came as lightning bolt out of the blue and I need some time to digest it."

Saying these last words, Henry turned around and disappeared.

"Henry, Henry," called Rose in an attempt to bring him back, but he was gone to the place she didn't know, and for a span of time she could only guess.

ESCAPE

Henry wanted to be as far as possible away from Rose. It was no matter where, as long as it was away from his reality that was crushing him. The place where he was supposed to feel safest suddenly became a place that every atom of his being was repelling. He had just come back from Earth and all the horror he had witnessed because of his loved one chose to become a human, and now his Rose, the love of his life, and the meaning of his existence was about to drag him back to hell. Turning his back on Rose, Henry closed his eyes, letting lady luck deal his hand of cards, and to deliver him to the place he most belonged. Regaining his vision Henry realized that he was standing in the glass cube.

"Where else!" he said to himself. "This makes perfect sense."

"I'm glad you see it that way," said a voice coming at him from all around. "Allow me to materialize myself into an older version of you since you already know who you are talking to."

"Was it your idea to bring me here?"

"Yes, we needed an escape, and I provided it."

"We'?"

'Yes."

"Forgive me, but this is weird. Am I talking to myself? Am I losing my mind?"

"Nothing has changed, Henry. You always used to talk to yourself. The only difference is that now you can see the one you were talking to."

"You're probably right."

"I am, but if you choose to, I can revoke it."

"You mean to erase the fact of your presence from my memory?"

"Yes."

"No, thank you."

"Is it the cube?"

"Maybe? I feel kind of trapped, or maybe too close to you."

"How about this then," asked the host.

Immediately the misty clouds disappeared, and Henry appeared in a green forest facing a waterfall.

"Where are we?" he asked.

"Doesn't this place look familiar to you?"

"Actually, yes it does."

"I transported you together with Soccy to this safe haven to escape the battlefield."

"Oh yes. I remember it now. The fact that I was the one who initiated the escape surprised me the most. So, it was you?"

"Yes, it was us."

Henry sat on a smooth rock on the banks of the river.

"So, it will be stupid to ask if you know what happened."

"Yes."

"So, what do you think?"

"She's free to choose her future."

"But she wants to go back to Earth with me, I mean with us."

"It's because she loves you."

"You mean us."

"No, you. If she knew us, I don't think she would have stayed in love."

"I see," said Henry. "So, what do you think?"

"Are you asking for my advice?"

"Yes."

"I will always encourage you to go back."

"So, you can learn more?"

"Exactly, but in this case, it would be us. If you think about it, what is a single life on Earth. You will be back before we know it."

"It doesn't feel so short when you are down there."

"Do it for Rose."

"You know I will do anything for her, but something deep inside is telling me not to do this."

"That should be my role!" teased the host.

"I think this is a decision that should be made all by myself. No offence, please, but allow me to lead you this time, and you will be pleasantly surprised."

"That's my boy," said Henry's bigger self, and he stepped back into the pattern that was sent by him from the time of Henry's soul's creation.

"Hello. Are you there?" called Henry, instinctively knowing that there would be no answer, and he wasn't mistaken.

"Home," said Henry, and stepping into Rose's space, he embraced her.

"Where did you go? I was worried sick. Don't do that to me ever again please. I cannot lose you again. If you want me to stay, I will do so. I am sure we can find lots of things to occupy ourselves with here."

"Shhh," said Henry. "I know what we are going to do."

Rose pulled back and looked into his eyes, "And, what's that?"

"We will go through the process, and then we will choose."

"What process?" asked Rose.

"Preparation."

"Preparation?"

"Yes, since we came back big changes have happened on the planet, and there will be even more by the time we are ready to descend."

"Thales didn't say anything about preparation."

"I am sorry to say this, just in case he can hear us, but Thales will take us down by all means. That's what he does. It is the purpose of his existence."

"Not only, my friend," Henry heard Thales behind him.

"I knew it!" Henry exclaimed loudly. Turning around Henry nodded his head with his hand against his chest.

"Hi there," greeted Thales, "Sorry for my intrusion, but whenever you say my name, I have to react.

"I was counting on it," Henry replied respectfully.

"How can I be of service?"

"Please, I am sure you are aware of our dilemma."

"It is old, like creation itself. But have no worries, I can assist to satisfy both of you."

"And what will that be?" asked Rose.

"Henry is right, you cannot go back to Earth without prior preparation. By the time you are fully ready, Earth will be unrecognizable to you."

"I understand that," said Rose, "But the relationships between humans will still be the same I hope."

"Oh yes, that is eternal," answered Thales.

"It's just that I can't send you down to the first available couple, eager to have a child."

"We understand that," agreed Henry.

"Good," said Thales rubbing his palms together. "Oh, one more thing," Thales said facing Rose.

"Yes?" asked Rose.

"Is it just you or…?"

"It will be both of us," leapt in Henry.

"Good, even better." And those were his last words before he disappeared.

"Please, don't do it for me," pleaded Rose. "I will be back in no time, and you will welcome me back like before."

Henry took both of Rose's hands into his, and looking straight into her eyes he said, "You can't step into the same river twice."

"What are you saying?"

"All the memories of our past will be wiped out from your mind, and on your return, I will be a stranger to you."

"No!" exclaimed Rose.

"Yes, my love. What we have now I have never had before in my past lives. I found what I was looking for through multiple lifetimes on Earth, and now that I finally have you, I cannot lose you. If you go down, I am coming with you, and it is not open for discussion."

Rose pressed her entire body against his and placed her head on his chest saying, "I just hope you will not regret it."

"I will if I do not follow you."

Seven Earth years later, in one of the cities on Earth, a baby girl was born, and six months later a boy arrived to the family of young medical students living in the same city, just a couple of blocks away from where the young girl was born.

THE END

About the Author

Artur Tadevosyan

Company Director, Author and Motivational Speaker

I am a Company Director of 30 staff members and an Armenian Polytechnic Masters Graduate.

I have owned my Business for 25 years, managing and training people from all walks of life. I lived the younger years of my life growing up in Soviet Union Armenia with my Wife and 2 daughters. We lived there in a time of difficulty and extreme poverty caused by the collapse of communism in the Soviet Union. My journey unexpectedly led myself and my family to Johannesburg, South Africa, to a land with a language I could not speak and a society that was completely new to me.

These difficult and challenging circumstances were colossal part of what led to the awakening of my spiritual journey and helping others through the trials and tribulations we face in everyday life.

My lifetime of self-studies in Philosophy and Religion gave me a greater understanding of life, humanity and our Soul's purpose. Leading me to writing my first Book, Croton, which came to me through conscious channelling.

Other Books by Ozark Mountain Publishing, Inc.

Dolores Cannon
A Soul Remembers Hiroshima
Between Death and Life
Conversations with Nostradamus, Volume I, II, III
The Convoluted Universe -Book One, Two, Three, Four, Five
The Custodians
Five Lives Remembered
Horns of the Goddess
Jesus and the Essenes
Keepers of the Garden
Legacy from the Stars
The Legend of Starcrash
The Search for Hidden Sacred Knowledge
They Walked with Jesus
The Three Waves of Volunteers and the New Earth
A Very Special Friend
Aron Abrahamsen
Holiday in Heaven
James Ream Adams
Little Steps
Justine Alessi & M. E. McMillan
Rebirth of the Oracle
Kathryn Andries
Time: The Second Secret
Will Alexander
Call Me Jonah
Cat Baldwin
Divine Gifts of Healing
The Forgiveness Workshop
Penny Barron
The Oracle of UR
The Oracle of UR, Book 2
P.E. Berg & Amanda Hemmingsen
The Birthmark Scar
The Birthmark Scar, Book 2
Dan Bird
Finding Your Way in the Spiritual Age
Waking Up in the Spiritual Age
Julia Cannon
Soul Speak – The Language of Your Body
Jack Cauley
Journey for Life
Ronald Chapman
Seeing True
Jack Churchward
Lifting the Veil on the Lost Continent of Mu
The Stone Tablets of Mu
Carolyn Greer Daly
Opening to Fullness of Spirit
Patrick De Haan
The Alien Handbook
Paulinne Delcour-Min
Divine Fire
Holly Ice
Spiritual Gold
Anthony DeNino
The Power of Giving and Gratitude
Joanne DiMaggio
Edgar Cayce and the Unfulfilled Destiny of Thomas Jefferson Reborn
Paul Fisher
Like a River to the Sea
Anita Holmes
Twidders
Aaron Hoopes
Reconnecting to the Earth
Edin Huskovic
God is a Woman
Patricia Irvine
In Light and In Shade
Kevin Killen
Ghosts and Me
Susan Linville
Blessings from Agnes
Donna Lynn
From Fear to Love
Curt Melliger
Heaven Here on Earth
Where the Weeds Grow
Henry Michaelson
And Jesus Said – A Conversation
Andy Myers
Not Your Average Angel Book
Holly Nadler
The Hobo Diaries
Guy Needler
The Anne Dialogues
Avoiding Karma
Beyond the Source – Book 1, Book 2
The Curators
The History of God
The OM
The Origin Speaks

For more information about any of the above titles, soon to be released titles, or other items in our catalog, write, phone or visit our website:
PO Box 754, Huntsville, AR 72740|479-738-2348/800-935-0045|www.ozarkmt.com

Other Books by Ozark Mountain Publishing, Inc.

Psycho Spiritual Healing
James Nussbaumer
And Then I Knew My Abundance
Each of You
Living Your Dram, Not Someone Else's
The Master of Everything
Mastering Your Own Spiritual Freedom
Sherry O'Brian
Peaks and Valley's
Gabrielle Orr
Akashic Records: One True Love
Let Miracles Happen
Nick Osborne
A Ronin's Tale
Nikki Pattillo
Children of the Stars
A Golden Compass
Victoria Pendragon
Being In A Body
Sleep Magic
The Sleeping Phoenix
Alexander Quinn
Starseeds What's It All About
Debra Rayburn
Let's Get Natural with Herbs
Charmian Redwood
A New Earth Rising
Coming Home to Lemuria
David Rousseau
Beyond Our World, Book 1
Beyond Our World, Book 2
Richard Rowe
Exploring the Divine Library
Imagining the Unimaginable
Garnet Schulhauser
Dance of Eternal Rapture
Dance of Heavenly Bliss
Dancing Forever with Spirit
Dancing on a Stamp
Dancing with Angels in Heaven
Annie Stillwater Gray
The Dawn Book
Education of a Guardian Angel
Joys of a Guardian Angel
Work of a Guardian Angel
Manuella Stoerzer
Headless Chicken
Blair Styra
Don't Change the Channel
Who Catharted
Natalie Sudman
Application of Impossible Things
L.R. Sumpter
Judy's Story
The Old is New
We Are the Creators
Artur Tradevosyan
Croton
Croton II
Jim Thomas
Tales from the Trance
Jolene and Jason Tierney
A Quest of Transcendence
Paul Travers
Dancing with the Mountains
Nicholas Vesey
Living the Life-Force
Dennis Wheatley/ Maria Wheatley
The Essential Dowsing Guide
Maria Wheatley
Druidic Soul Star Astrology
Sherry Wilde
The Forgotten Promise
Lyn Willmott
A Small Book of Comfort
Beyond all Boundaries Book 1
Beyond all Boundaries Book 2
Beyond all Boundaries Book 3
D. Arthur Wilson
You Selfish Bastard
Stuart Wilson & Joanna Prentis
Atlantis and the New Consciousness
Beyond Limitations
The Essenes -Children of the Light
The Magdalene Version
Power of the Magdalene
Sally Wolf
Life of a Military Psychologist

For more information about any of the above titles, soon to be released titles,
or other items in our catalog, write, phone or visit our website:
PO Box 754, Huntsville, AR 72740|479-738-2348/800-935-0045|www.ozarkmt.com